Skip·Beat!

34
Story & Art by Yoshiki Nakamura

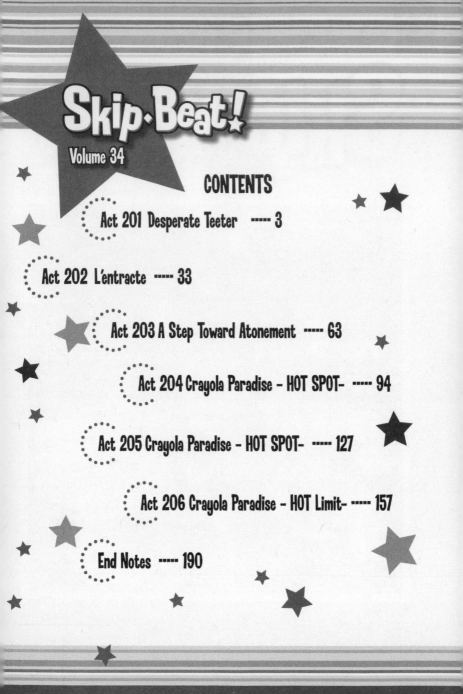

Skip·Beat!
Volume 34

CONTENTS

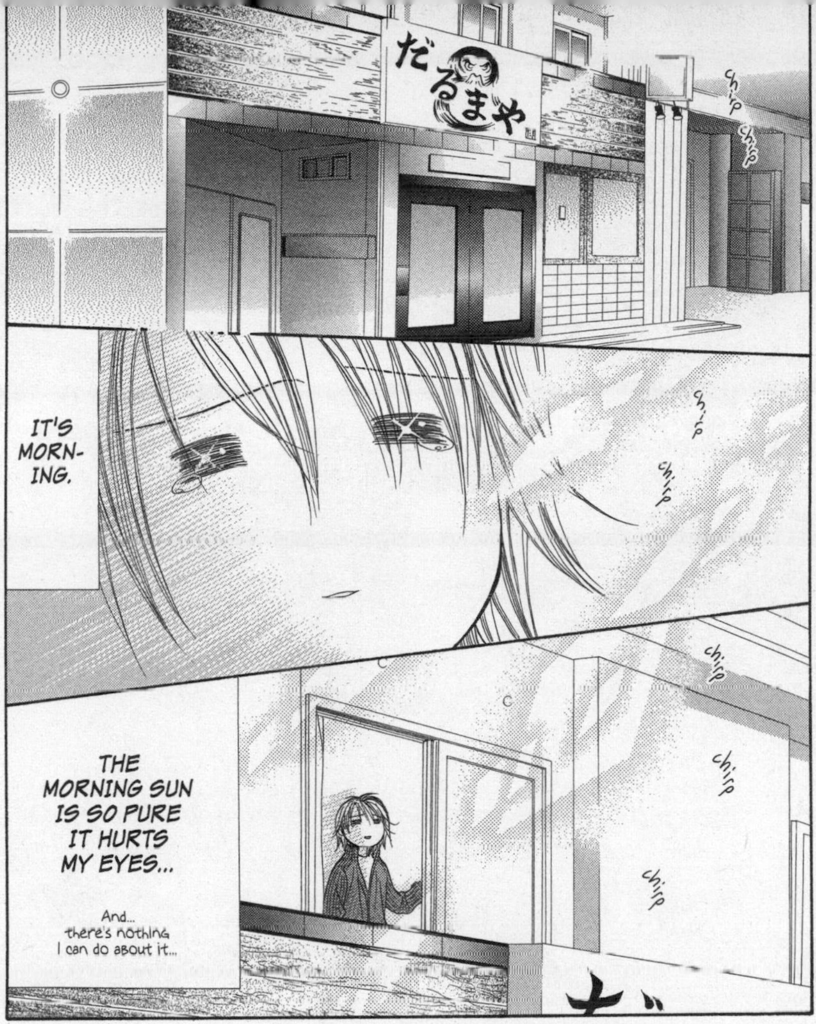
だるまや
chirp chirp
chirp
chirp
IT'S MORNING.
chirp
chirp
chirp
THE MORNING SUN IS SO PURE IT HURTS MY EYES...
And... there's nothing I can do about it...

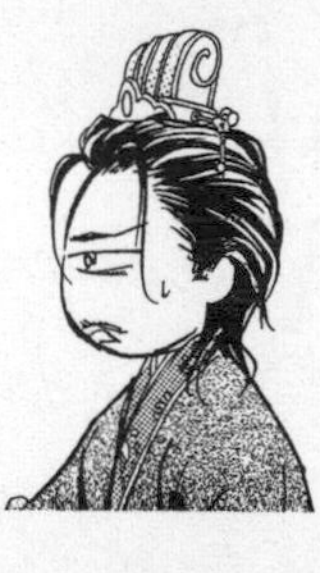

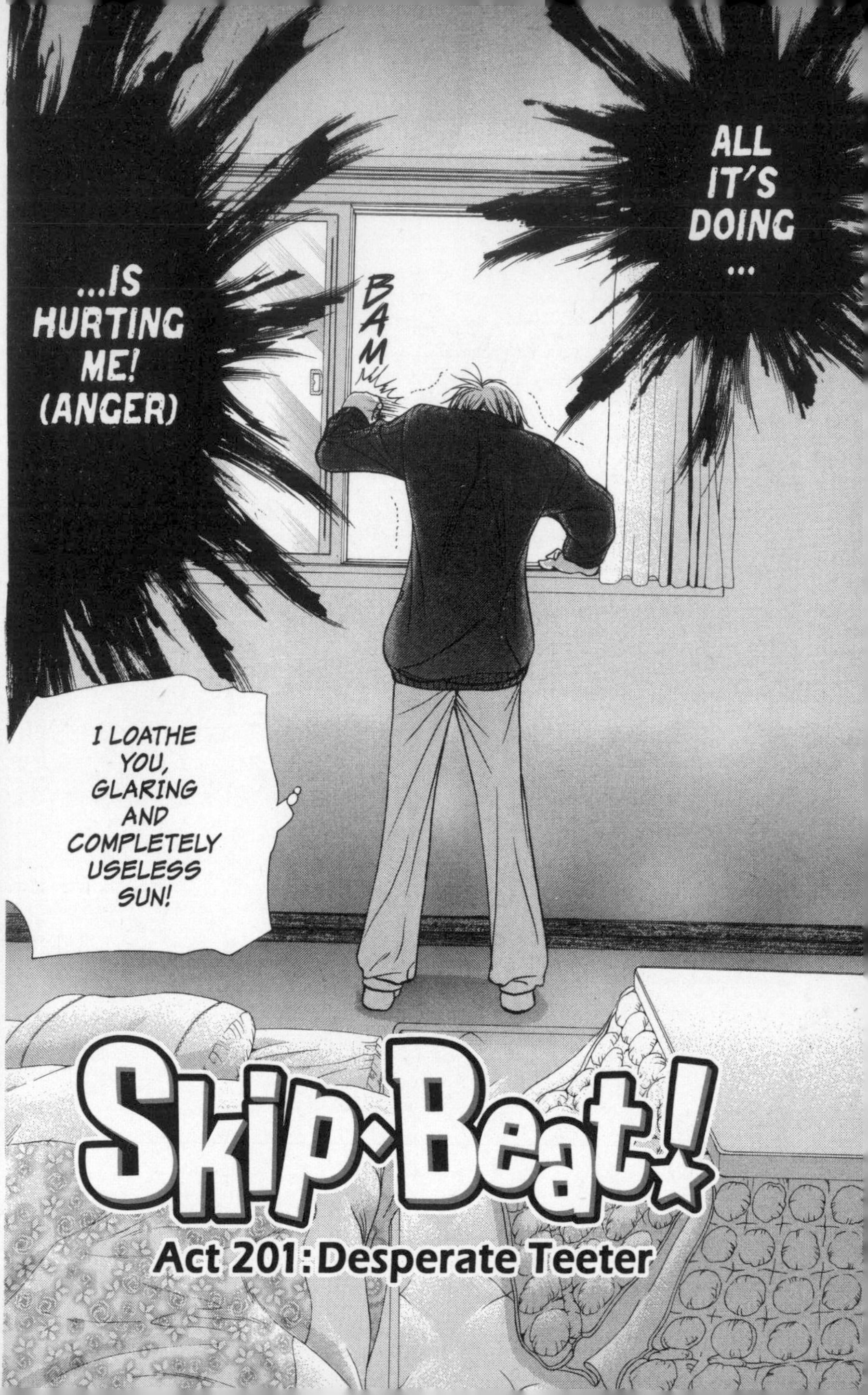
ALL IT'S DOING ...
...IS HURTING ME! (ANGER)
BAM
I LOATHE YOU, GLARING AND COMPLETELY USELESS SUN!
Skip·Beat!
Act 201: Desperate Teeter

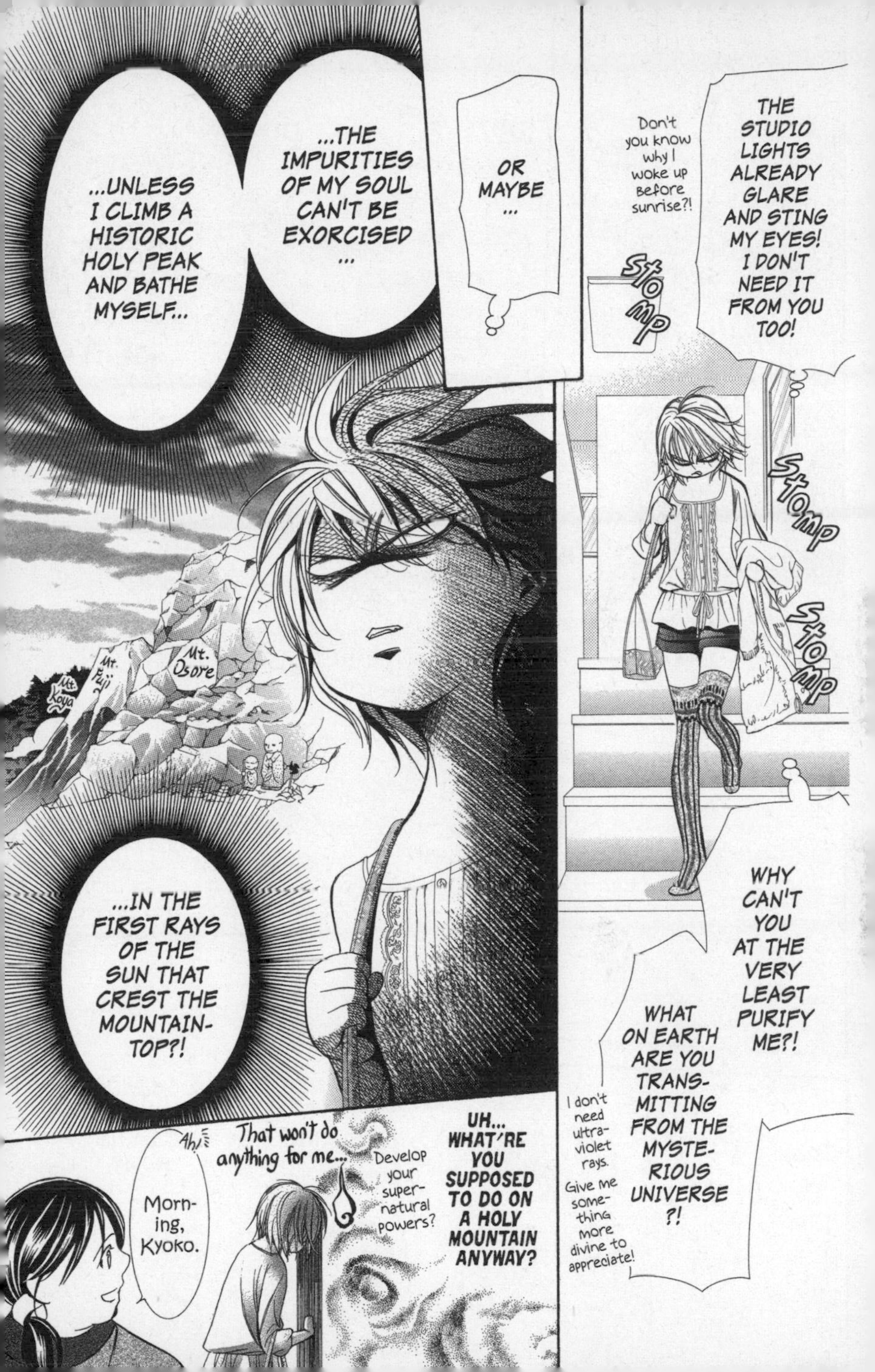
THE STUDIO LIGHTS ALREADY GLARE AND STING MY EYES! I DON'T NEED IT FROM YOU TOO!
Don't you know why I woke up before sunrise?!
Stomp
Stomp
Stomp
WHY CAN'T YOU AT THE VERY LEAST PURIFY ME?!
WHAT ON EARTH ARE YOU TRANSMITTING FROM THE MYSTERIOUS UNIVERSE?!
I don't need ultraviolet rays.
Give me something more divine to appreciate!
OR MAYBE...
...THE IMPURITIES OF MY SOUL CAN'T BE EXORCISED...
...UNLESS I CLIMB A HISTORIC HOLY PEAK AND BATHE MYSELF...
Mt. Osore
Mt. Fuji
Mt. Koya
...IN THE FIRST RAYS OF THE SUN THAT CREST THE MOUNTAINTOP?!
UH... WHAT'RE YOU SUPPOSED TO DO ON A HOLY MOUNTAIN ANYWAY?
Develop your supernatural powers?
That won't do anything for me...
Ah!
Morning, Kyoko.

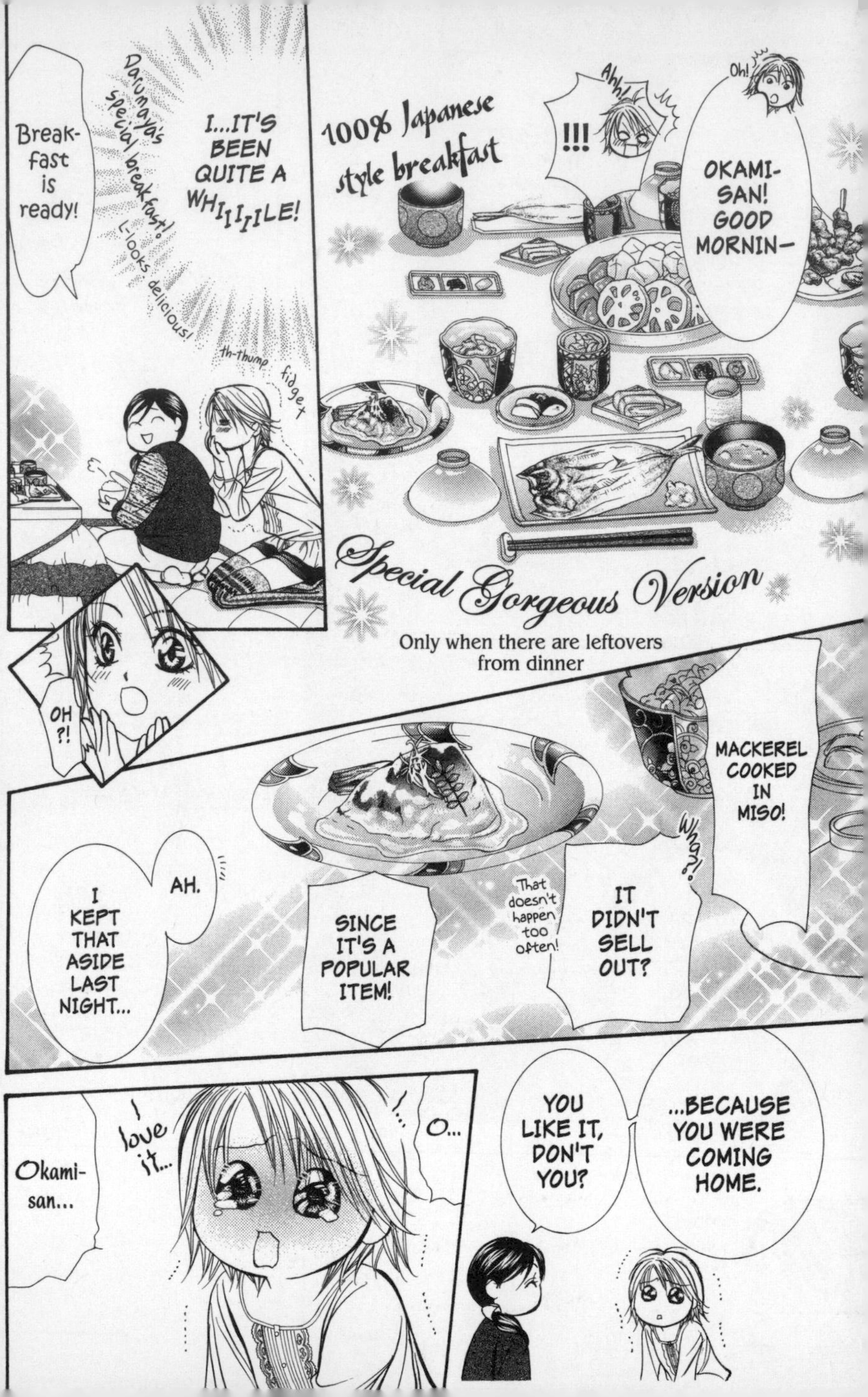
Oh!
OKAMI-SAN! GOOD MORNIN—
Ahh!
!!!
100% Japanese style breakfast
Special Gorgeous Version
Only when there are leftovers from dinner
I...IT'S BEEN QUITE A WHIIIIILE!
Darumaya's special breakfast! L-looks delicious!
th-thump
fidget
Break-fast is ready!
OH ?!
MACKEREL COOKED IN MISO!
What?!
IT DIDN'T SELL OUT?
That doesn't happen too often!
SINCE IT'S A POPULAR ITEM!
AH.
I KEPT THAT ASIDE LAST NIGHT...
...BECAUSE YOU WERE COMING HOME.
YOU LIKE IT, DON'T YOU?
O...
I love it...
Okami-san...

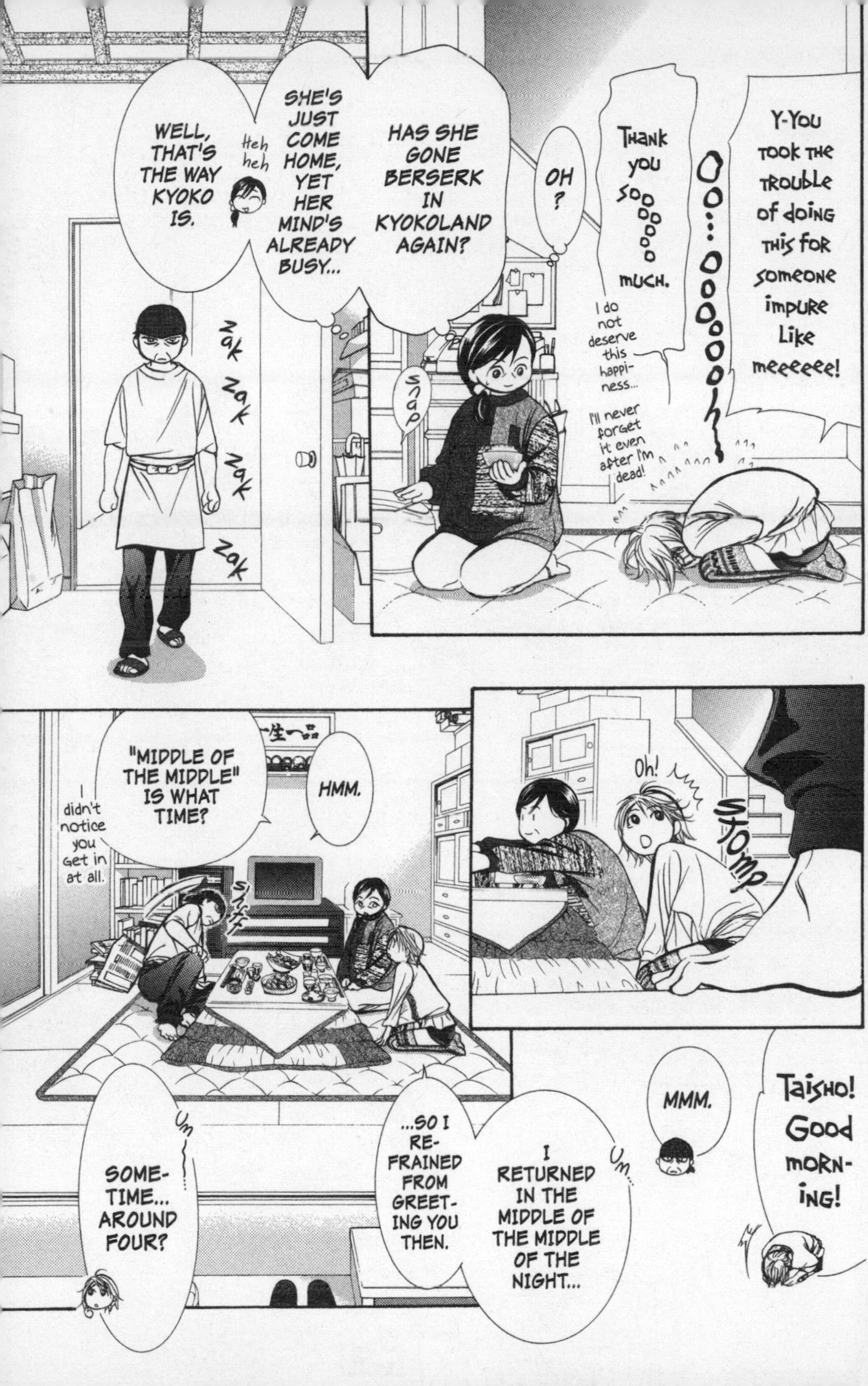
Y-You took the trouble of doing this for someone impure like meeeeee!
Oo... Ooooooh
Thank you soooooooo much.
I do not deserve this happiness...
I'll never forget it even after I'm dead!
Oh?
Snap
Has she gone berserk in Kyokoland again?
She's just come home, yet her mind's already busy...
Heh heh
Well, that's the way Kyoko is.
Zak Zak Zak Zak
Stomp
Oh!
Taisho! Good morning!
Mmm.
I returned in the middle of the middle of the night...
Um...
...so I refrained from greeting you then.
"Middle of the middle" is what time?
Um...
Sometime... around four?
Hmm.
I didn't notice you get in at all.
Shff

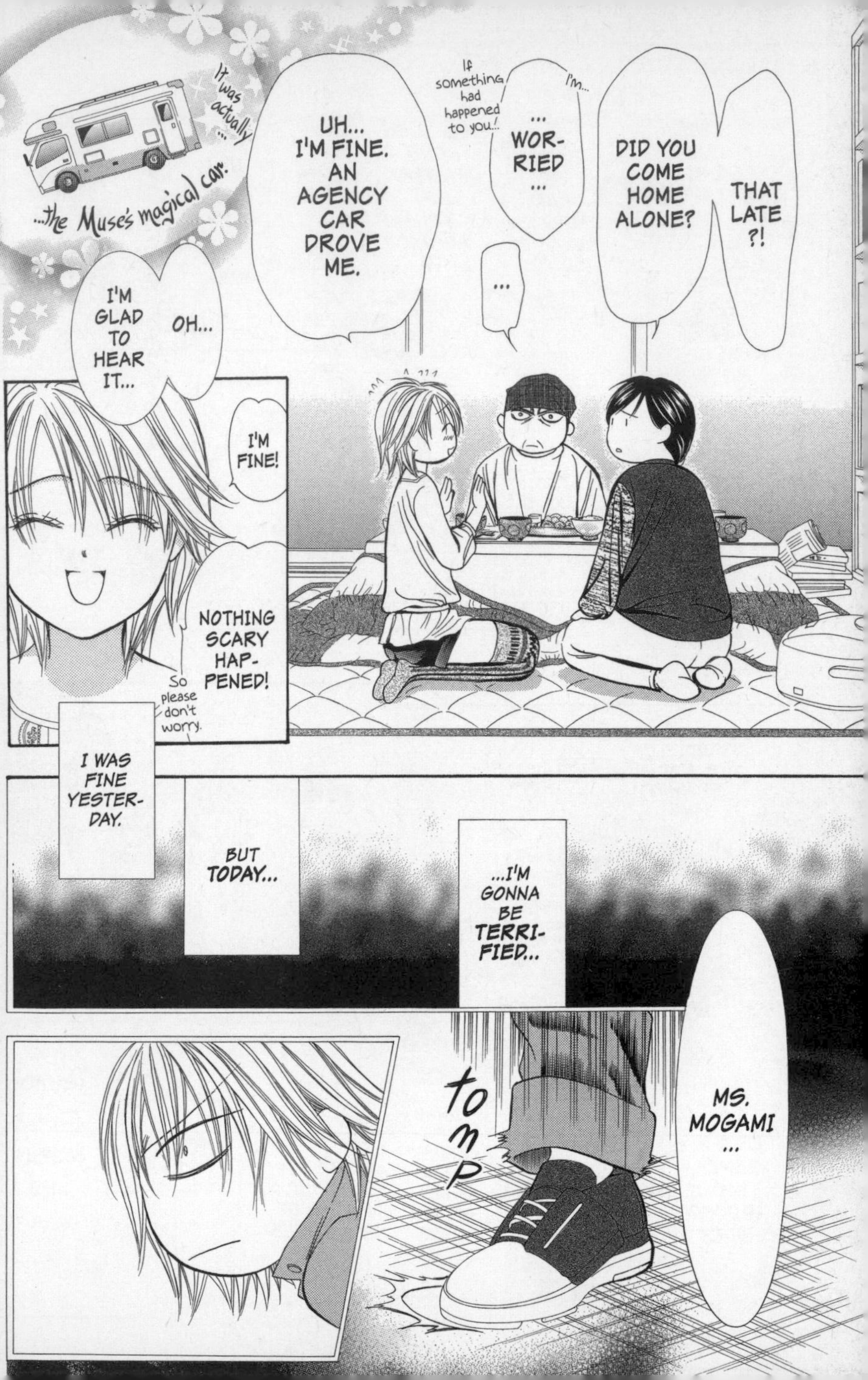
DID YOU COME HOME ALONE?
THAT LATE?!
I'm...
... WORRIED ...
If something had happened to you..!
...
UH... I'M FINE. AN AGENCY CAR DROVE ME.
It was actually...
...the Muse's magical car.
OH...
I'M GLAD TO HEAR IT...
I'M FINE!
NOTHING SCARY HAPPENED!
So please don't worry.
I WAS FINE YESTERDAY.
BUT TODAY...
...I'M GONNA BE TERRIFIED...
MS. MOGAMI ...
TOMP

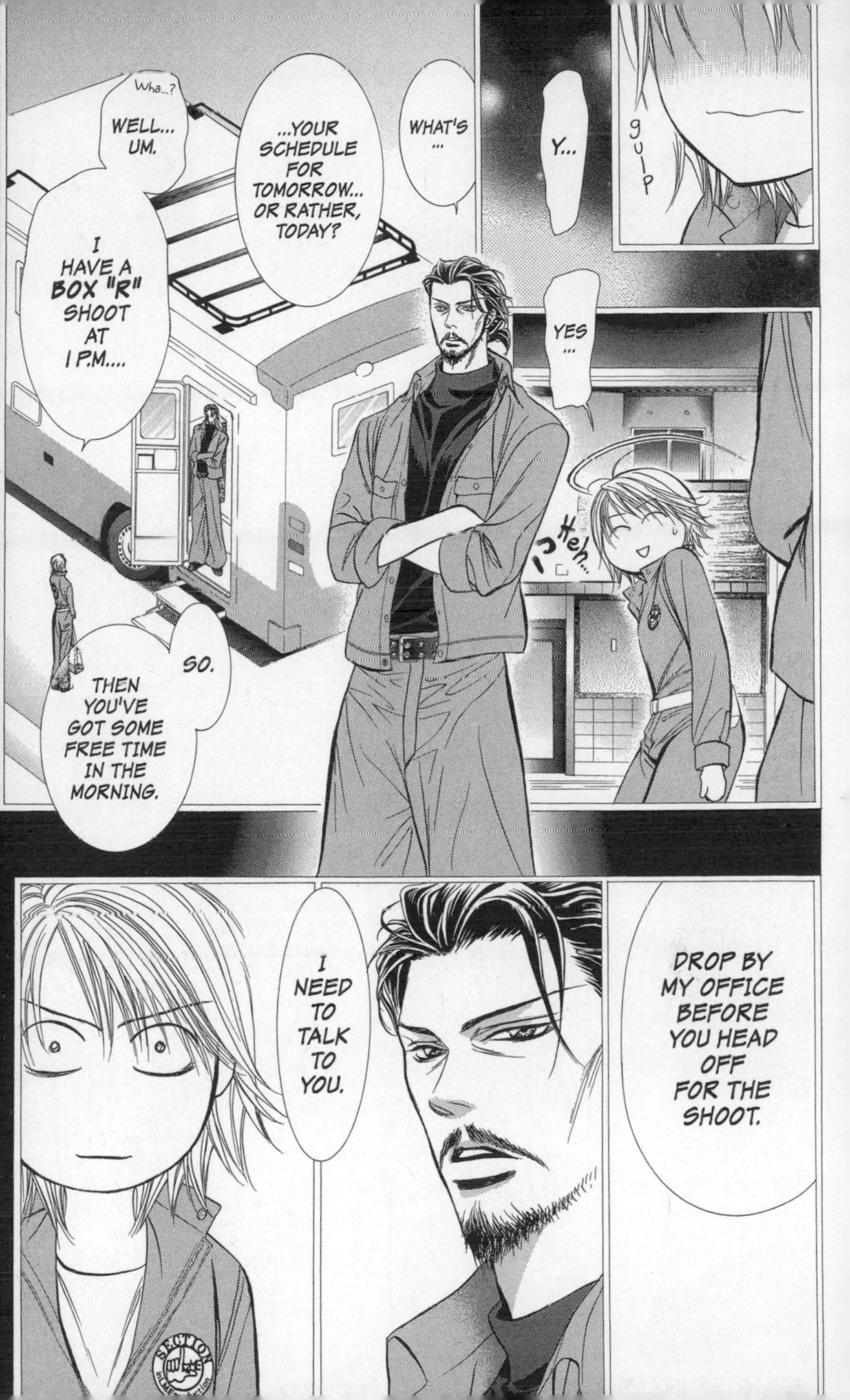

gulp
Y...
YES...
Heh...
WHAT'S...
...YOUR SCHEDULE FOR TOMORROW... OR RATHER, TODAY?
Wha...?
WELL... UM.
I HAVE A BOX "R" SHOOT AT 1 P.M....
SO.
THEN YOU'VE GOT SOME FREE TIME IN THE MORNING.
DROP BY MY OFFICE BEFORE YOU HEAD OFF FOR THE SHOOT.
I NEED TO TALK TO YOU.

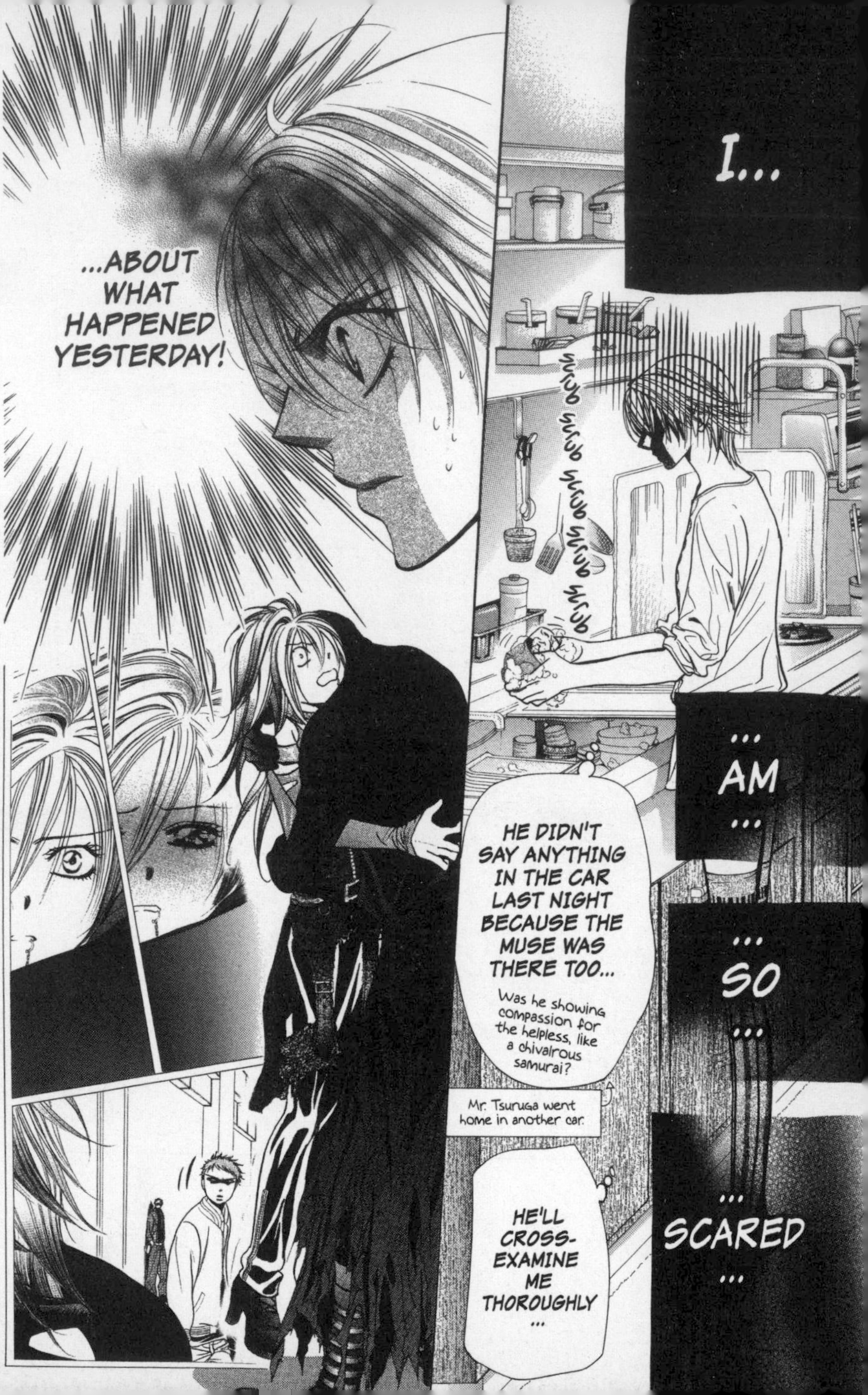
I...
...AM...
...SO...
...SCARED...
scrub scrub scrub scrub scrub
HE DIDN'T SAY ANYTHING IN THE CAR LAST NIGHT BECAUSE THE MUSE WAS THERE TOO...
Was he showing compassion for the helpless, like a chivalrous samurai?
Mr. Tsuruga went home in another car.
HE'LL CROSS-EXAMINE ME THOROUGHLY...
...ABOUT WHAT HAPPENED YESTERDAY!

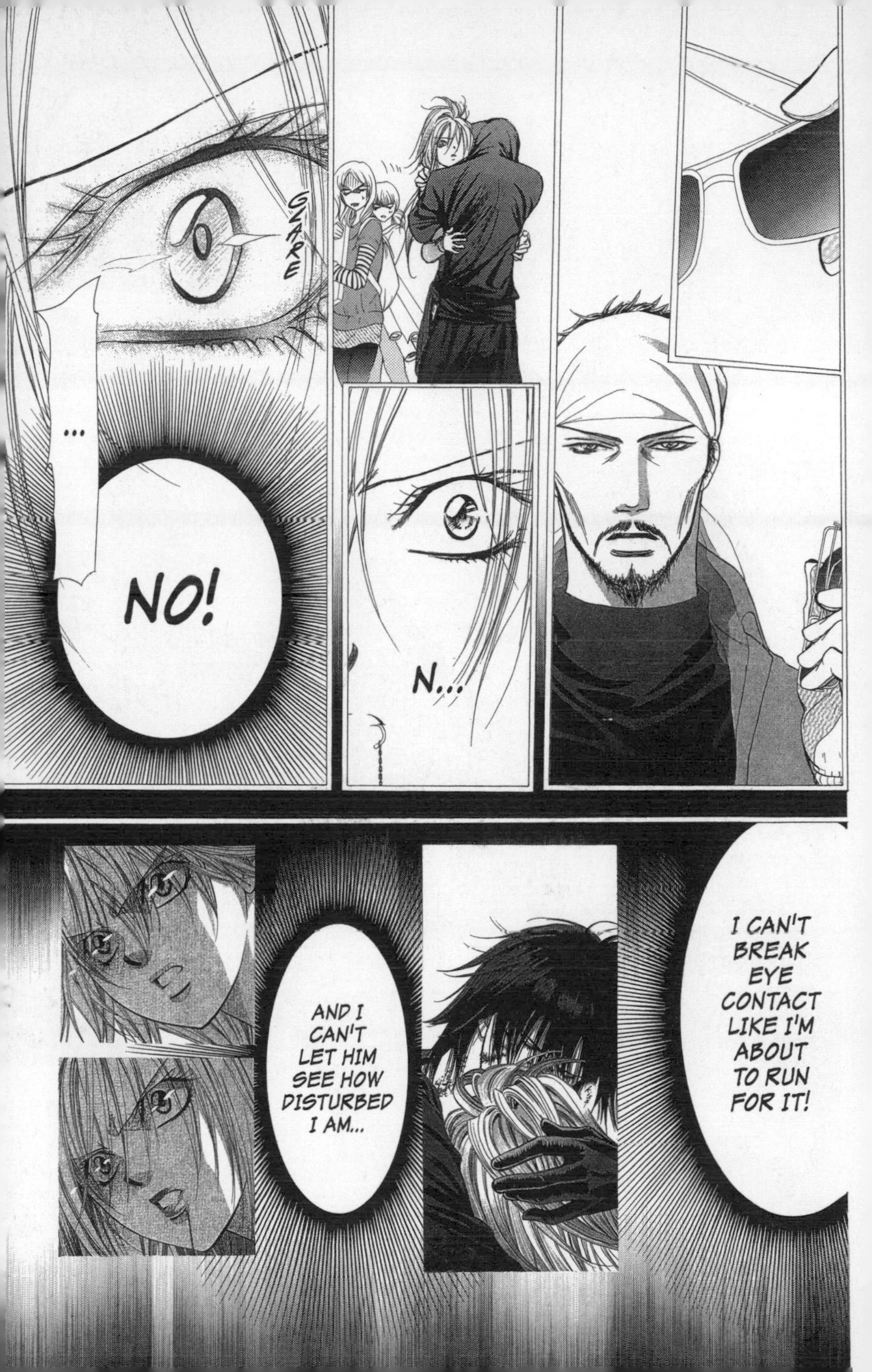
N...
GLARE
...
NO!
I CAN'T BREAK EYE CONTACT LIKE I'M ABOUT TO RUN FOR IT!
AND I CAN'T LET HIM SEE HOW DISTURBED I AM...

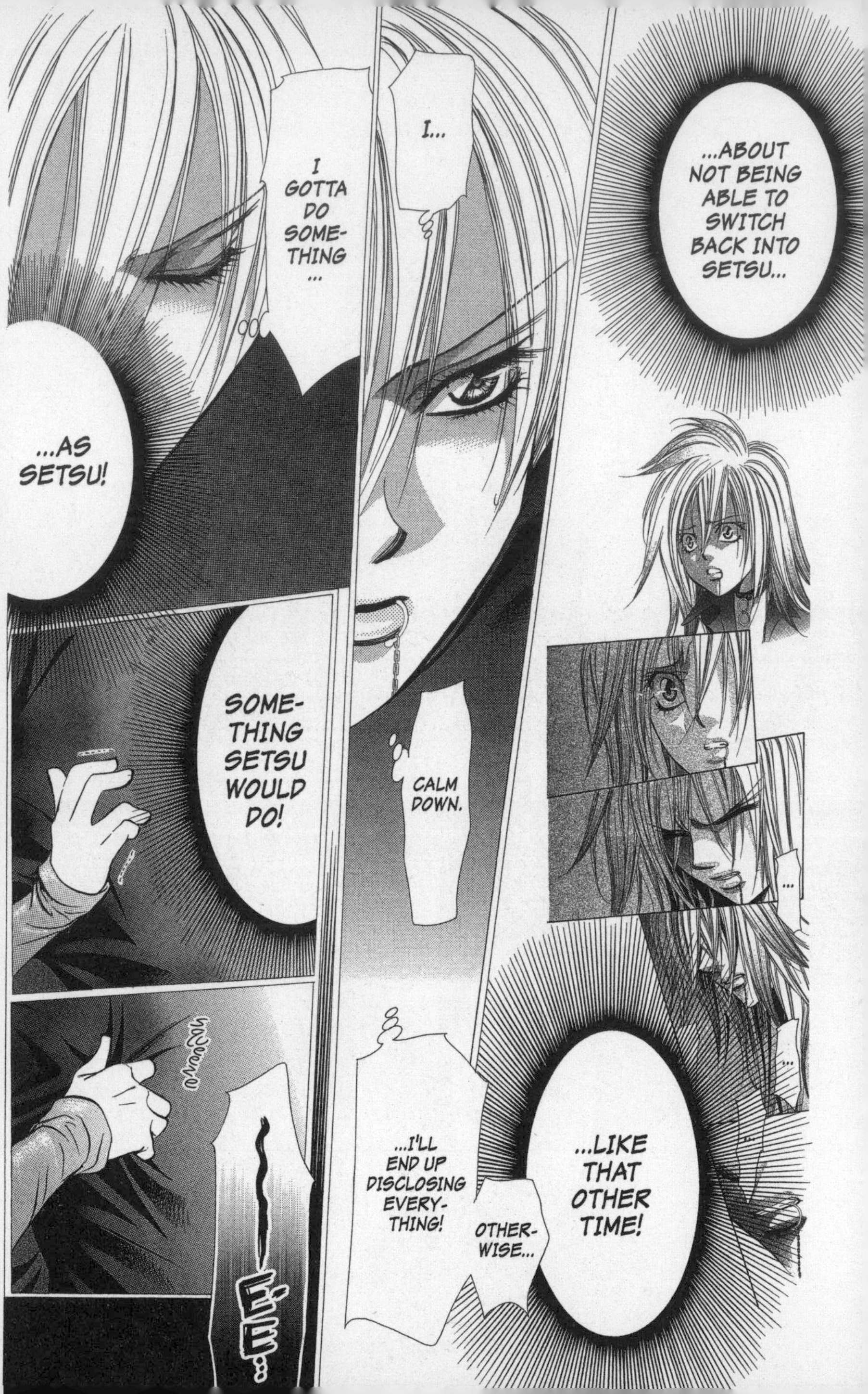
...ABOUT NOT BEING ABLE TO SWITCH BACK INTO SETSU...
...
...
...LIKE THAT OTHER TIME!
I...
CALM DOWN.
OTHERWISE...
...I'LL END UP DISCLOSING EVERY-THING!
I GOTTA DO SOME-THING...
...AS SETSU!
SOME-THING SETSU WOULD DO!

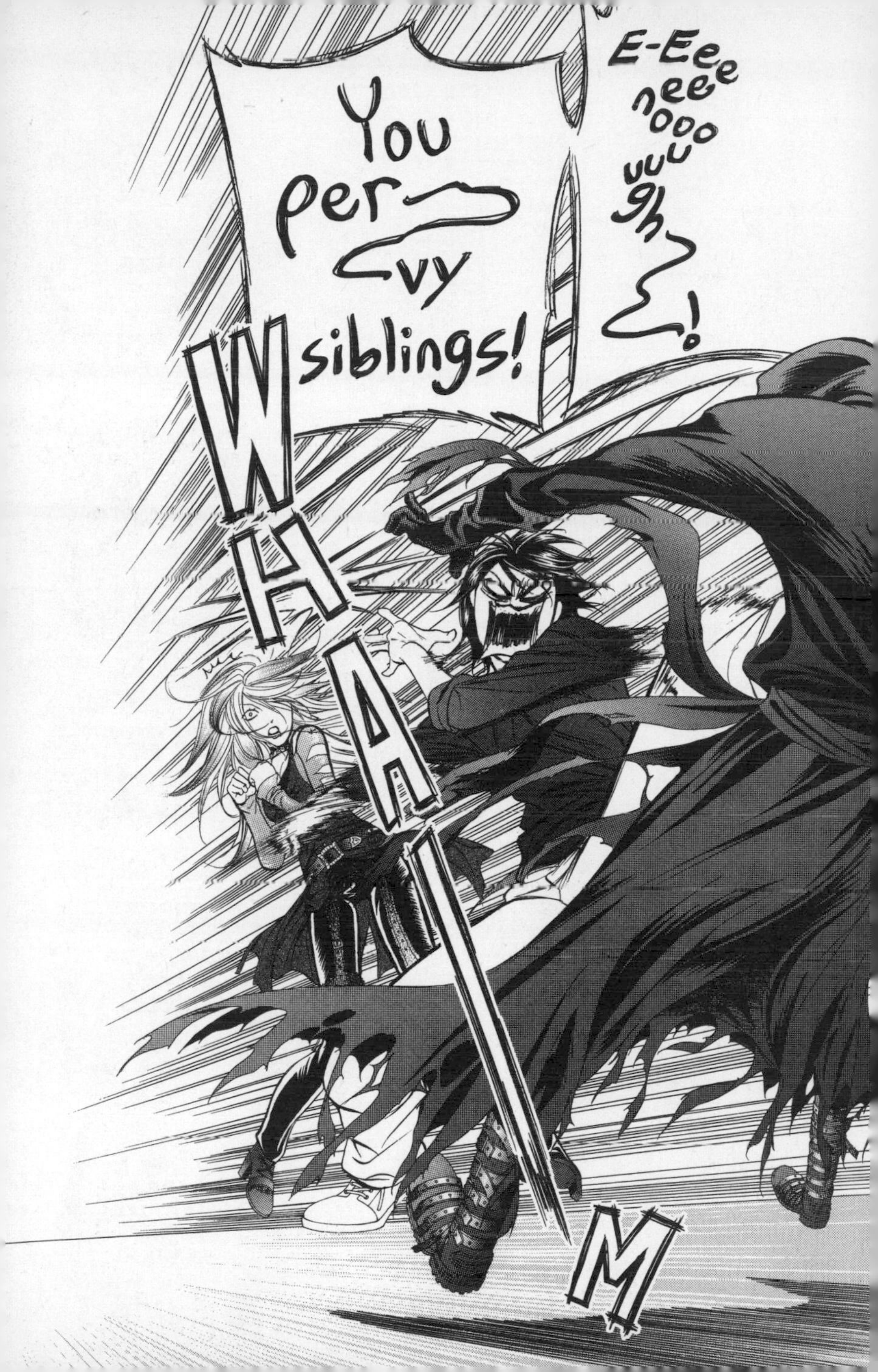

E-Eeeneeenooouuugh!
You per—vy siblings!
WHAAAM

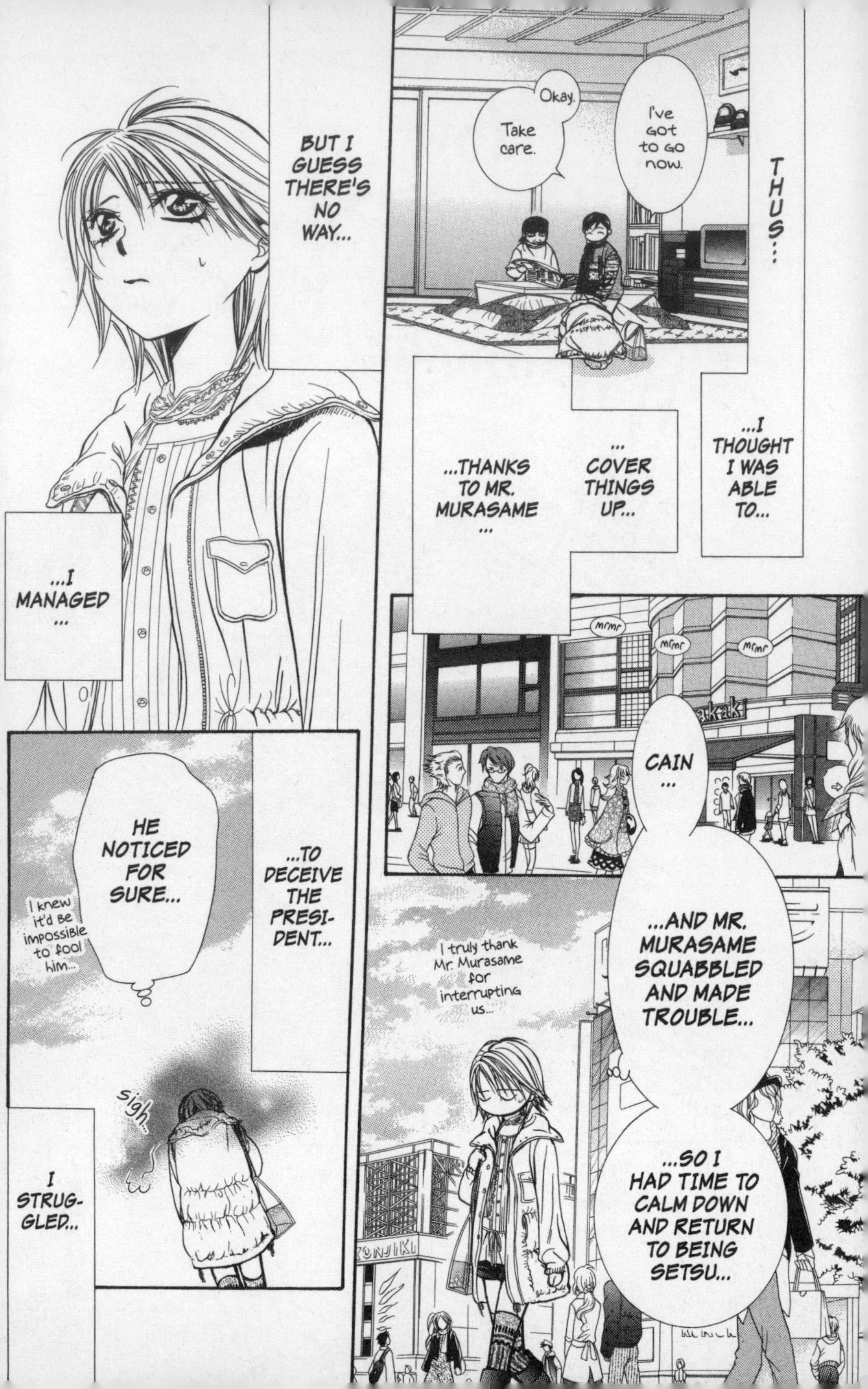
THUS...
I've got to go now.
Okay.
Take care.
...I THOUGHT I WAS ABLE TO...
...COVER THINGS UP...
...THANKS TO MR. MURASAME...
mrmr
mrmr
mrmr
CAIN...
...AND MR. MURASAME SQUABBLED AND MADE TROUBLE...
...SO I HAD TIME TO CALM DOWN AND RETURN TO BEING SETSU...
I truly thank Mr. Murasame for interrupting us...
BUT I GUESS THERE'S NO WAY...
...I MANAGED...
...TO DECEIVE THE PRESIDENT...
HE NOTICED FOR SURE...
I knew it'd be impossible to fool him...
sigh...
I STRUGGLED...

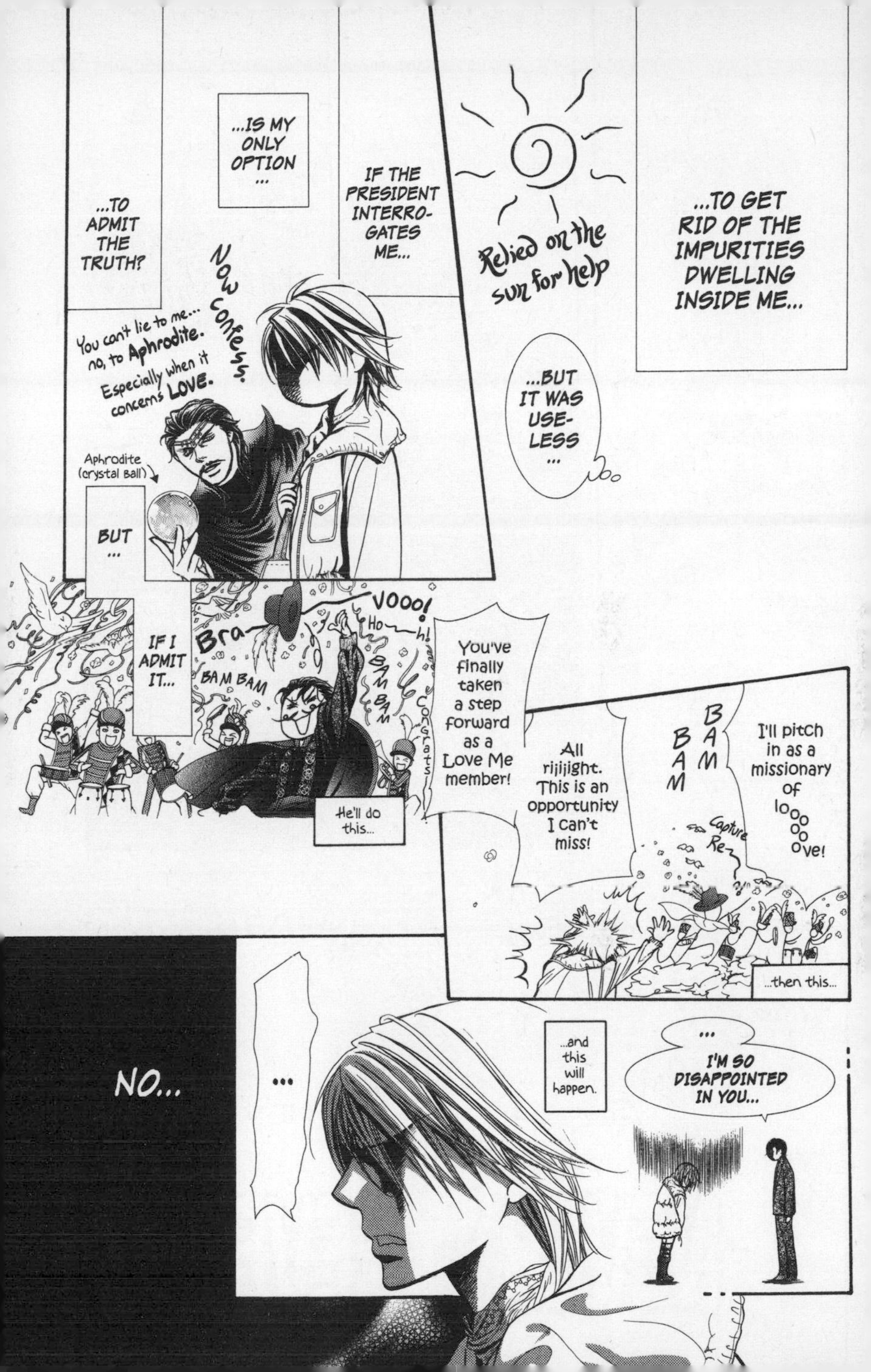
...TO GET RID OF THE IMPURITIES DWELLING INSIDE ME...
Relied on the sun for help
...BUT IT WAS USELESS...
IF THE PRESIDENT INTERROGATES ME...
...IS MY ONLY OPTION...
...TO ADMIT THE TRUTH?
Now confess.
You can't lie to me... no, to Aphrodite. Especially when it concerns LOVE.
Aphrodite (crystal ball)
BUT...
IF I ADMIT IT...
Bra—VOOO!
Ho—h!
BAM BAM
BAM BAM
Congrats!
You've finally taken a step forward as a Love Me member!
He'll do this...
I'll pitch in as a missionary of looooove!
BAM BAM
All riiiiight. This is an opportunity I can't miss!
Capture Re—
...then this...
...and this will happen.
... I'M SO DISAPPOINTED IN YOU...
...
NO...

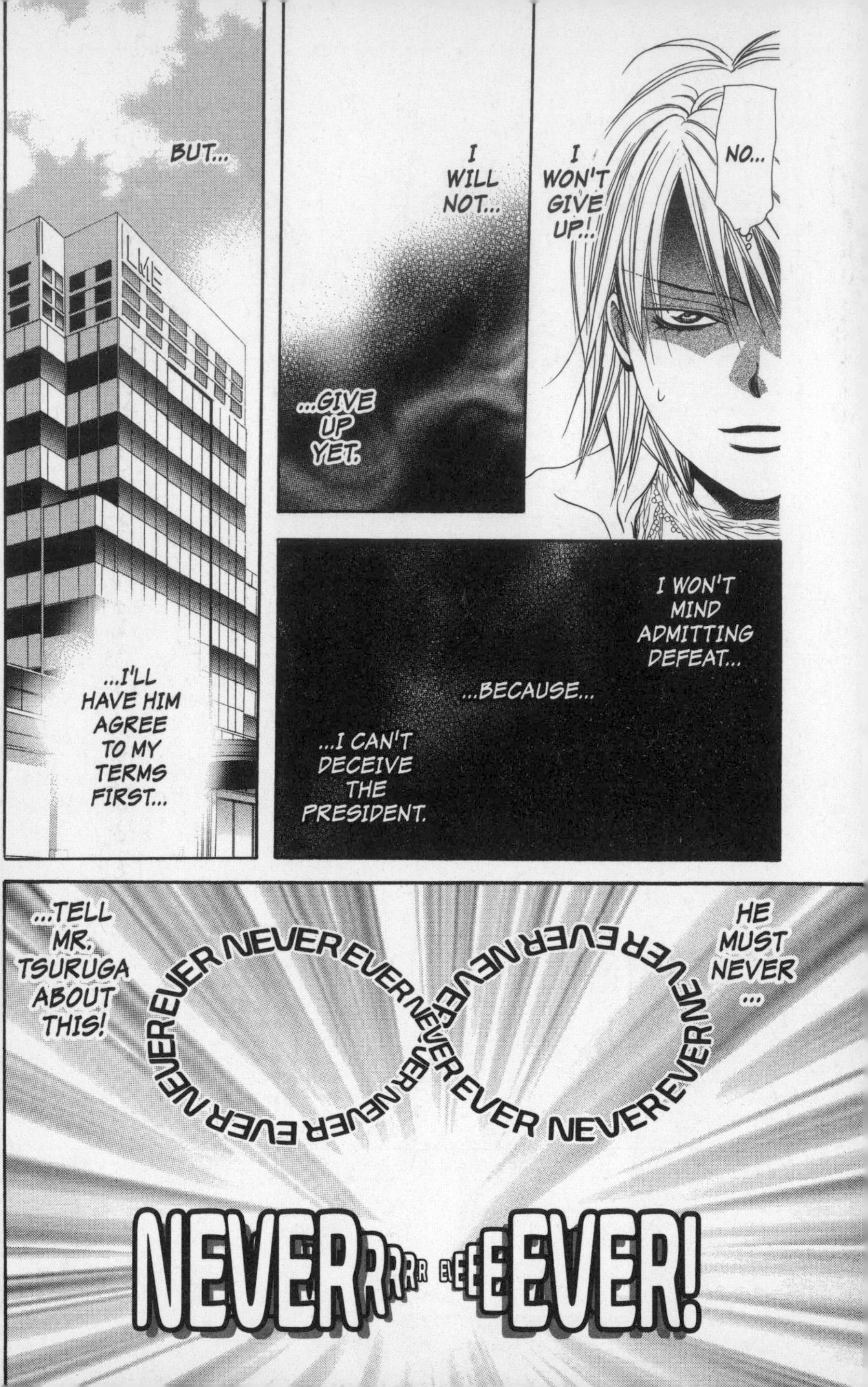
NO...
I WON'T GIVE UP!!
I WILL NOT...
...GIVE UP YET.
I WON'T MIND ADMITTING DEFEAT...
...BECAUSE...
...I CAN'T DECEIVE THE PRESIDENT.
BUT...
...I'LL HAVE HIM AGREE TO MY TERMS FIRST...
HE MUST NEVER...
...TELL MR. TSURUGA ABOUT THIS!
NEVERRRRR EEEEVER!

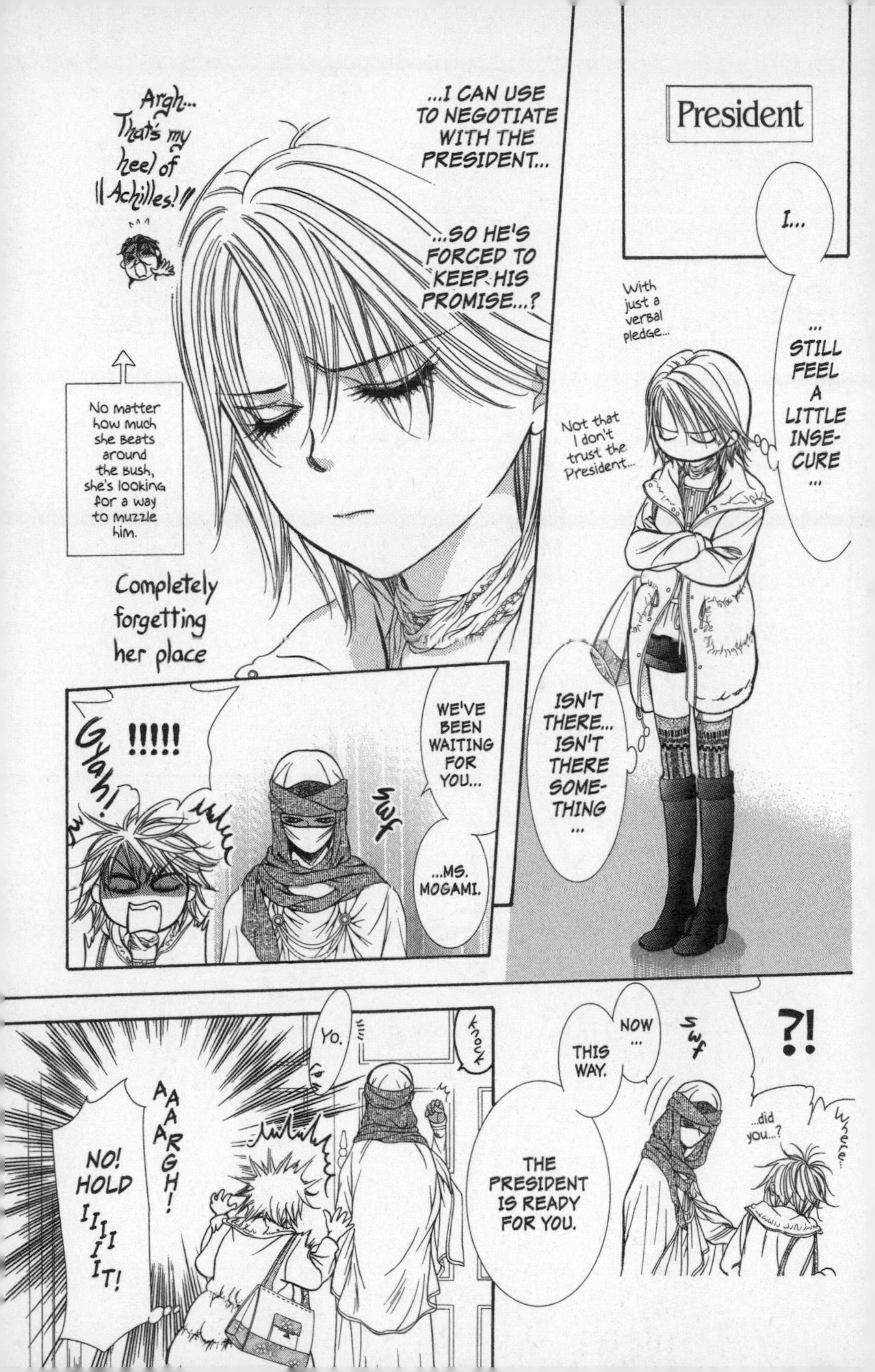
President
I...
... STILL FEEL A LITTLE INSE-CURE ...
With just a verbal pledge...
Not that I don't trust the President...
ISN'T THERE... ISN'T THERE SOME-THING ...
...I CAN USE TO NEGOTIATE WITH THE PRESIDENT...
...SO HE'S FORCED TO KEEP HIS PROMISE...?
Argh... That's my heel of Achilles!!
No matter how much she beats around the bush, she's looking for a way to muzzle him.
Completely forgetting her place
WE'VE BEEN WAITING FOR YOU...
...MS. MOGAMI.
swf
!!!!!
Gyah!
?!
Where...
...did you...?
swf
NOW ...
THIS WAY.
THE PRESIDENT IS READY FOR YOU.
knock
Yo.
AAAARGH!
NO! HOLD IIIIIT!

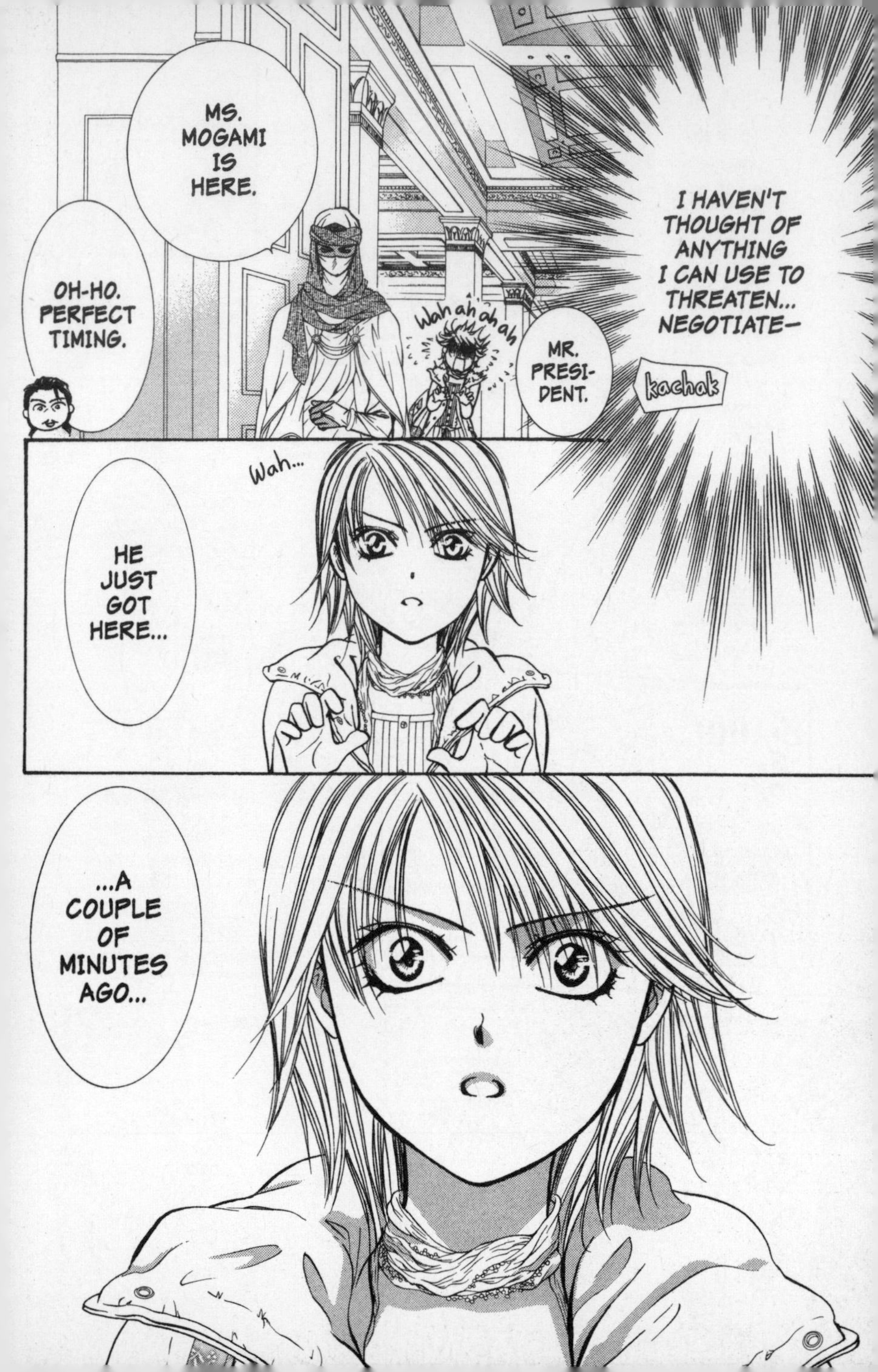
I HAVEN'T THOUGHT OF ANYTHING I CAN USE TO THREATEN... NEGOTIATE–
kachak
MR. PRESI-DENT.
Wah ah ah ah
MS. MOGAMI IS HERE.
OH-HO. PERFECT TIMING.
Wah...
HE JUST GOT HERE...
...A COUPLE OF MINUTES AGO...

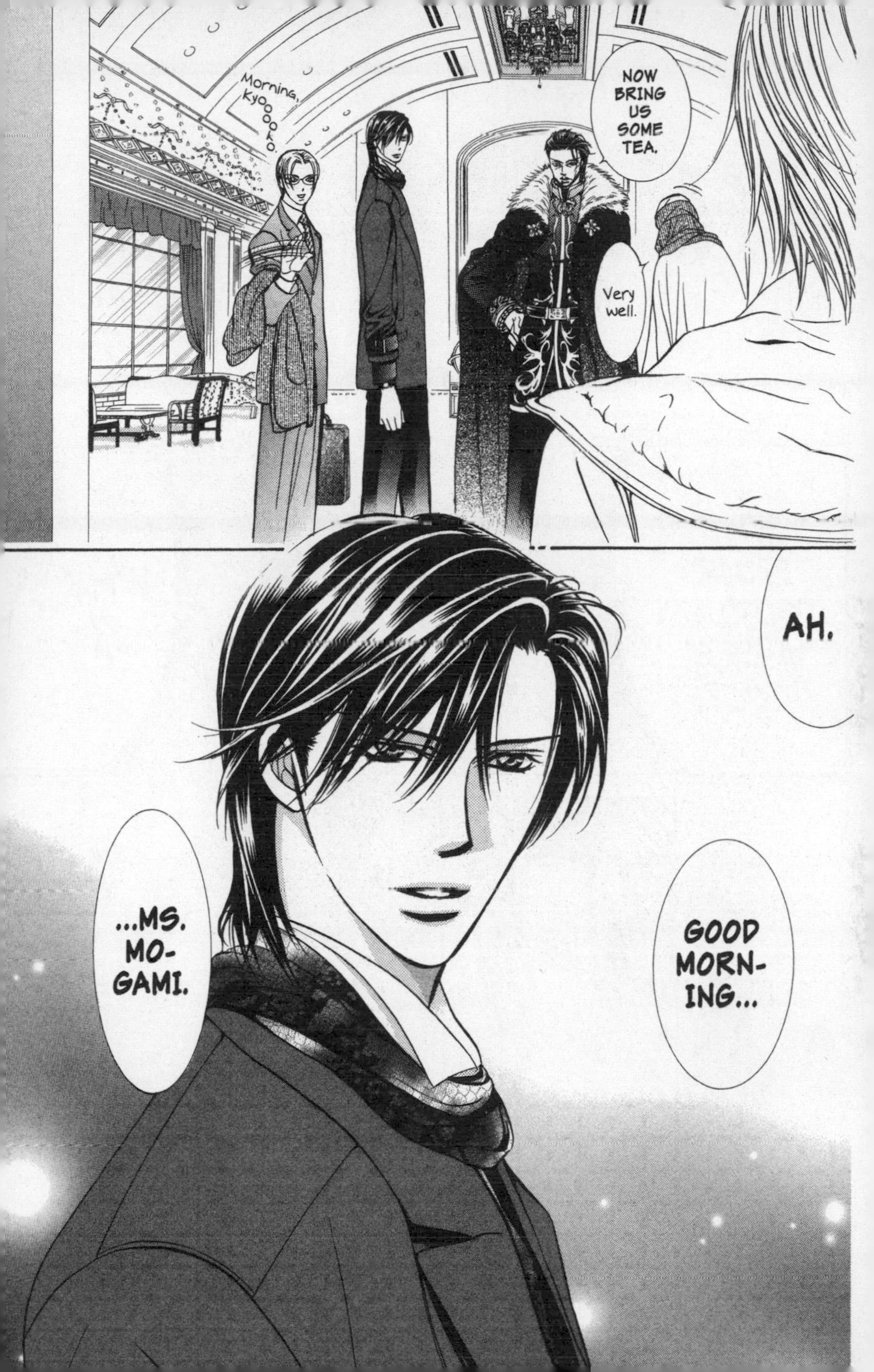
NOW BRING US SOME TEA.
Very well.
Morning, Kyooooko.
AH.
GOOD MORNING...
...MS. MOGAMI.

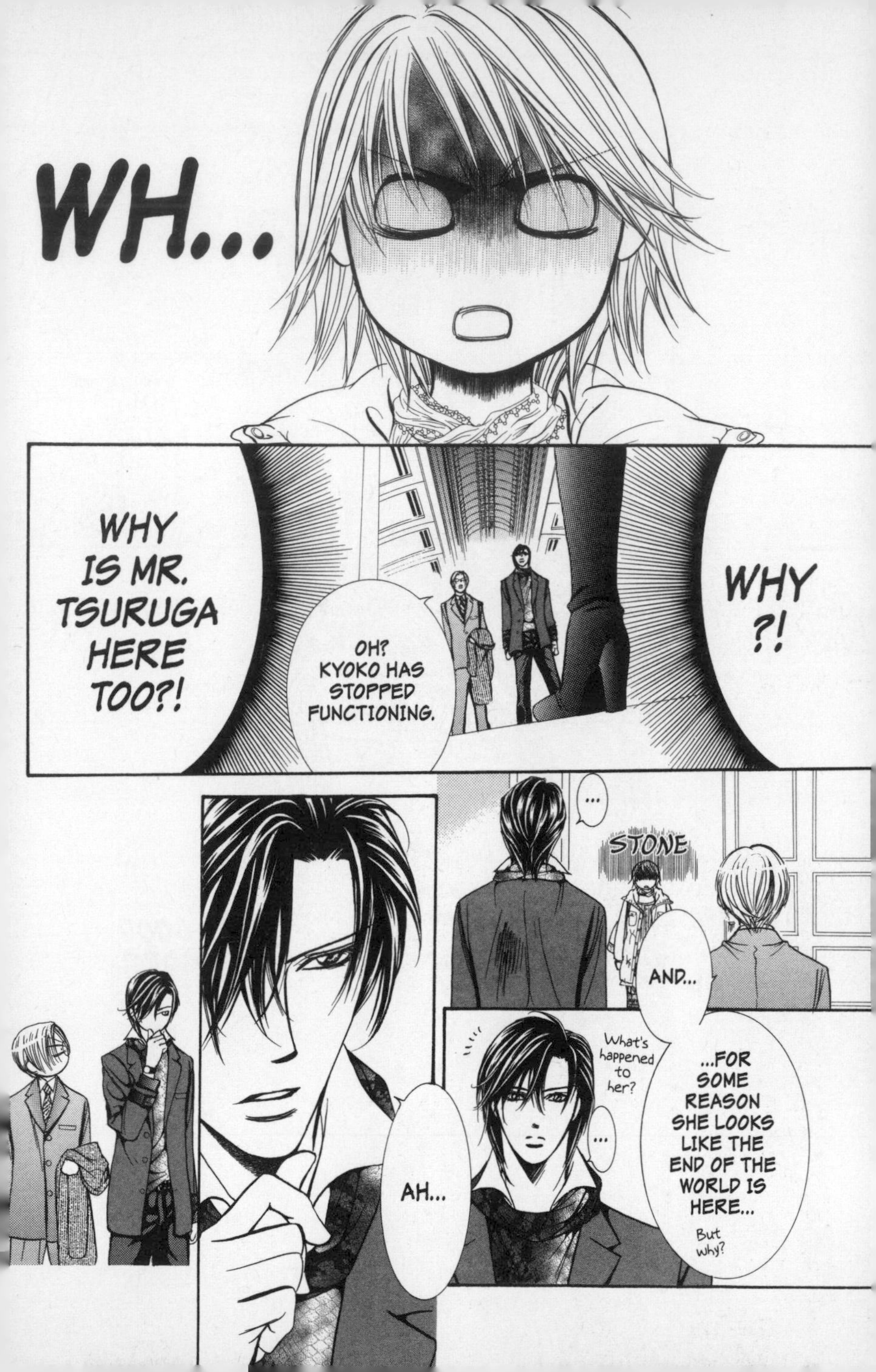
WH...
WHY ?!
WHY IS MR. TSURUGA HERE TOO?!
OH? KYOKO HAS STOPPED FUNCTIONING.
...
STONE
AND...
...FOR SOME REASON SHE LOOKS LIKE THE END OF THE WORLD IS HERE...
What's happened to her?
...
But why?
AH...

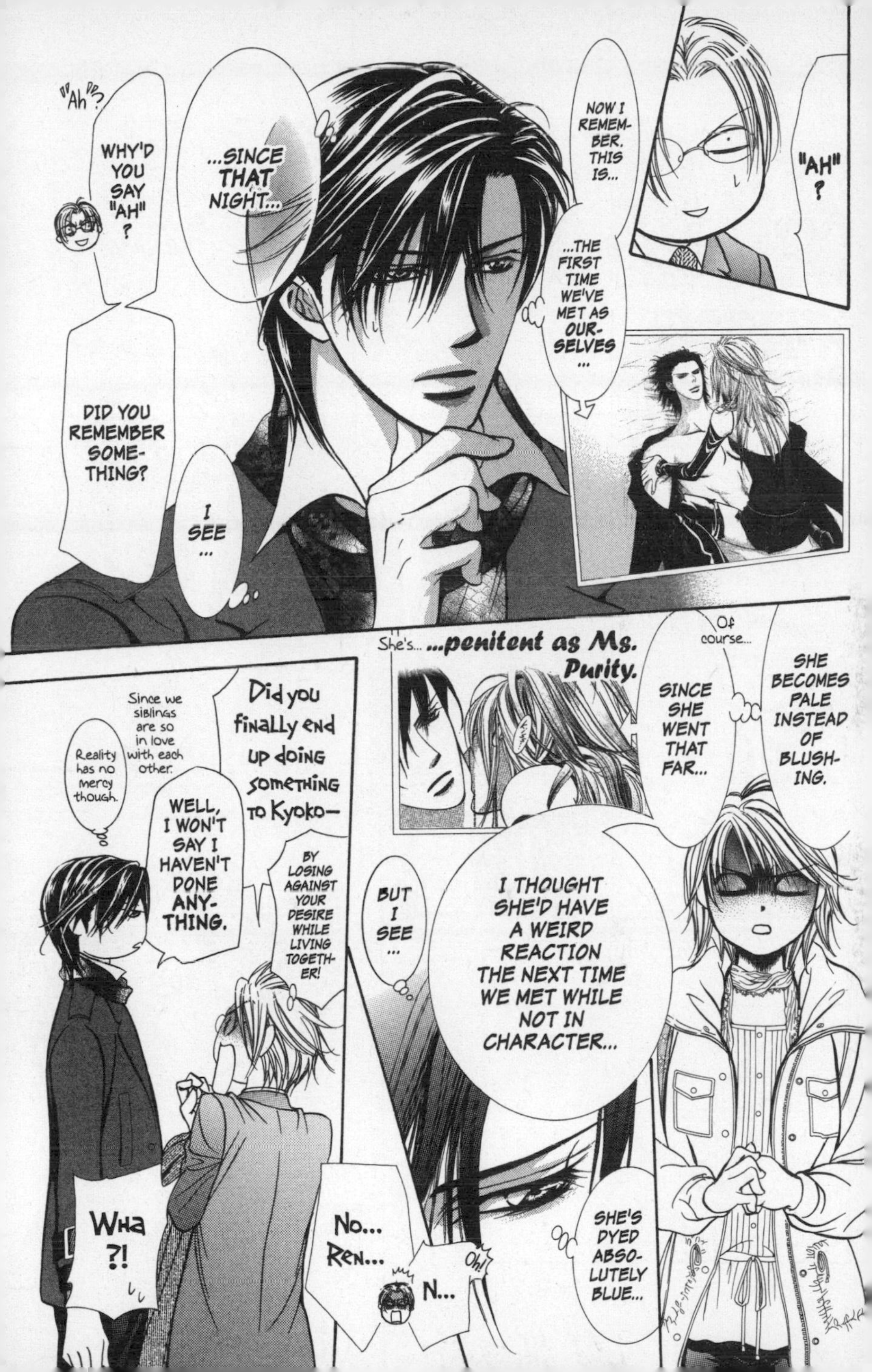
"AH"?
NOW I REMEMBER. THIS IS...
...THE FIRST TIME WE'VE MET AS OURSELVES...
...SINCE THAT NIGHT...
I SEE...
"Ah"?
WHY'D YOU SAY "AH"?
DID YOU REMEMBER SOMETHING?
Of course...
SHE BECOMES PALE INSTEAD OF BLUSHING.
SINCE SHE WENT THAT FAR...
She's... ...penitent as Ms. Purity.
I THOUGHT SHE'D HAVE A WEIRD REACTION THE NEXT TIME WE MET WHILE NOT IN CHARACTER...
BUT I SEE...
SHE'S DYED ABSOLUTELY BLUE...
Did you finally end up doing something to Kyoko—
BY LOSING AGAINST YOUR DESIRE WHILE LIVING TOGETHER!
Since we siblings are so in love with each other.
Reality has no mercy though.
WELL, I WON'T SAY I HAVEN'T DONE ANYTHING.
Wha?!
No... Ren...
Oh!
N...

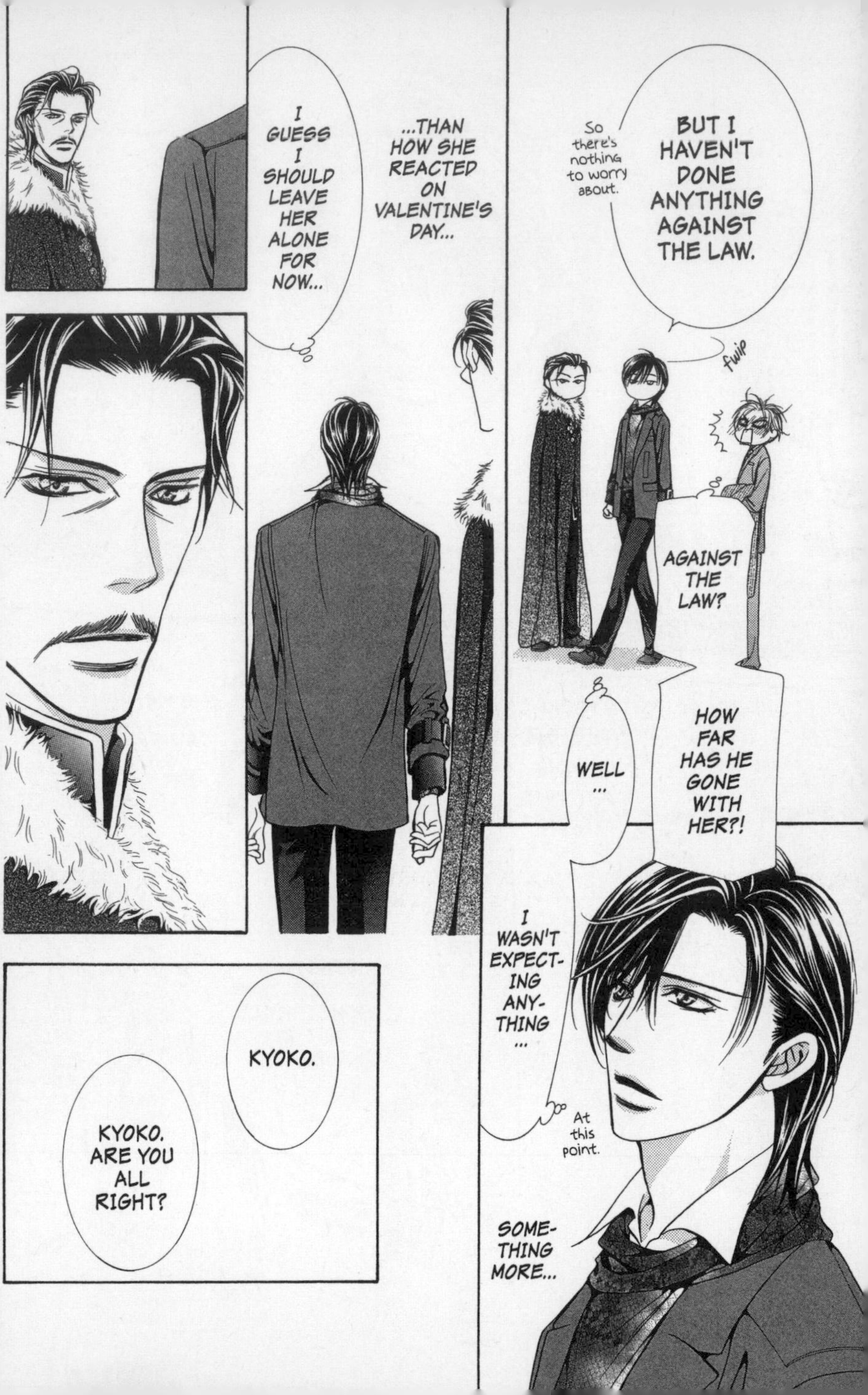
BUT I HAVEN'T DONE ANYTHING AGAINST THE LAW.
So there's nothing to worry about.
fwip
AGAINST THE LAW?
HOW FAR HAS HE GONE WITH HER?!
WELL...
I WASN'T EXPECTING ANYTHING...
At this point.
SOMETHING MORE...
...THAN HOW SHE REACTED ON VALENTINE'S DAY...
I GUESS I SHOULD LEAVE HER ALONE FOR NOW...
KYOKO.
KYOKO. ARE YOU ALL RIGHT?

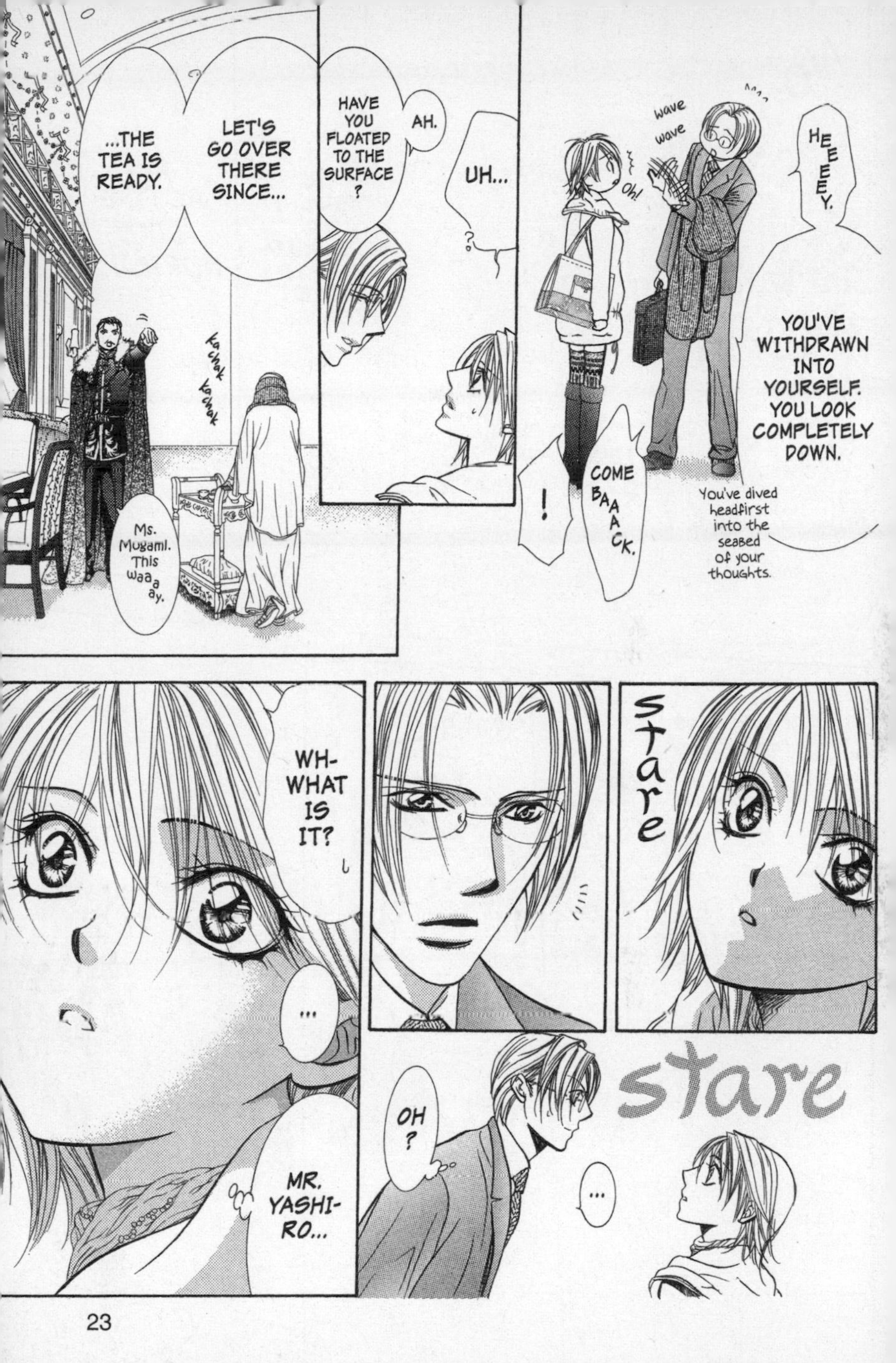
HEEEEEY.
wave wave
Oh!
YOU'VE WITHDRAWN INTO YOURSELF. YOU LOOK COMPLETELY DOWN.
You've dived headfirst into the seabed of your thoughts.
!
COME BAAAACK.
UH...
?
AH.
HAVE YOU FLOATED TO THE SURFACE?
LET'S GO OVER THERE SINCE...
...THE TEA IS READY.
ka chak ka chak
Ms. Mugami. This waaaay.
stare
WH-WHAT IS IT?
...
stare
...
OH?
MR. YASHIRO...

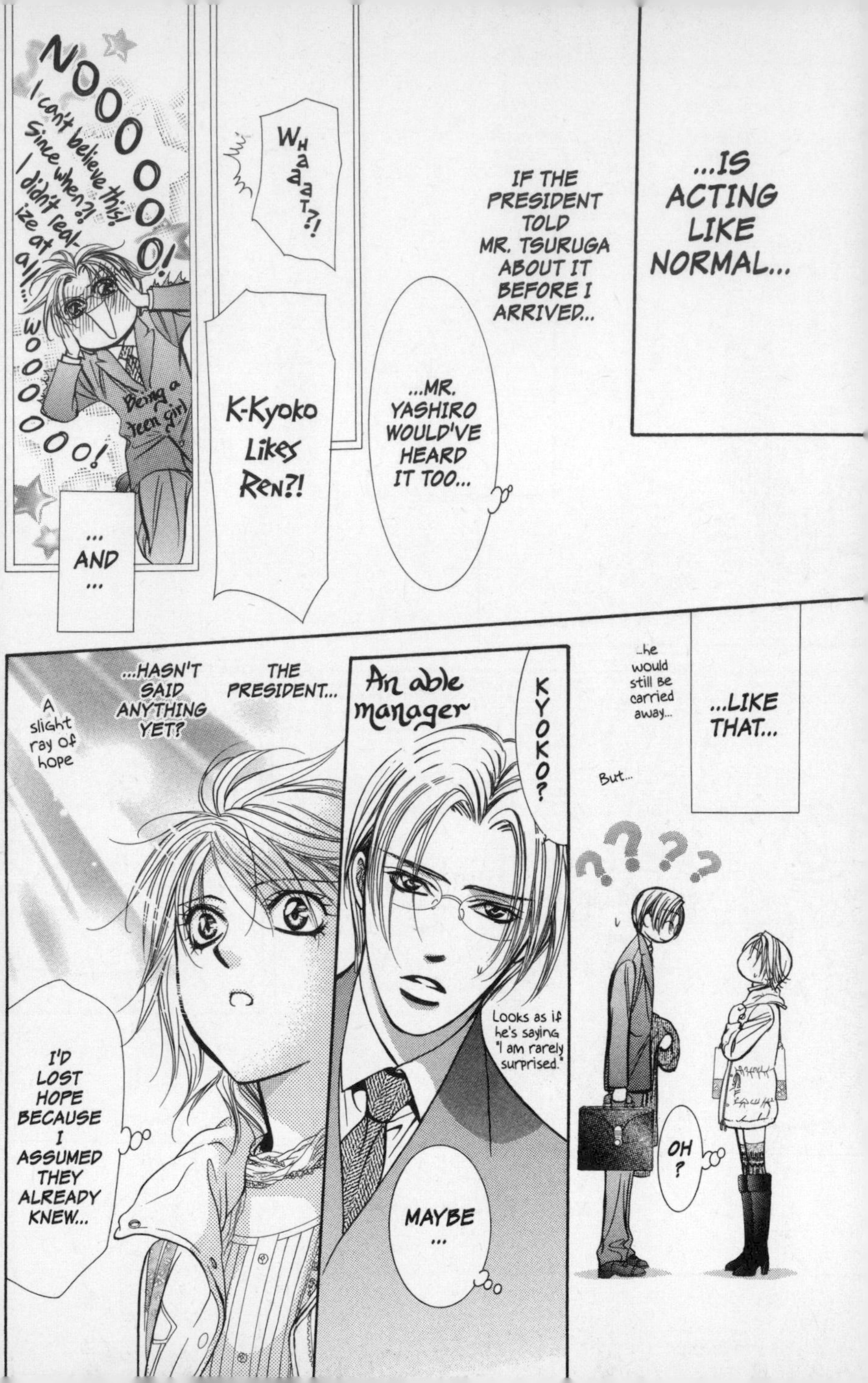
...IS ACTING LIKE NORMAL...
IF THE PRESIDENT TOLD MR. TSURUGA ABOUT IT BEFORE I ARRIVED...
...MR. YASHIRO WOULD'VE HEARD IT TOO...
Whaaat?!
K-Kyoko Likes Ren?!
NOOOOOOO!
I can't believe this! Since when?! I didn't realize at all...
WOOOOOOOO!
Being a teen girl
...AND...
...LIKE THAT...
...he would still be carried away...
But...
OH?
KYOKO?
An able manager
Looks as if he's saying "I am rarely surprised."
MAYBE...
THE PRESIDENT...
...HASN'T SAID ANYTHING YET?
A slight ray of hope
I'D LOST HOPE BECAUSE I ASSUMED THEY ALREADY KNEW...

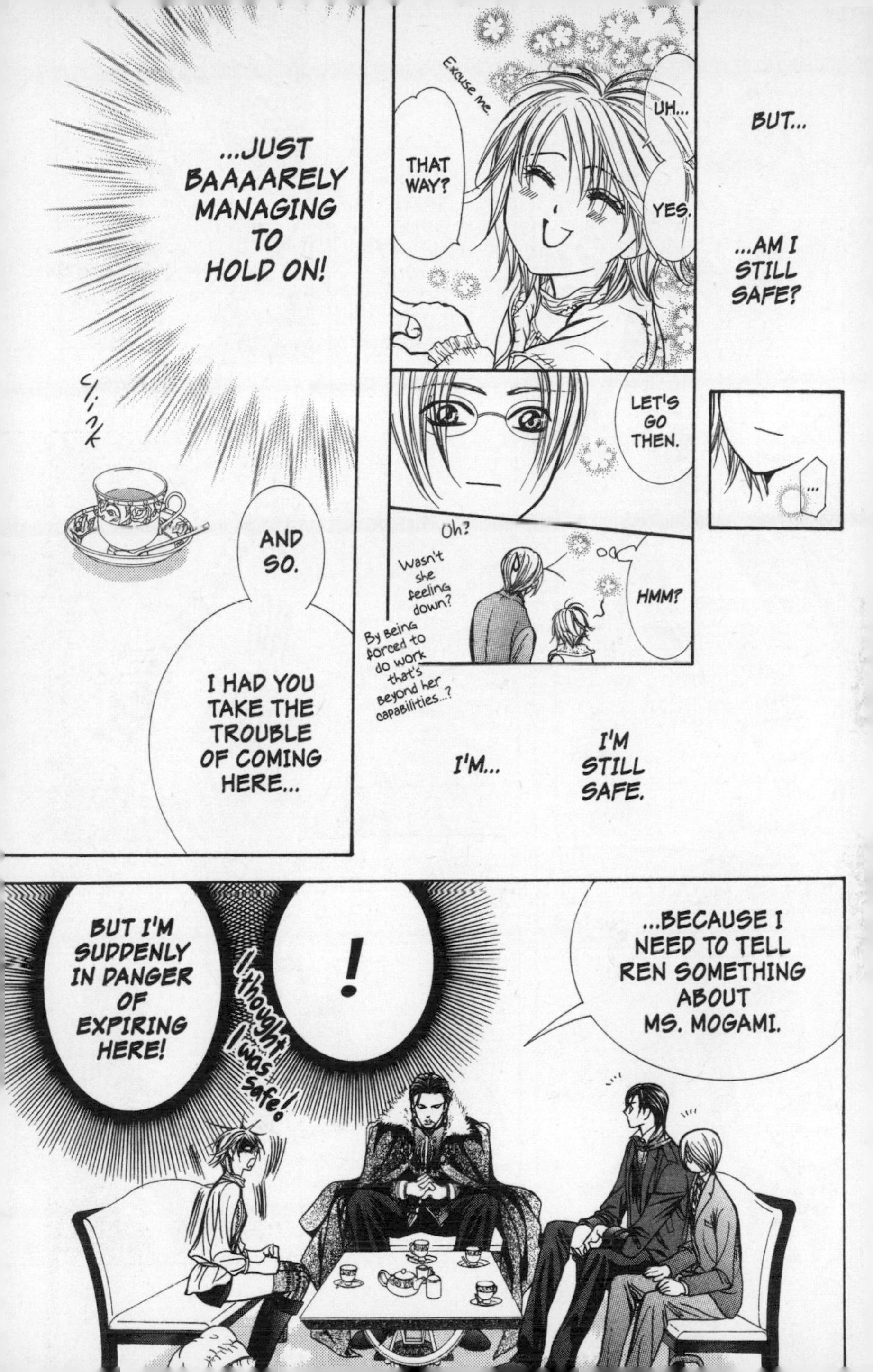
BUT...
...AM I STILL SAFE?
UH...
YES.
Excuse me.
THAT WAY?
...
LET'S GO THEN.
HMM?
Oh?
Wasn't she feeling down?
By being forced to do work that's beyond her capabilities...?
I'M STILL SAFE.
I'M...
...JUST BAAAARELY MANAGING TO HOLD ON!
Clink
AND SO.
I HAD YOU TAKE THE TROUBLE OF COMING HERE...
...BECAUSE I NEED TO TELL REN SOMETHING ABOUT MS. MOGAMI.
!
I thought I was safe!
BUT I'M SUDDENLY IN DANGER OF EXPIRING HERE!

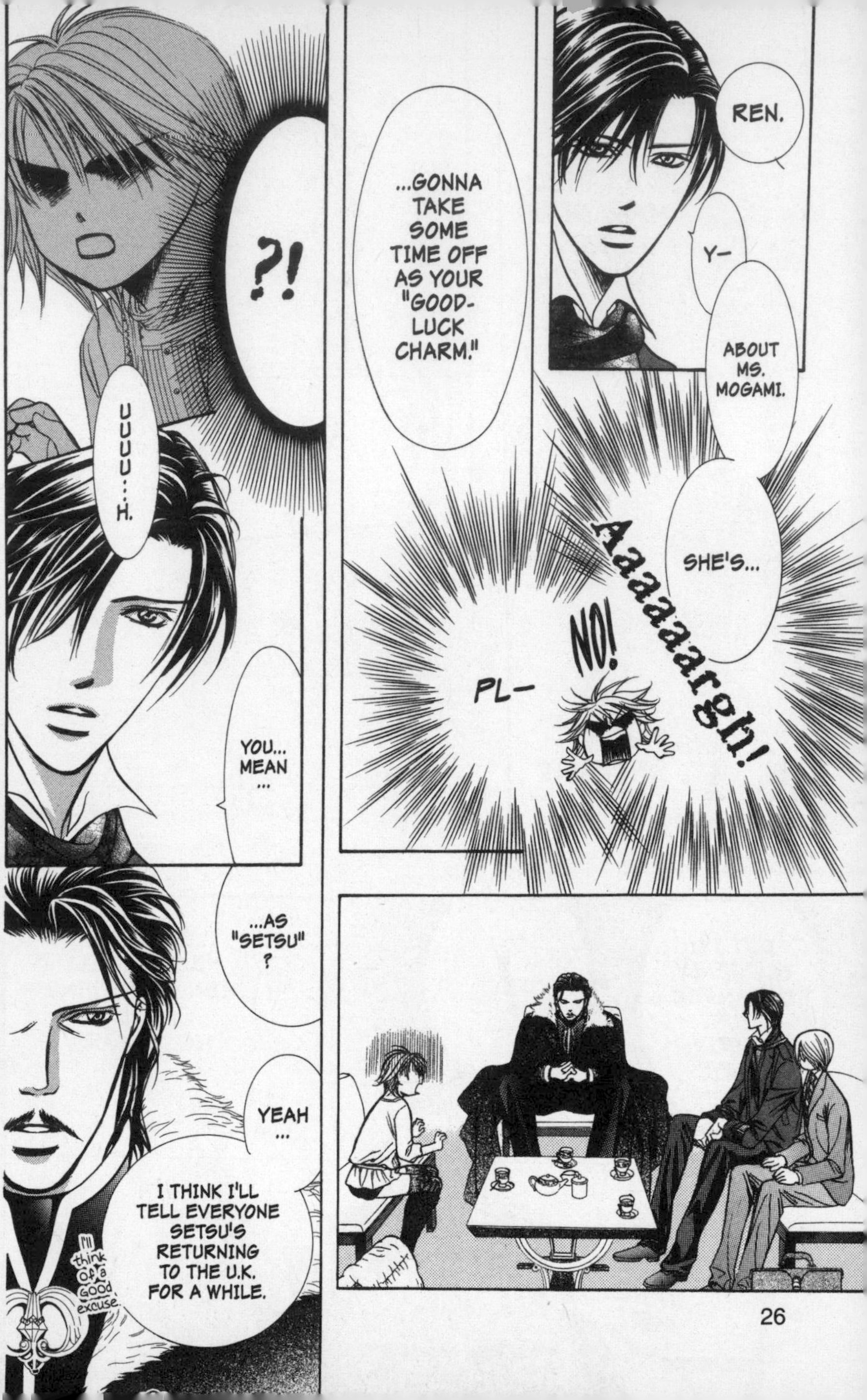
REN.
Y–
ABOUT MS. MOGAMI.
SHE'S...
Aaaaaargh!
NO!
PL–
...GONNA TAKE SOME TIME OFF AS YOUR "GOOD-LUCK CHARM."
?!
UUUU...H.
YOU... MEAN ...
...AS "SETSU"?
YEAH ...
I THINK I'LL TELL EVERYONE SETSU'S RETURNING TO THE U.K. FOR A WHILE.
I'll think of a good excuse.

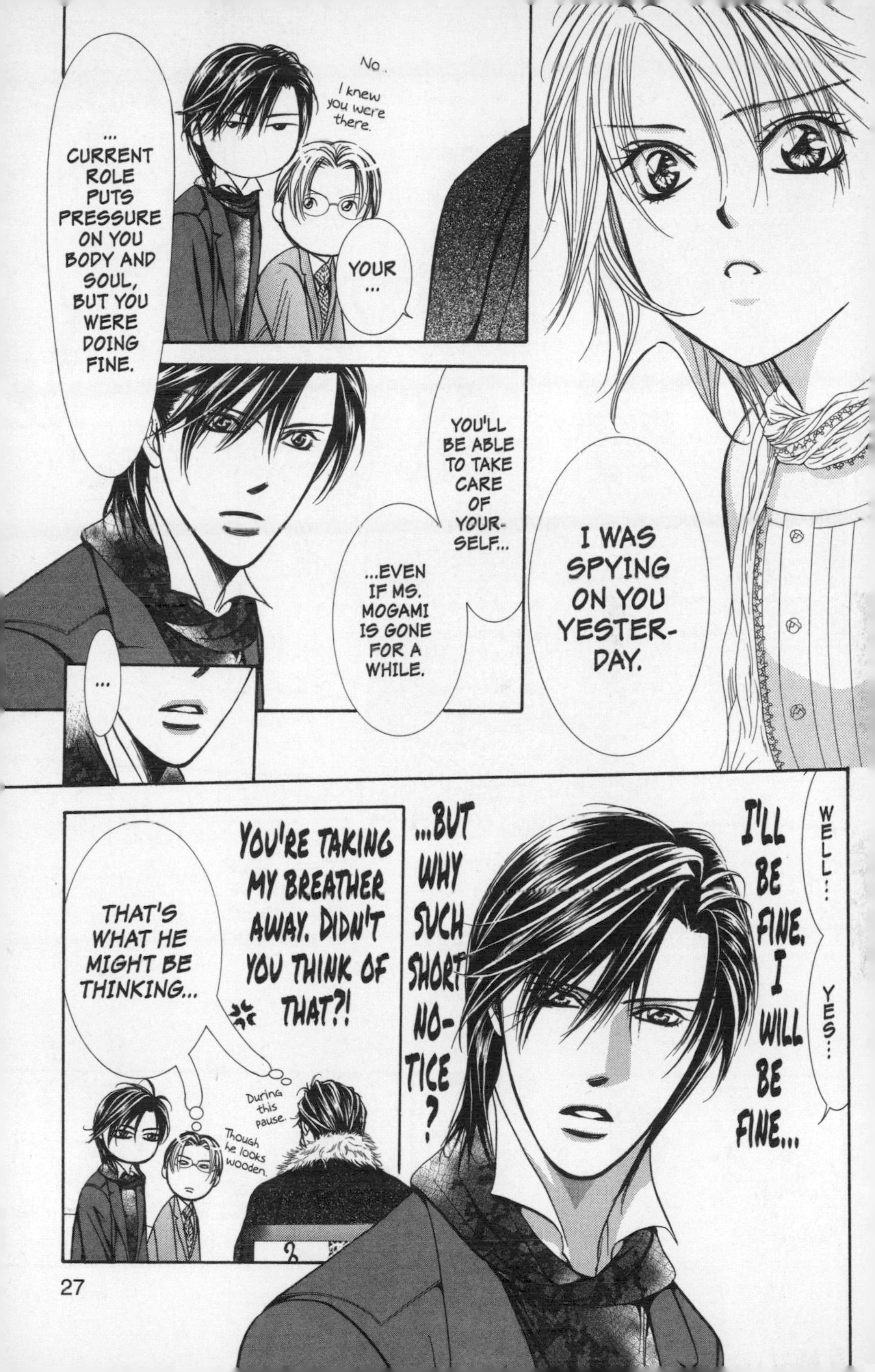
I WAS SPYING ON YOU YESTERDAY.
No.. I knew you were there.
YOUR ...
... CURRENT ROLE PUTS PRESSURE ON YOU BODY AND SOUL, BUT YOU WERE DOING FINE.
YOU'LL BE ABLE TO TAKE CARE OF YOURSELF...
...EVEN IF MS. MOGAMI IS GONE FOR A WHILE.
...
WELL... YES...
I'LL BE FINE. I WILL BE FINE...
...BUT WHY SUCH SHORT NOTICE?
YOU'RE TAKING MY BREATHER AWAY. DIDN'T YOU THINK OF THAT?!
THAT'S WHAT HE MIGHT BE THINKING...
During this pause.
Though he looks wooden.

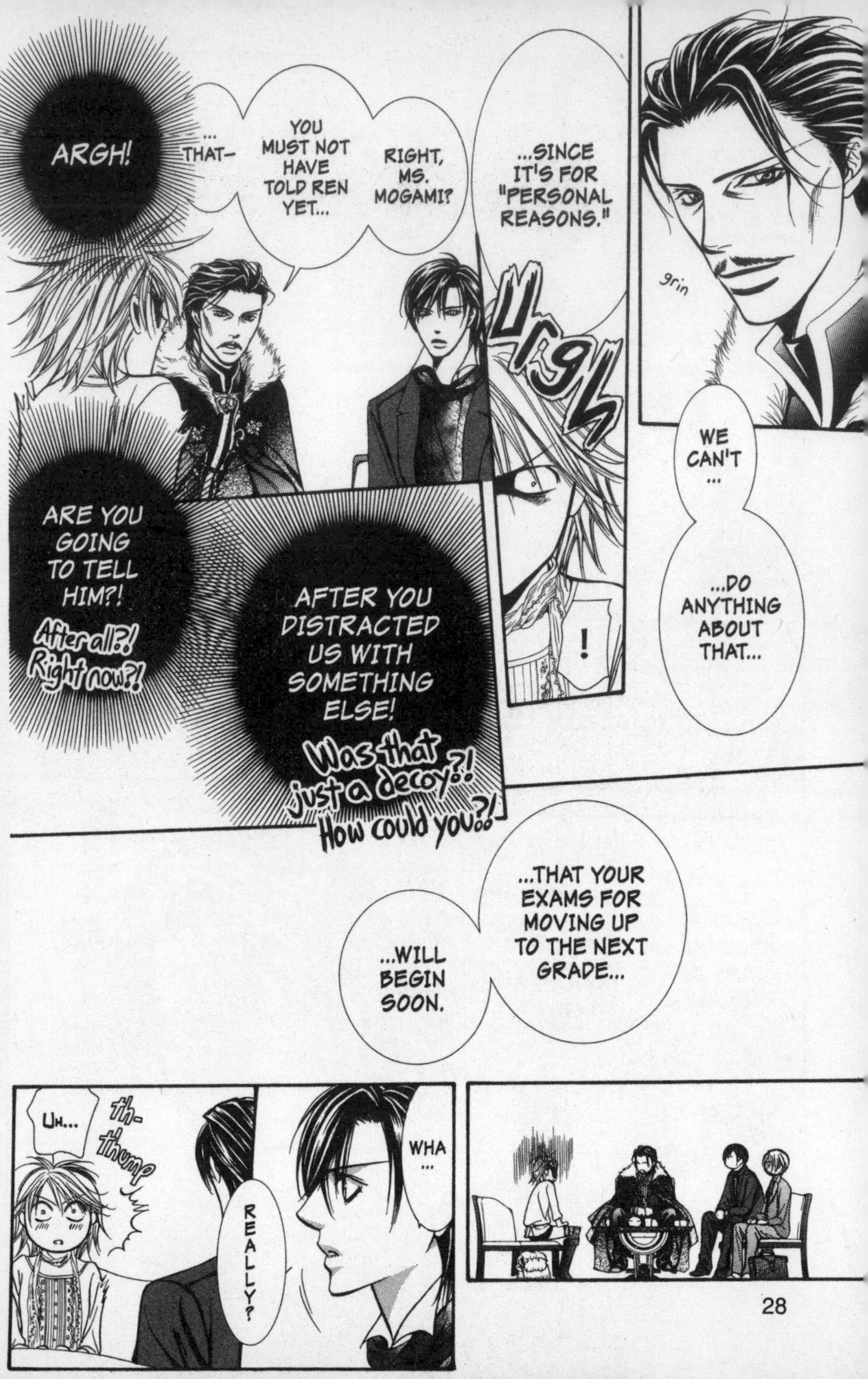
grin
WE CAN'T ...
...DO ANYTHING ABOUT THAT...
...SINCE IT'S FOR "PERSONAL REASONS."
RIGHT, MS. MOGAMI?
YOU MUST NOT HAVE TOLD REN YET...
... THAT-
ARGH!
Argh
!
AFTER YOU DISTRACTED US WITH SOMETHING ELSE!
Was that just a decoy?! How could you?!
ARE YOU GOING TO TELL HIM?!
After all?! Right now?!
...THAT YOUR EXAMS FOR MOVING UP TO THE NEXT GRADE...
...WILL BEGIN SOON.
WHA ...
REALLY?
th-thump
Uh...

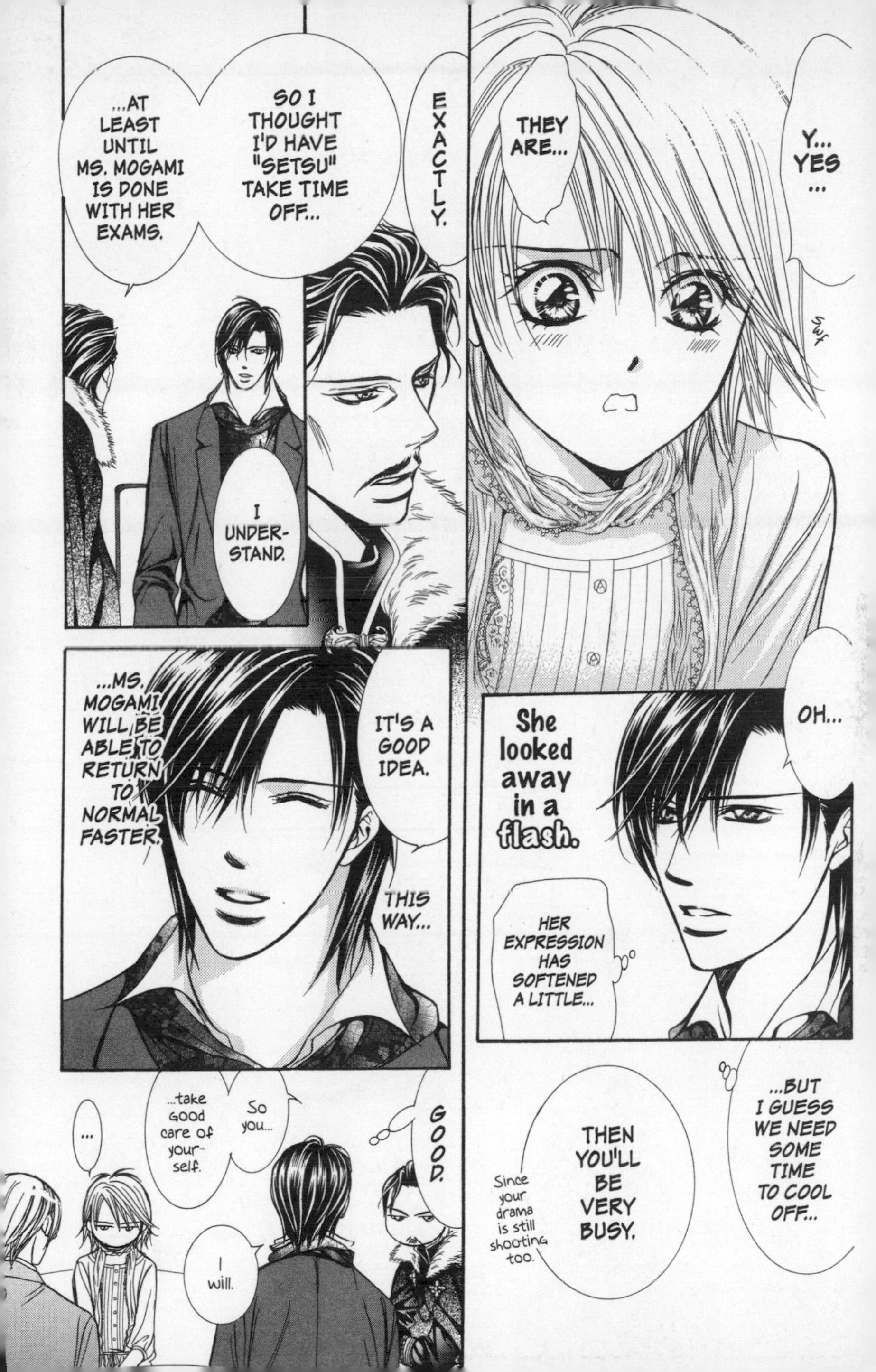
Y... YES ...
THEY ARE...
swf
EXACTLY.
SO I THOUGHT I'D HAVE "SETSU" TAKE TIME OFF...
...AT LEAST UNTIL MS. MOGAMI IS DONE WITH HER EXAMS.
I UNDER-STAND.
OH...
She looked away in a flash.
HER EXPRESSION HAS SOFTENED A LITTLE...
IT'S A GOOD IDEA.
THIS WAY...
...MS. MOGAMI WILL BE ABLE TO RETURN TO NORMAL FASTER.
...BUT I GUESS WE NEED SOME TIME TO COOL OFF...
THEN YOU'LL BE VERY BUSY.
Since your drama is still shooting too.
GOOD.
So you...
...take good care of your-self.
...
I will.

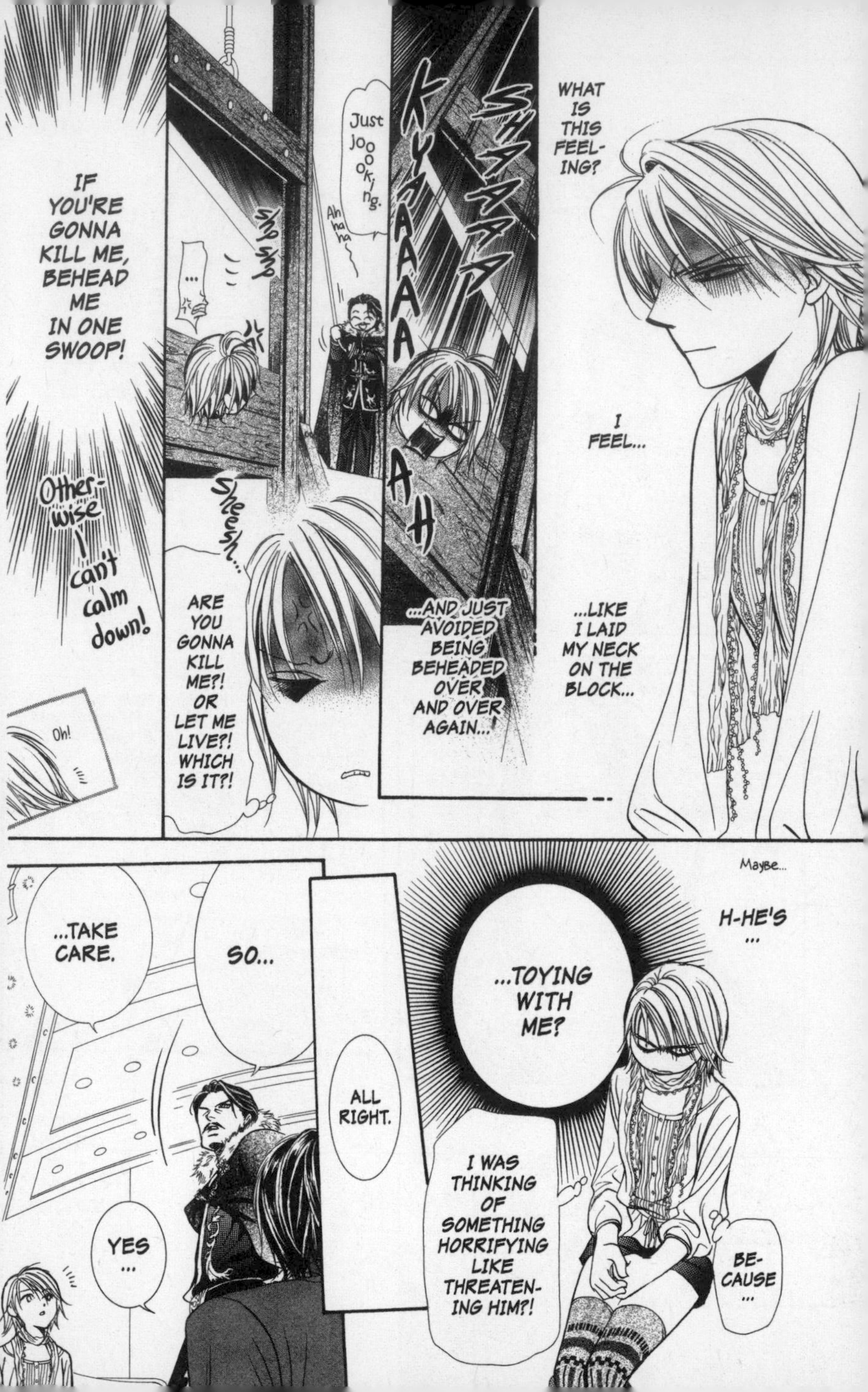
WHAT IS THIS FEELING?
I FEEL...
...LIKE I LAID MY NECK ON THE BLOCK...
SHAAAAA
KYAAAAAAH
...AND JUST AVOIDED BEING BEHEADED OVER AND OVER AGAIN...
Just joooooking.
Ah ha ha
slip slip
...
Sheesh...
ARE YOU GONNA KILL ME?! OR LET ME LIVE?! WHICH IS IT?!
IF YOU'RE GONNA KILL ME, BEHEAD ME IN ONE SWOOP!
Otherwise I can't calm down!
Oh!
Maybe...
H-HE'S ...
...TOYING WITH ME?
I WAS THINKING OF SOMETHING HORRIFYING LIKE THREATENING HIM?!
BE-CAUSE ...
ALL RIGHT.
SO...
...TAKE CARE.
YES ...

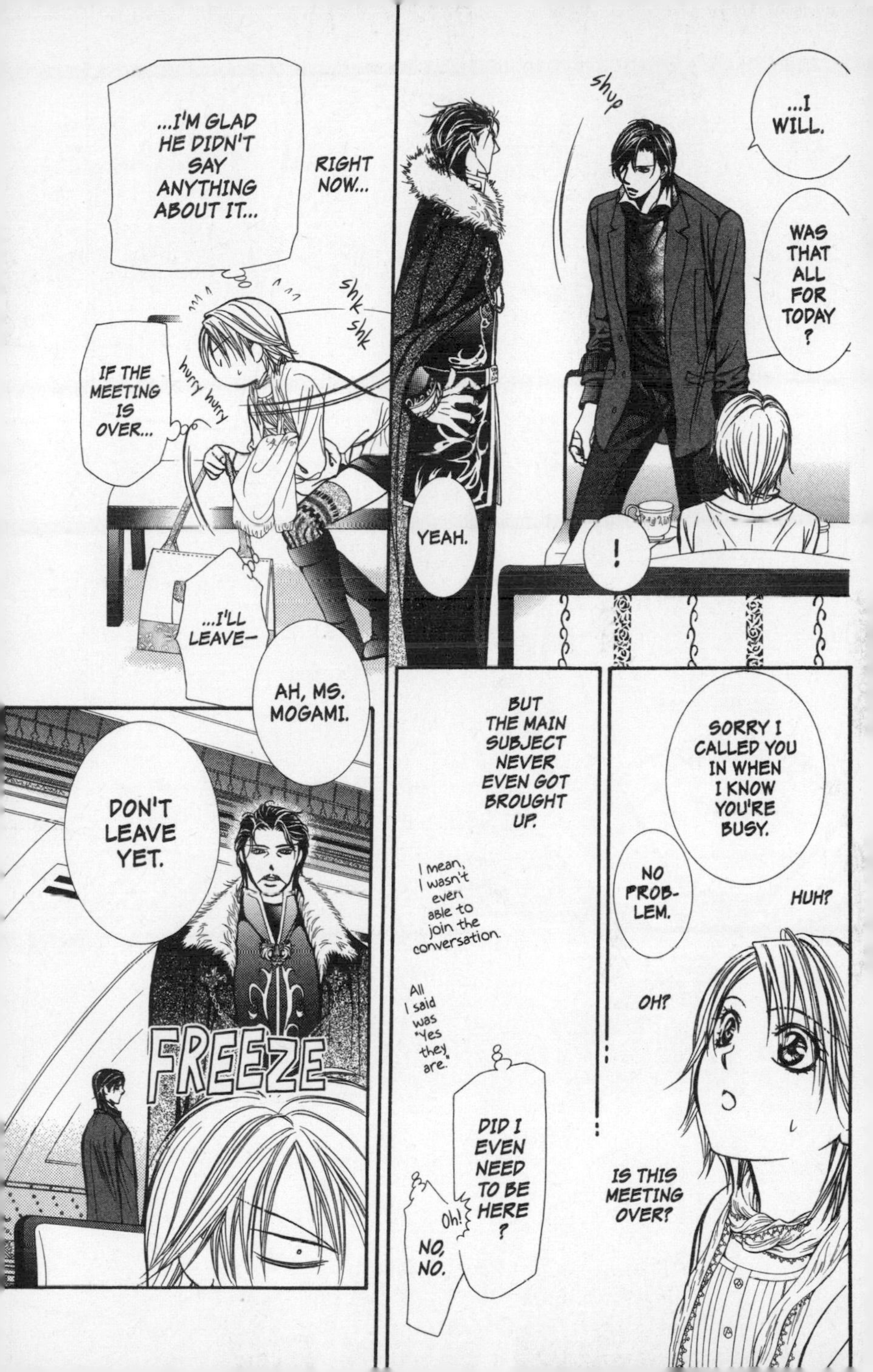
shup
...I WILL.
WAS THAT ALL FOR TODAY?
YEAH.
!
...I'M GLAD HE DIDN'T SAY ANYTHING ABOUT IT...
RIGHT NOW...
shk shk
hurry hurry
IF THE MEETING IS OVER...
...I'LL LEAVE—
SORRY I CALLED YOU IN WHEN I KNOW YOU'RE BUSY.
NO PROBLEM.
HUH?
OH?
IS THIS MEETING OVER?
BUT THE MAIN SUBJECT NEVER EVEN GOT BROUGHT UP.
I mean, I wasn't even able to join the conversation.
All I said was "Yes they are."
DID I EVEN NEED TO BE HERE?
Oh!
NO, NO.
AH, MS. MOGAMI.
DON'T LEAVE YET.
FREEZE

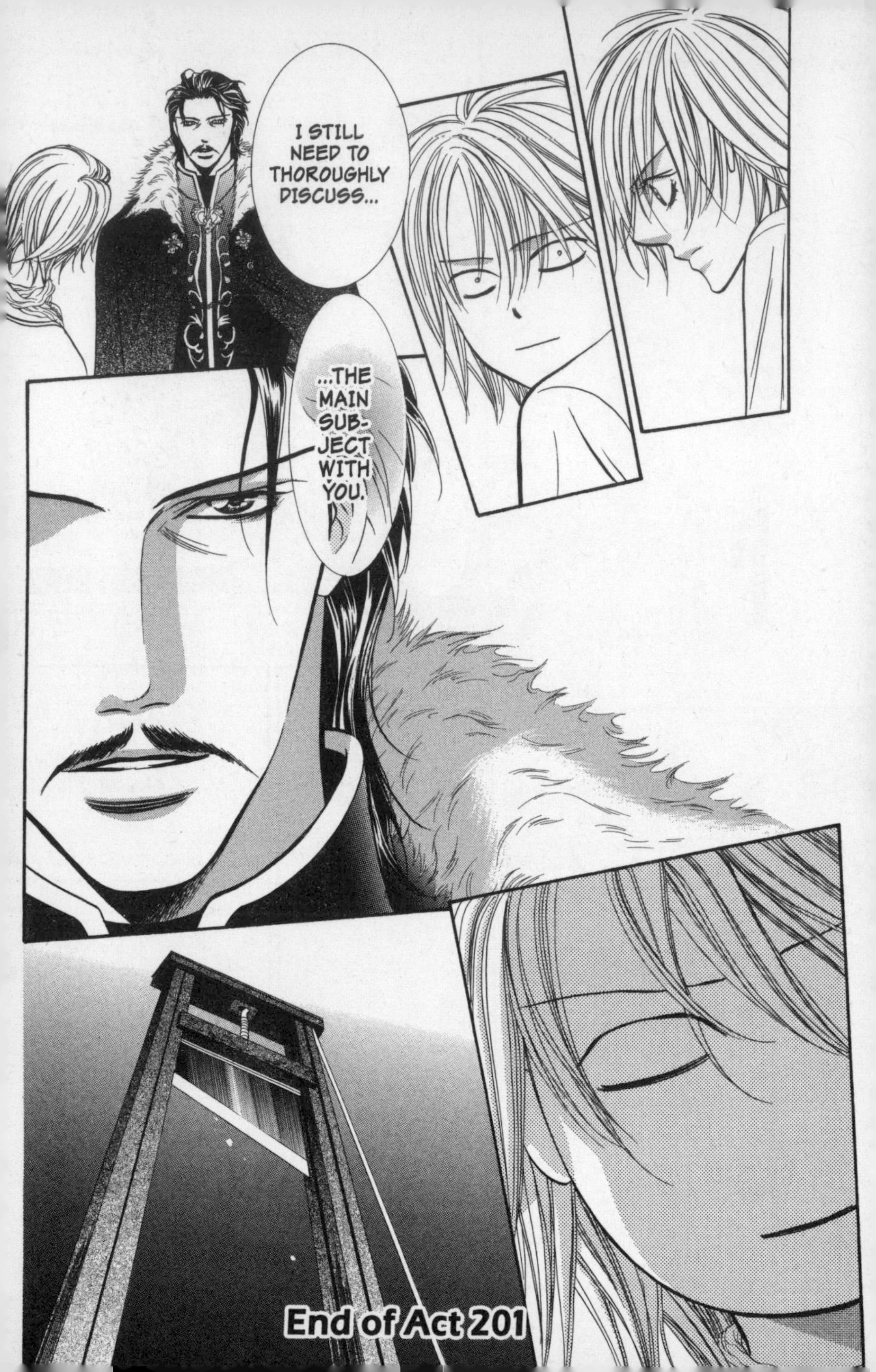
I STILL NEED TO THOROUGHLY DISCUSS...
...THE MAIN SUB-JECT WITH YOU.
End of Act 201

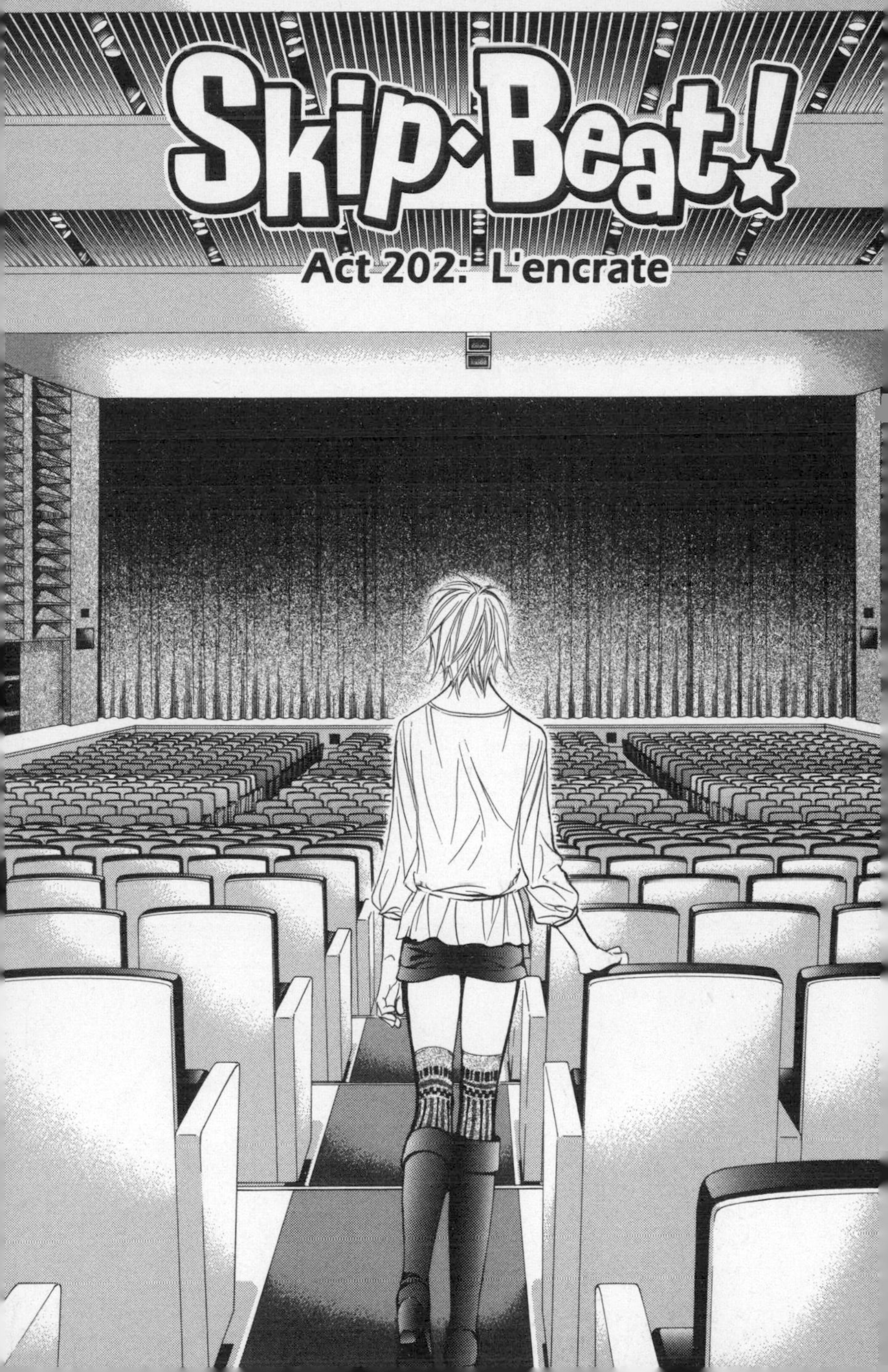
Skip·Beat!
Act 202: L'encrate

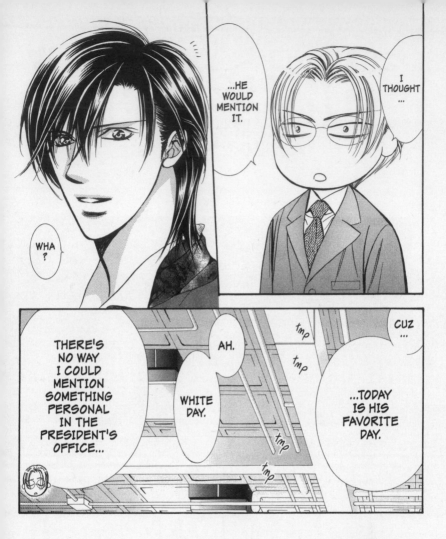

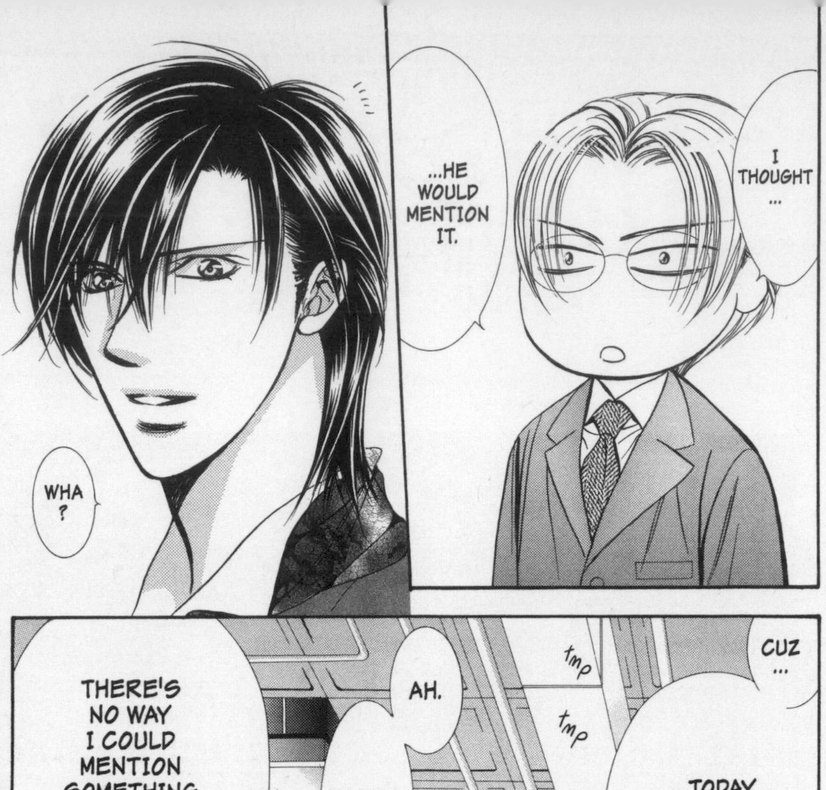
I THOUGHT ...
...HE WOULD MENTION IT.
WHA ?
CUZ ...
...TODAY IS HIS FAVORITE DAY.
tmp
tmp
tmp
tmp
AH.
WHITE DAY.
THERE'S NO WAY I COULD MENTION SOMETHING PERSONAL IN THE PRESIDENT'S OFFICE...

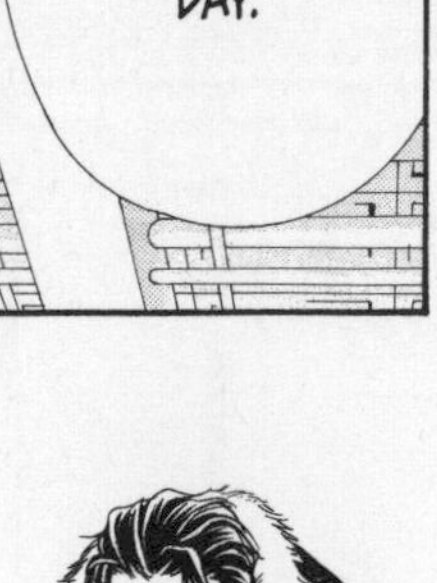

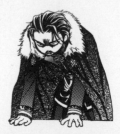

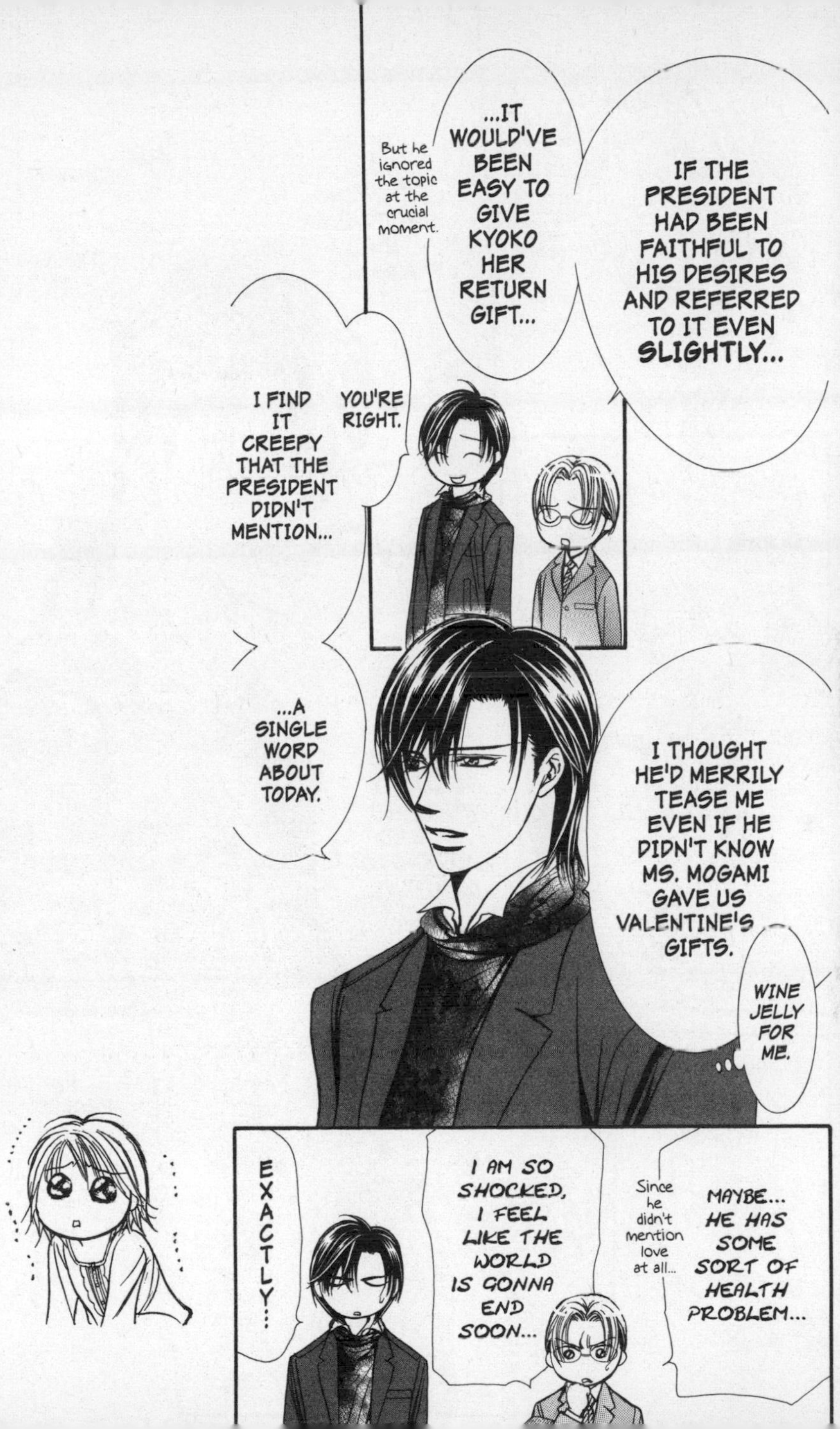
IF THE PRESIDENT HAD BEEN FAITHFUL TO HIS DESIRES AND REFERRED TO IT EVEN SLIGHTLY...
...IT WOULD'VE BEEN EASY TO GIVE KYOKO HER RETURN GIFT...
But he ignored the topic at the crucial moment.
YOU'RE RIGHT.
I FIND IT CREEPY THAT THE PRESIDENT DIDN'T MENTION...
...A SINGLE WORD ABOUT TODAY.
I THOUGHT HE'D MERRILY TEASE ME EVEN IF HE DIDN'T KNOW MS. MOGAMI GAVE US VALENTINE'S GIFTS.
WINE JELLY FOR ME.
MAYBE... HE HAS SOME SORT OF HEALTH PROBLEM...
Since he didn't mention love at all...
I AM SO SHOCKED, I FEEL LIKE THE WORLD IS GONNA END SOON...
EXACTLY...

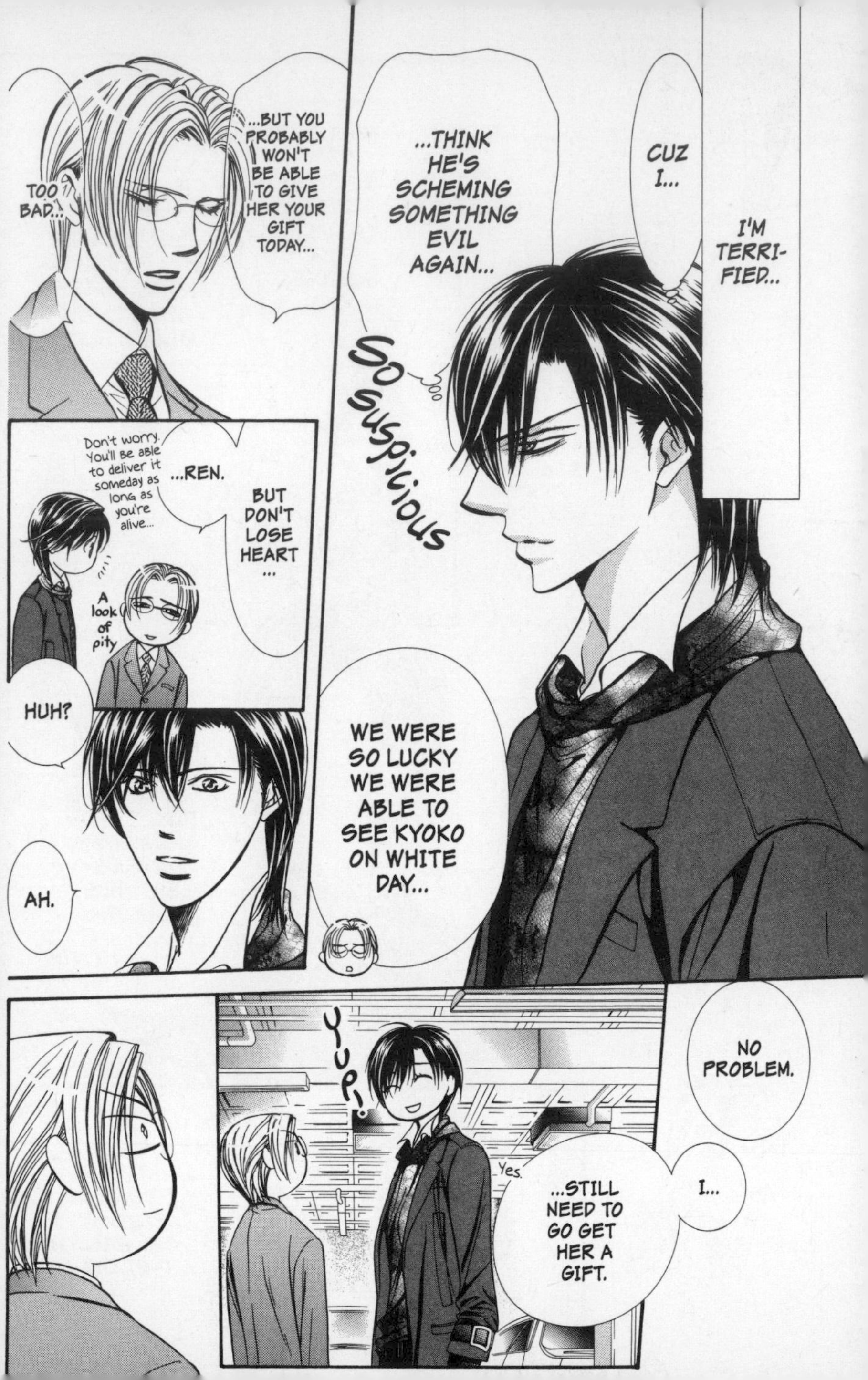
I'M TERRIFIED...
CUZ I...
...THINK HE'S SCHEMING SOMETHING EVIL AGAIN...
So suspicious
WE WERE SO LUCKY WE WERE ABLE TO SEE KYOKO ON WHITE DAY...
...BUT YOU PROBABLY WON'T BE ABLE TO GIVE HER YOUR GIFT TODAY...
TOO BAD...
BUT DON'T LOSE HEART...
...REN.
Don't worry. You'll be able to deliver it someday as long as you're alive...
A look of pity
HUH?
AH.
NO PROBLEM.
I...
...STILL NEED TO GO GET HER A GIFT.
Yes.
YUP!

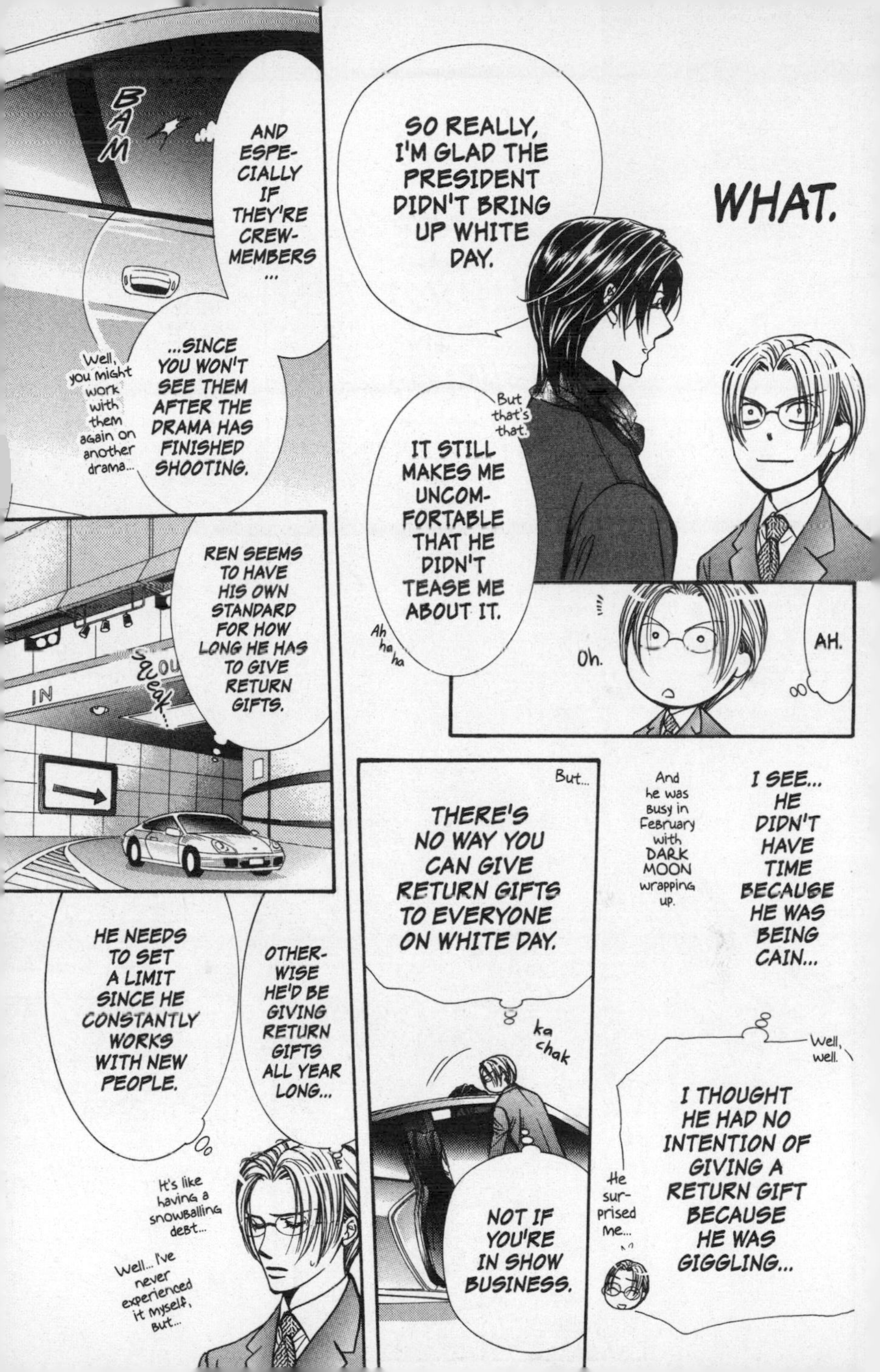
WHAT.
SO REALLY, I'M GLAD THE PRESIDENT DIDN'T BRING UP WHITE DAY.
But that's that.
IT STILL MAKES ME UNCOMFORTABLE THAT HE DIDN'T TEASE ME ABOUT IT.
Ah ha ha
AH.
Oh.
I SEE... HE DIDN'T HAVE TIME BECAUSE HE WAS BEING CAIN...
And he was busy in February with DARK MOON wrapping up.
But...
THERE'S NO WAY YOU CAN GIVE RETURN GIFTS TO EVERYONE ON WHITE DAY.
Well, well.
I THOUGHT HE HAD NO INTENTION OF GIVING A RETURN GIFT BECAUSE HE WAS GIGGLING...
He surprised me...
ka chak
NOT IF YOU'RE IN SHOW BUSINESS.
BAM
AND ESPECIALLY IF THEY'RE CREW-MEMBERS...
...SINCE YOU WON'T SEE THEM AFTER THE DRAMA HAS FINISHED SHOOTING.
Well, you might work with them again on another drama...
REN SEEMS TO HAVE HIS OWN STANDARD FOR HOW LONG HE HAS TO GIVE RETURN GIFTS.
IN
squeak...
OTHERWISE HE'D BE GIVING RETURN GIFTS ALL YEAR LONG...
HE NEEDS TO SET A LIMIT SINCE HE CONSTANTLY WORKS WITH NEW PEOPLE.
It's like having a snowballing debt...
Well... I've never experienced it myself, but...

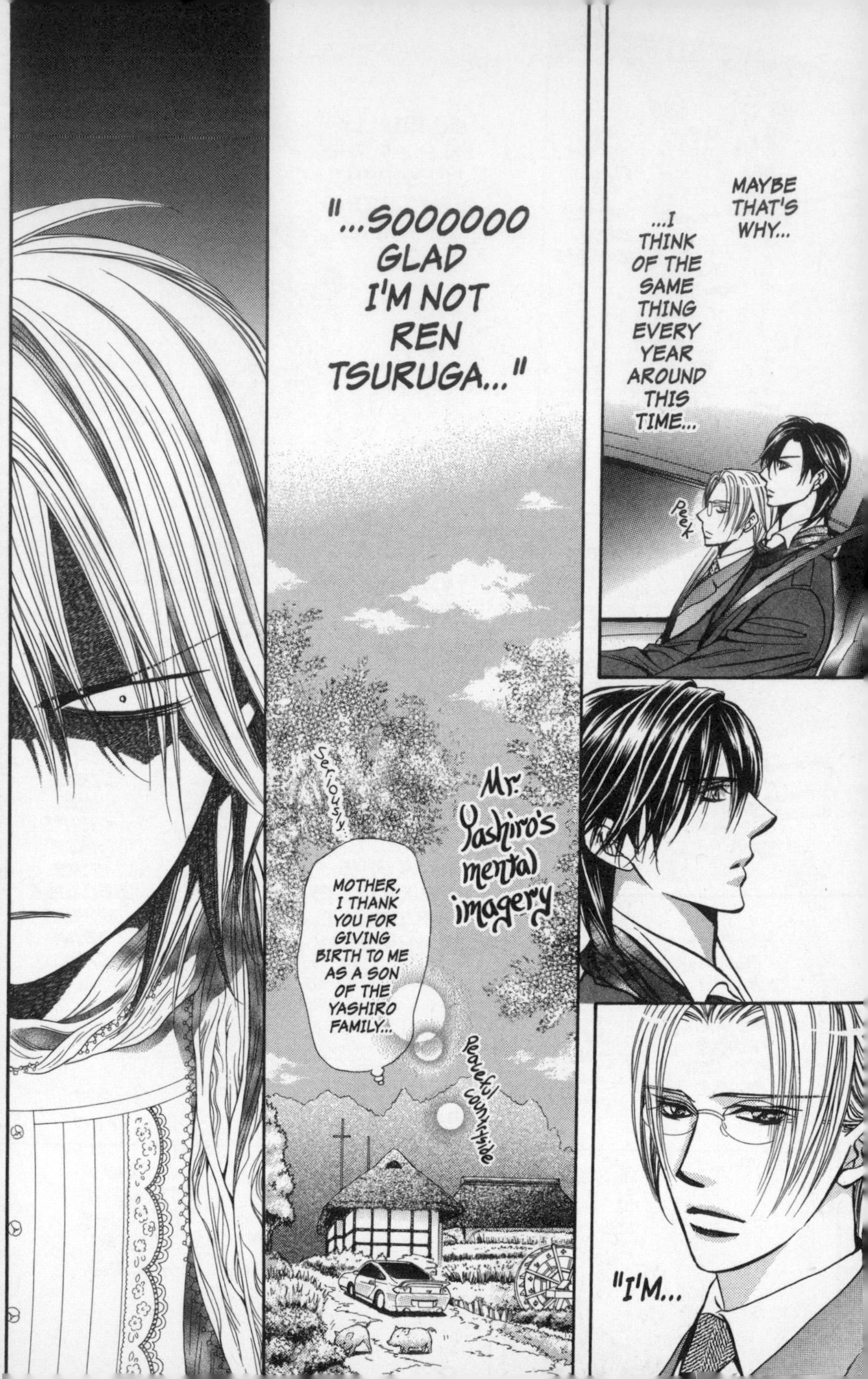
MAYBE THAT'S WHY...
...I THINK OF THE SAME THING EVERY YEAR AROUND THIS TIME...
Peek
"I'M...
"...SOOOOOO GLAD I'M NOT REN TSURUGA..."
Mr. Yashiro's mental imagery
Seriously.
MOTHER, I THANK YOU FOR GIVING BIRTH TO ME AS A SON OF THE YASHIRO FAMILY...
Peaceful countryside

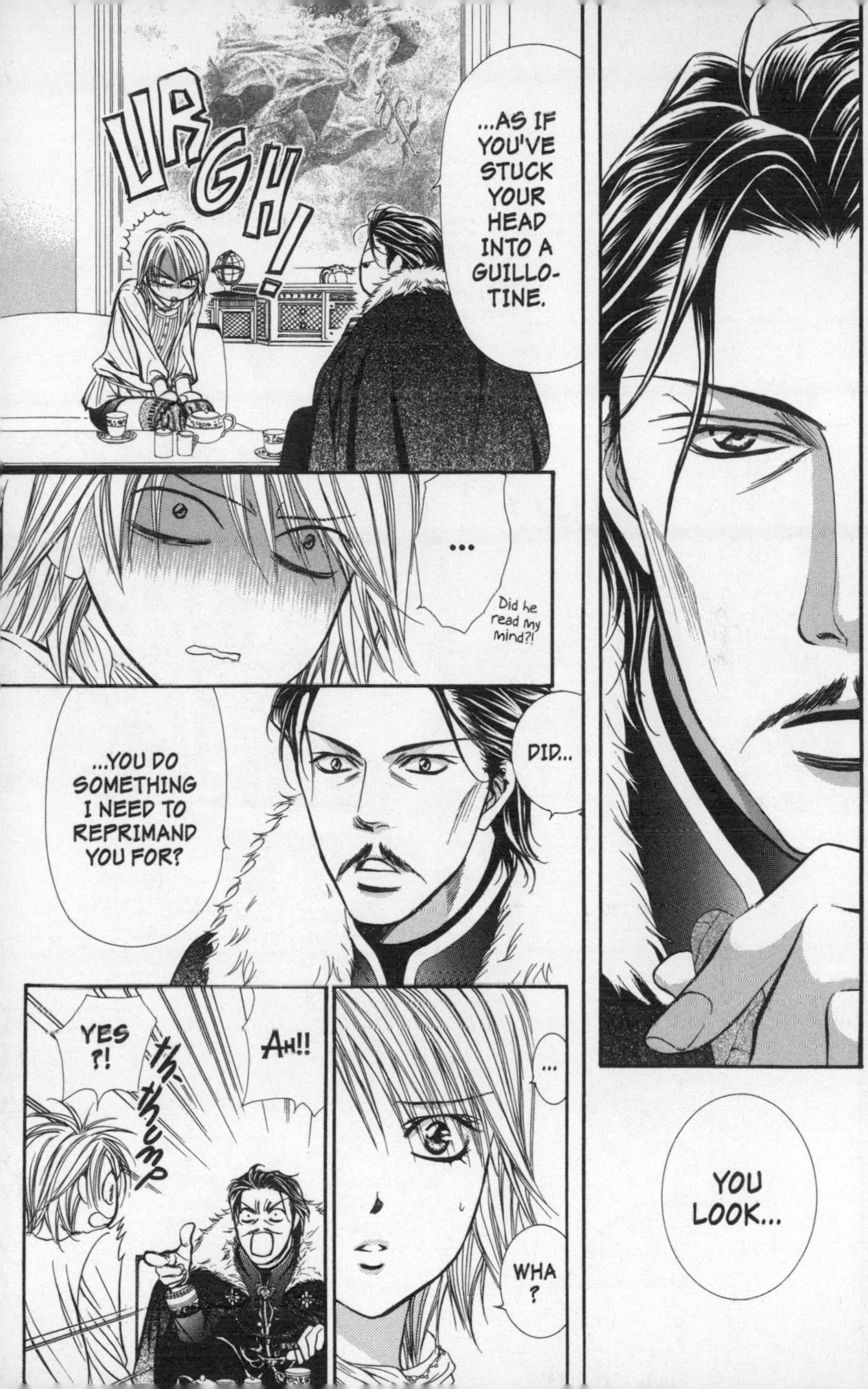
YOU LOOK...
...AS IF YOU'VE STUCK YOUR HEAD INTO A GUILLOTINE.
URGH!
...
Did he read my mind?!
DID...
...YOU DO SOMETHING I NEED TO REPRIMAND YOU FOR?
...
WHA?
AH!!
th-thump
YES?!

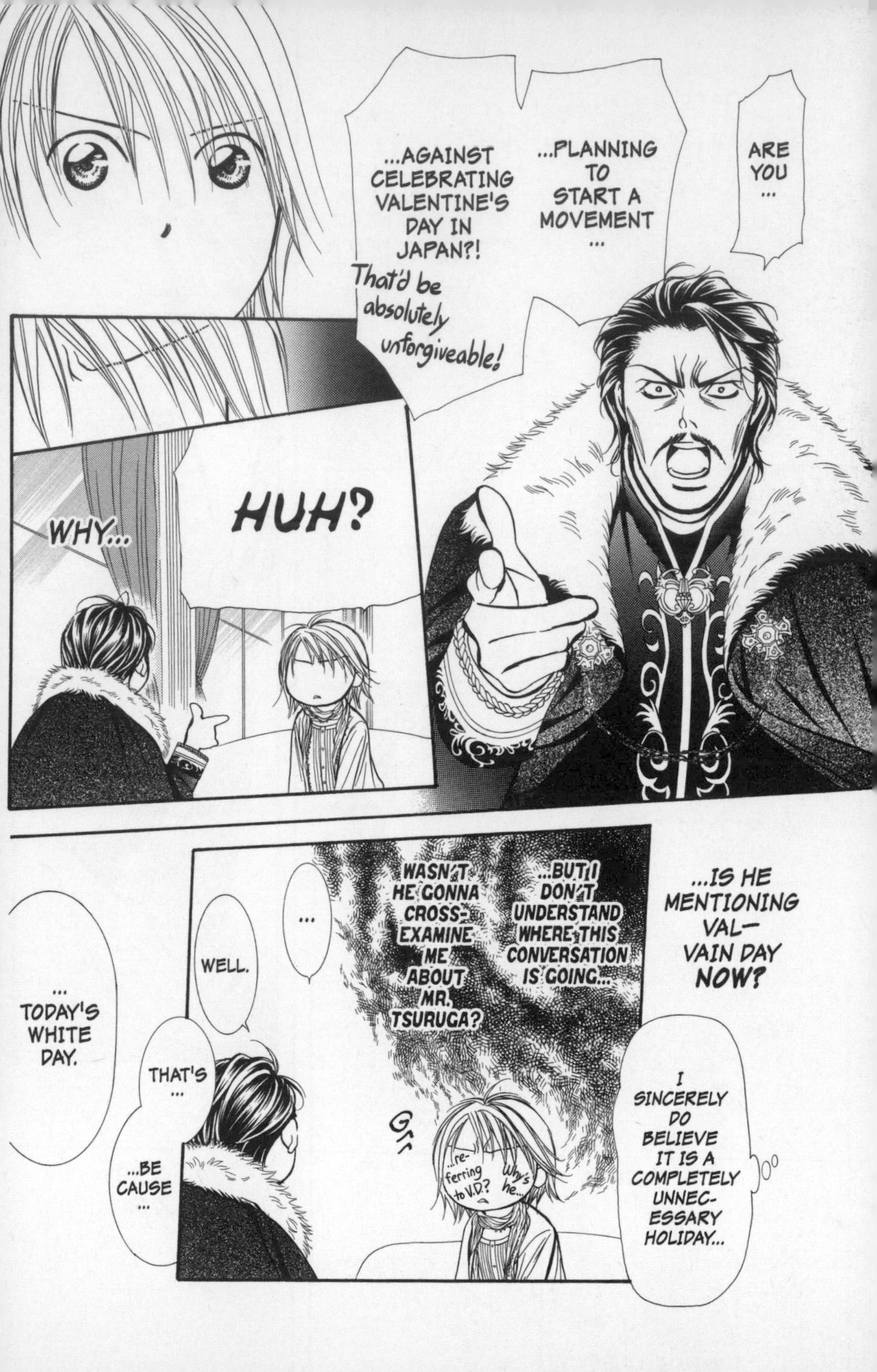
ARE YOU ...
...PLANNING TO START A MOVEMENT ...
...AGAINST CELEBRATING VALENTINE'S DAY IN JAPAN?!
That'd be absolutely unforgiveable!
HUH?
WHY...
...IS HE MENTIONING VAL— VAIN DAY NOW?
I SINCERELY DO BELIEVE IT IS A COMPLETELY UNNEC-ESSARY HOLIDAY...
...BUT I DON'T UNDERSTAND WHERE THIS CONVERSATION IS GOING...
WASN'T HE GONNA CROSS-EXAMINE ME ABOUT MR. TSURUGA?
...
Why's he...
...re-ferring to V.D.?
Grr
WELL.
THAT'S ...
...BE CAUSE ...
... TODAY'S WHITE DAY.

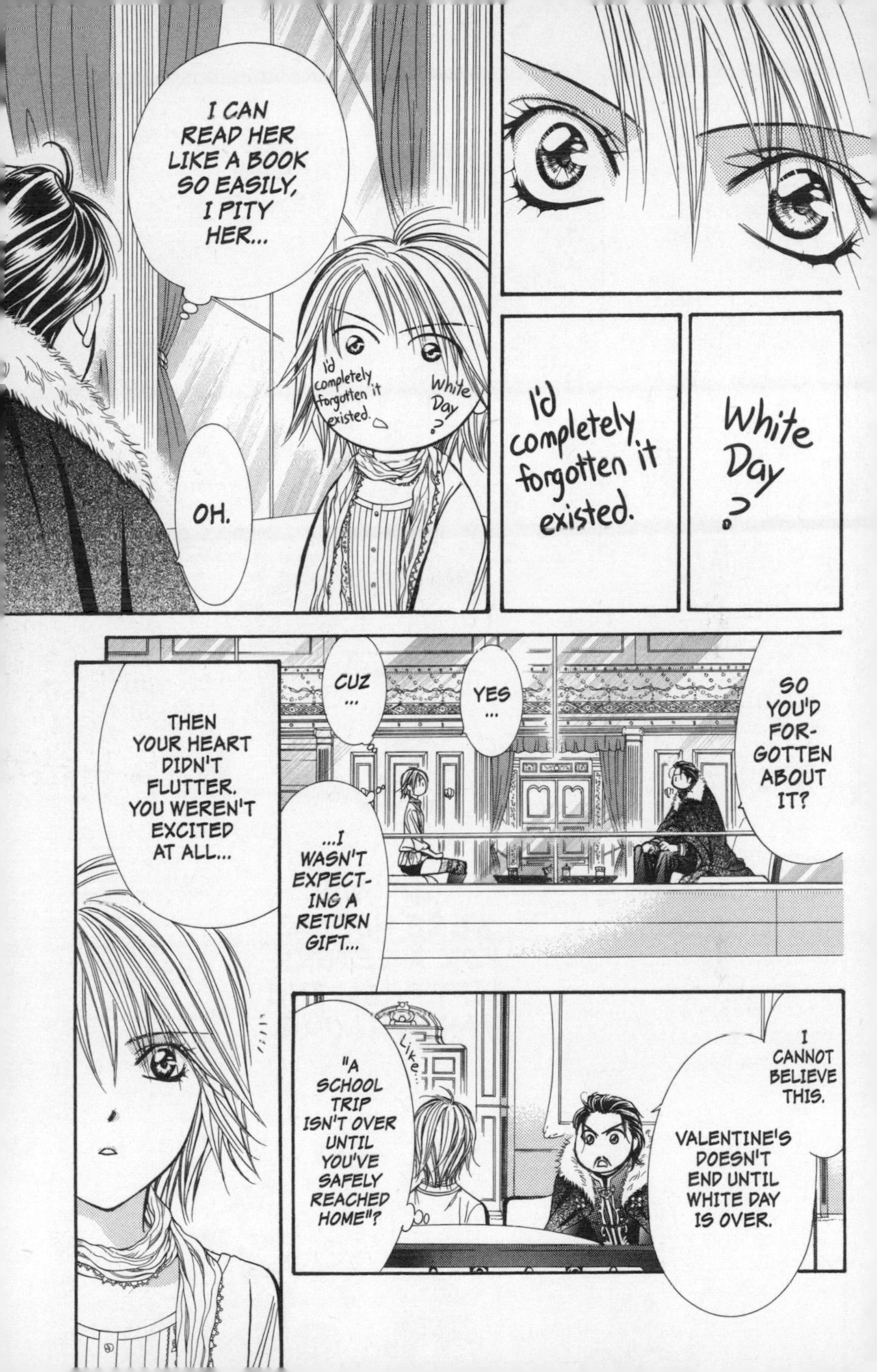
White Day?
I'd completely forgotten it existed.
I CAN READ HER LIKE A BOOK SO EASILY, I PITY HER...
White Day?
I'd completely forgotten it existed.
OH.
SO YOU'D FOR-GOTTEN ABOUT IT?
YES...
CUZ...
...I WASN'T EXPECT-ING A RETURN GIFT...
I CANNOT BELIEVE THIS.
VALENTINE'S DOESN'T END UNTIL WHITE DAY IS OVER.
Like...
"A SCHOOL TRIP ISN'T OVER UNTIL YOU'VE SAFELY REACHED HOME"?
THEN YOUR HEART DIDN'T FLUTTER. YOU WEREN'T EXCITED AT ALL...

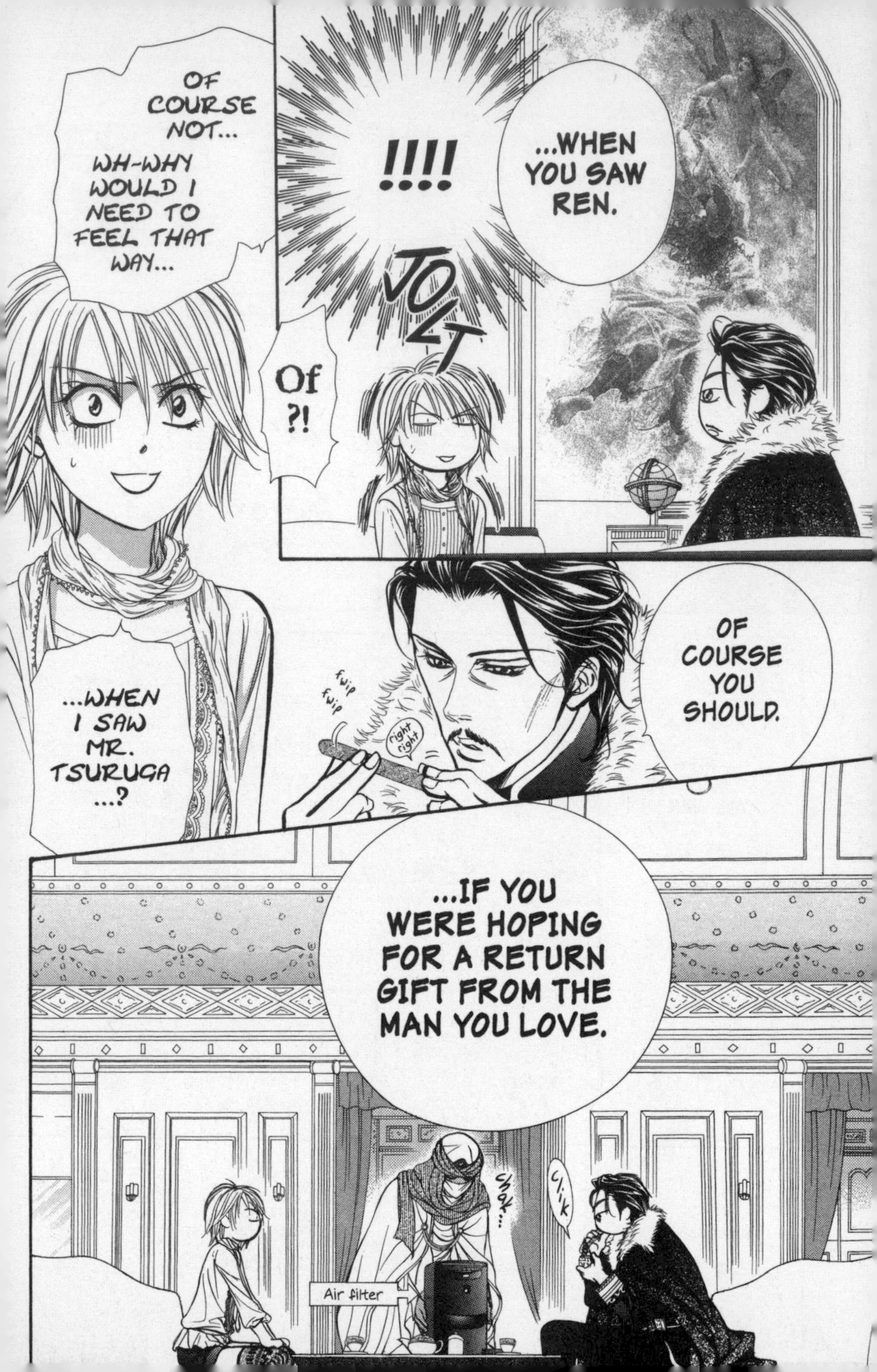
...WHEN YOU SAW REN.
!!!!
JOLT
Of ?!
OF COURSE YOU SHOULD.
fwip fwip
right right
OF COURSE NOT... WH-WHY WOULD I NEED TO FEEL THAT WAY...
...WHEN I SAW MR. TSURUGA ...?
...IF YOU WERE HOPING FOR A RETURN GIFT FROM THE MAN YOU LOVE.
clik
chok...
Air filter

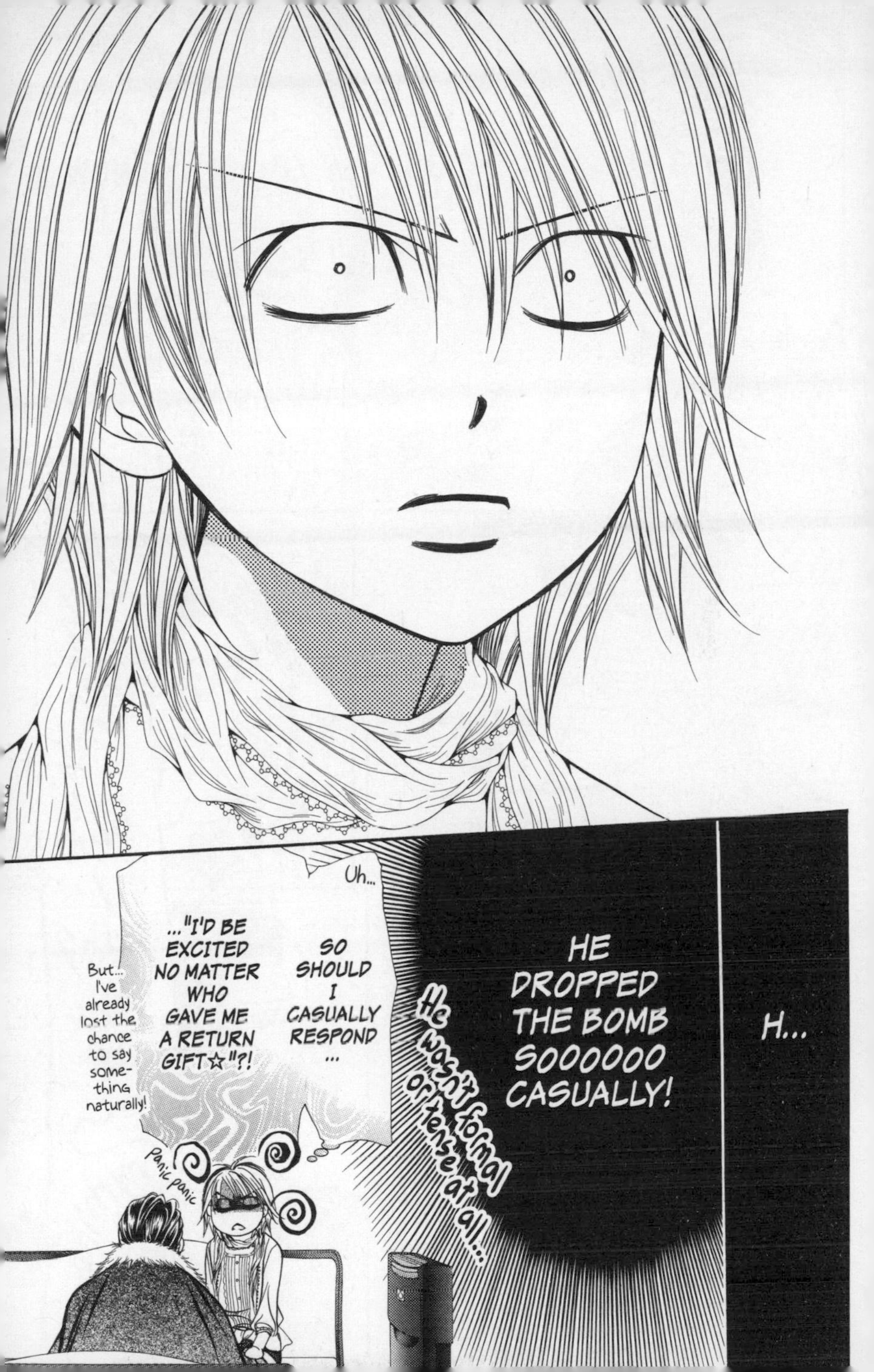
H...
HE DROPPED THE BOMB SOOOOOO CASUALLY!
He wasn't formal or tense at all...
Uh...
SO SHOULD I CASUALLY RESPOND...
..."I'D BE EXCITED NO MATTER WHO GAVE ME A RETURN GIFT☆"?!
But... I've already lost the chance to say something naturally!
Panic panic

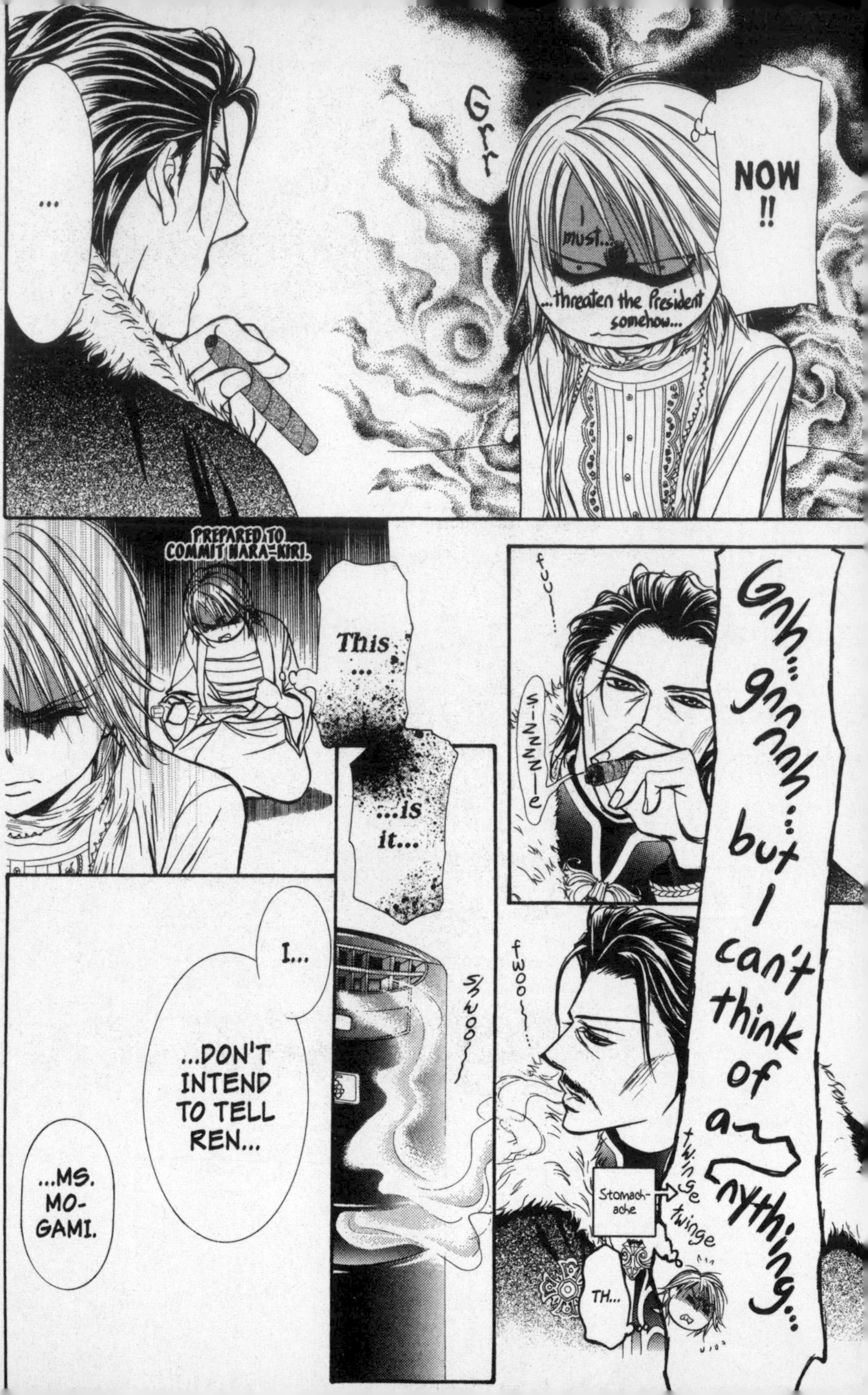
NOW!!
Grrr
I must...
...threaten the President somehow...
...
fuu...
SIZZZZle
Gnh... gnnnnh... but I can't think of anything...
PREPARED TO COMMIT HARA-KIRI.
This...
...is it...
fwoo...
Stomach-ache
twinge twinge
TH...
shwoo
I...
...DON'T INTEND TO TELL REN...
...MS. MOGAMI.

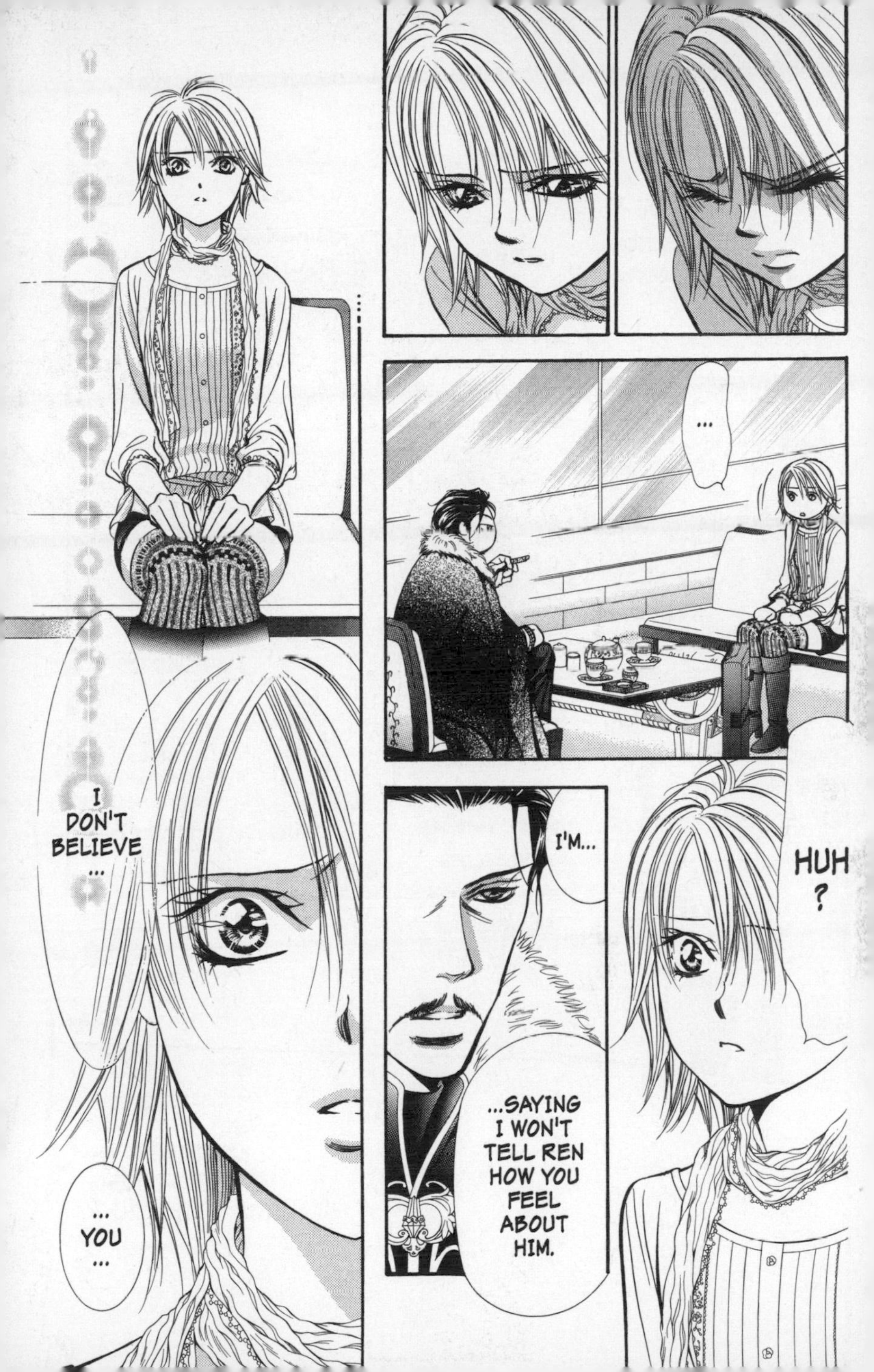
...
HUH ?
I'M...
...SAYING I WON'T TELL REN HOW YOU FEEL ABOUT HIM.
I DON'T BELIEVE ...
... YOU ...

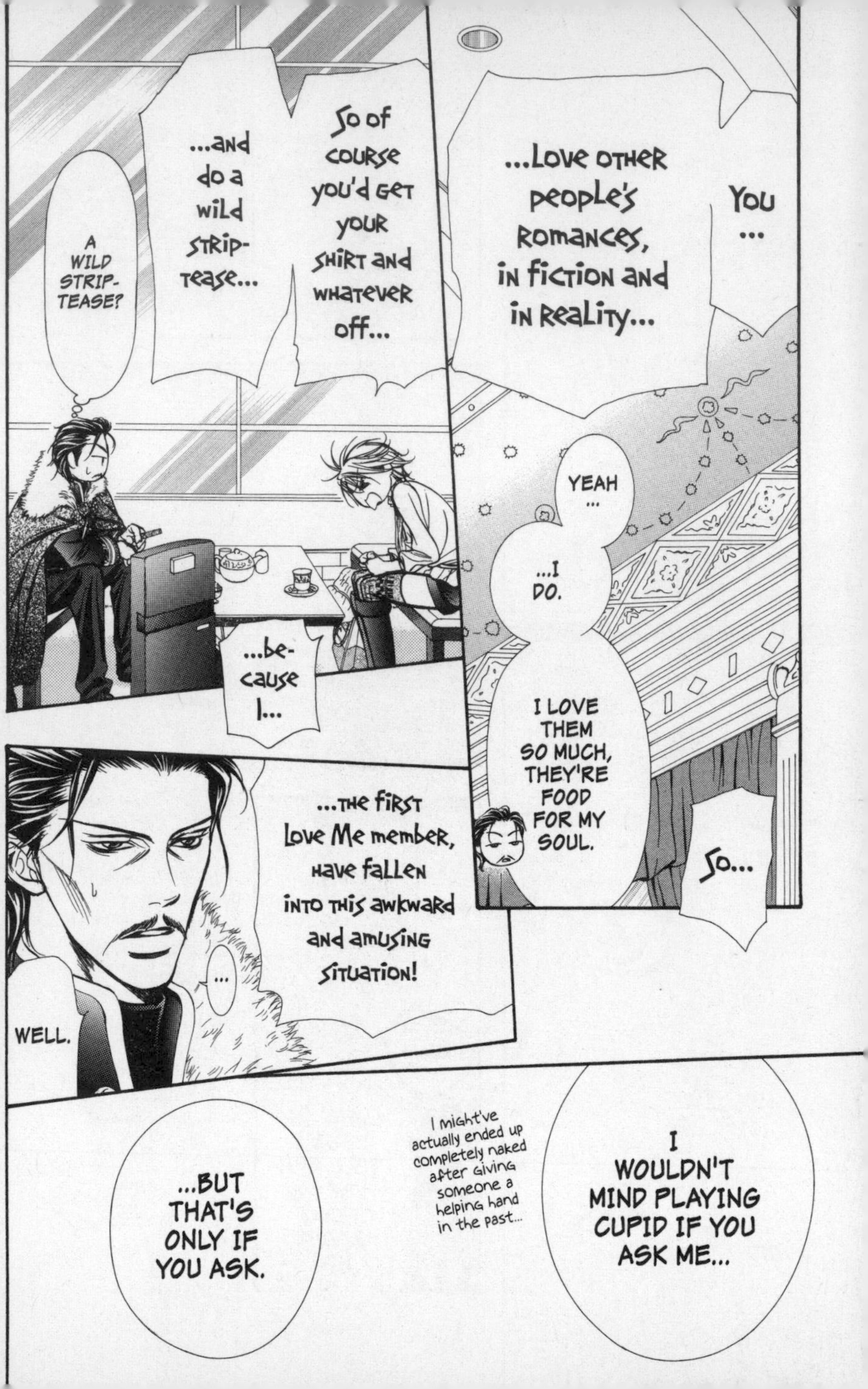
You ...
...Love other people's romances, in fiction and in reality...
YEAH ...
...I DO.
I LOVE THEM SO MUCH, THEY'RE FOOD FOR MY SOUL.
So...
So of course you'd get your shirt and whatever off...
...and do a wild strip-tease...
A WILD STRIP-TEASE?
...be-cause I...
...the first Love Me member, have fallen into this awkward and amusing situation!
...
WELL.
I WOULDN'T MIND PLAYING CUPID IF YOU ASK ME...
I might've actually ended up completely naked after giving someone a helping hand in the past...
...BUT THAT'S ONLY IF YOU ASK.

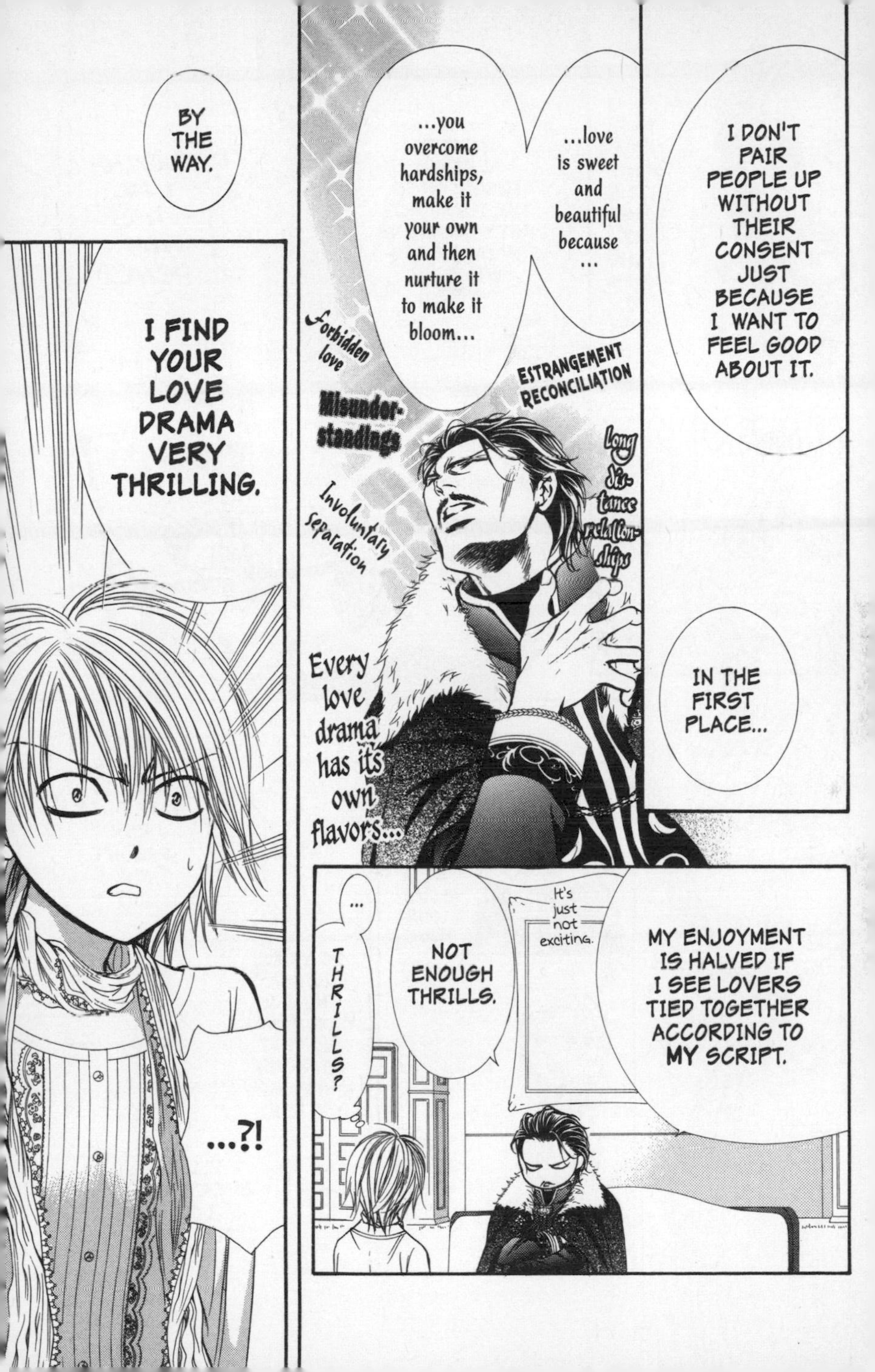
I DON'T PAIR PEOPLE UP WITHOUT THEIR CONSENT JUST BECAUSE I WANT TO FEEL GOOD ABOUT IT.
IN THE FIRST PLACE...
...love is sweet and beautiful because ...
...you overcome hardships, make it your own and then nurture it to make it bloom...
Forbidden love
ESTRANGEMENT RECONCILIATION
Misunder-standings
Long dis-tance relation-ships
Involuntary separation
Every love drama has its own flavors...
MY ENJOYMENT IS HALVED IF I SEE LOVERS TIED TOGETHER ACCORDING TO MY SCRIPT.
It's just not exciting.
NOT ENOUGH THRILLS.
...
THRILLS?
BY THE WAY.
I FIND YOUR LOVE DRAMA VERY THRILLING.
...?!

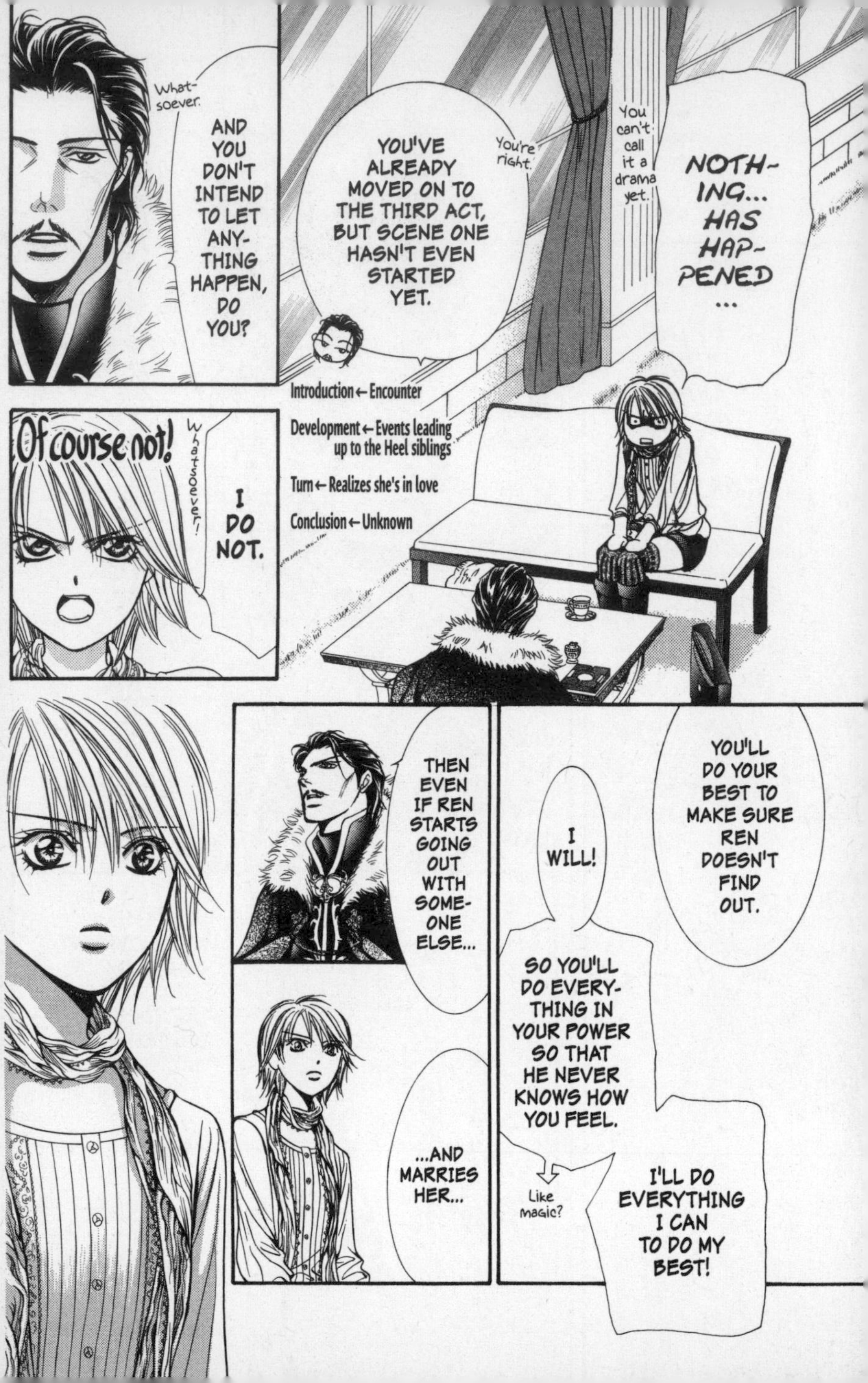
NOTHING... HAS HAPPENED...
You can't call it a drama yet.
You're right.
YOU'VE ALREADY MOVED ON TO THE THIRD ACT, BUT SCENE ONE HASN'T EVEN STARTED YET.
Introduction ← Encounter
Development ← Events leading up to the Heel siblings
Turn ← Realizes she's in love
Conclusion ← Unknown
AND YOU DON'T INTEND TO LET ANYTHING HAPPEN, DO YOU?
Whatsoever.
I DO NOT.
Whatsoever!
Of course not!
YOU'LL DO YOUR BEST TO MAKE SURE REN DOESN'T FIND OUT.
I WILL!
SO YOU'LL DO EVERYTHING IN YOUR POWER SO THAT HE NEVER KNOWS HOW YOU FEEL.
I'LL DO EVERYTHING I CAN TO DO MY BEST!
Like magic?
THEN EVEN IF REN STARTS GOING OUT WITH SOMEONE ELSE...
...AND MARRIES HER...

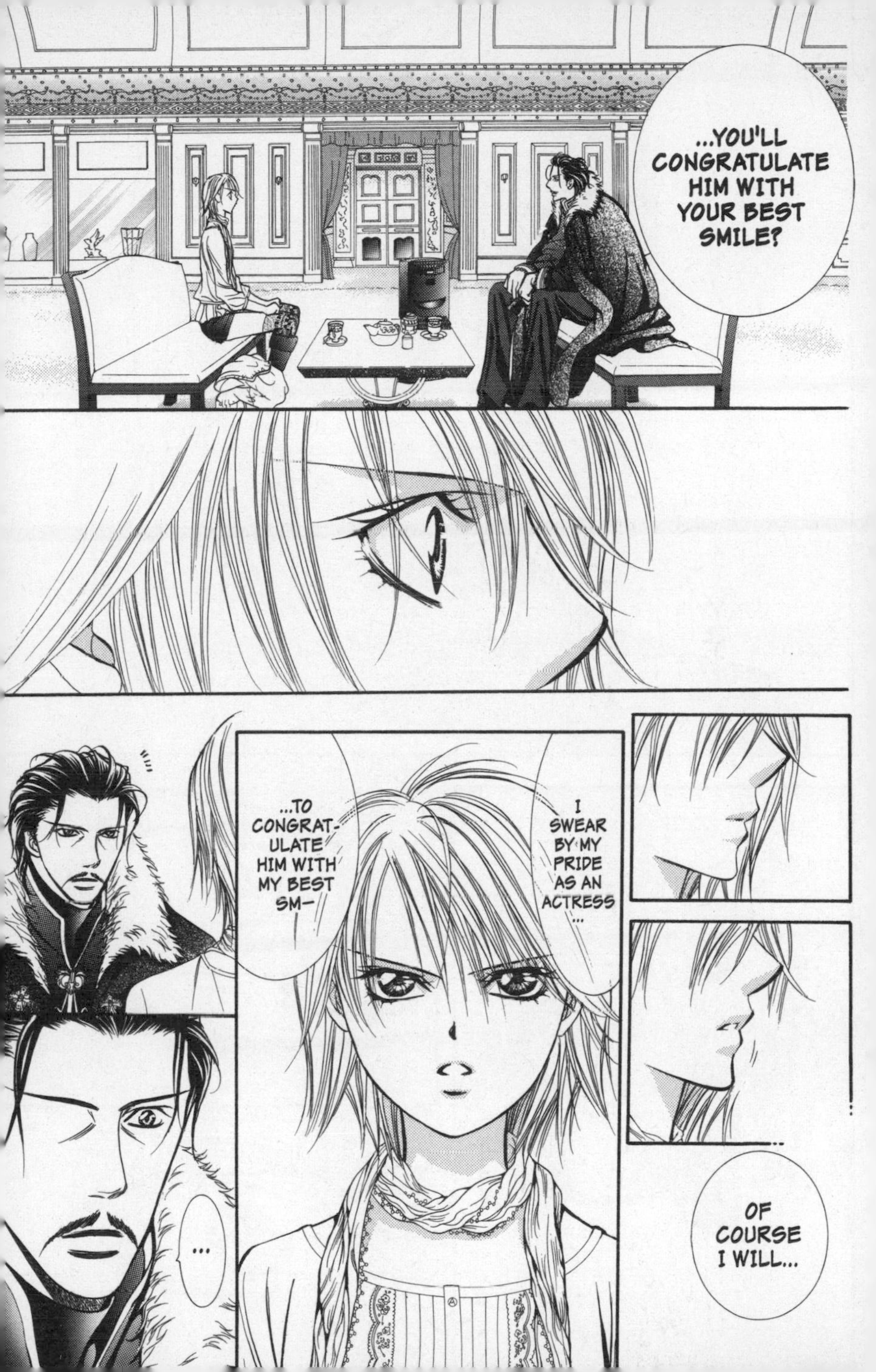
...YOU'LL CONGRATULATE HIM WITH YOUR BEST SMILE?
OF COURSE I WILL...
I SWEAR BY MY PRIDE AS AN ACTRESS...
...TO CONGRATULATE HIM WITH MY BEST SM—
...

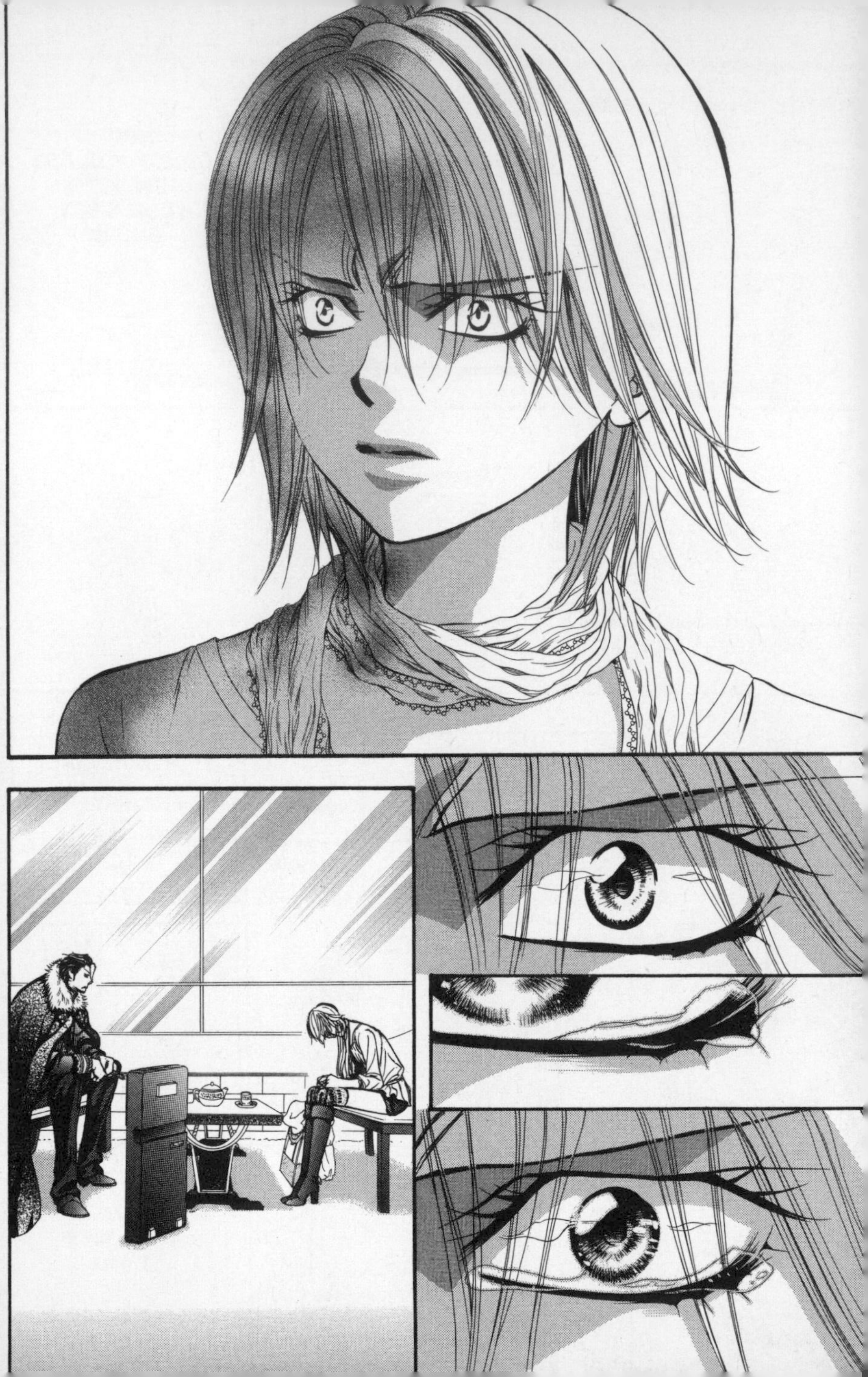

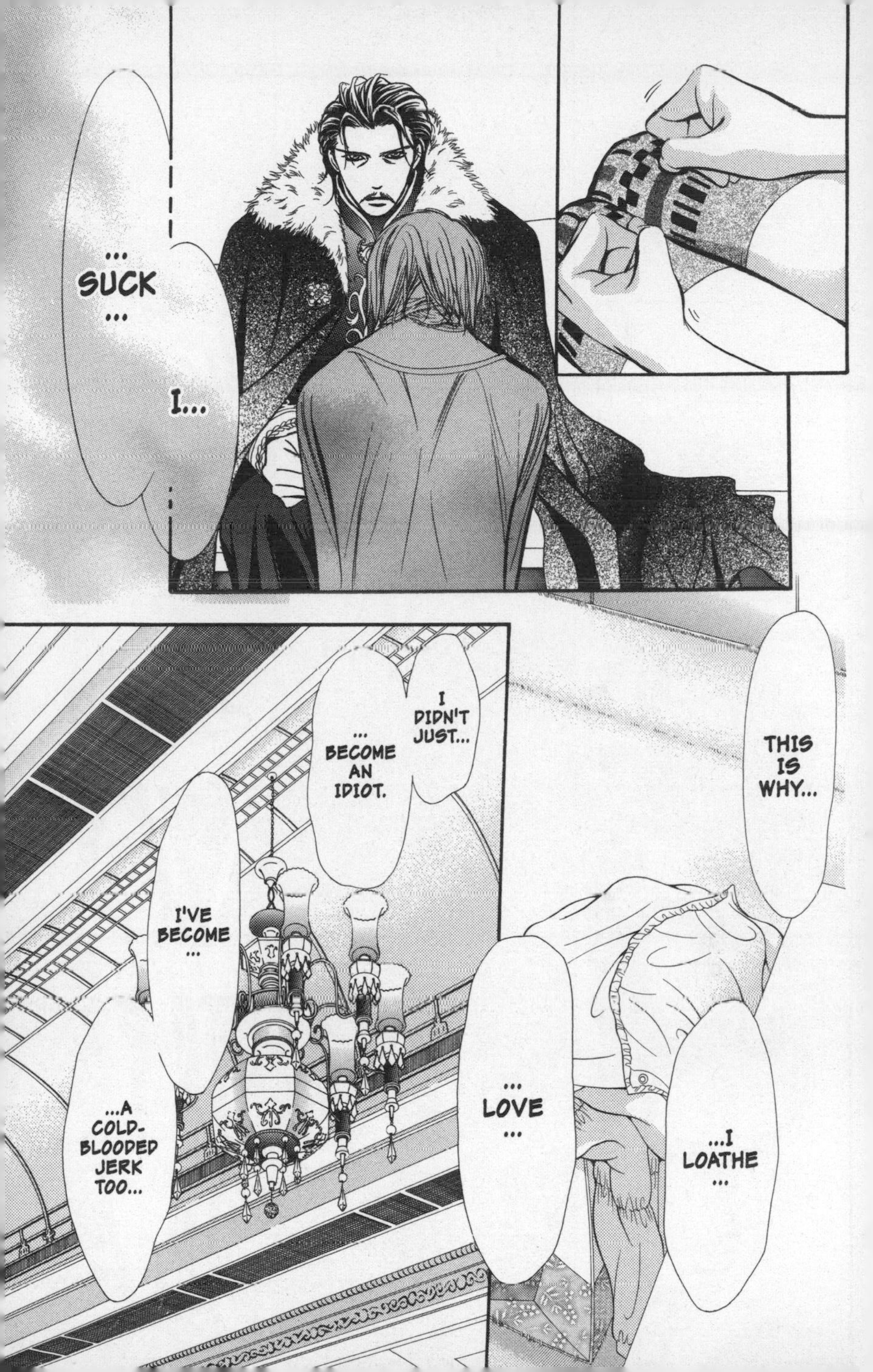
I...
... SUCK ...
THIS IS WHY...
...I LOATHE ...
... LOVE ...
I DIDN'T JUST...
... BECOME AN IDIOT.
I'VE BECOME ...
...A COLD-BLOODED JERK TOO...

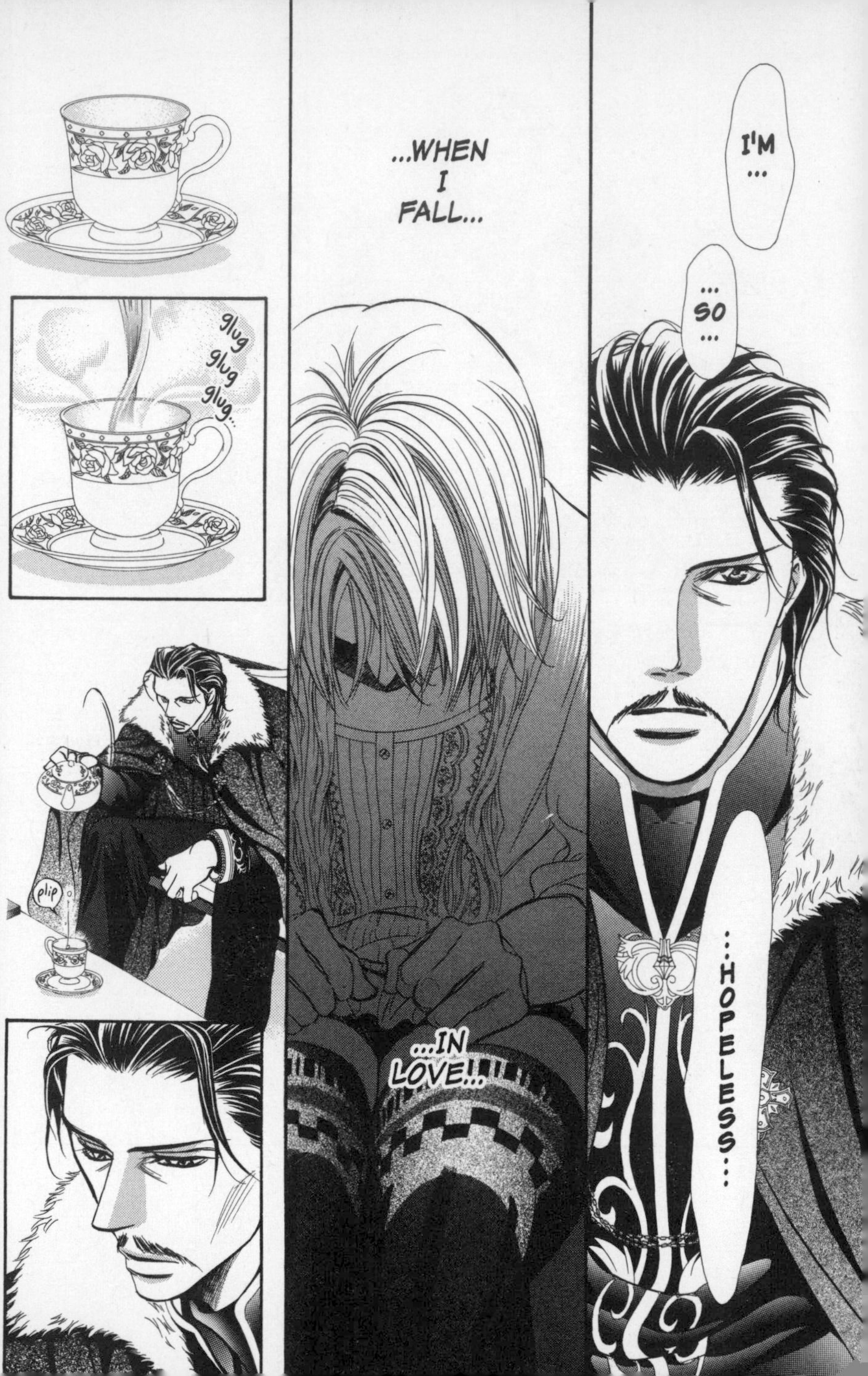
I'M ...
... SO ...
...HOPELESS...
...WHEN I FALL...
...IN LOVE!...
glug glug glug...
plip

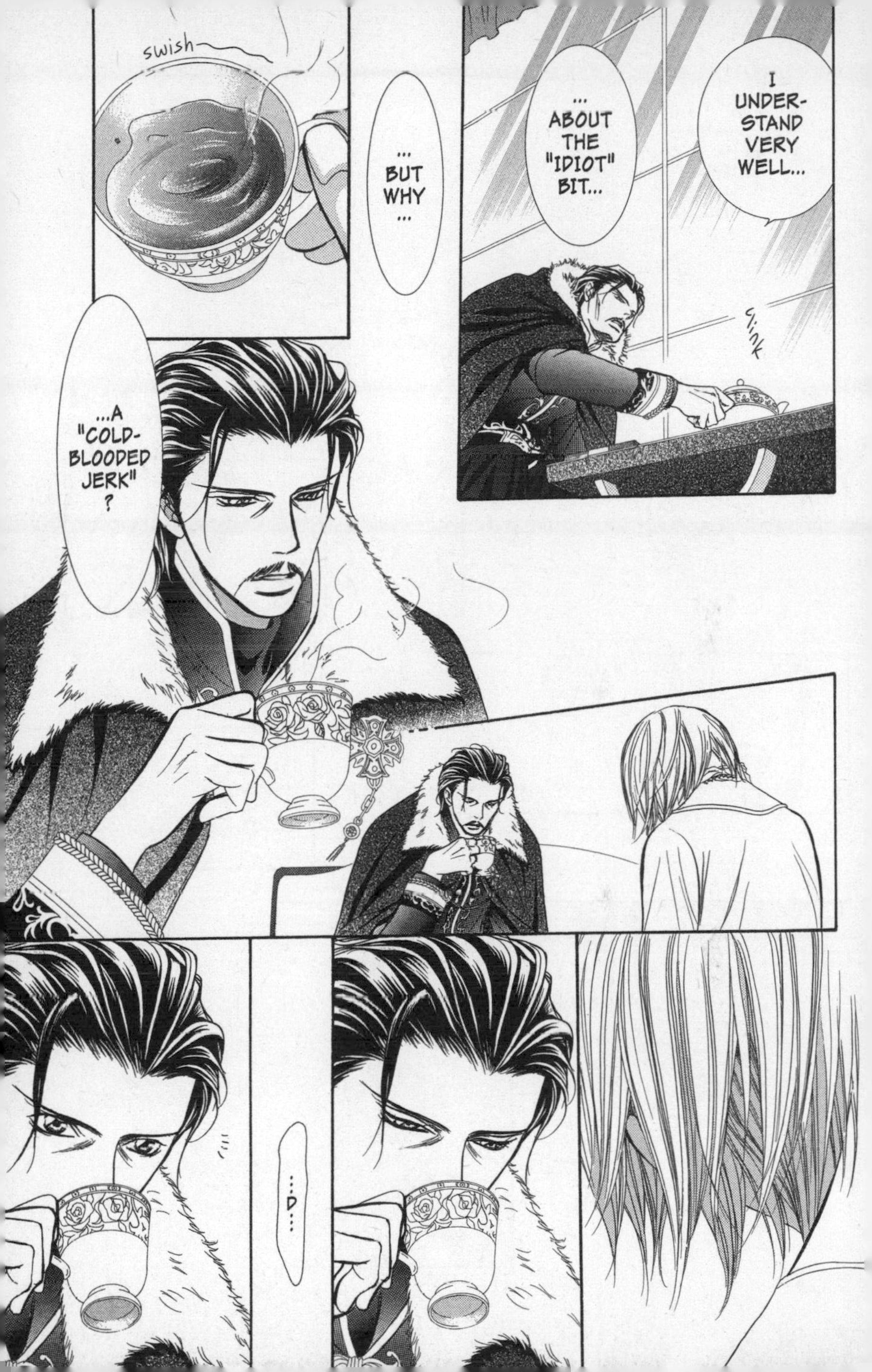
I UNDER-STAND VERY WELL...
...ABOUT THE "IDIOT" BIT...
clink
...BUT WHY...
swish
...A "COLD-BLOODED JERK"?
...D...

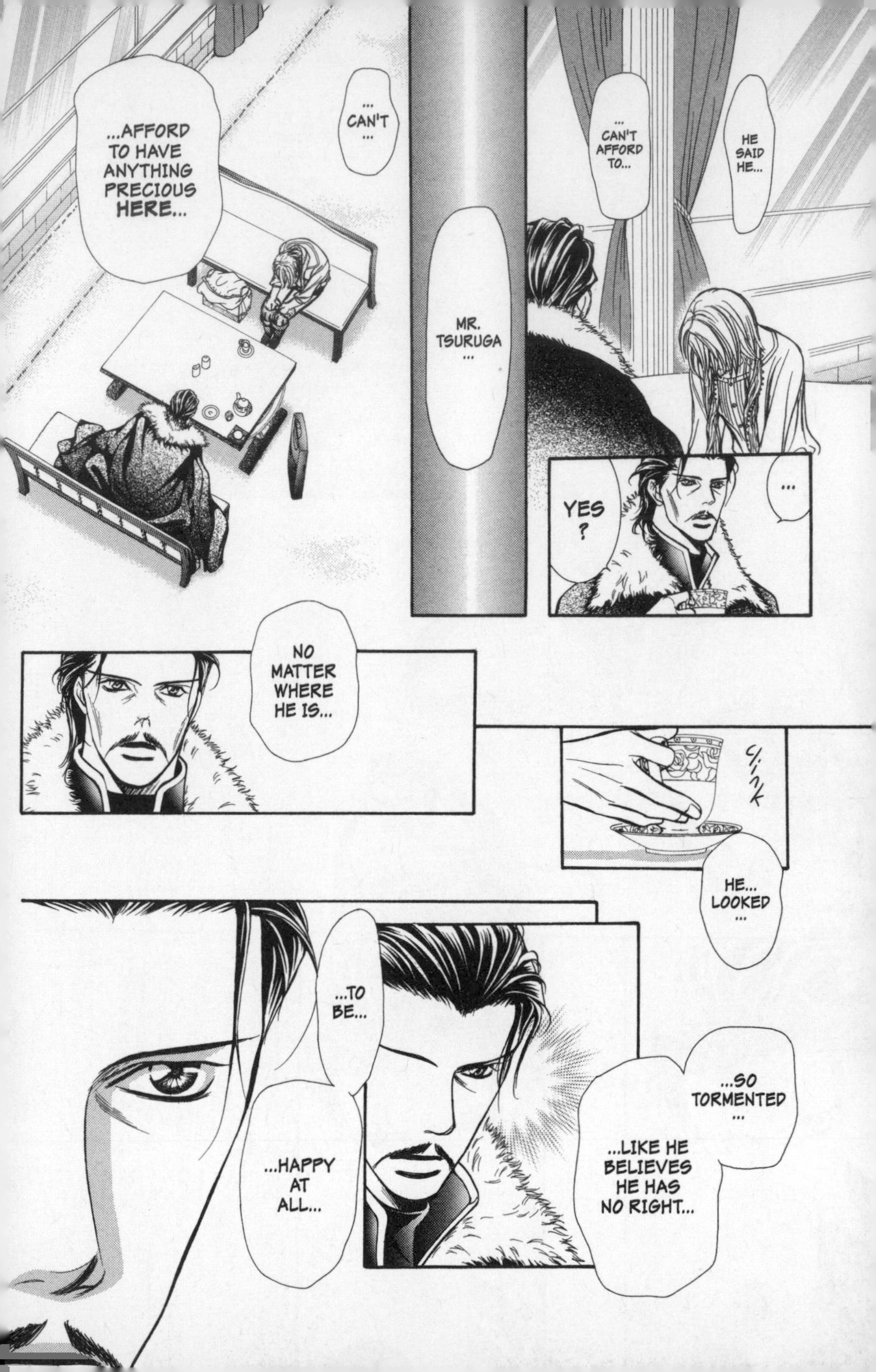
HE SAID HE...
...CAN'T AFFORD TO...
...CAN'T...
...AFFORD TO HAVE ANYTHING PRECIOUS HERE...
MR. TSURUGA...
YES?
...
CLINK
HE... LOOKED...
NO MATTER WHERE HE IS...
...SO TORMENTED...
...LIKE HE BELIEVES HE HAS NO RIGHT...
...TO BE...
...HAPPY AT ALL...

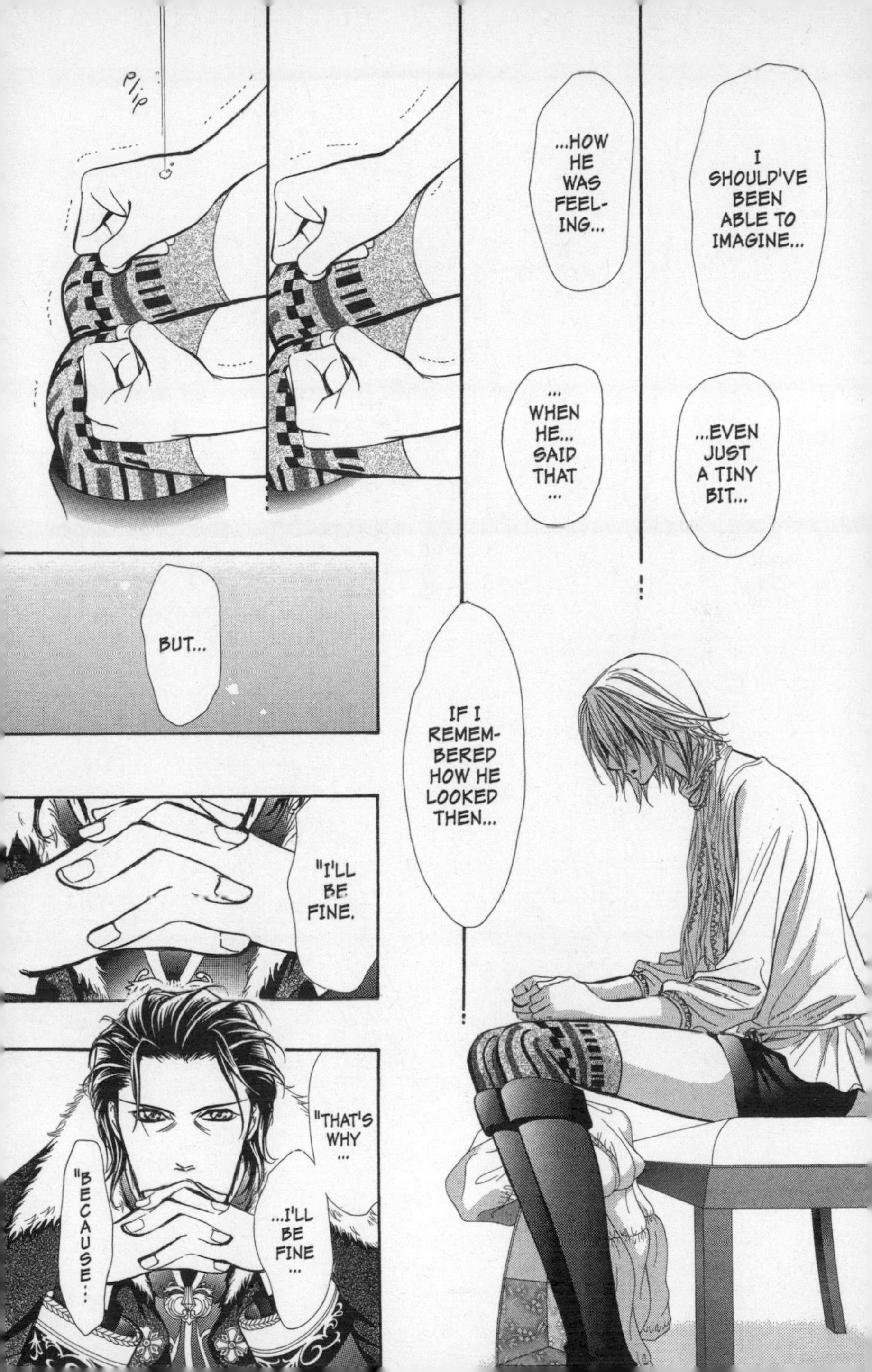
I SHOULD'VE BEEN ABLE TO IMAGINE...
...EVEN JUST A TINY BIT...
...HOW HE WAS FEELING...
...WHEN HE... SAID THAT...
IF I REMEMBERED HOW HE LOOKED THEN...
plip
BUT...
"I'LL BE FINE.
"THAT'S WHY...
...I'LL BE FINE...
"BECAUSE...

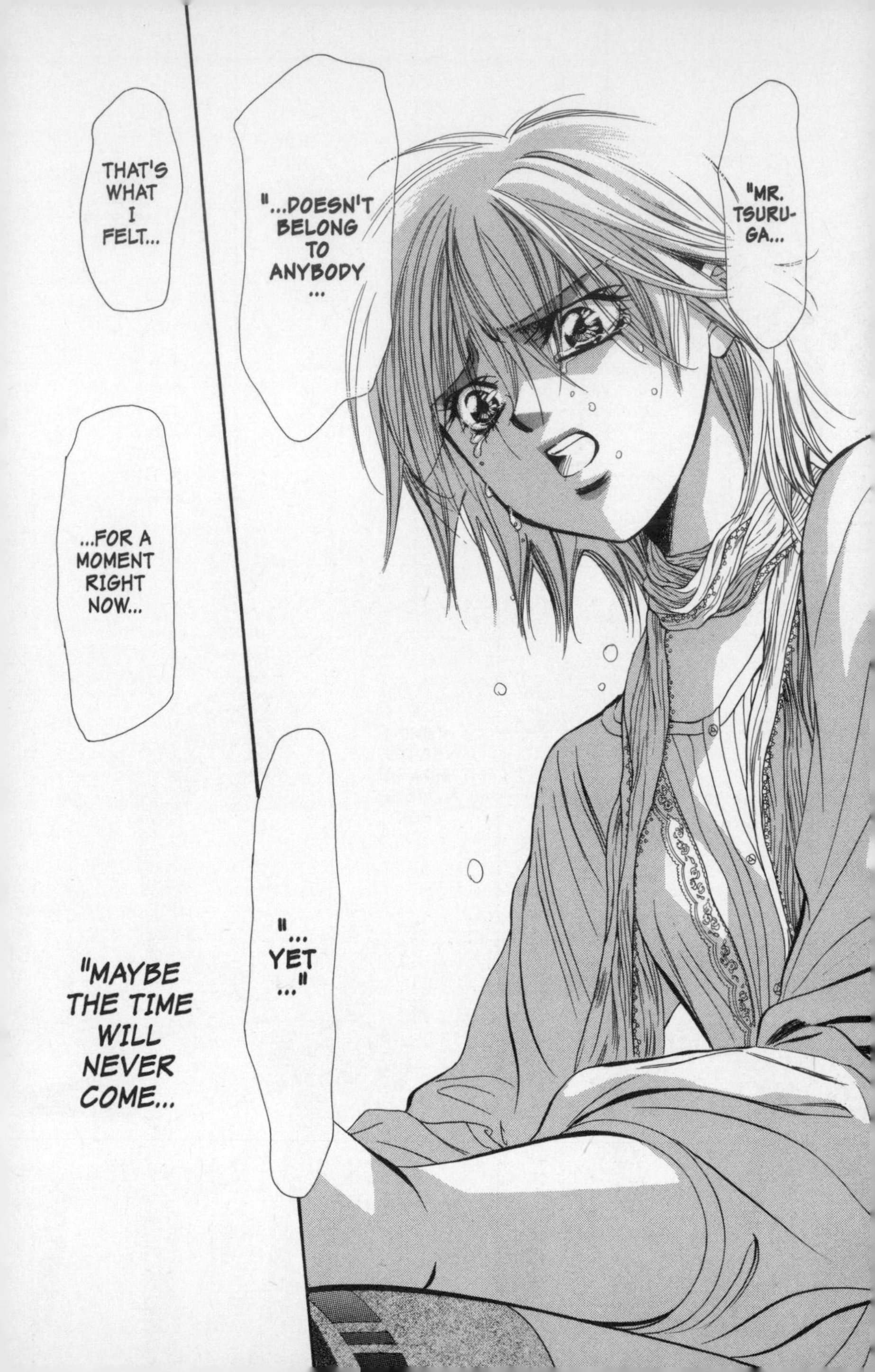
"MR. TSURUGA...
"...DOESN'T BELONG TO ANYBODY...
"...YET..."
"MAYBE THE TIME WILL NEVER COME...
THAT'S WHAT I FELT...
...FOR A MOMENT RIGHT NOW...

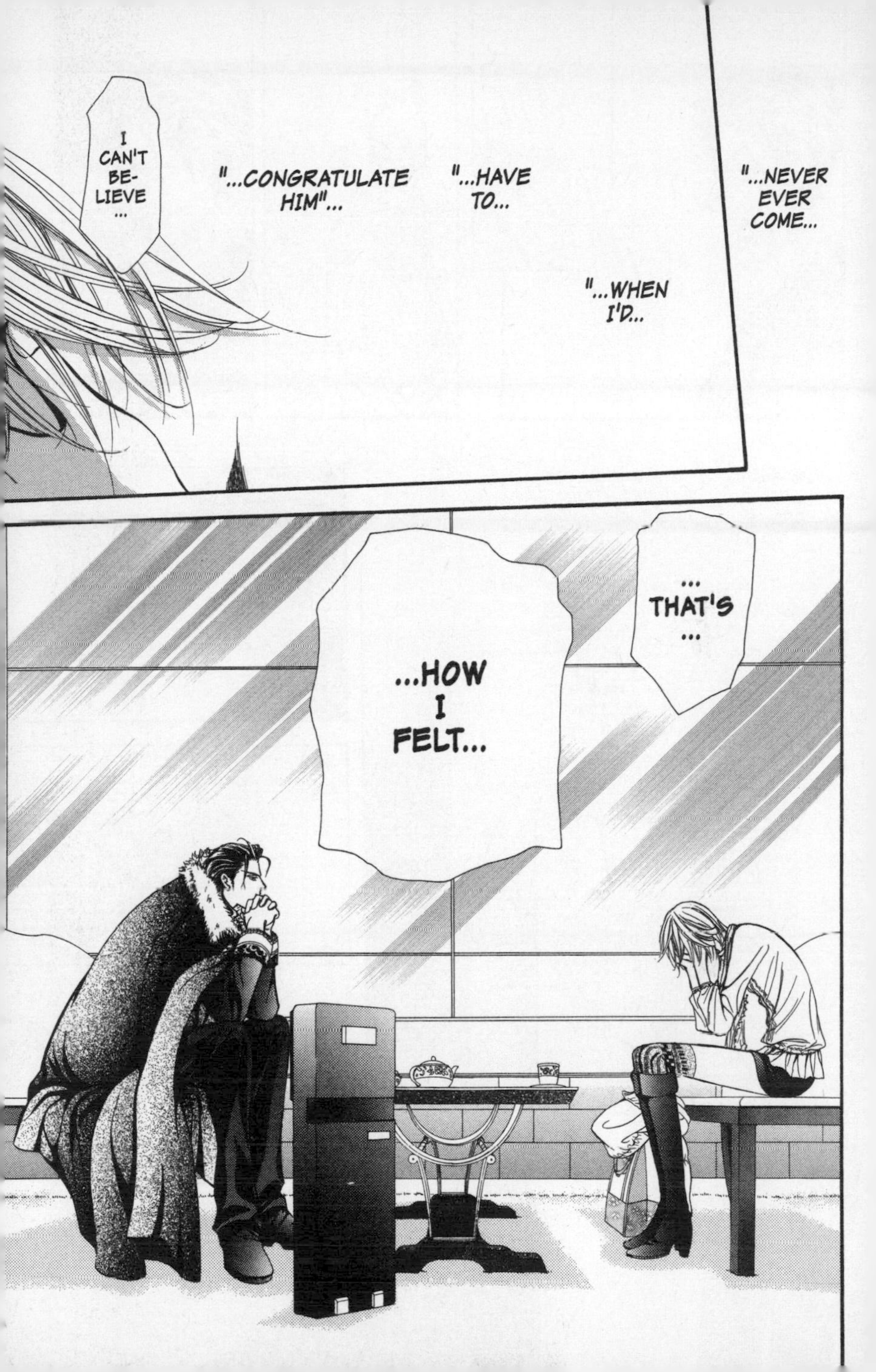
"...NEVER EVER COME...
"...WHEN I'D...
"...HAVE TO...
"...CONGRATULATE HIM"...
I CAN'T BE- LIEVE ...
... THAT'S ...
...HOW I FELT...

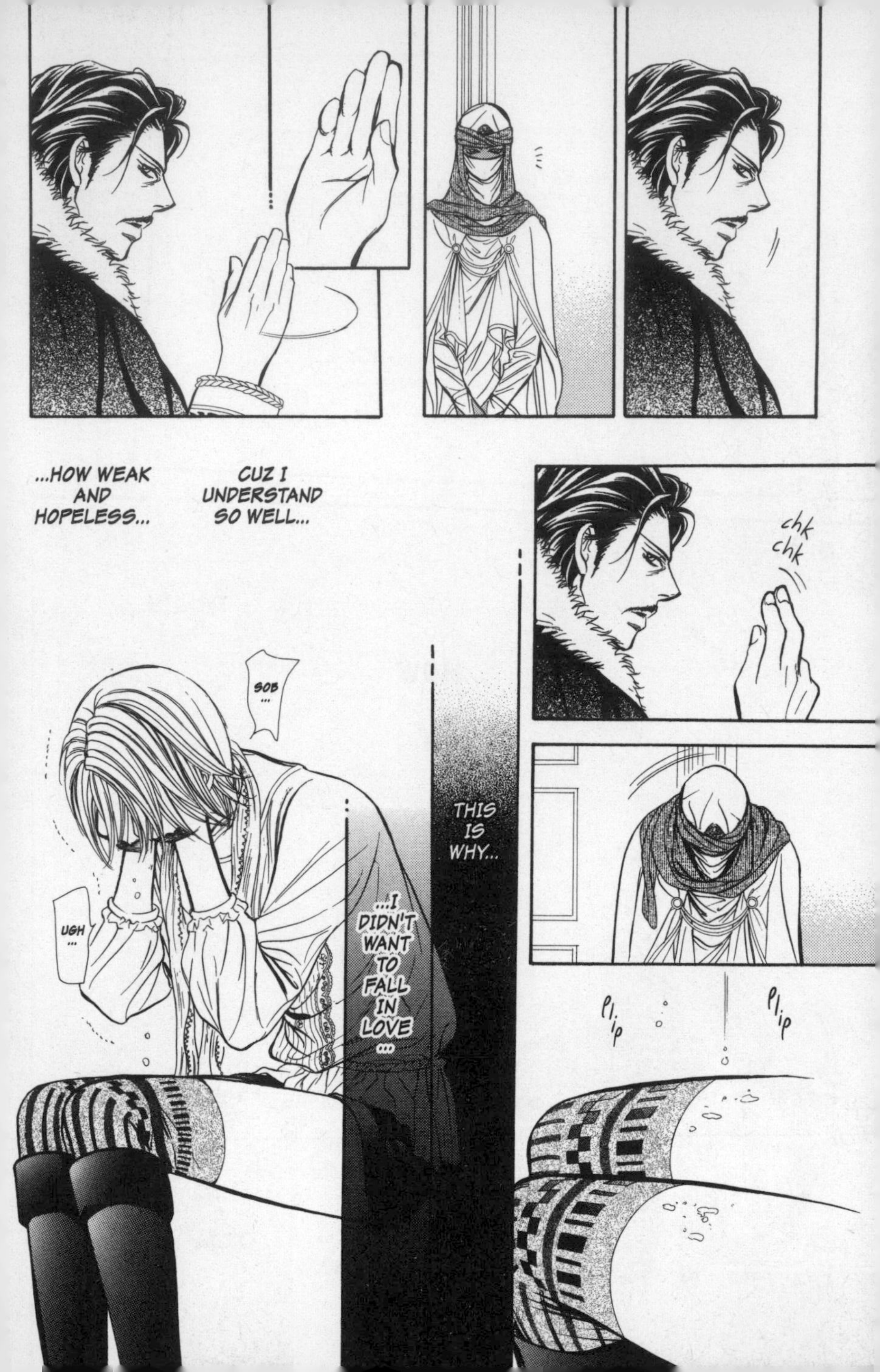
chk chk
Plip
Plip
THIS IS WHY...
...I DIDN'T WANT TO FALL IN LOVE...
CUZ I UNDERSTAND SO WELL...
...HOW WEAK AND HOPELESS...
SOB...
UGH...

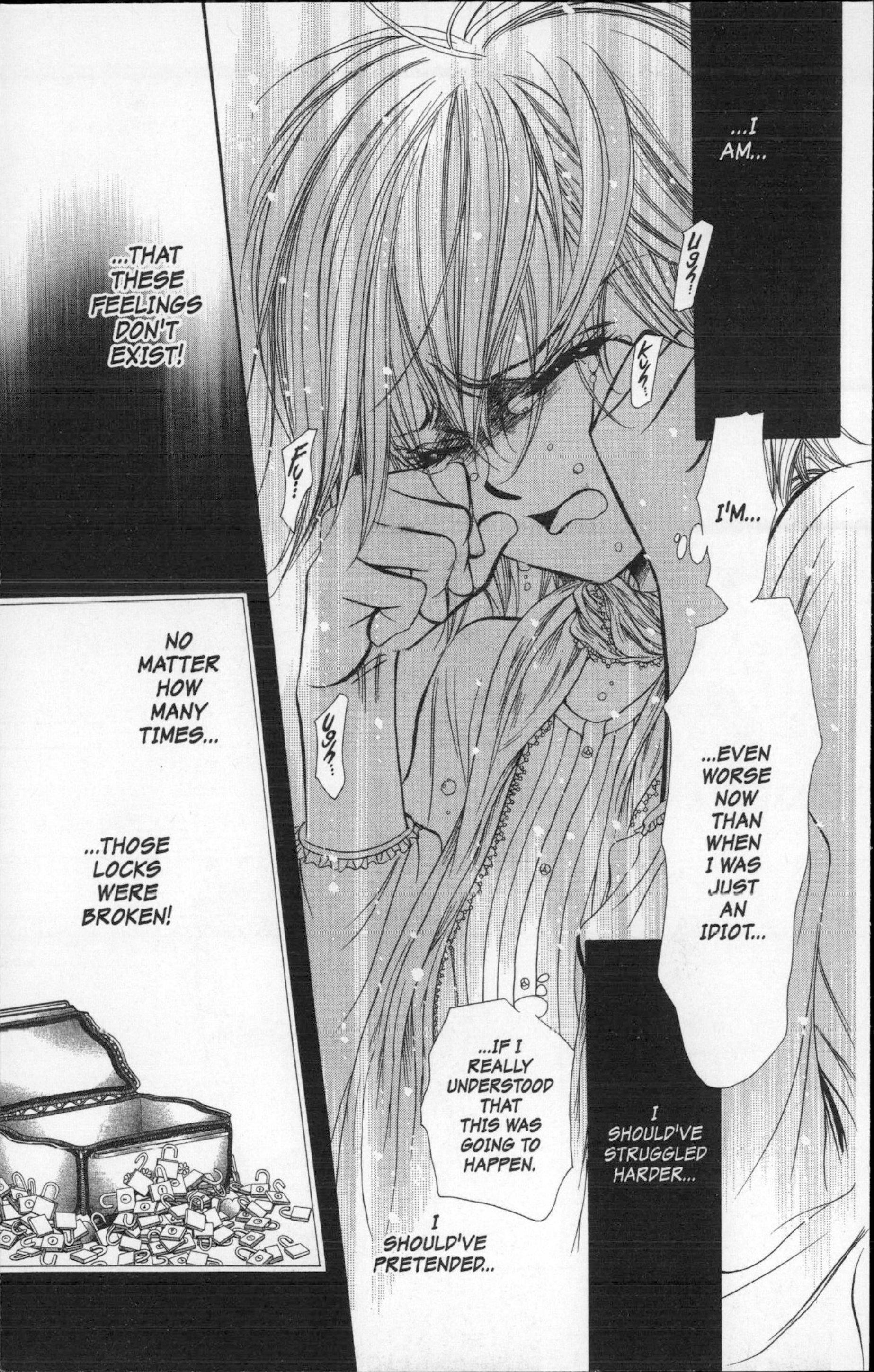
...I AM...
Ugh...
Kuh...
I'M...
...EVEN WORSE NOW THAN WHEN I WAS JUST AN IDIOT...
I SHOULD'VE STRUGGLED HARDER...
...IF I REALLY UNDERSTOOD THAT THIS WAS GOING TO HAPPEN.
I SHOULD'VE PRETENDED...
Fu...
Ugh...
...THAT THESE FEELINGS DON'T EXIST!
NO MATTER HOW MANY TIMES...
...THOSE LOCKS WERE BROKEN!

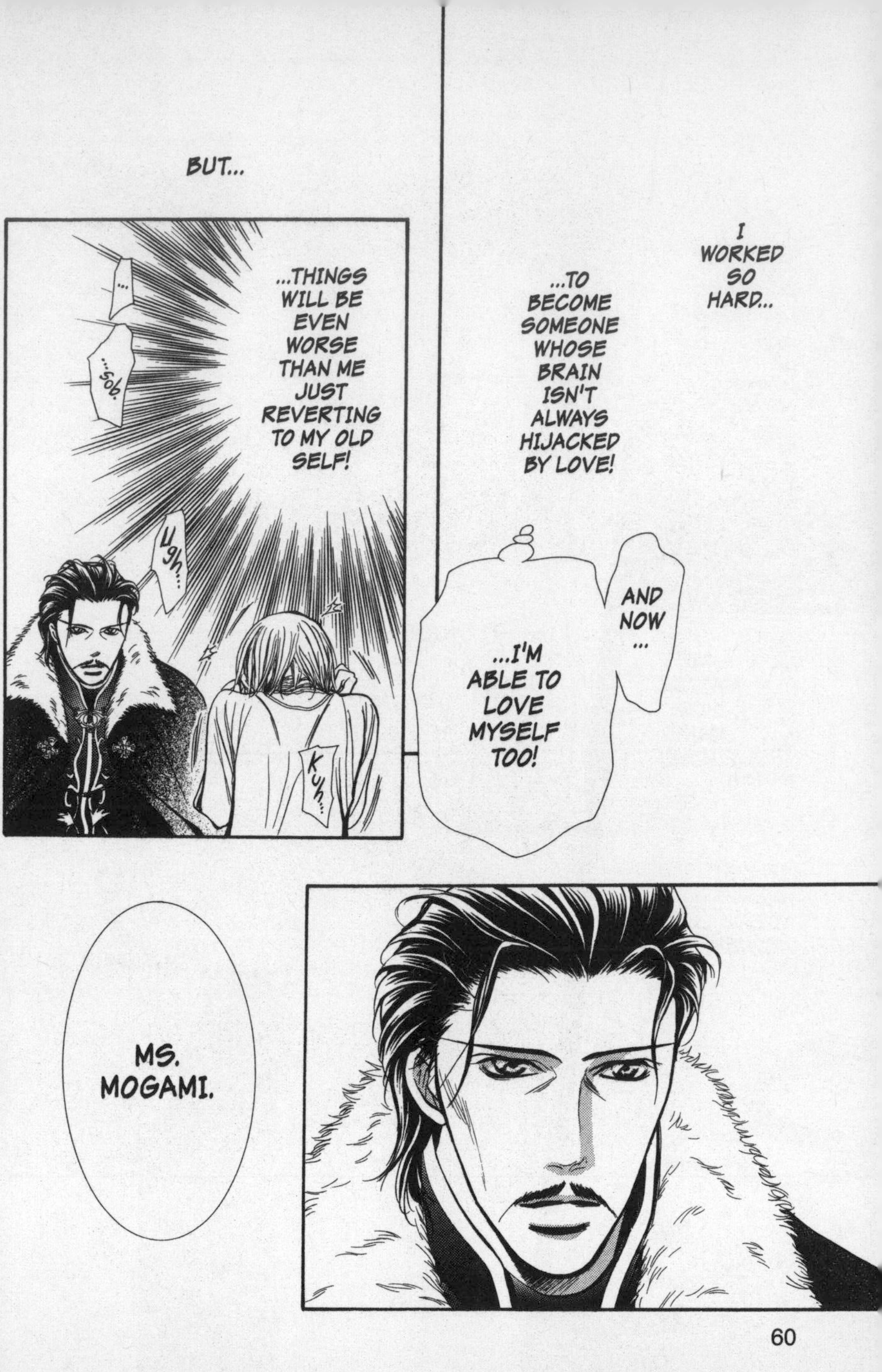
I WORKED SO HARD...
...TO BECOME SOMEONE WHOSE BRAIN ISN'T ALWAYS HIJACKED BY LOVE!
AND NOW...
...I'M ABLE TO LOVE MYSELF TOO!
BUT...
...THINGS WILL BE EVEN WORSE THAN ME JUST REVERTING TO MY OLD SELF!
...
...sob...
Ugh...
Kuh...
MS. MOGAMI.

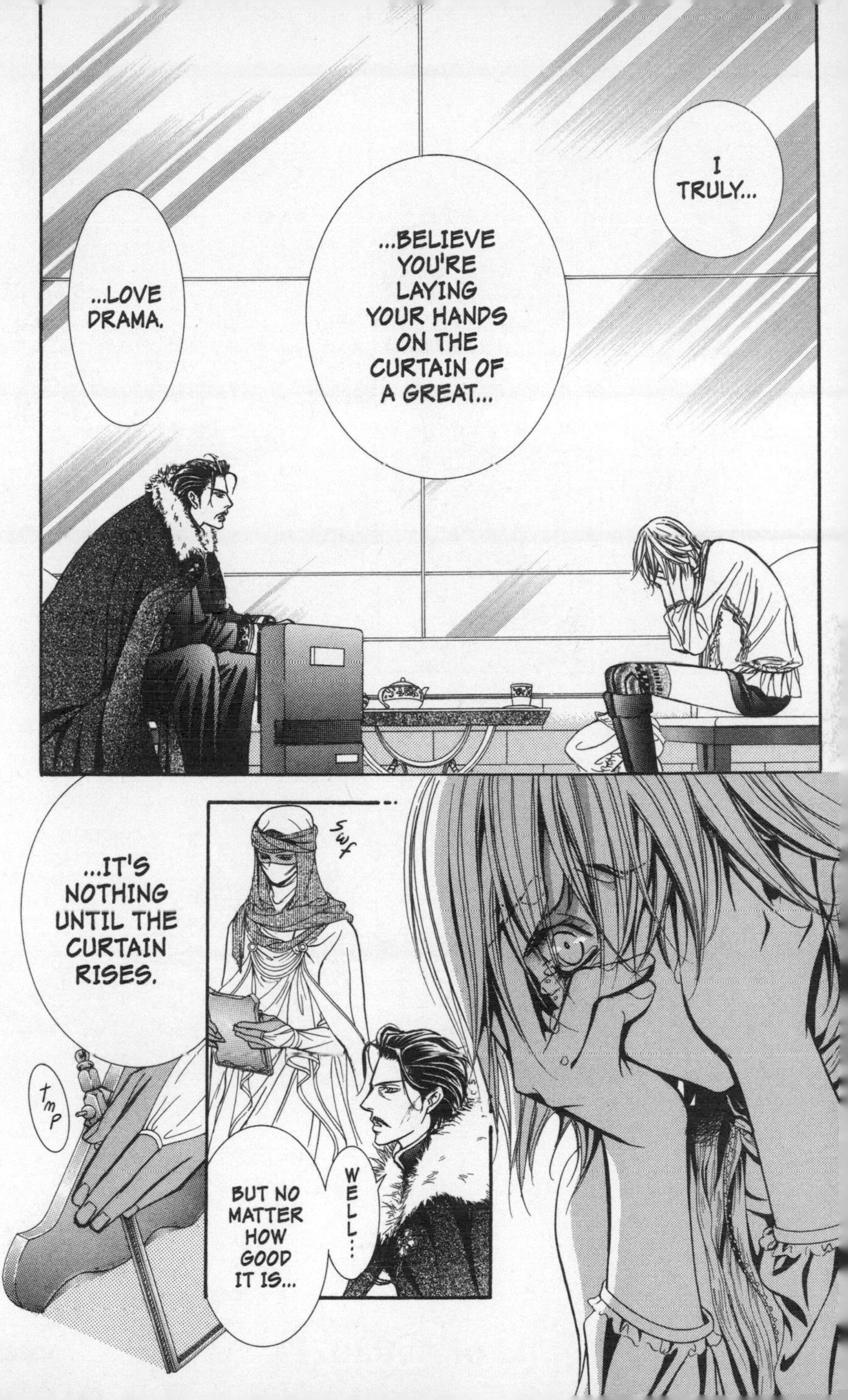
I TRULY...
...BELIEVE YOU'RE LAYING YOUR HANDS ON THE CURTAIN OF A GREAT...
...LOVE DRAMA.
swf
WELL...
BUT NO MATTER HOW GOOD IT IS...
...IT'S NOTHING UNTIL THE CURTAIN RISES.
tmp

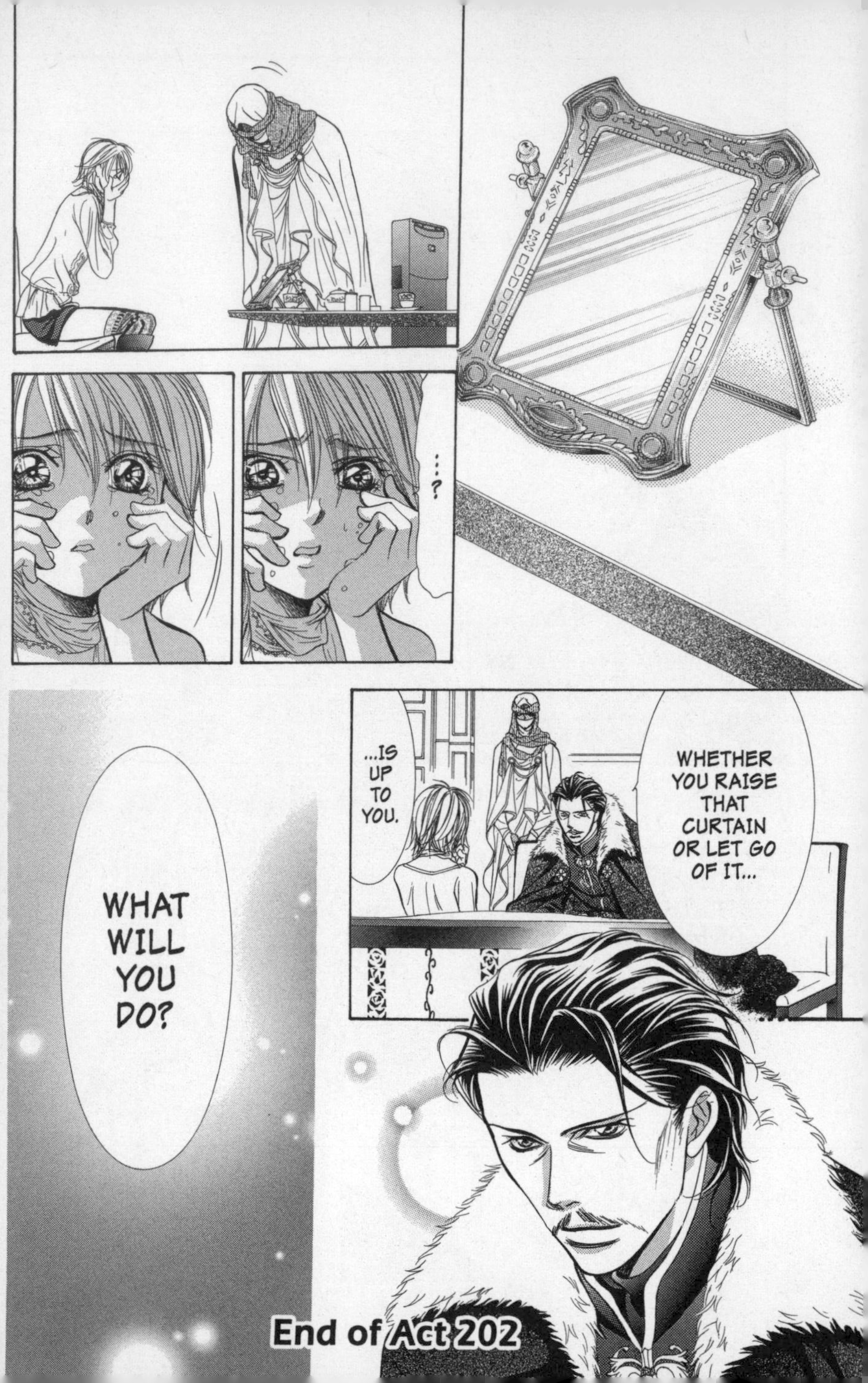
...?
WHETHER YOU RAISE THAT CURTAIN OR LET GO OF IT...
...IS UP TO YOU.
WHAT WILL YOU DO?
End of Act 202

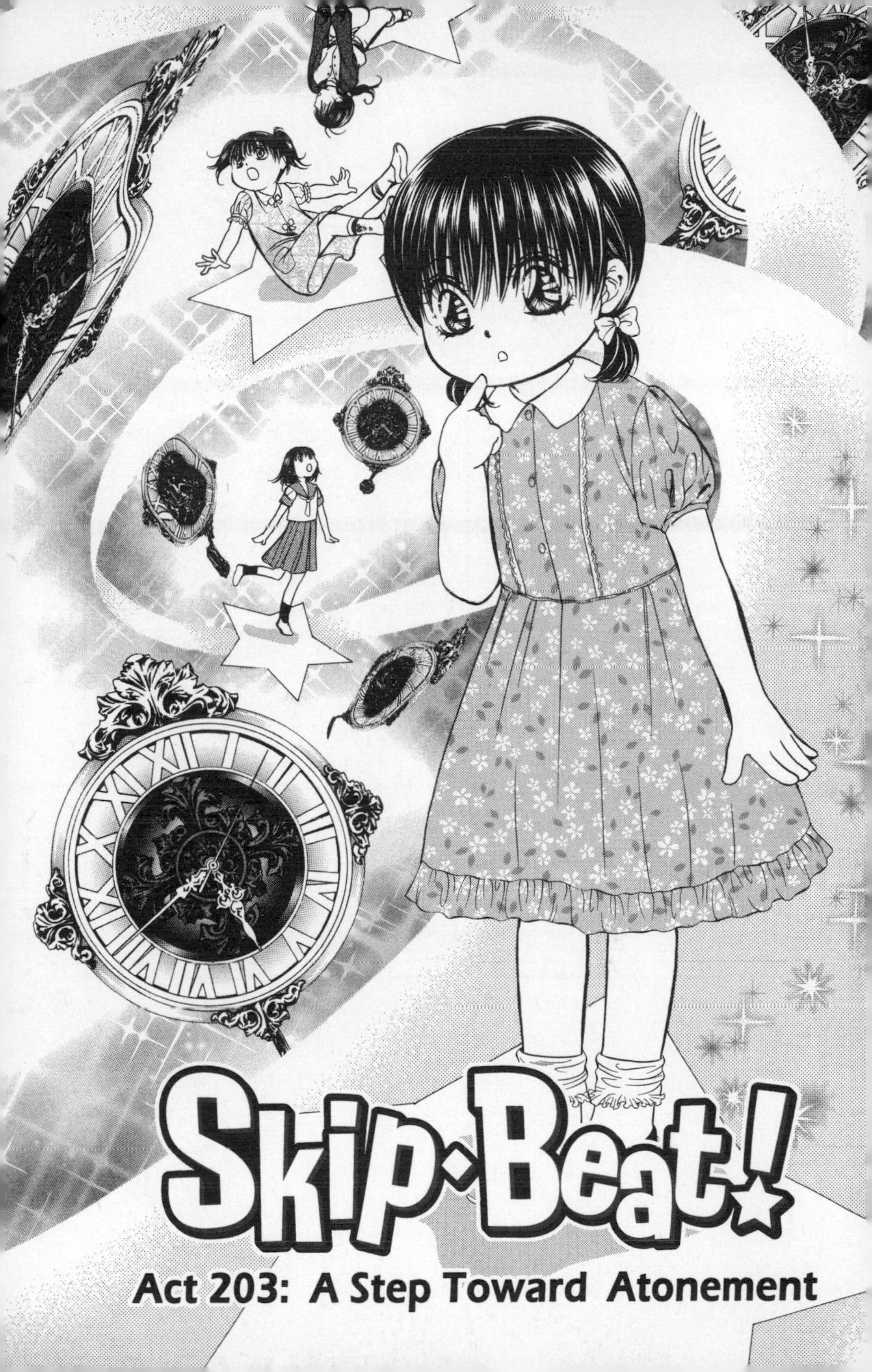
Skip·Beat!
Act 203: A Step Toward Atonement

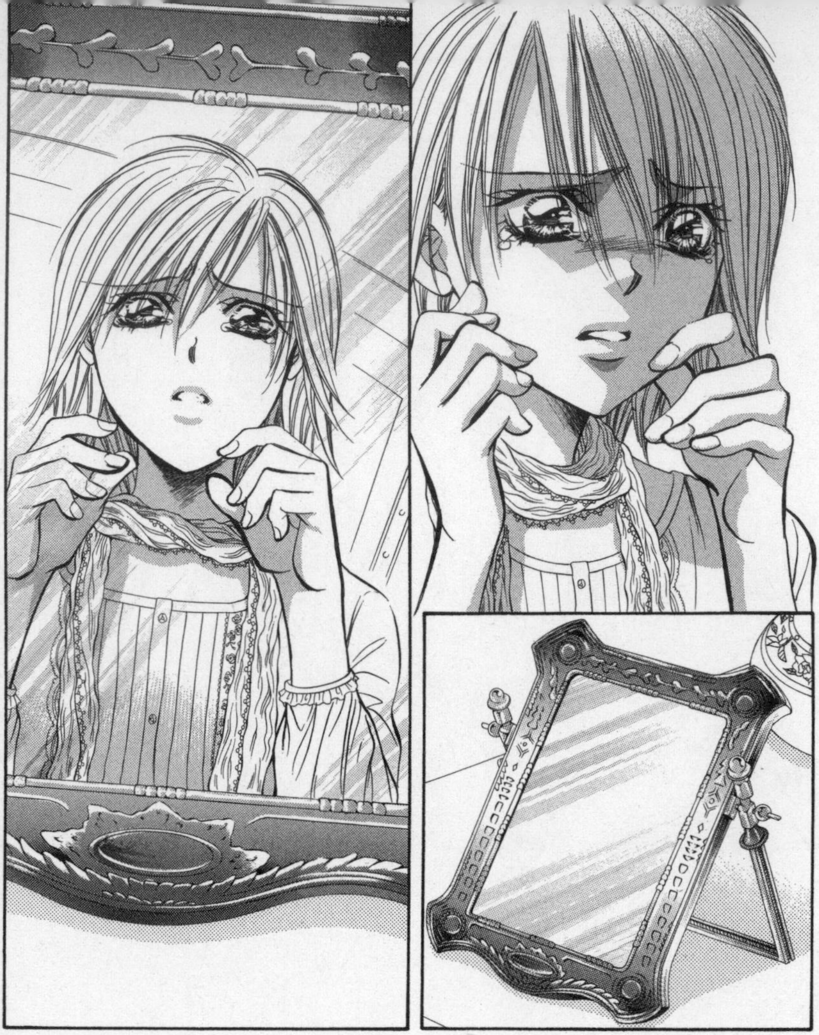
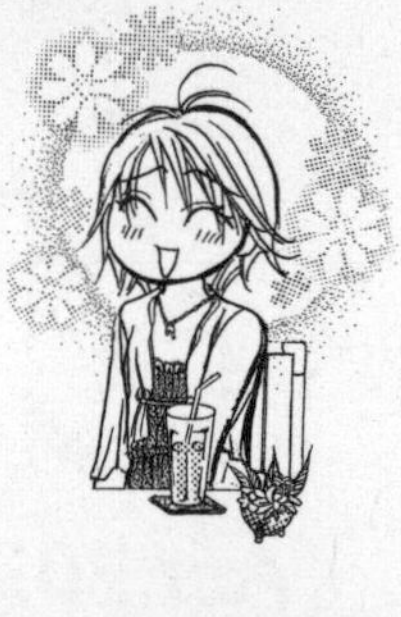

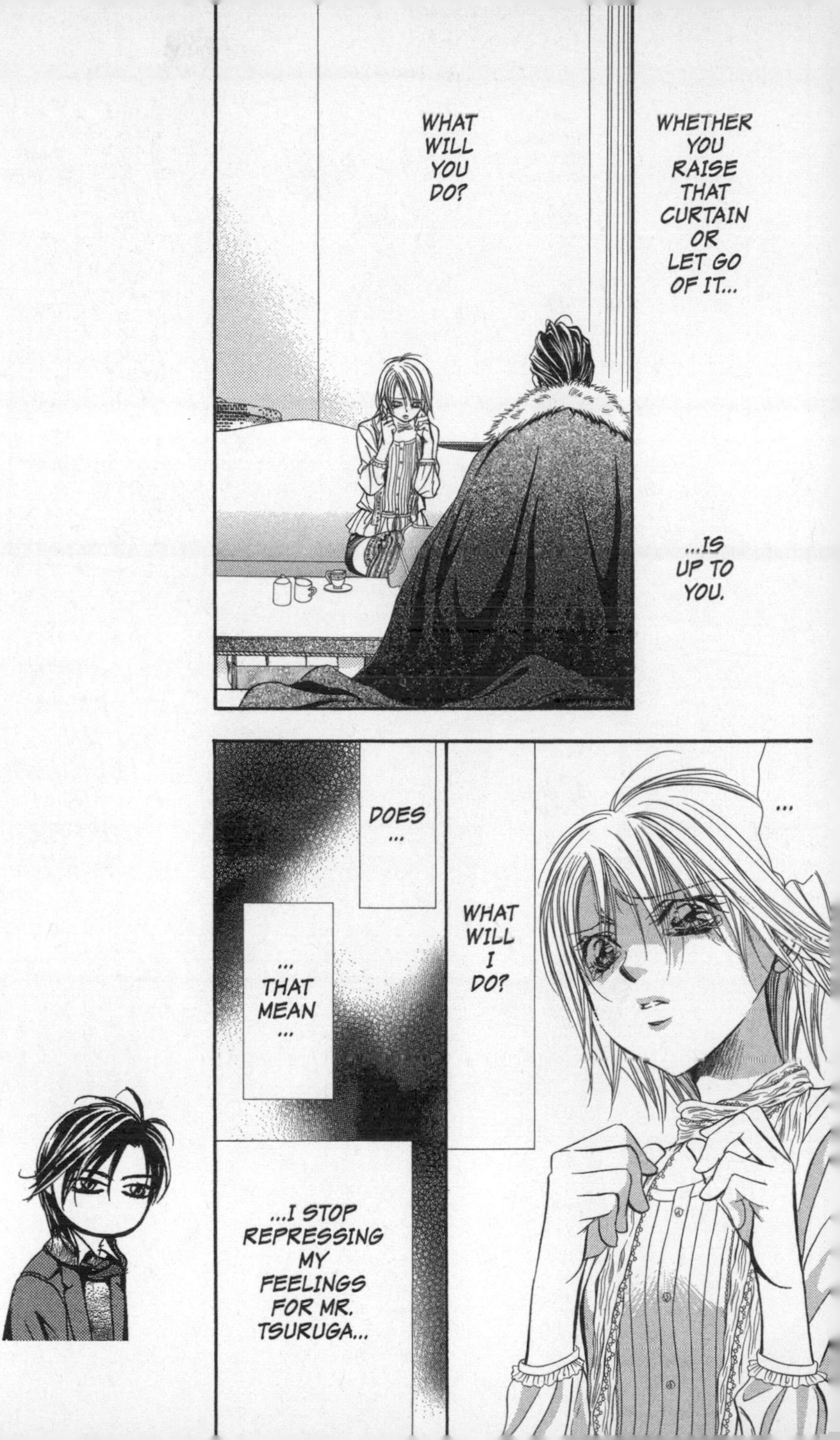
WHETHER YOU RAISE THAT CURTAIN OR LET GO OF IT...
WHAT WILL YOU DO?
...IS UP TO YOU.
...
WHAT WILL I DO?
DOES ...
... THAT MEAN ...
...I STOP REPRESSING MY FEELINGS FOR MR. TSURUGA...

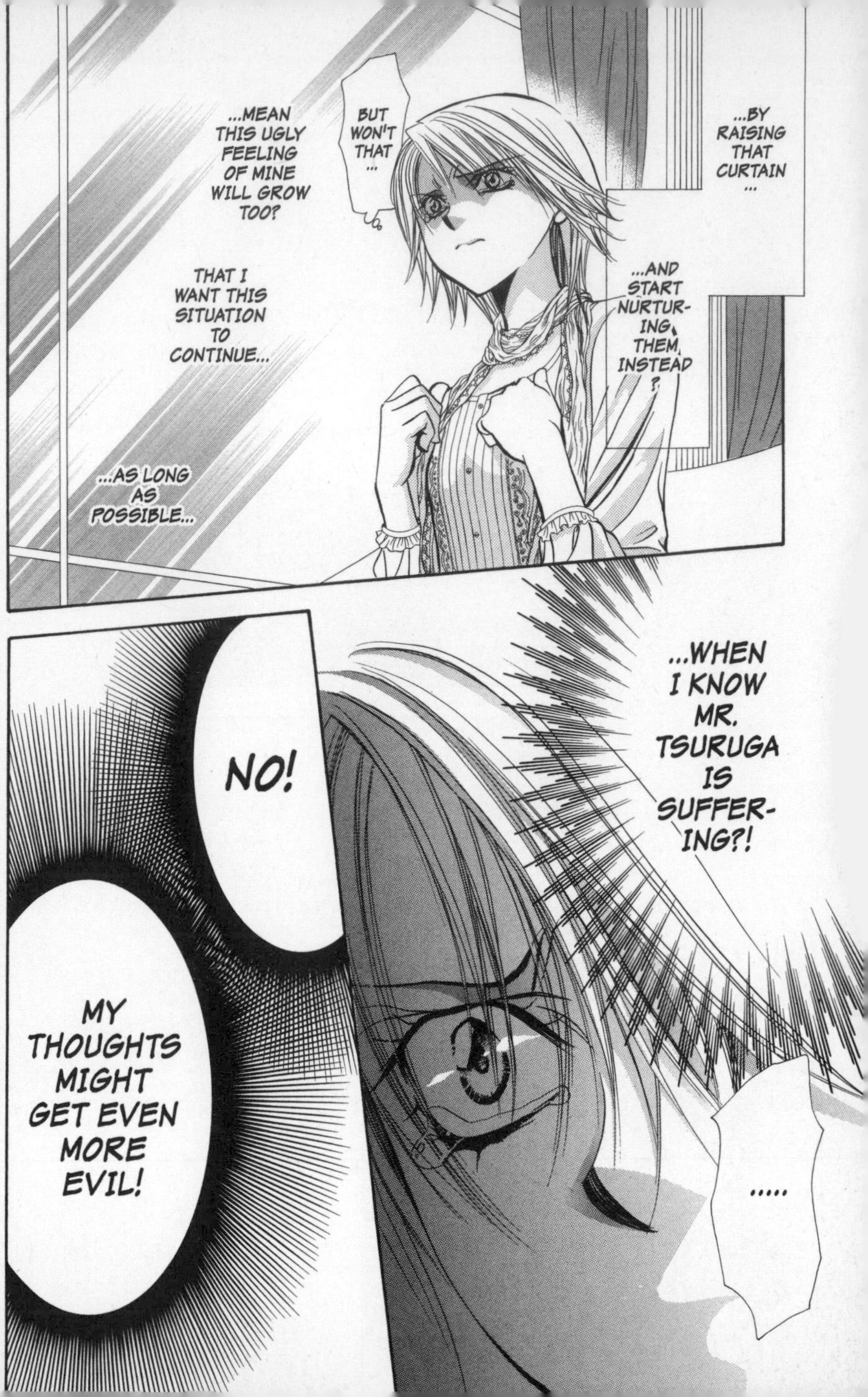
...BY RAISING THAT CURTAIN...
...AND START NURTURING THEM INSTEAD?
BUT WON'T THAT...
...MEAN THIS UGLY FEELING OF MINE WILL GROW TOO?
THAT I WANT THIS SITUATION TO CONTINUE...
...AS LONG AS POSSIBLE...
...WHEN I KNOW MR. TSURUGA IS SUFFERING?!
.....
NO!
MY THOUGHTS MIGHT GET EVEN MORE EVIL!

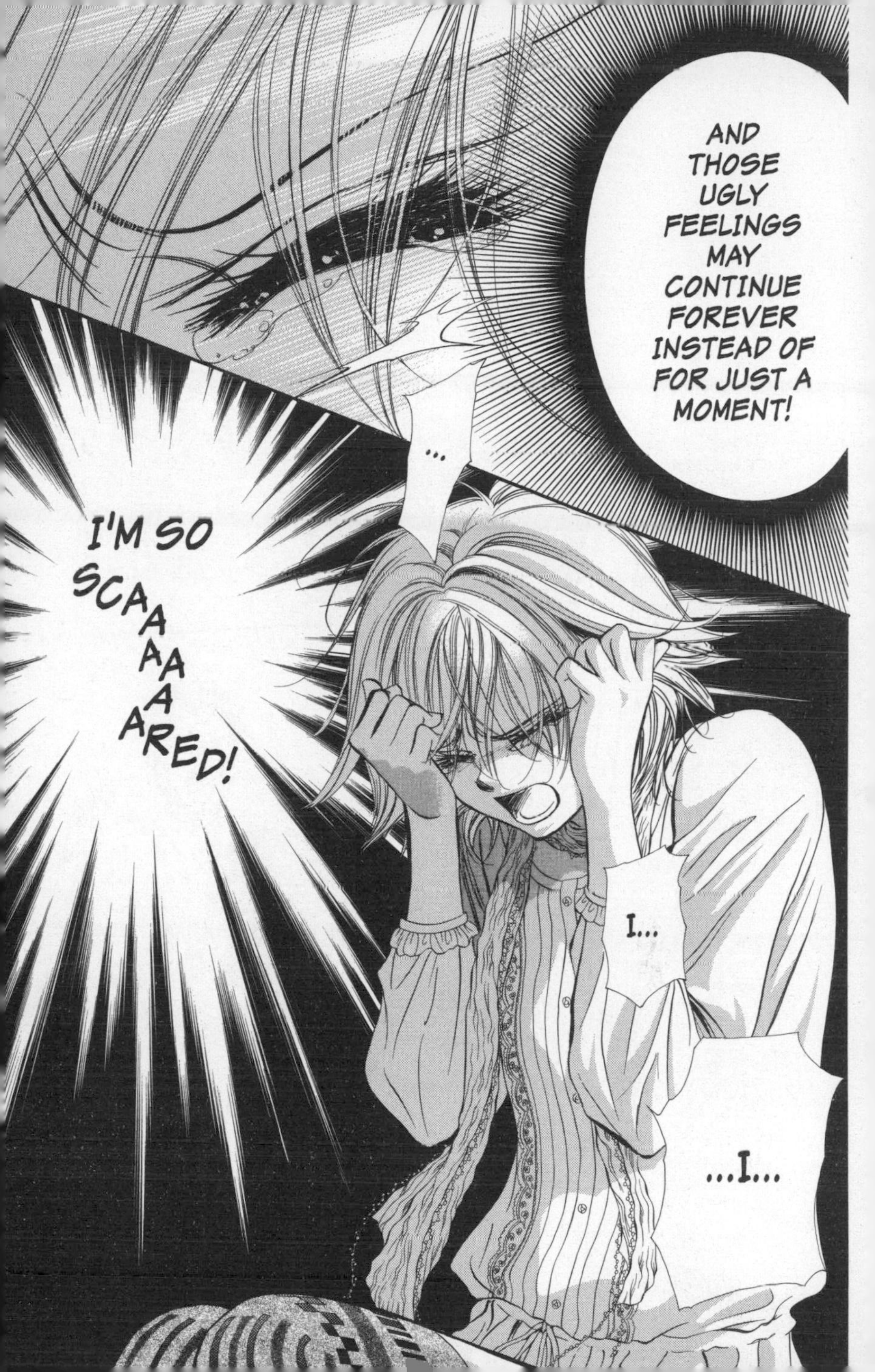
AND THOSE UGLY FEELINGS MAY CONTINUE FOREVER INSTEAD OF FOR JUST A MOMENT!
...
I'M SO SCAAAAAARED!
I...
...I...

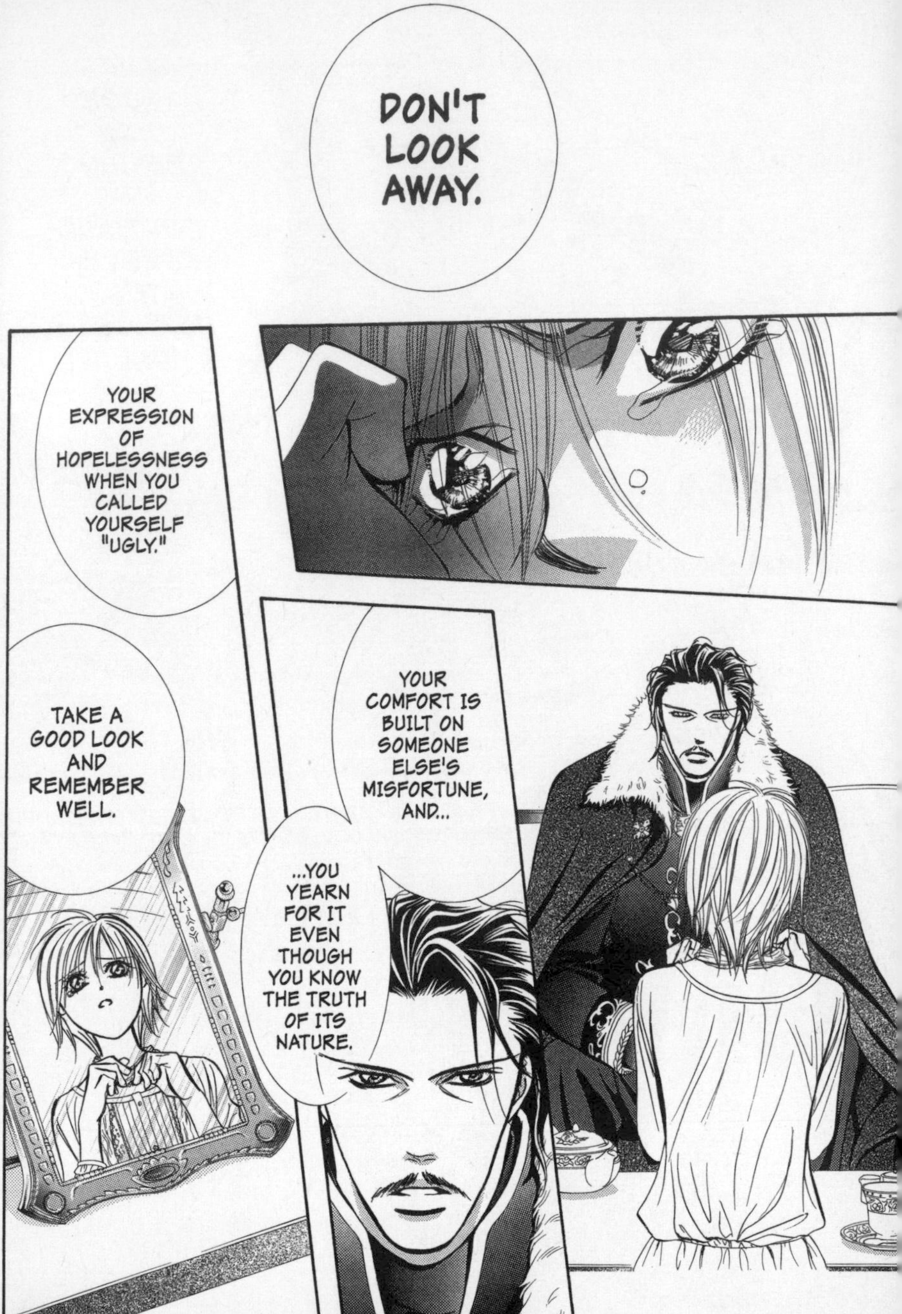
DON'T LOOK AWAY.
YOUR COMFORT IS BUILT ON SOMEONE ELSE'S MISFORTUNE, AND...
...YOU YEARN FOR IT EVEN THOUGH YOU KNOW THE TRUTH OF ITS NATURE.
YOUR EXPRESSION OF HOPELESSNESS WHEN YOU CALLED YOURSELF "UGLY."
TAKE A GOOD LOOK AND REMEMBER WELL.

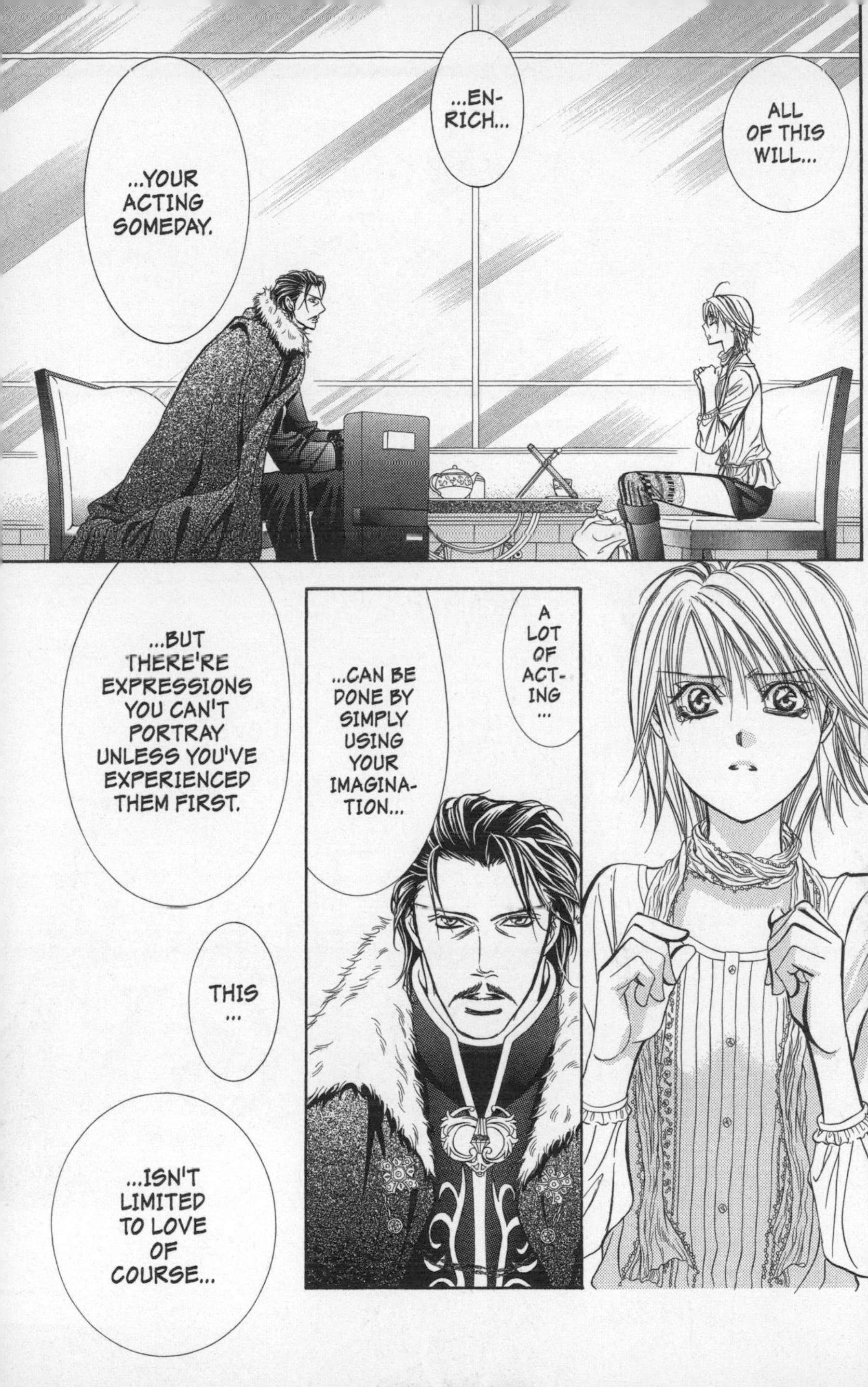
ALL OF THIS WILL...
...EN-RICH...
...YOUR ACTING SOMEDAY.
A LOT OF ACT-ING...
...CAN BE DONE BY SIMPLY USING YOUR IMAGINA-TION...
...BUT THERE'RE EXPRESSIONS YOU CAN'T PORTRAY UNLESS YOU'VE EXPERIENCED THEM FIRST.
THIS...
...ISN'T LIMITED TO LOVE OF COURSE...

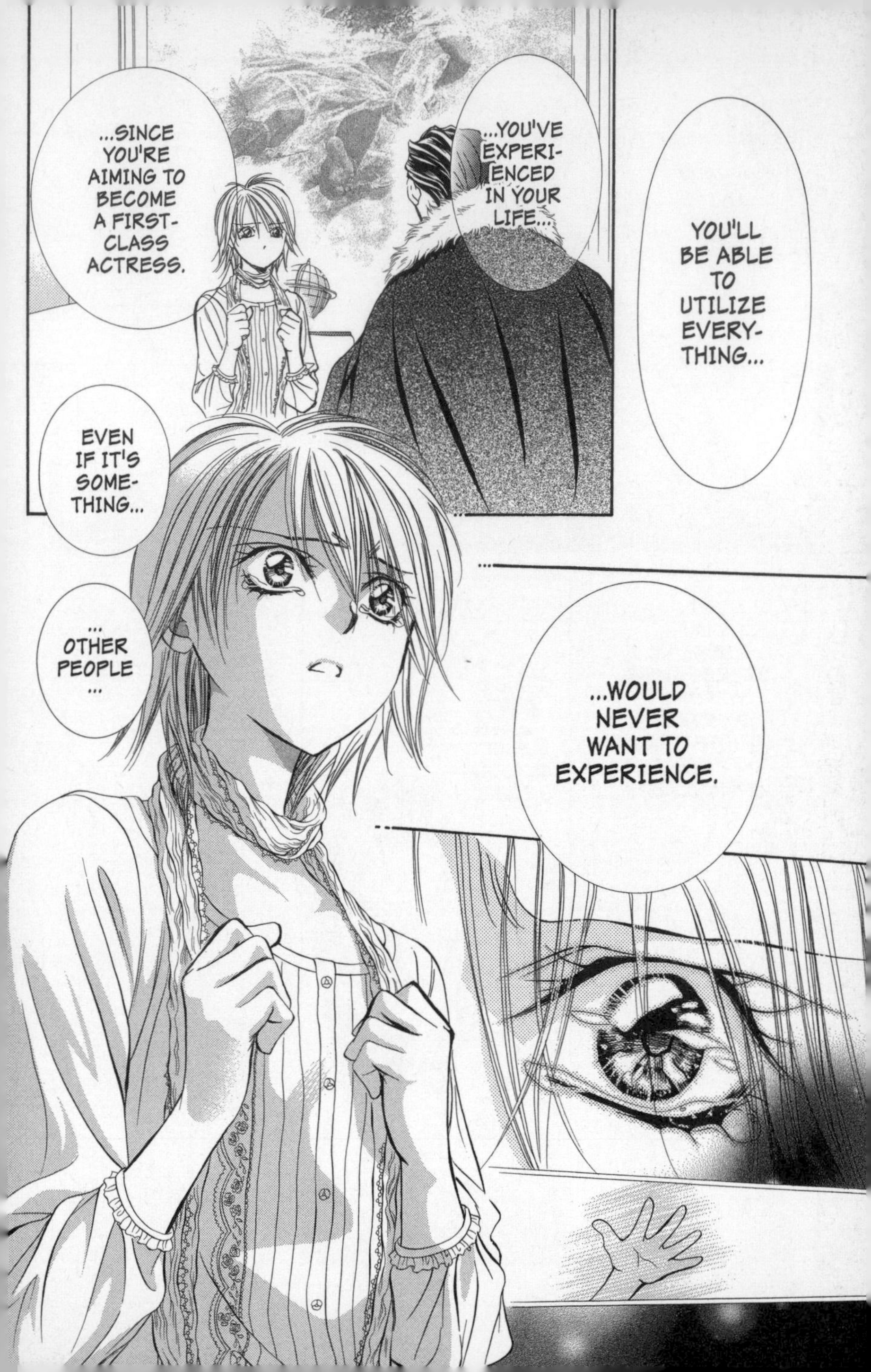
YOU'LL BE ABLE TO UTILIZE EVERY-THING...
...YOU'VE EXPERI-ENCED IN YOUR LIFE...
...SINCE YOU'RE AIMING TO BECOME A FIRST-CLASS ACTRESS.
EVEN IF IT'S SOME-THING...
... OTHER PEOPLE ...
...WOULD NEVER WANT TO EXPERIENCE.

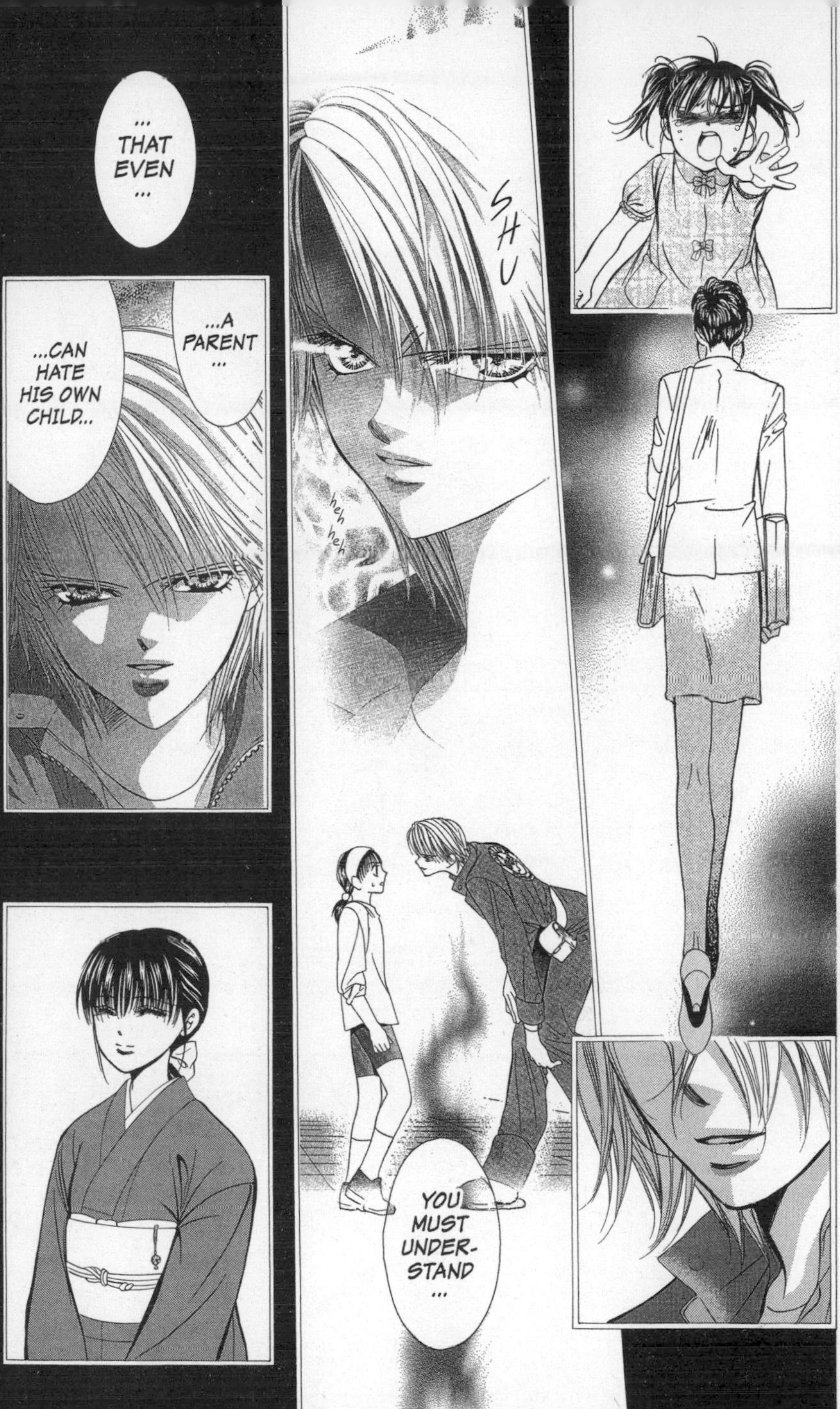
SHU
heh heh
YOU MUST UNDERSTAND...
...THAT EVEN...
...A PARENT...
...CAN HATE HIS OWN CHILD...

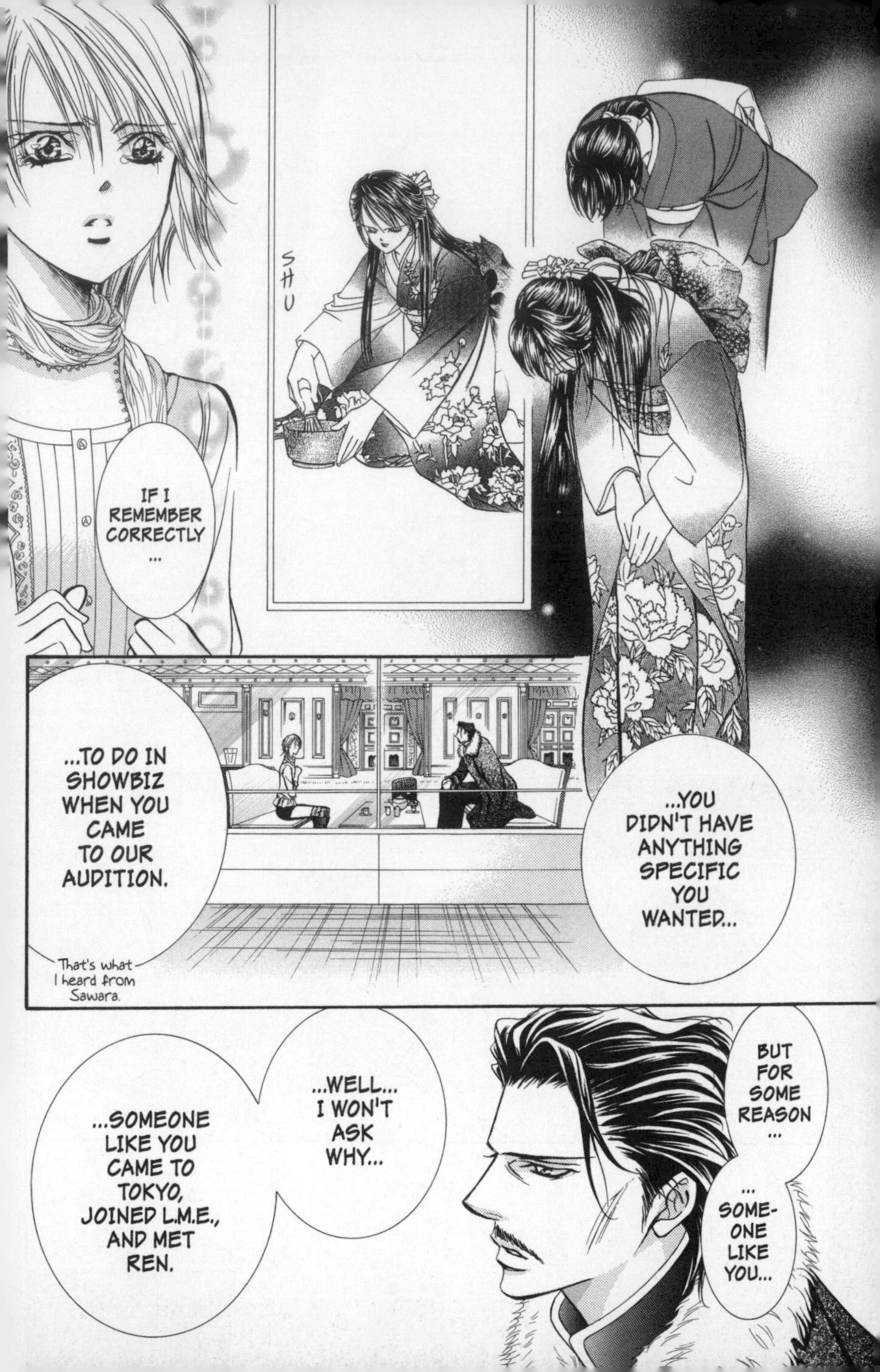
SHU
IF I REMEMBER CORRECTLY ...
...YOU DIDN'T HAVE ANYTHING SPECIFIC YOU WANTED...
...TO DO IN SHOWBIZ WHEN YOU CAME TO OUR AUDITION.
That's what I heard from Sawara.
BUT FOR SOME REASON ...
... SOME-ONE LIKE YOU...
...WELL... I WON'T ASK WHY...
...SOMEONE LIKE YOU CAME TO TOKYO, JOINED L.M.E., AND MET REN.

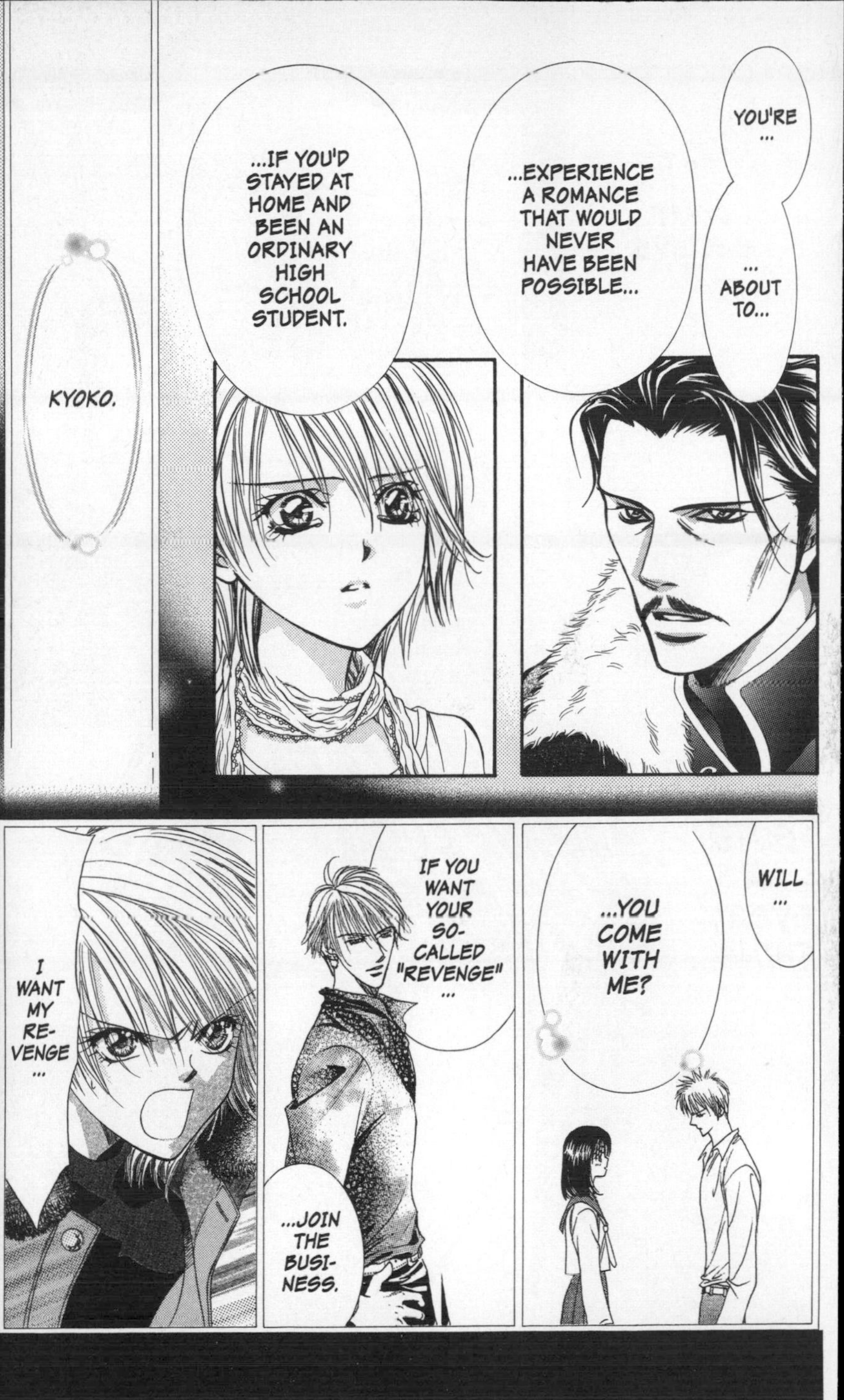
YOU'RE ... ... ABOUT TO...
...EXPERIENCE A ROMANCE THAT WOULD NEVER HAVE BEEN POSSIBLE...
...IF YOU'D STAYED AT HOME AND BEEN AN ORDINARY HIGH SCHOOL STUDENT.
KYOKO.
WILL ...
...YOU COME WITH ME?
IF YOU WANT YOUR SO-CALLED "REVENGE" ...
...JOIN THE BUSINESS.
I WANT MY REVENGE ...

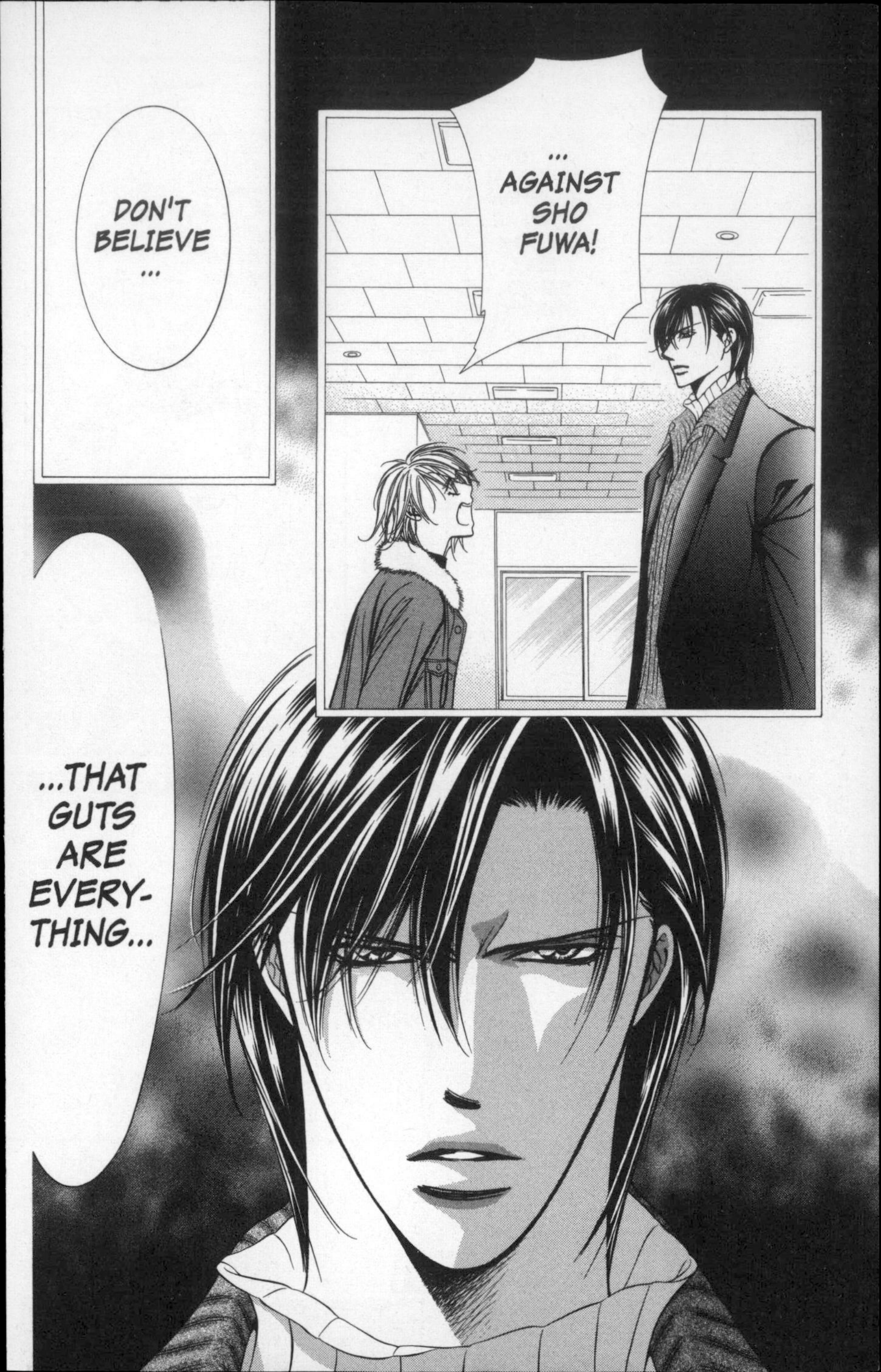
...AGAINST SHO FUWA!
DON'T BELIEVE ...
...THAT GUTS ARE EVERY-THING...

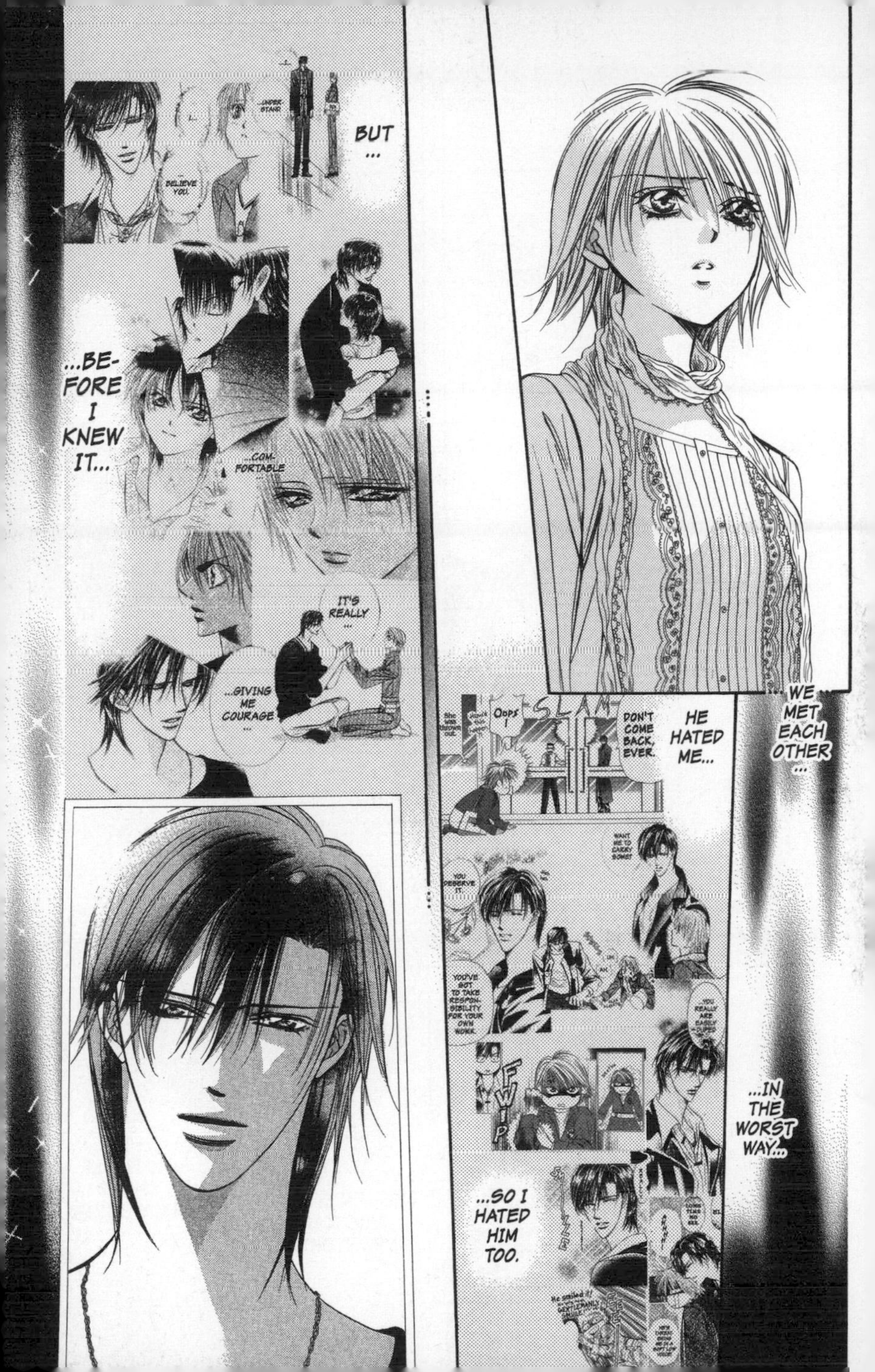

...WE MET EACH OTHER...
HE HATED ME...
DON'T COME BACK, EVER.
Oops!
She was thrown out.
SLAM
WANT ME TO CARRY SOME?
YOU DESERVE IT.
YOU'VE GOT TO TAKE RESPONSIBILITY FOR YOUR OWN WORK.
...YOU REALLY ARE EASILY DUPED...
FWIP
...IN THE WORST WAY...
...SO I HATED HIM TOO.
He nailed it!
GENTLEMANLY
BUT...
...UNDERSTAND
...BELIEVE YOU.
...BEFORE I KNEW IT...
...COMFORTABLE...
IT'S REALLY...
...GIVING ME COURAGE...

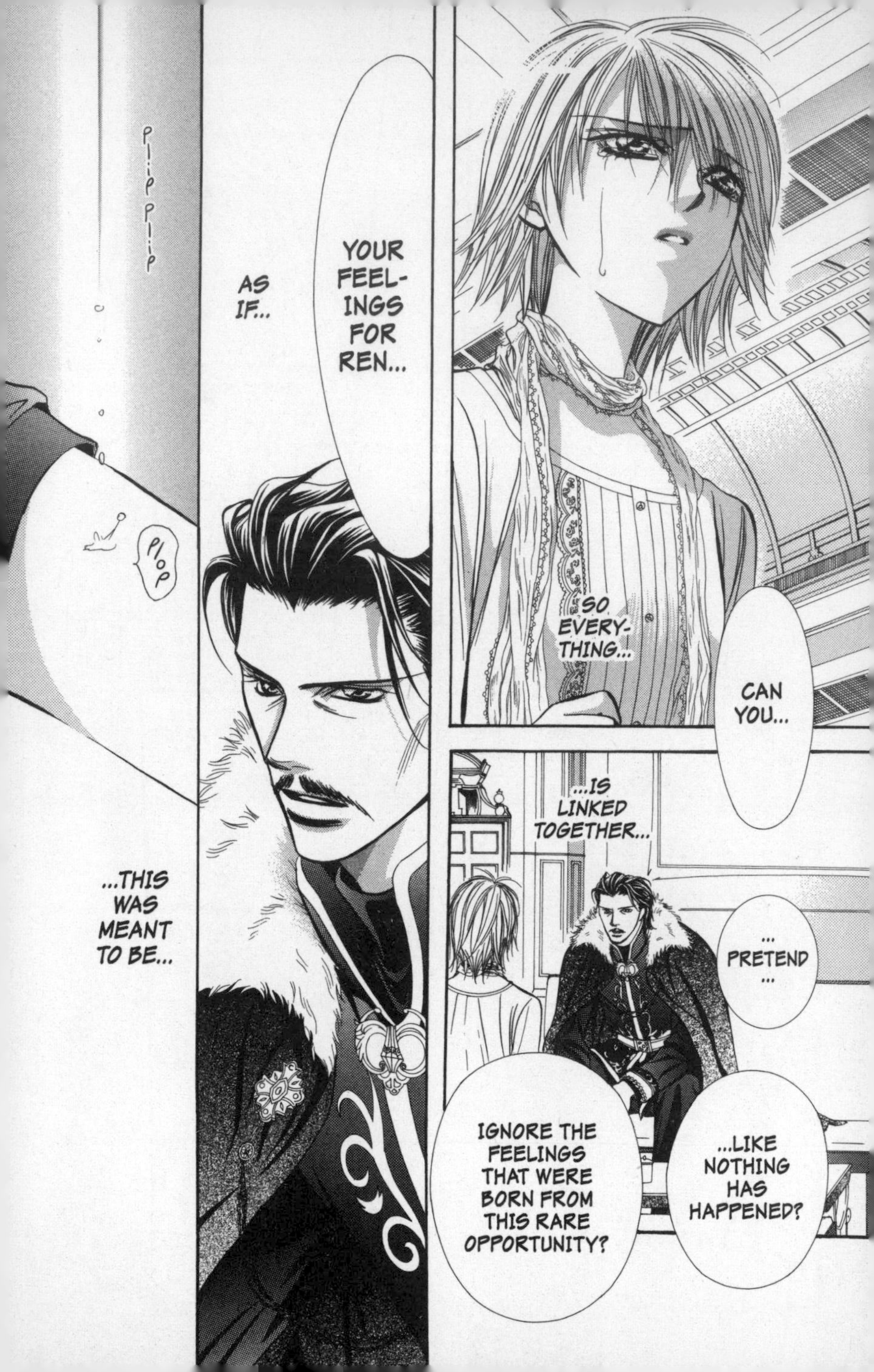
SO EVERY-THING...
...IS LINKED TOGETHER...
CAN YOU...
...PRETEND...
...LIKE NOTHING HAS HAPPENED?
IGNORE THE FEELINGS THAT WERE BORN FROM THIS RARE OPPORTUNITY?
YOUR FEEL-INGS FOR REN...
AS IF...
PLIP PLIP
PLOP
...THIS WAS MEANT TO BE...

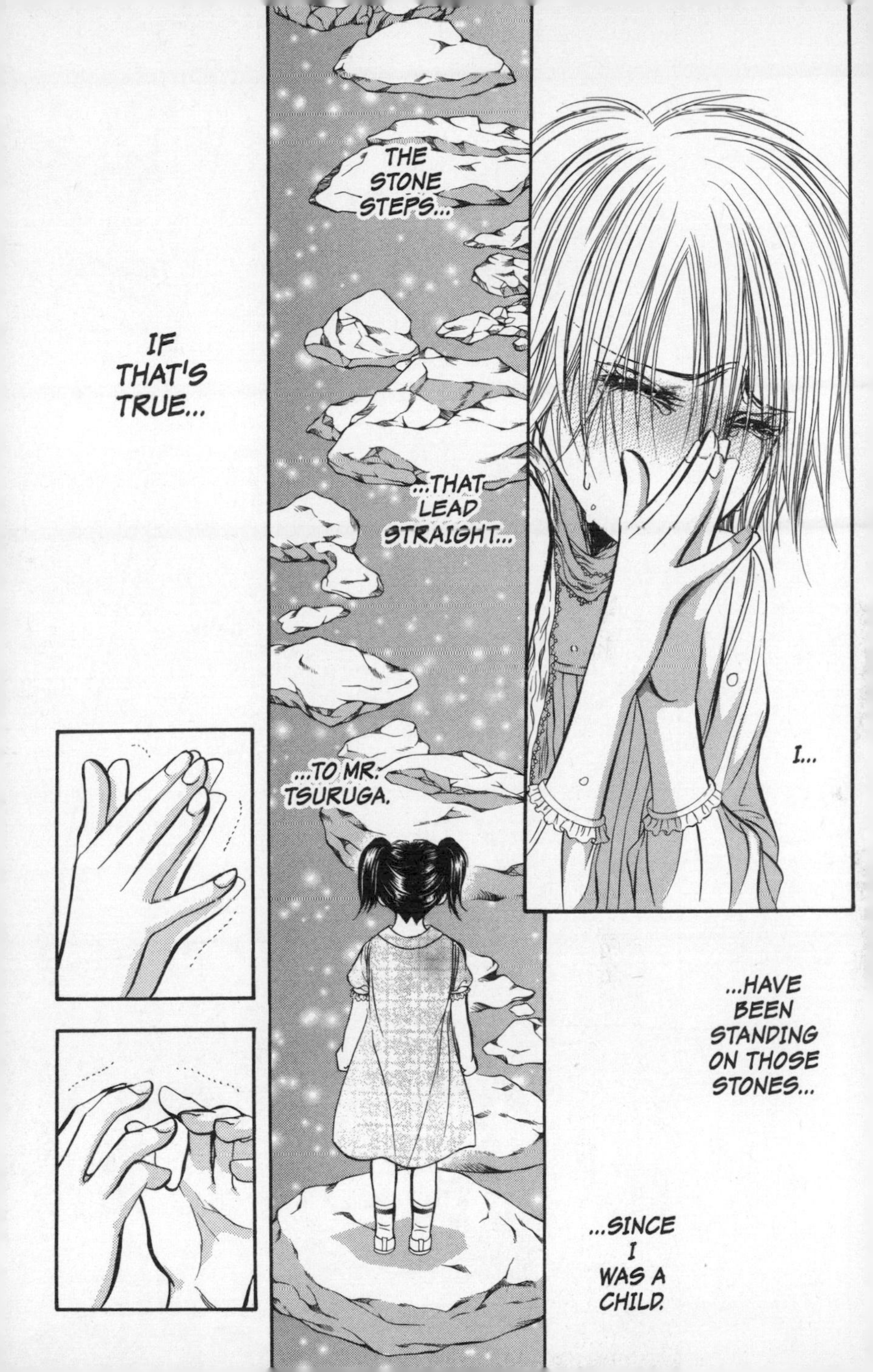
IF THAT'S TRUE...
THE STONE STEPS...
...THAT LEAD STRAIGHT...
...TO MR. TSURUGA.
I...
...HAVE BEEN STANDING ON THOSE STONES...
...SINCE I WAS A CHILD.

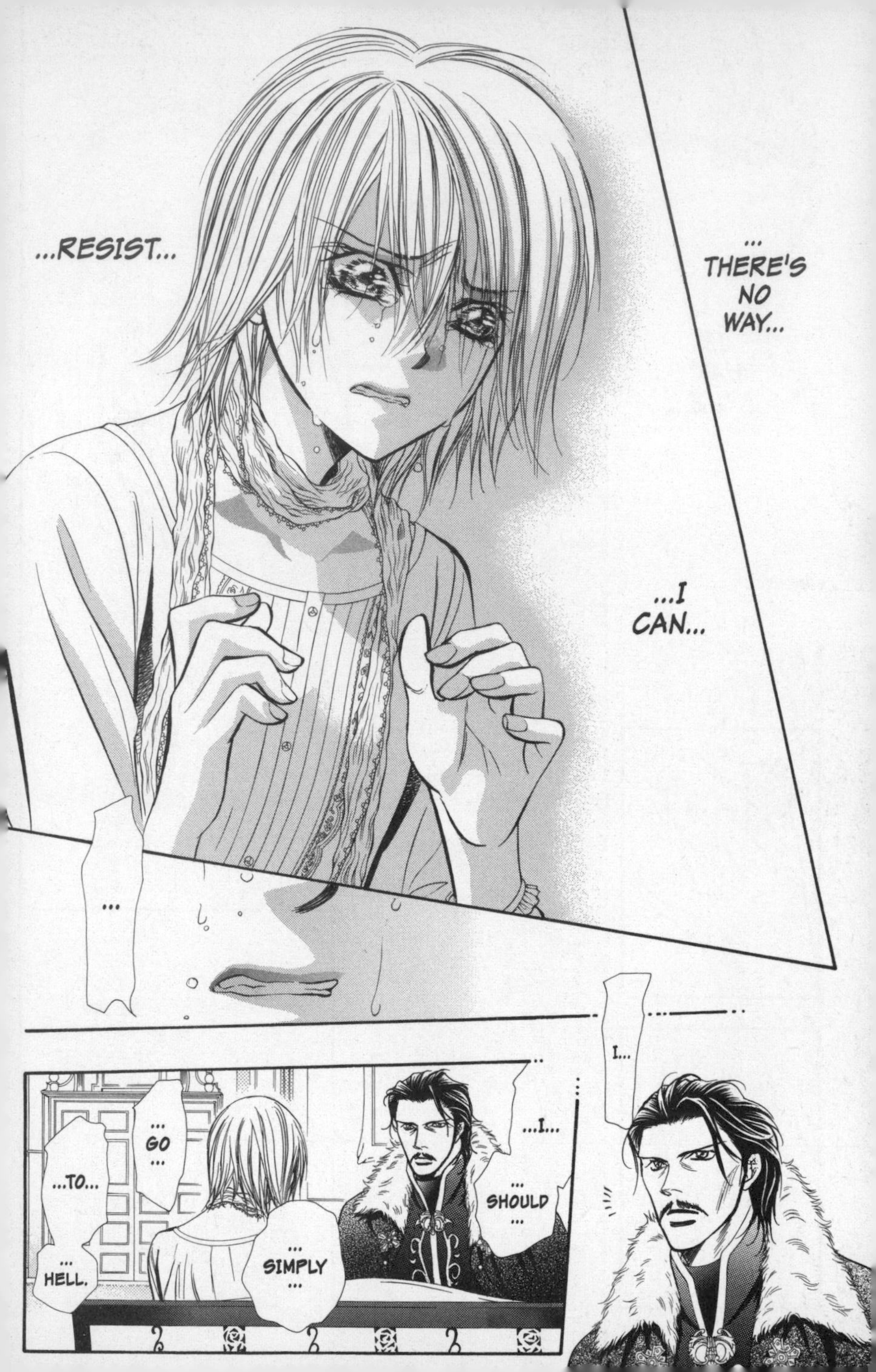
...THERE'S NO WAY...
...I CAN...
...RESIST...
...
I...
...I...
...SHOULD...
...SIMPLY...
...GO...
...TO...
...HELL.

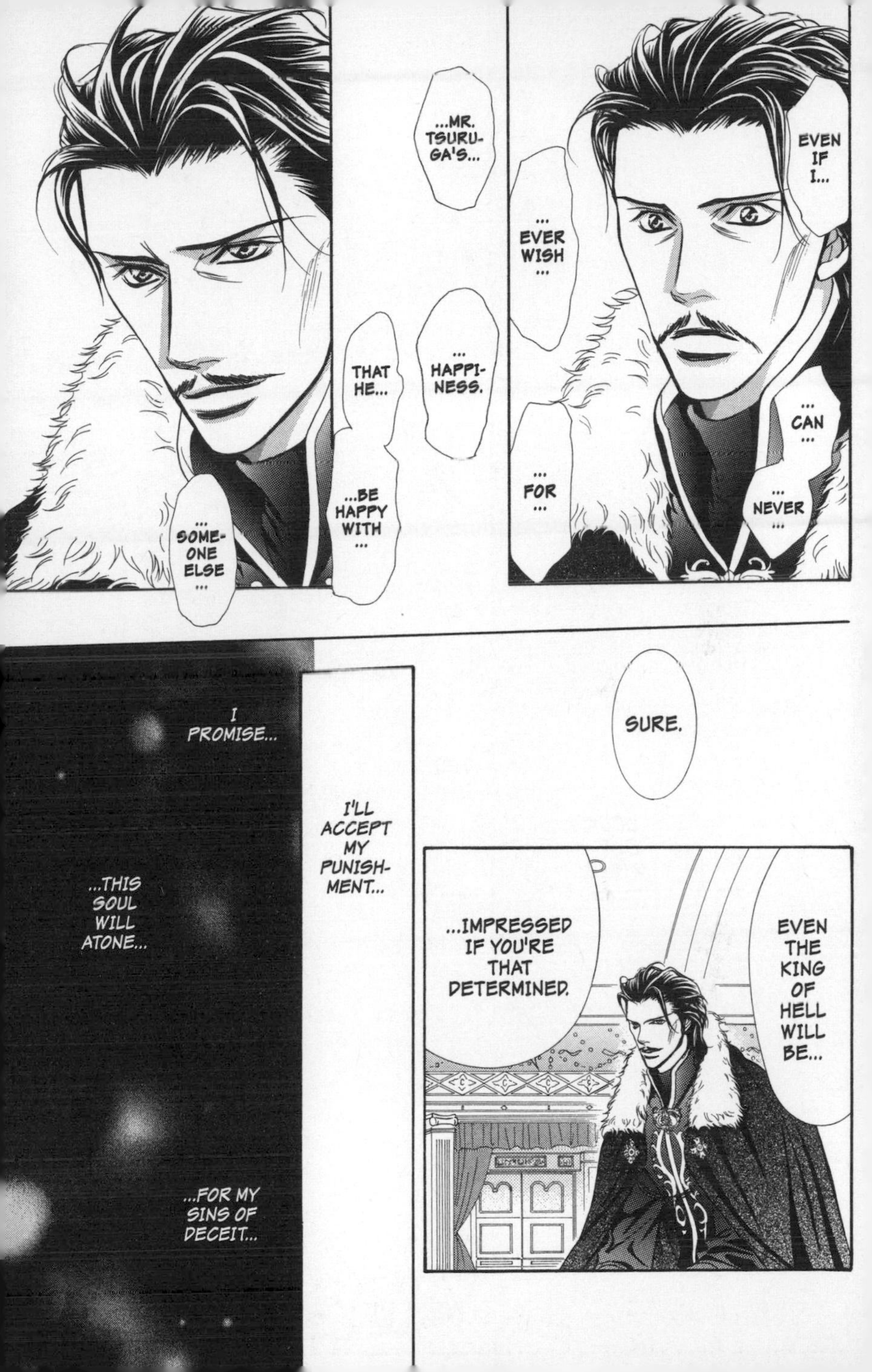
EVEN IF I...
...CAN...
...NEVER...
...EVER WISH...
...FOR...
...MR. TSURU-GA'S...
...HAPPI-NESS.
THAT HE...
...BE HAPPY WITH...
...SOME-ONE ELSE...
SURE.
EVEN THE KING OF HELL WILL BE...
...IMPRESSED IF YOU'RE THAT DETERMINED.
I'LL ACCEPT MY PUNISH-MENT...
I PROMISE...
...THIS SOUL WILL ATONE...
...FOR MY SINS OF DECEIT...

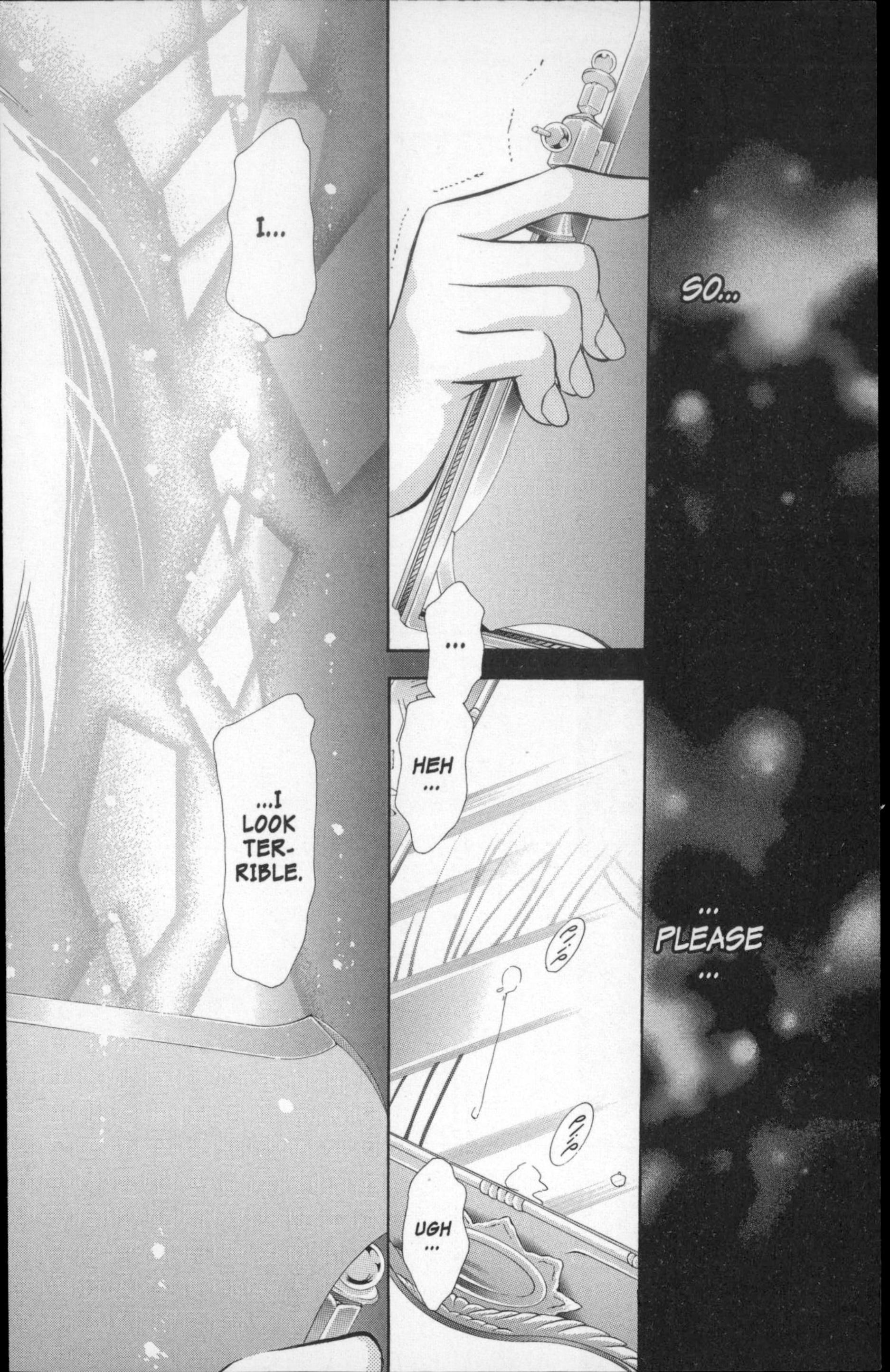
SO...
...PLEASE...
...
HEH...
drip
drip
UGH...
I...
...I LOOK TERRIBLE.

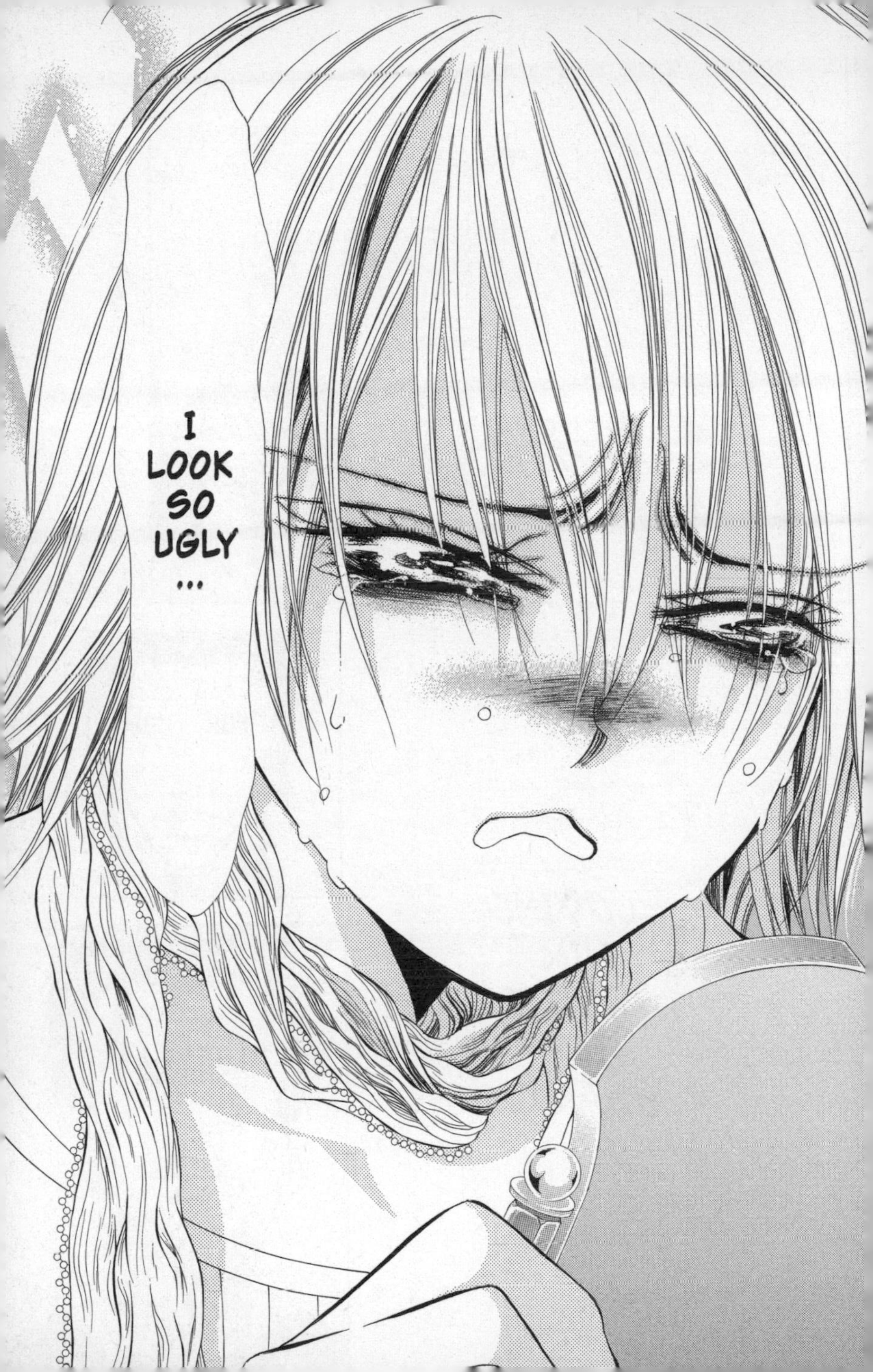
I LOOK SO UGLY...

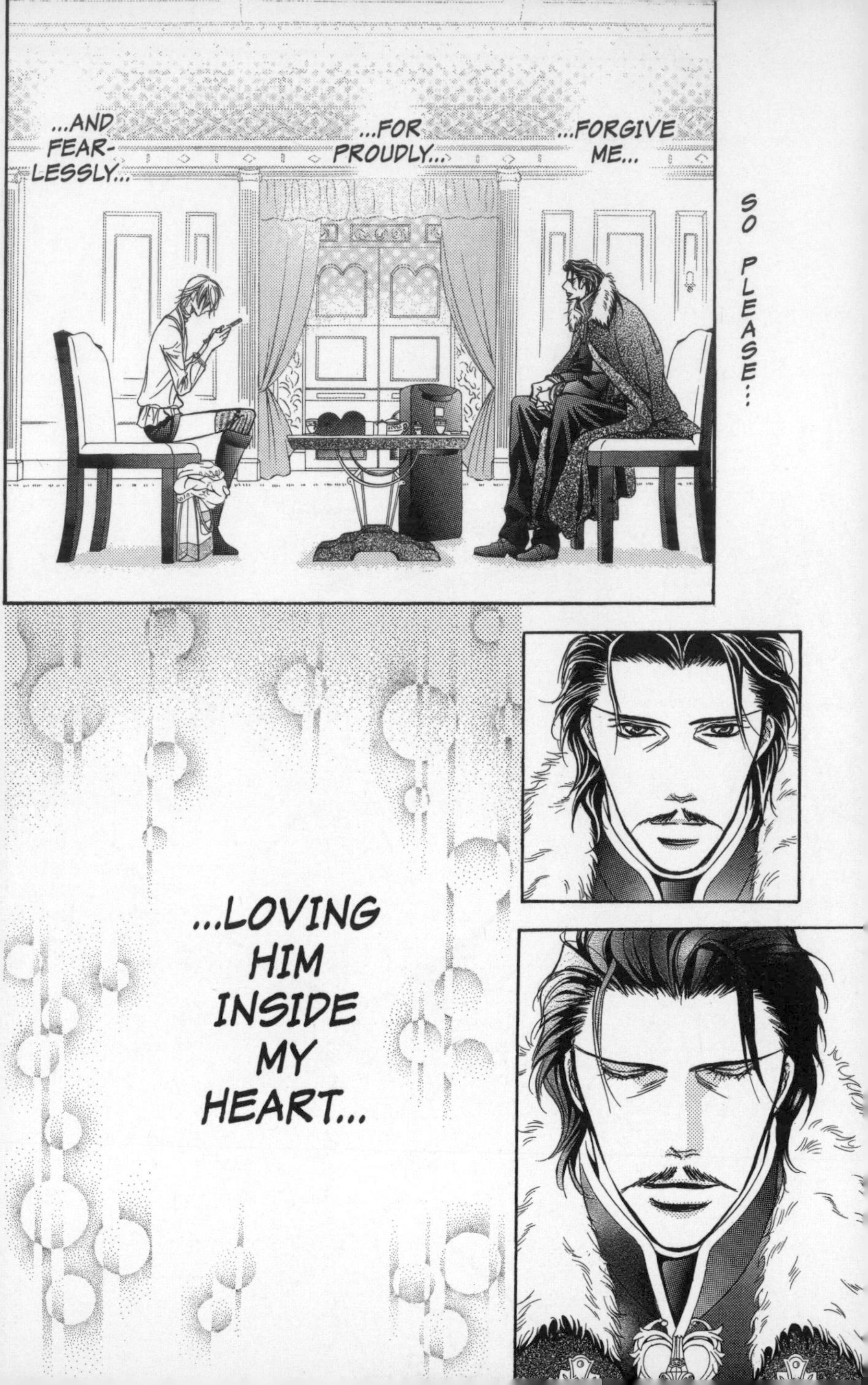
SO PLEASE...
...FORGIVE ME...
...FOR PROUDLY...
...AND FEAR-LESSLY...
...LOVING HIM INSIDE MY HEART...

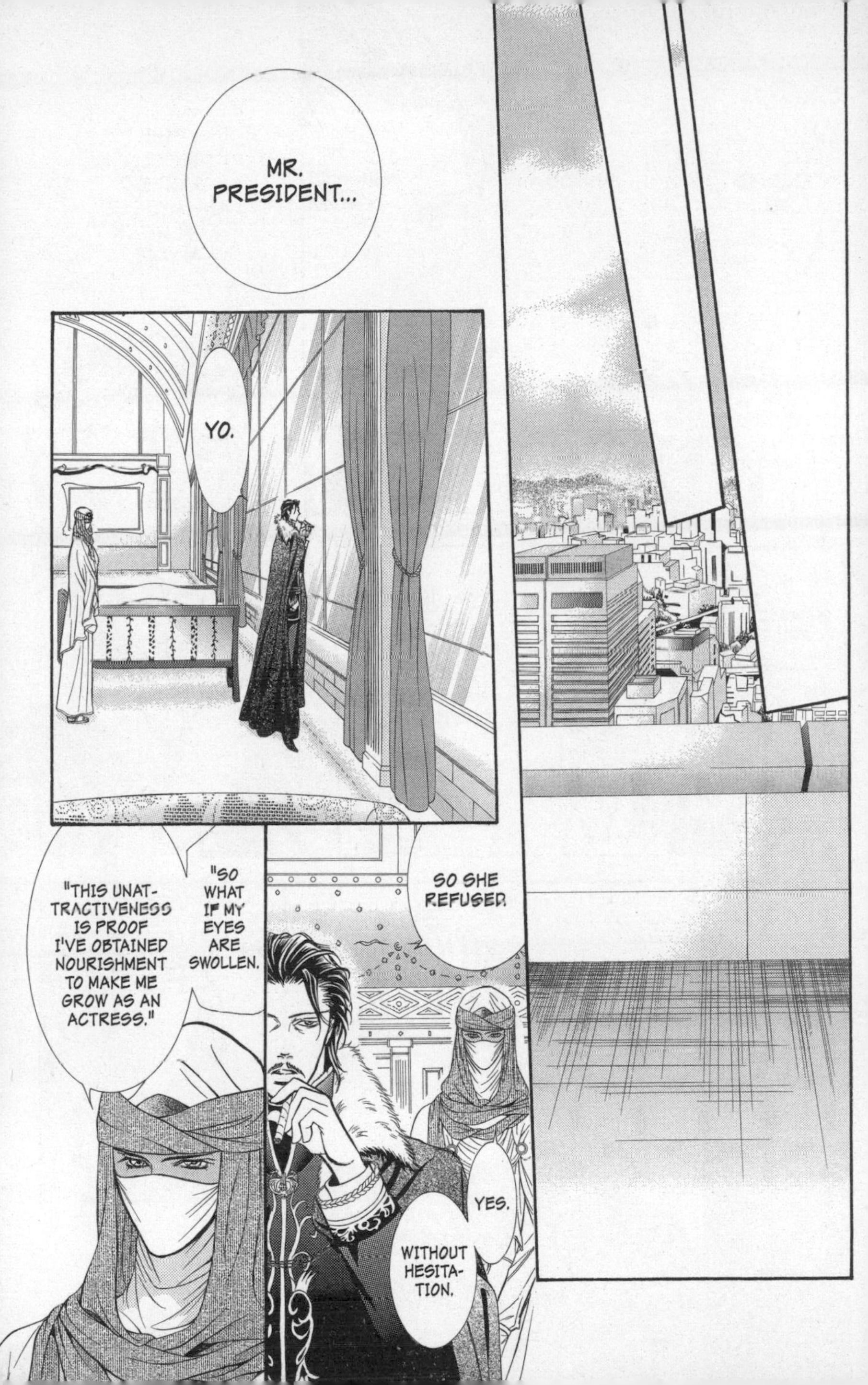
MR. PRESIDENT...
YO.
SO SHE REFUSED.
YES.
WITHOUT HESITATION.
"SO WHAT IF MY EYES ARE SWOLLEN.
"THIS UNATTRACTIVENESS IS PROOF I'VE OBTAINED NOURISHMENT TO MAKE ME GROW AS AN ACTRESS."

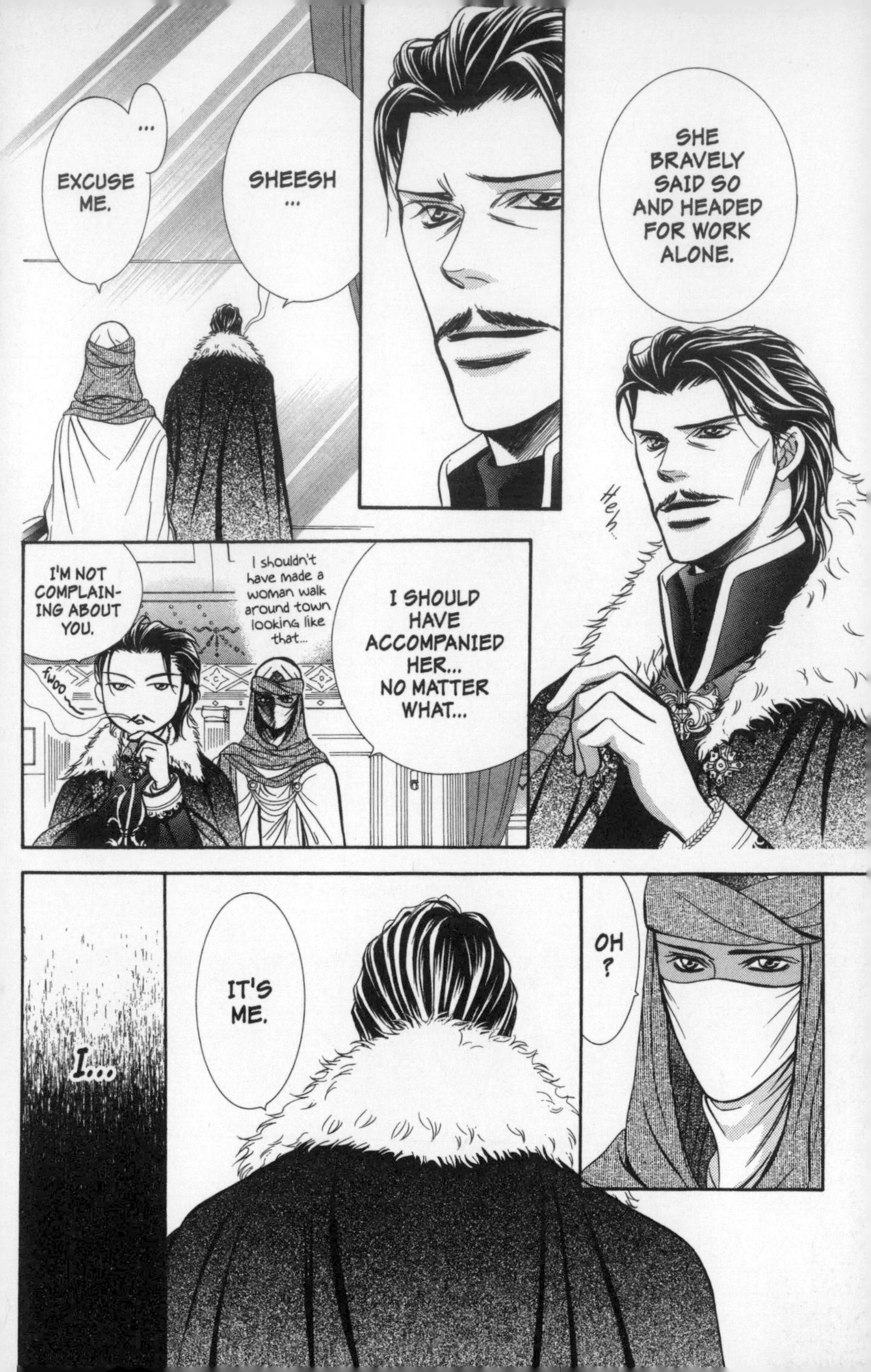
SHE BRAVELY SAID SO AND HEADED FOR WORK ALONE.
Heh...
SHEESH...
... EXCUSE ME.
I SHOULD HAVE ACCOMPANIED HER... NO MATTER WHAT...
I shouldn't have made a woman walk around town looking like that...
I'M NOT COMPLAINING ABOUT YOU.
fwoo
OH?
IT'S ME.
I...

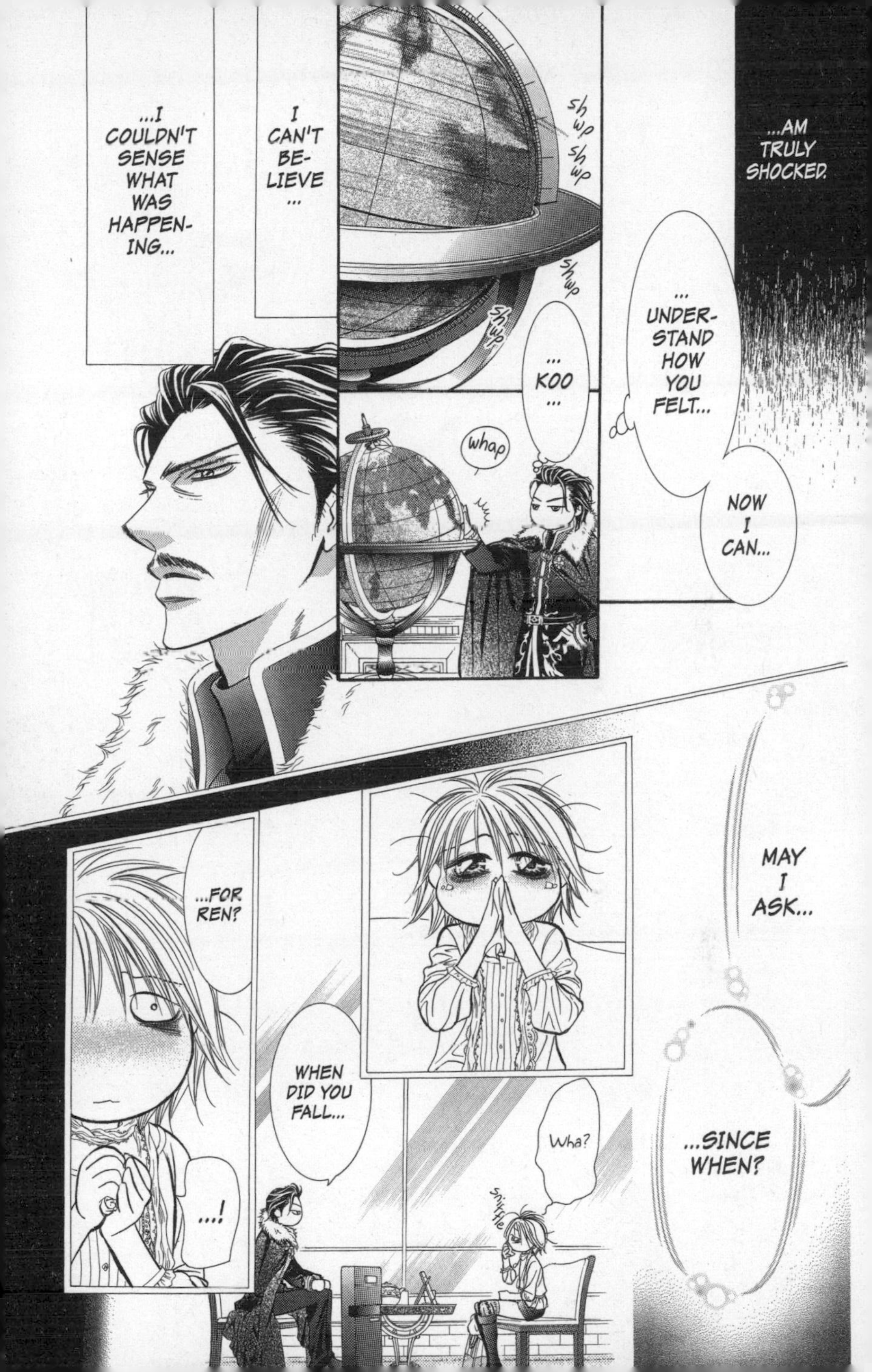
...AM TRULY SHOCKED.
NOW I CAN...
...UNDERSTAND HOW YOU FELT...
shwp shwp
shwp
shwp
...KOO...
whap
I CAN'T BELIEVE...
...I COULDN'T SENSE WHAT WAS HAPPENING...
MAY I ASK...
...SINCE WHEN?
WHEN DID YOU FALL...
...FOR REN?
...!
Wha?

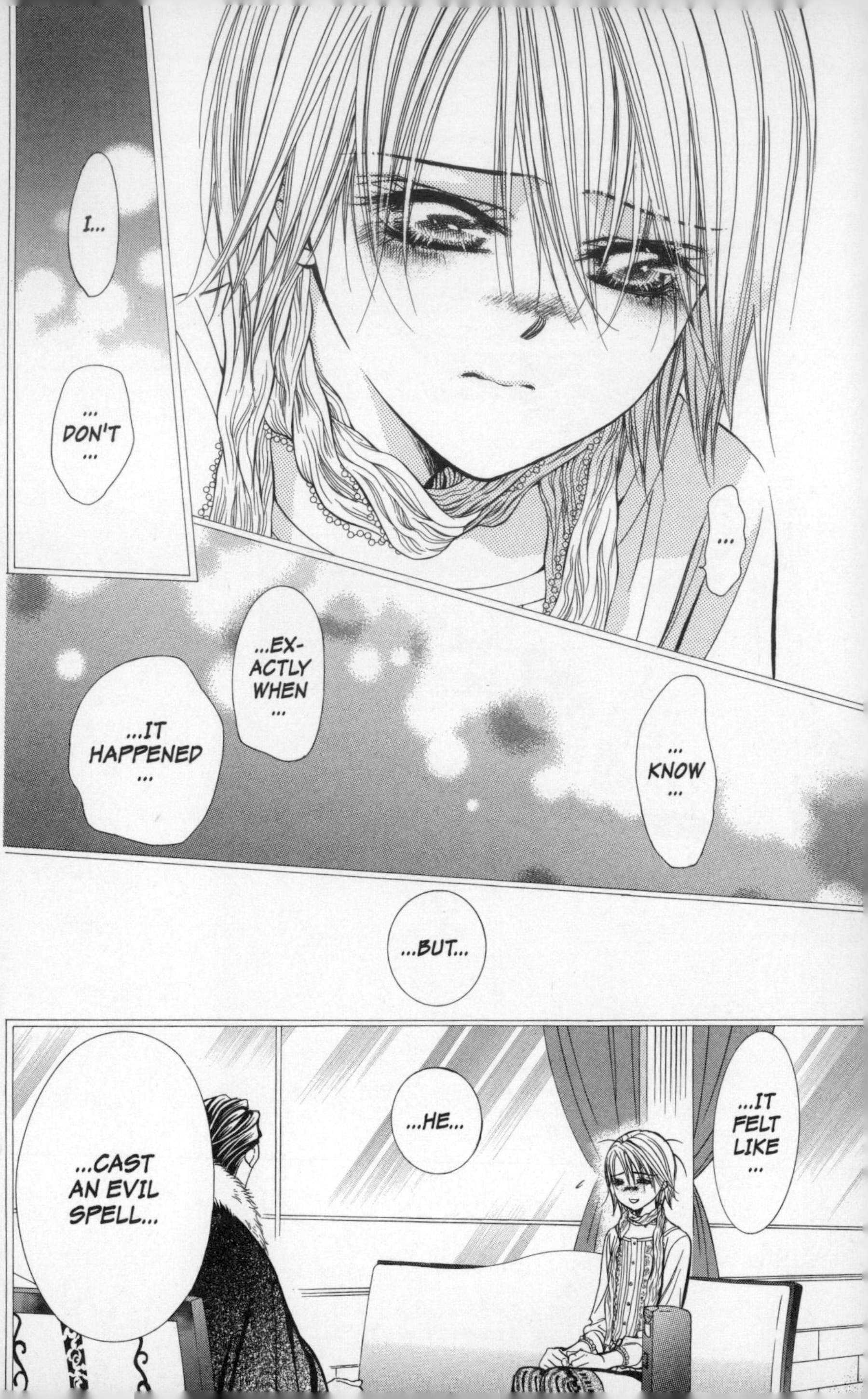
...
I...
...DON'T...
...KNOW...
...EX-ACTLY WHEN...
...IT HAPPENED...
...BUT...
...IT FELT LIKE...
...HE...
...CAST AN EVIL SPELL...

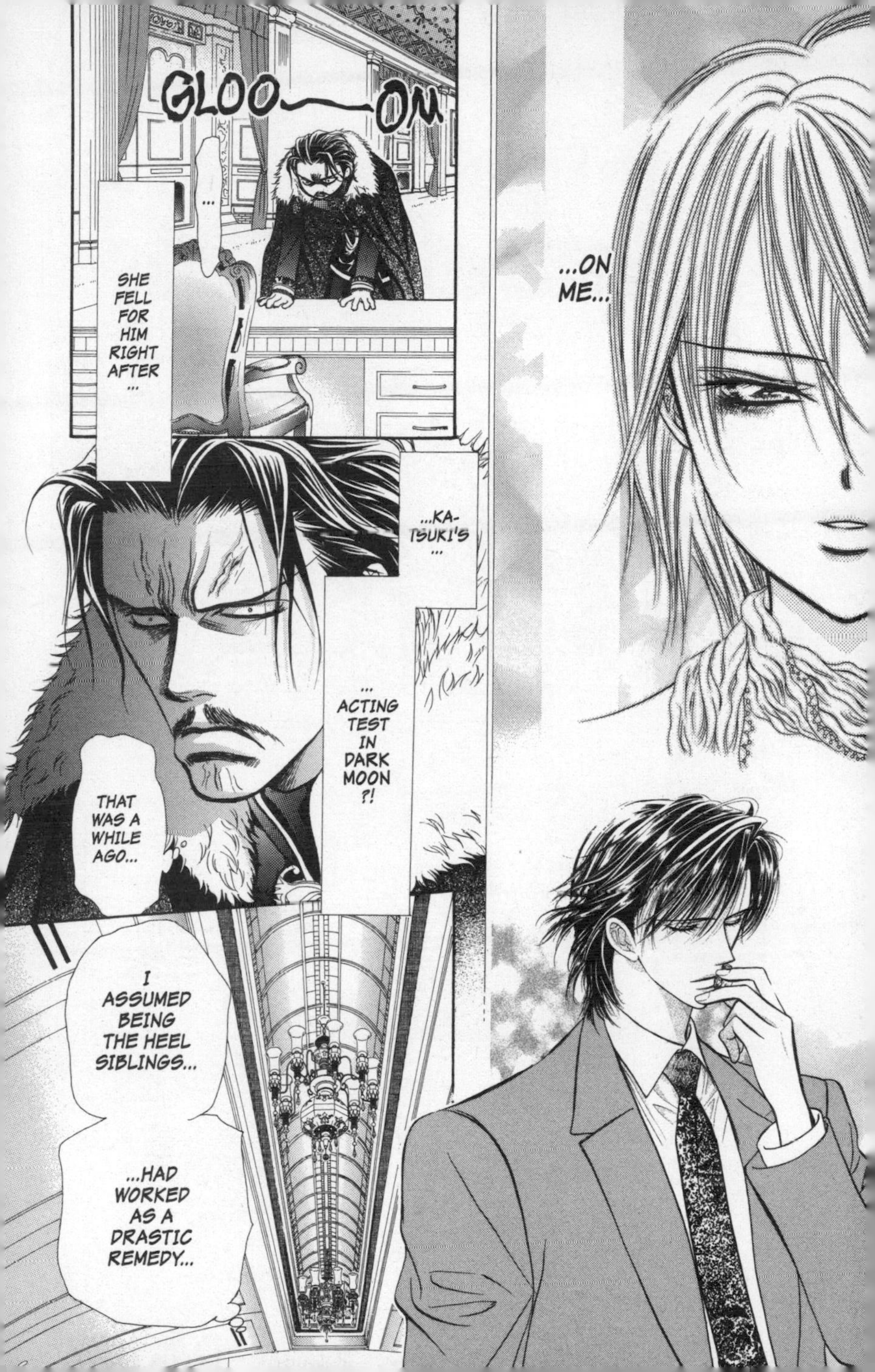
GLOO——ON
...
SHE FELL FOR HIM RIGHT AFTER...
...KA-TSUKI'S...
...ACTING TEST IN DARK MOON?!
THAT WAS A WHILE AGO...
I ASSUMED BEING THE HEEL SIBLINGS...
...HAD WORKED AS A DRASTIC REMEDY...
...ON ME...

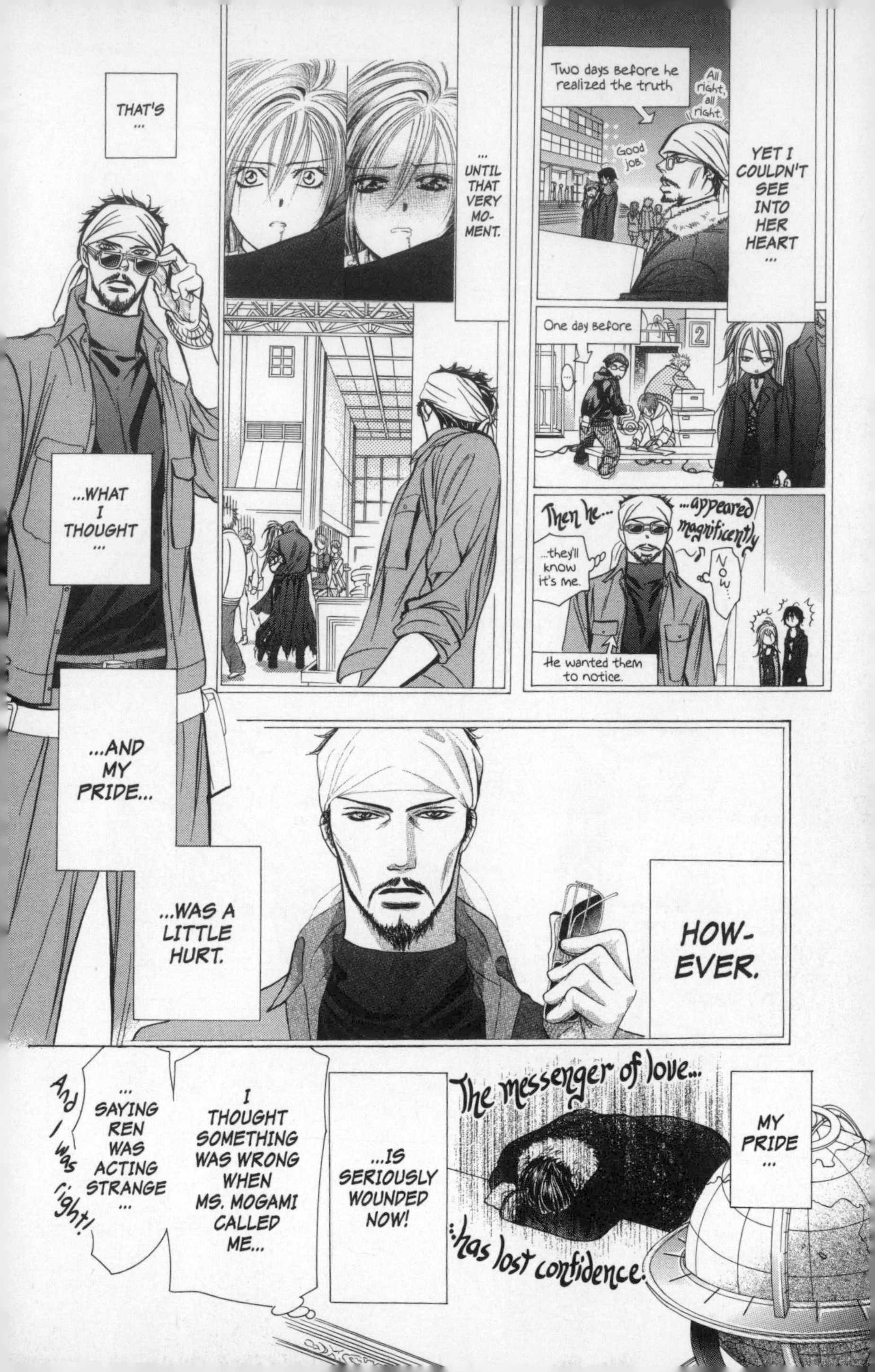

YET I COULDN'T SEE INTO HER HEART ...
Two days before he realized the truth
All right, all right.
Good job.
One day before
...
Then he...
...appeared magnificently
Now...
...they'll know it's me.
He wanted them to notice.
... UNTIL THAT VERY MOMENT.
THAT'S ...
...WHAT I THOUGHT ...
...AND MY PRIDE...
...WAS A LITTLE HURT.
HOW-EVER.
MY PRIDE ...
The messenger of love...
...has lost confidence.
...IS SERIOUSLY WOUNDED NOW!
I THOUGHT SOMETHING WAS WRONG WHEN MS. MOGAMI CALLED ME...
... SAYING REN WAS ACTING STRANGE ...
And I was right!

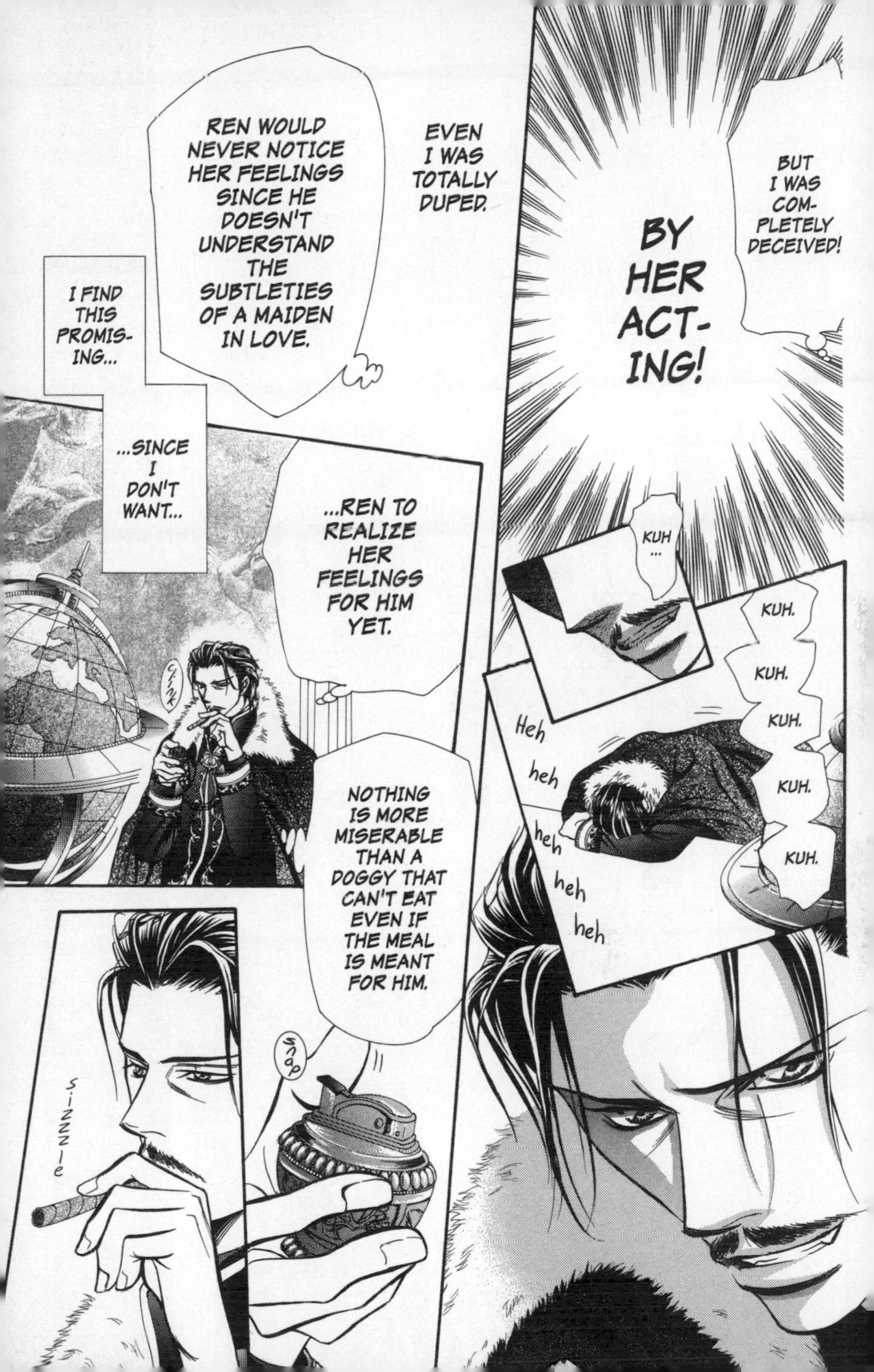
BUT I WAS COM-PLETELY DECEIVED!
BY HER ACT-ING!
KUH...
KUH.
KUH.
KUH.
KUH.
KUH.
Heh heh heh heh heh
EVEN I WAS TOTALLY DUPED.
REN WOULD NEVER NOTICE HER FEELINGS SINCE HE DOESN'T UNDERSTAND THE SUBTLETIES OF A MAIDEN IN LOVE.
I FIND THIS PROMIS-ING...
...SINCE I DON'T WANT...
...REN TO REALIZE HER FEELINGS FOR HIM YET.
NOTHING IS MORE MISERABLE THAN A DOGGY THAT CAN'T EAT EVEN IF THE MEAL IS MEANT FOR HIM.
snap
sizzle

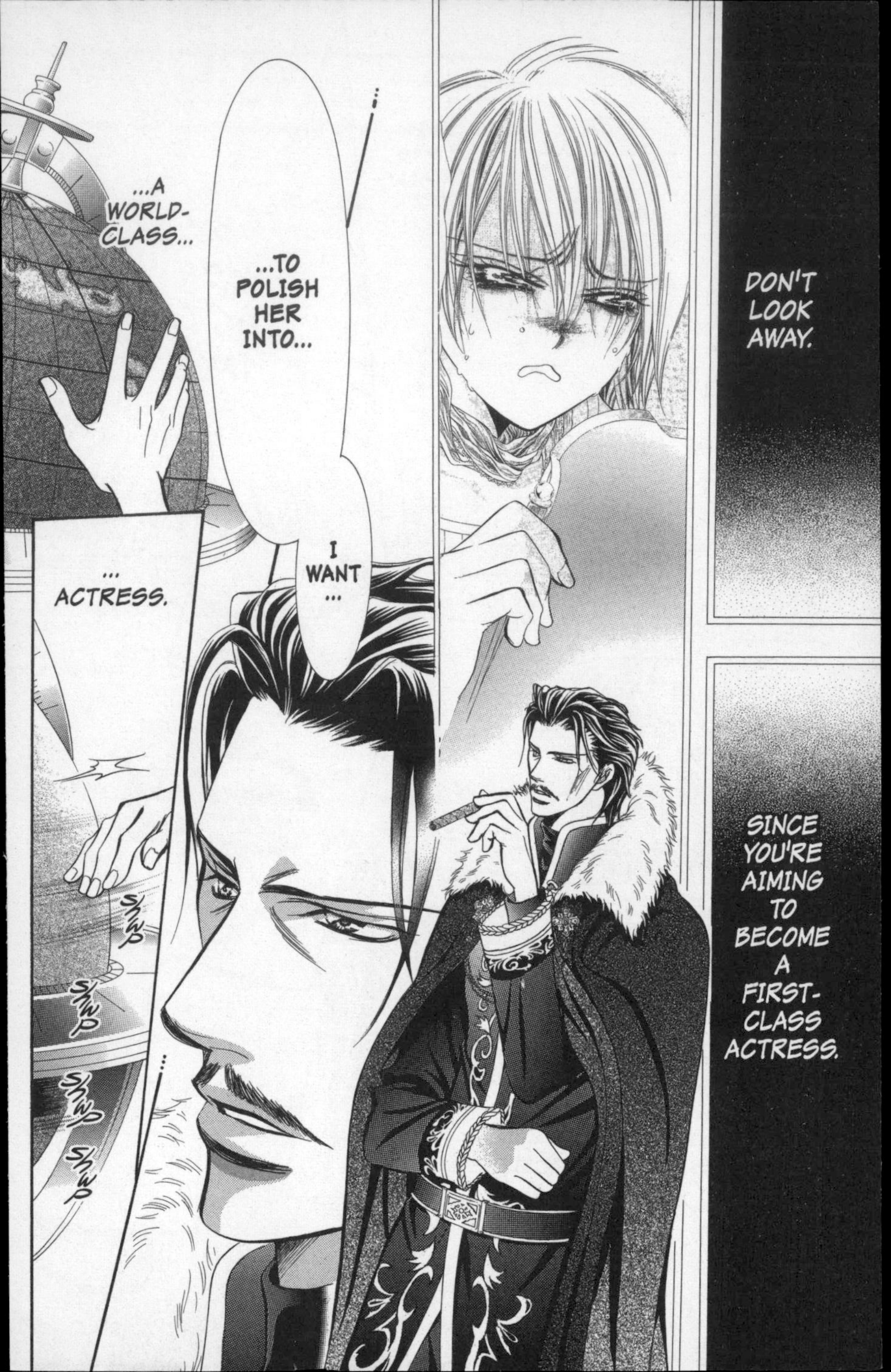
DON'T LOOK AWAY.
SINCE YOU'RE AIMING TO BECOME A FIRST-CLASS ACTRESS.
I WANT ...
...TO POLISH HER INTO...
...A WORLD-CLASS...
... ACTRESS.
SHWP
SHWP
SHWP
SHWP

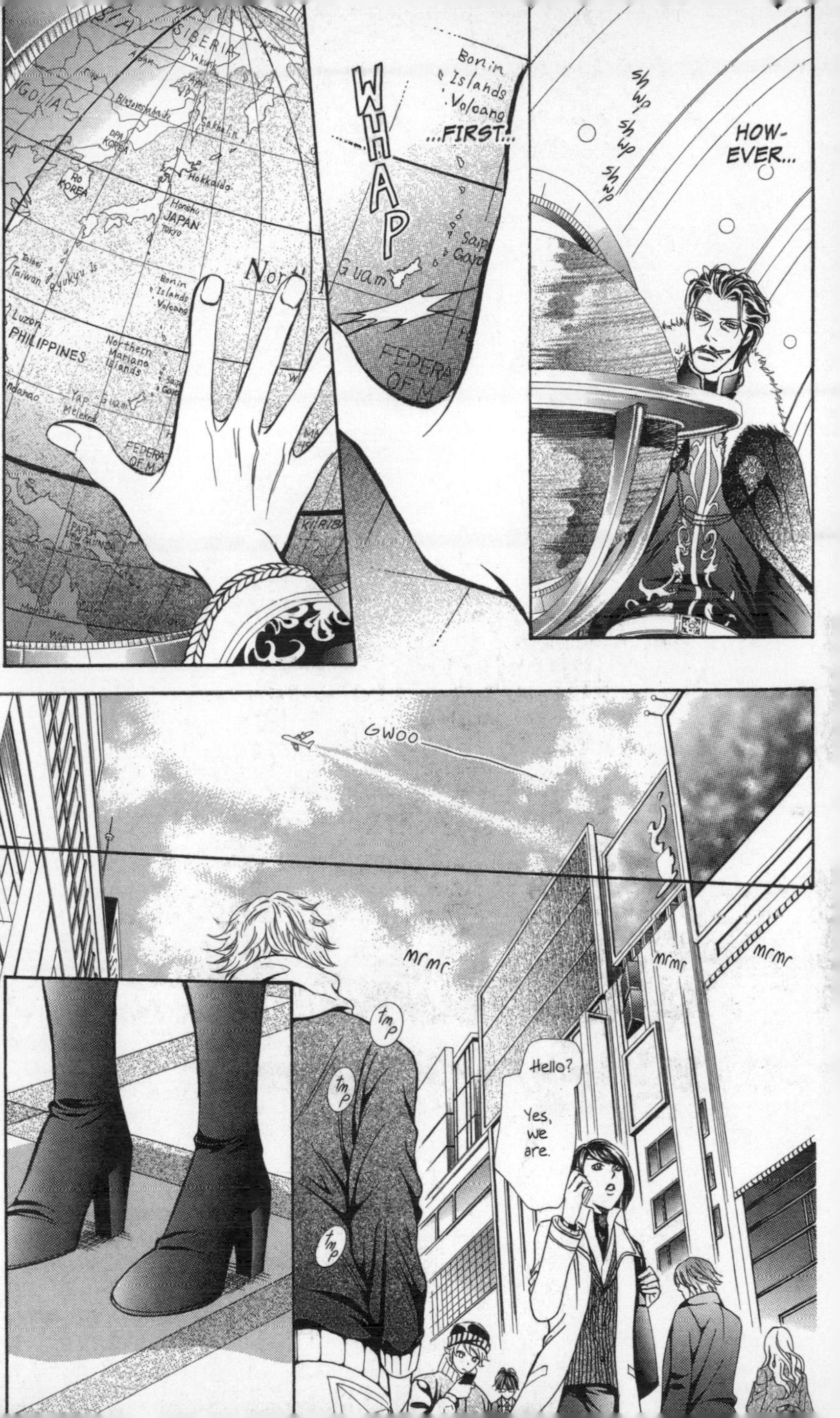
shwp shwp shwp
HOW-EVER...
WHAP
...FIRST...
Bonin Islands Volcano
Guam
FEDERA OF M
SIBERIA
Yakutsk
MONGOLIA
Sakhalin
DPR KOREA
Ro KOREA
Hokkaido
Honshu
JAPAN
Tokyo
Taipei
Taiwan
Ryukyu Is
Bonin Islands Volcano
Luzon
PHILIPPINES
Northern Mariana Islands
Yap
Guam
FEDERA OF M
KIRIBA
GWOO
mrmr
mrmr
mrmr
tmp
tmp
tmp
Hello?
Yes, we are.

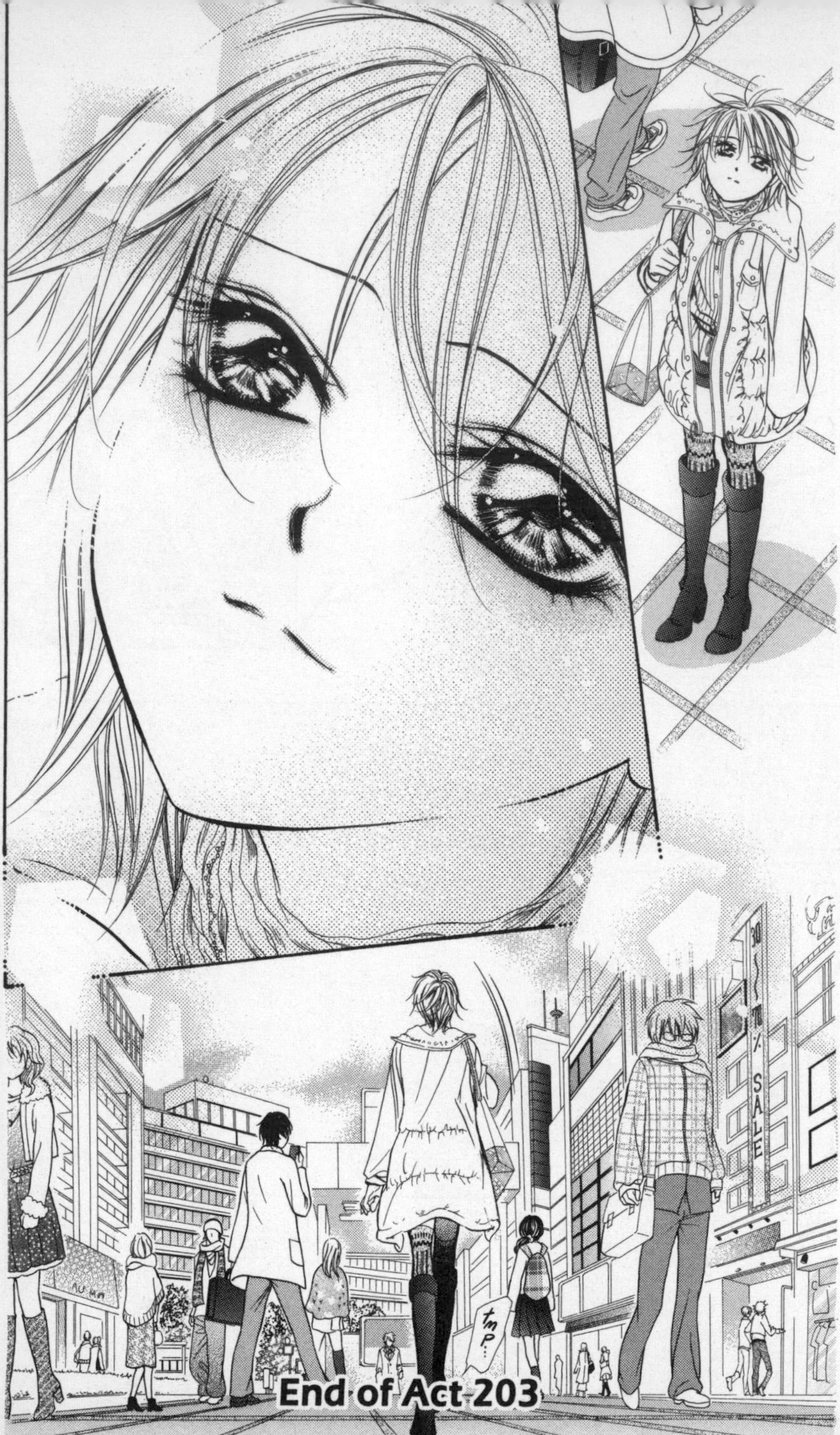
tmp...
SALE
End of Act 203

An encounter beyond their wildest dreams

(According to me, Nakamura)

This is only a "what if" episode since the plot and situation are impossible in the main story.

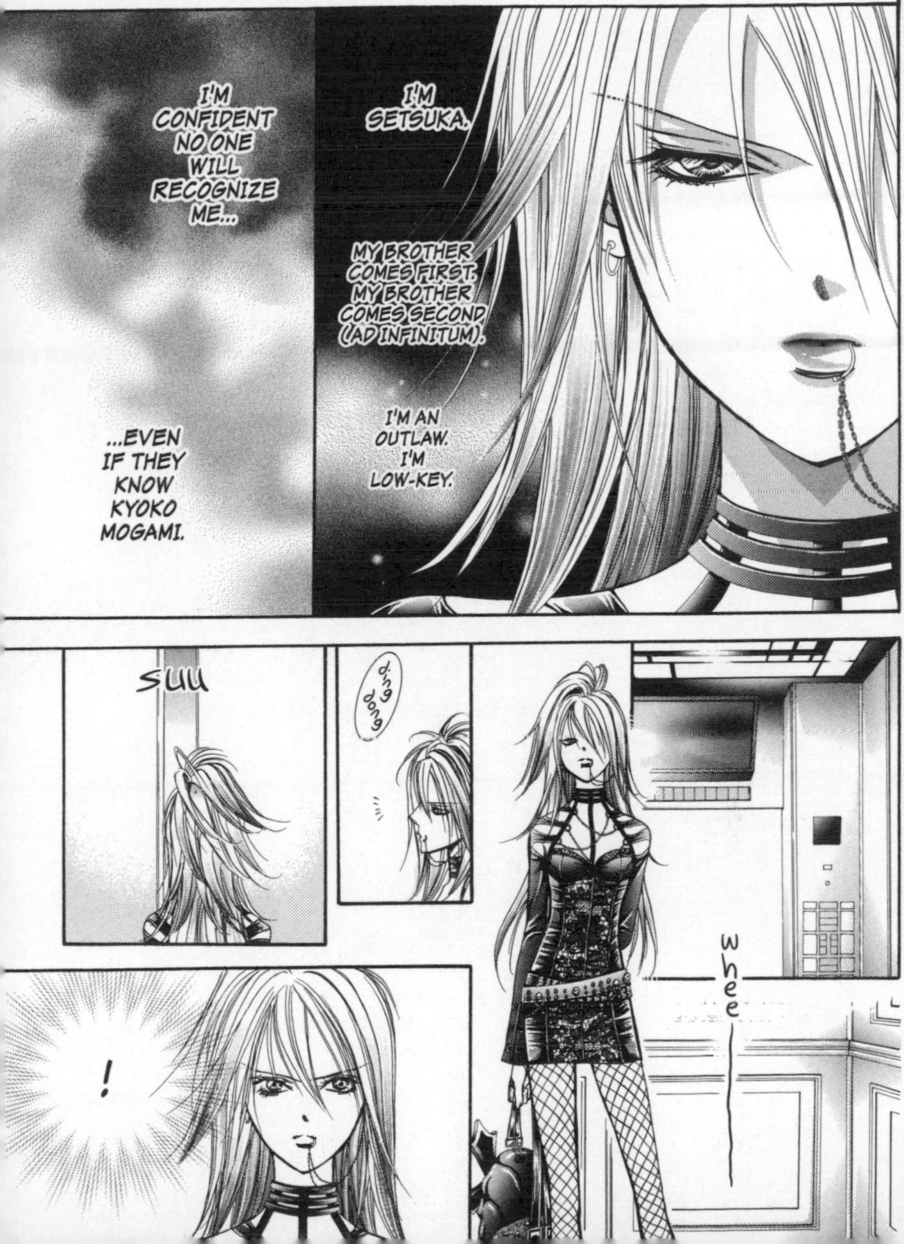

I'M SETSUKA.
MY BROTHER COMES FIRST. MY BROTHER COMES SECOND (AD INFINITUM).
I'M AN OUTLAW. I'M LOW-KEY.
I'M CONFIDENT NO ONE WILL RECOGNIZE ME...
...EVEN IF THEY KNOW KYOKO MOGAMI.
wheee—
ding dong
SUU
!

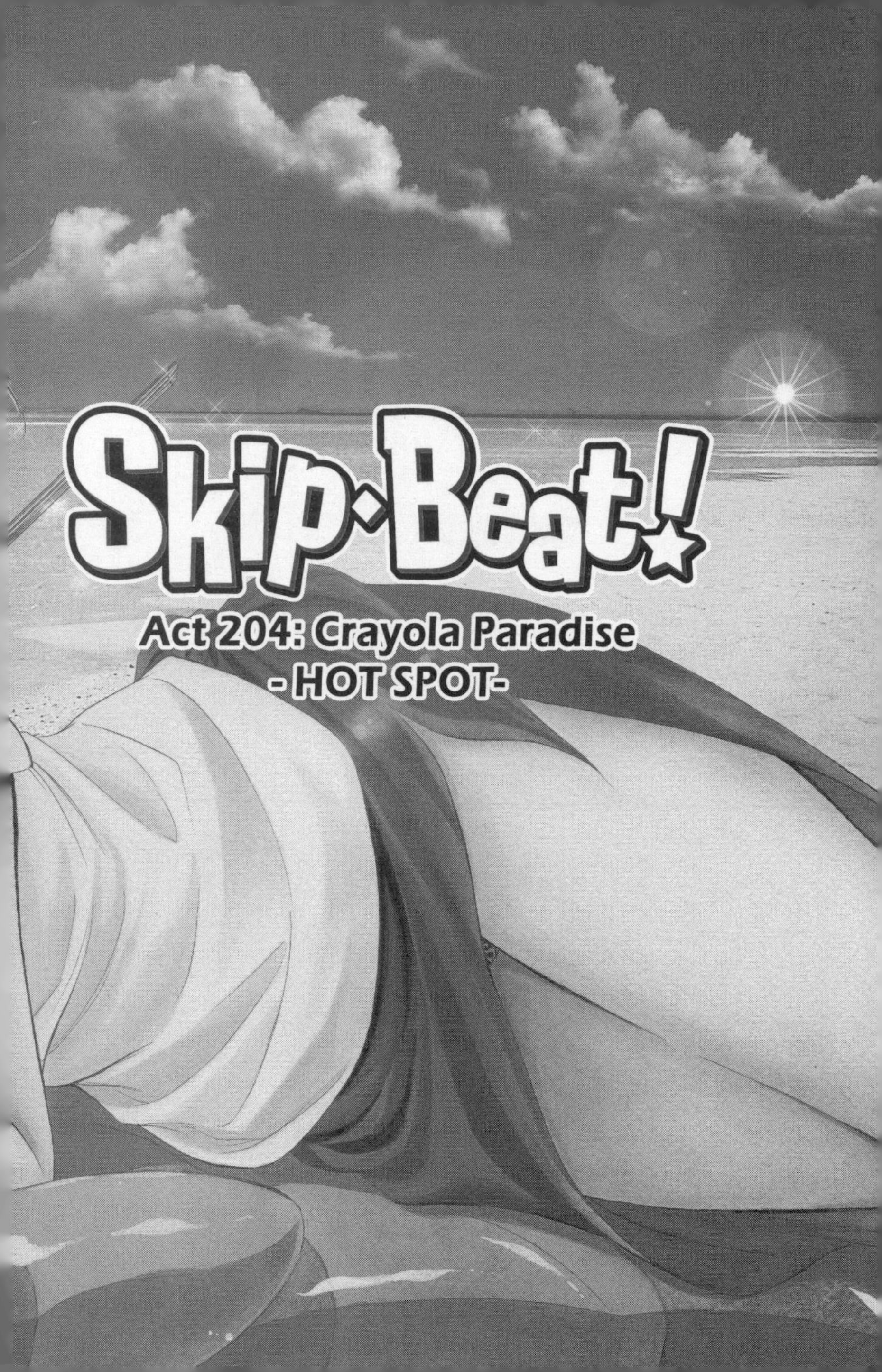
Skip·Beat!
Act 204: Crayola Paradise
- HOT SPOT-

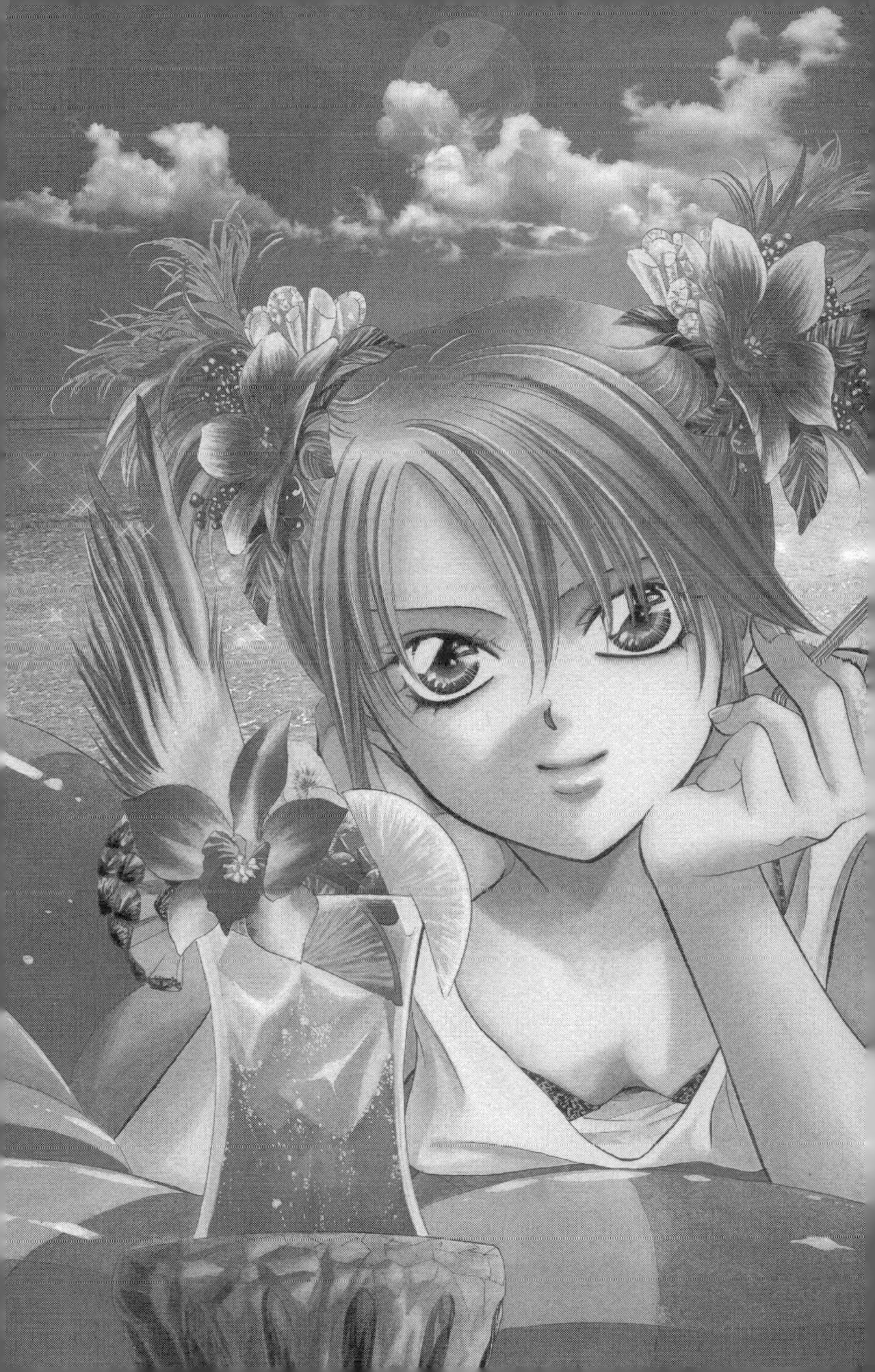

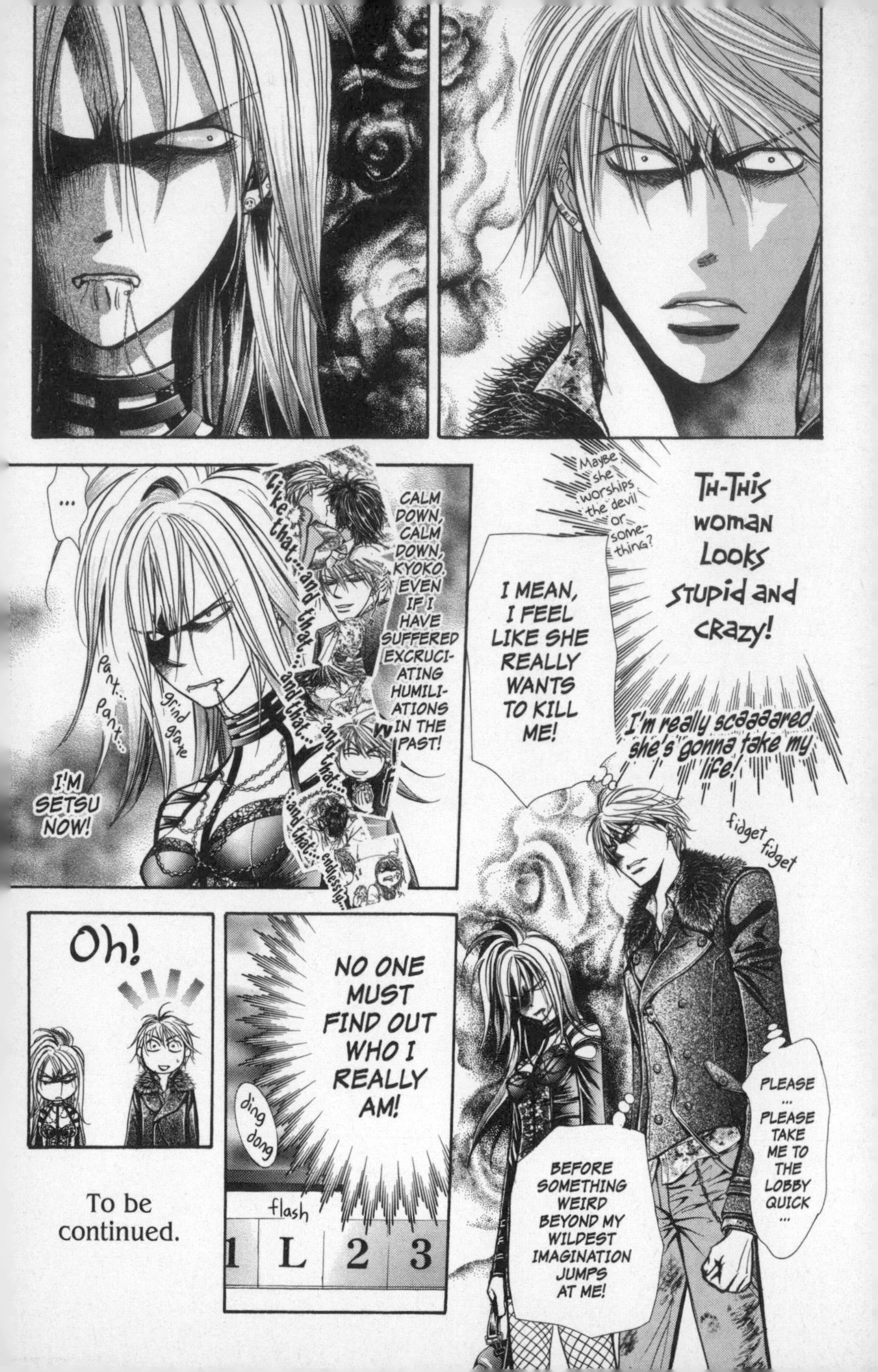
Maybe she worships the devil or some-thing?
Th-This woman looks stupid and crazy!
I MEAN, I FEEL LIKE SHE REALLY WANTS TO KILL ME!
I'm really scaaaared she's gonna take my life!
fidget fidget
PLEASE ... PLEASE TAKE ME TO THE LOBBY QUICK ...
BEFORE SOMETHING WEIRD BEYOND MY WILDEST IMAGINATION JUMPS AT ME!
...
CALM DOWN, CALM DOWN, KYOKO. EVEN IF I HAVE SUFFERED EXCRUCI-ATING HUMILI-ATIONS IN THE PAST!
Like that... and that... and that... and that... and that... and that... endlessly...
Pant... Pant...
grind grate
I'M SETSU NOW!
NO ONE MUST FIND OUT WHO I REALLY AM!
ding dong
flash
1 L 2 3
Oh!

To be continued.

EVERY
INCIDENT
THAT
OCCURS
IN
LIFE...

...IS
INEVITABLE.
THERE
ARE NO
COINCIDENCES.

I HEARD
A
SUPPOSEDLY
FAMOUS...

...SPIRITUAL
ADVISOR
SAY SO
ONCE.

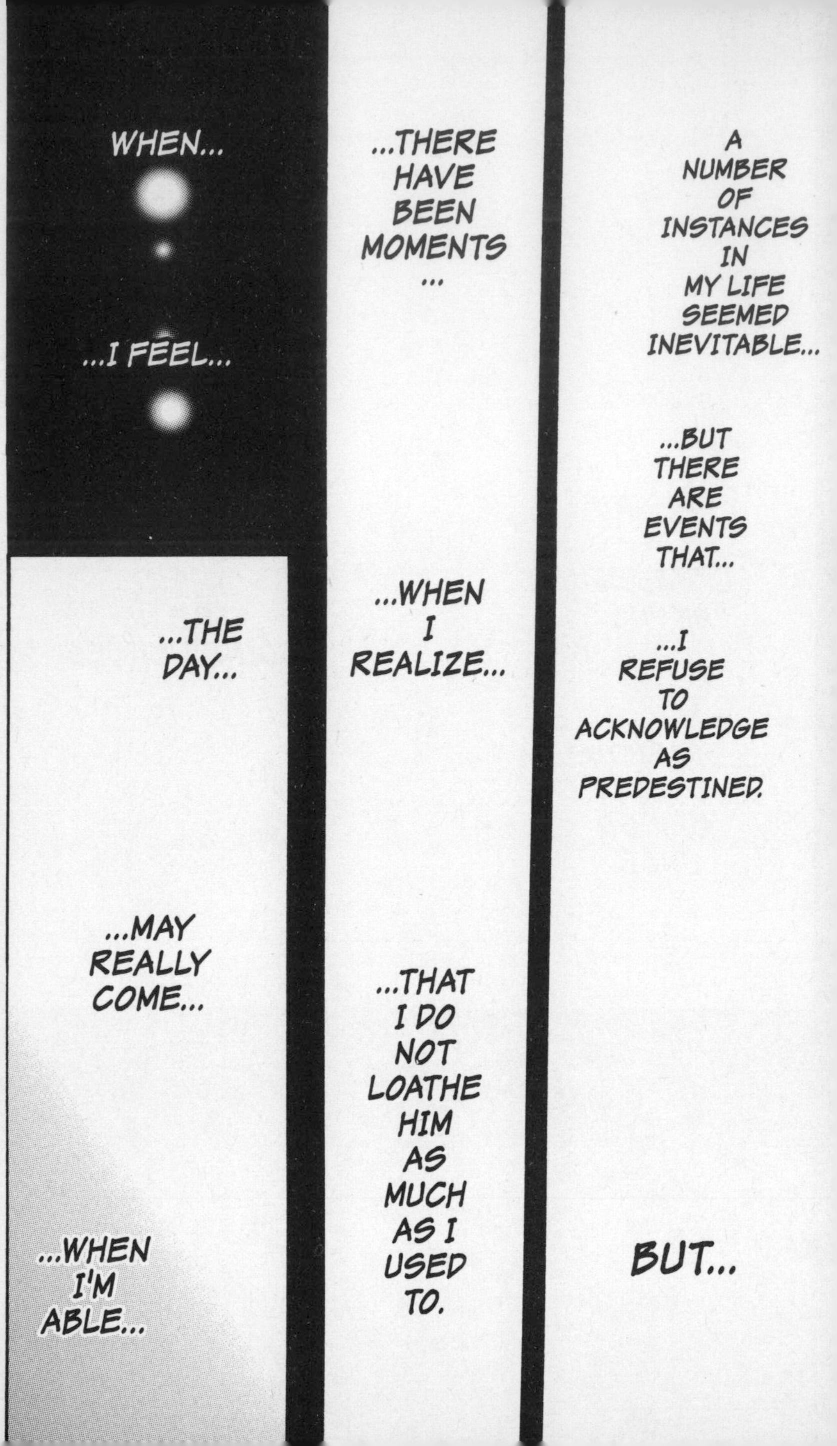
A NUMBER OF INSTANCES IN MY LIFE SEEMED INEVITABLE...
...BUT THERE ARE EVENTS THAT...
...I REFUSE TO ACKNOWLEDGE AS PREDESTINED.
BUT...
...THERE HAVE BEEN MOMENTS...
...WHEN I REALIZE...
...THAT I DO NOT LOATHE HIM AS MUCH AS I USED TO.
WHEN...
...I FEEL...
...THE DAY...
...MAY REALLY COME...
...WHEN I'M ABLE...

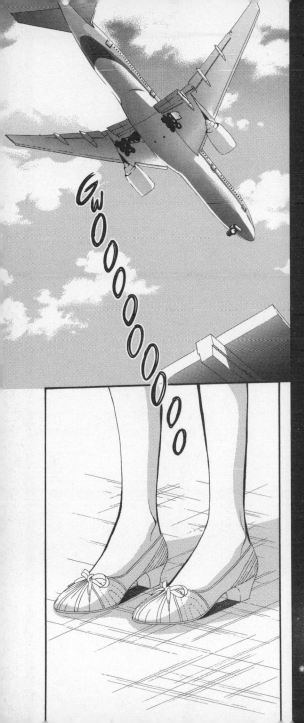

...TO
ACCEPT
THE
FACT...

...THAT
HE
EXISTS...

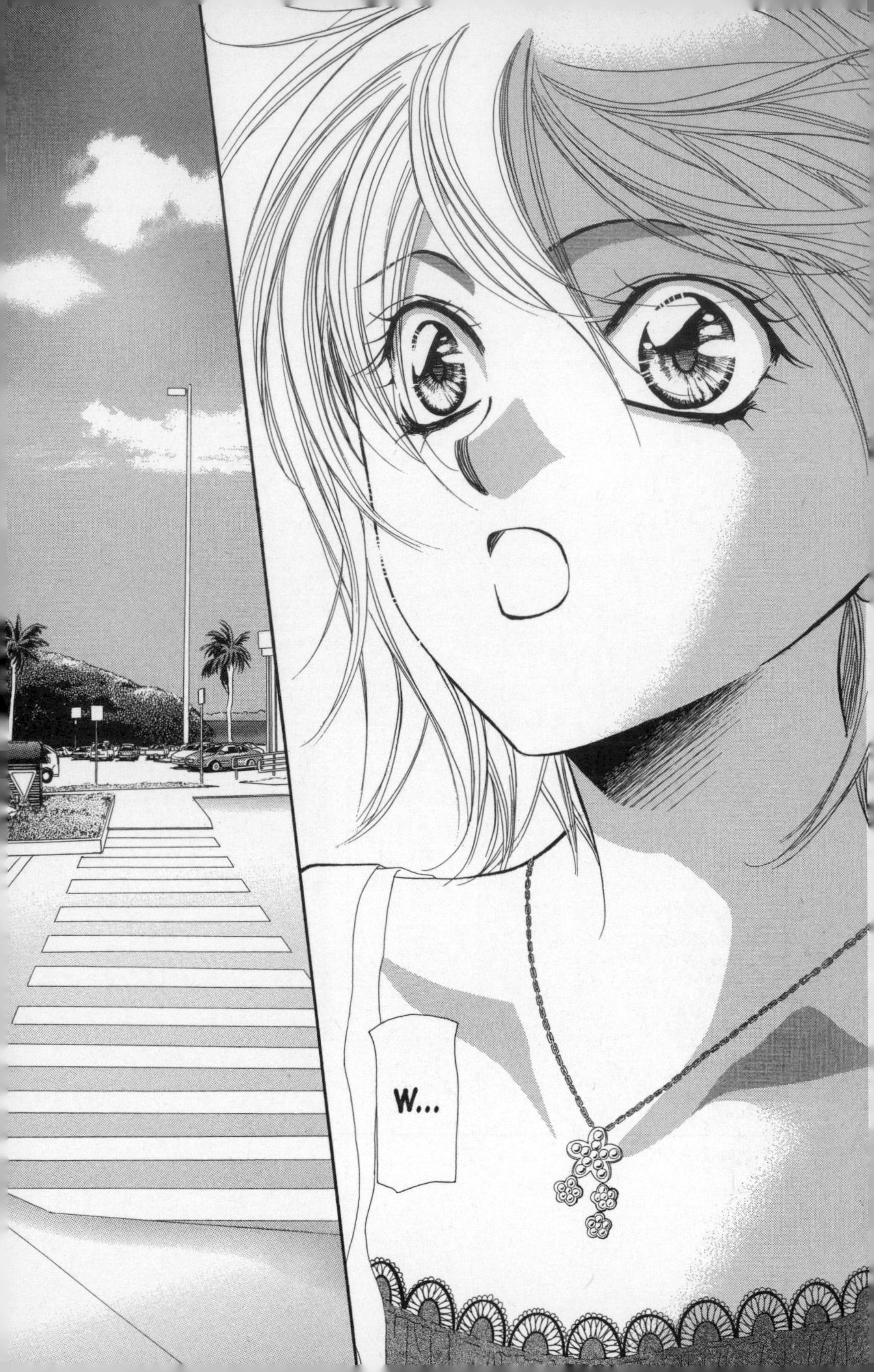
W...

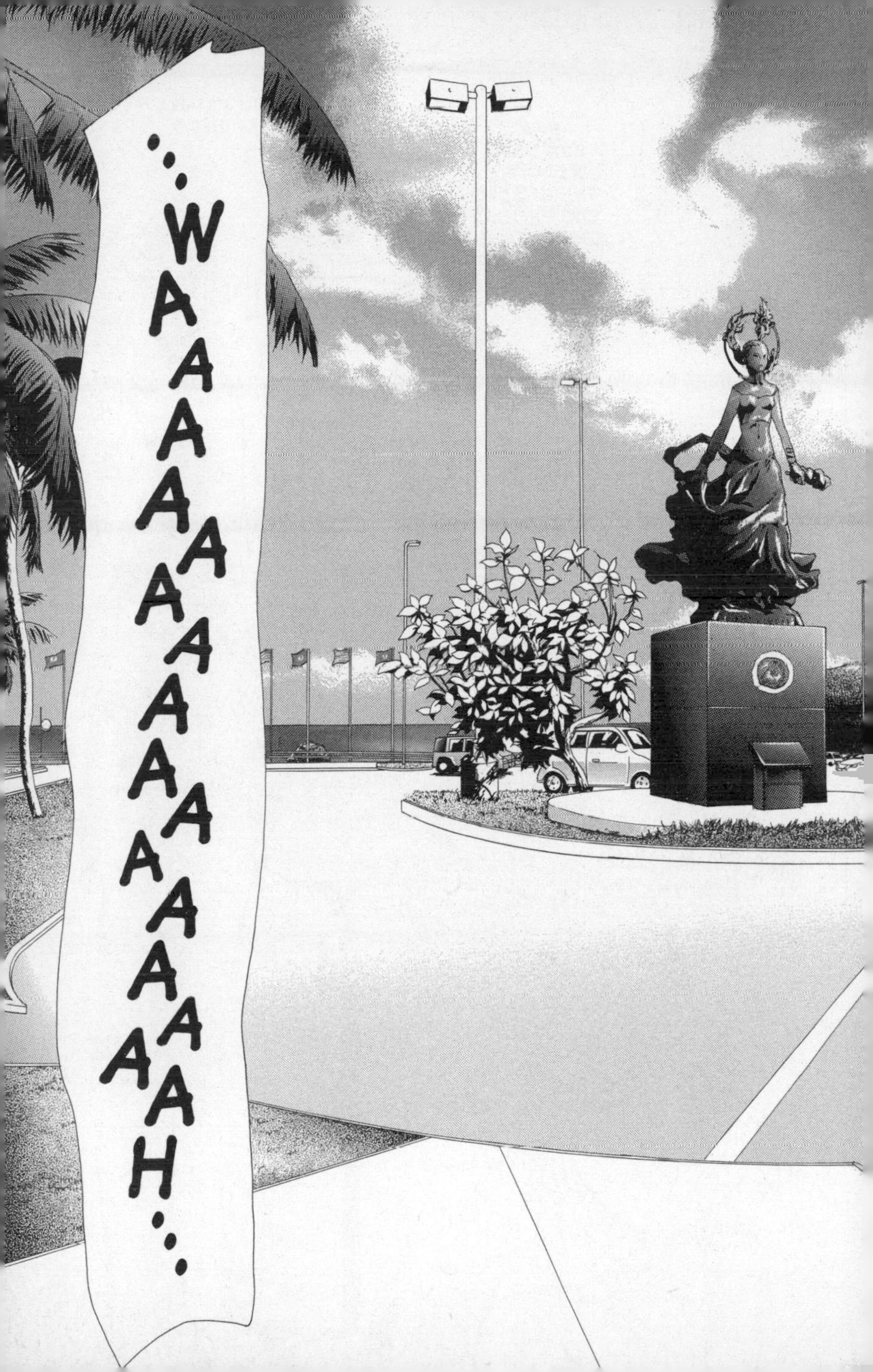
...WAAAAAAAAAAAAAAAAH...

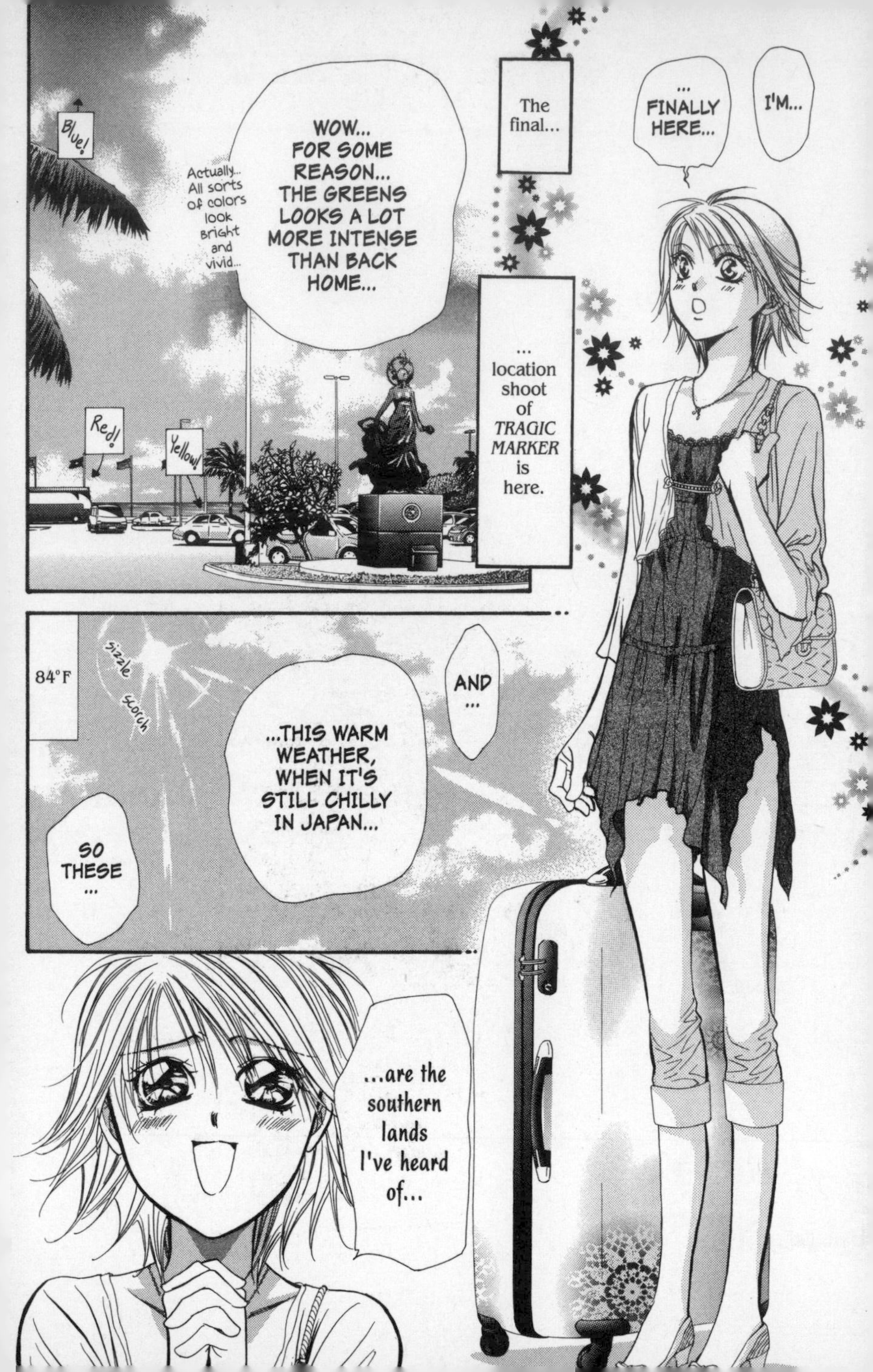
I'M...
... FINALLY HERE...
The final...
... location shoot of *TRAGIC MARKER* is here.
WOW... FOR SOME REASON... THE GREENS LOOKS A LOT MORE INTENSE THAN BACK HOME...
Actually... All sorts of colors look bright and vivid...
Blue!
Red!
Yellow!
84°F
sizzle
scorch
AND ...
...THIS WARM WEATHER, WHEN IT'S STILL CHILLY IN JAPAN...
SO THESE ...
...are the southern lands I've heard of...

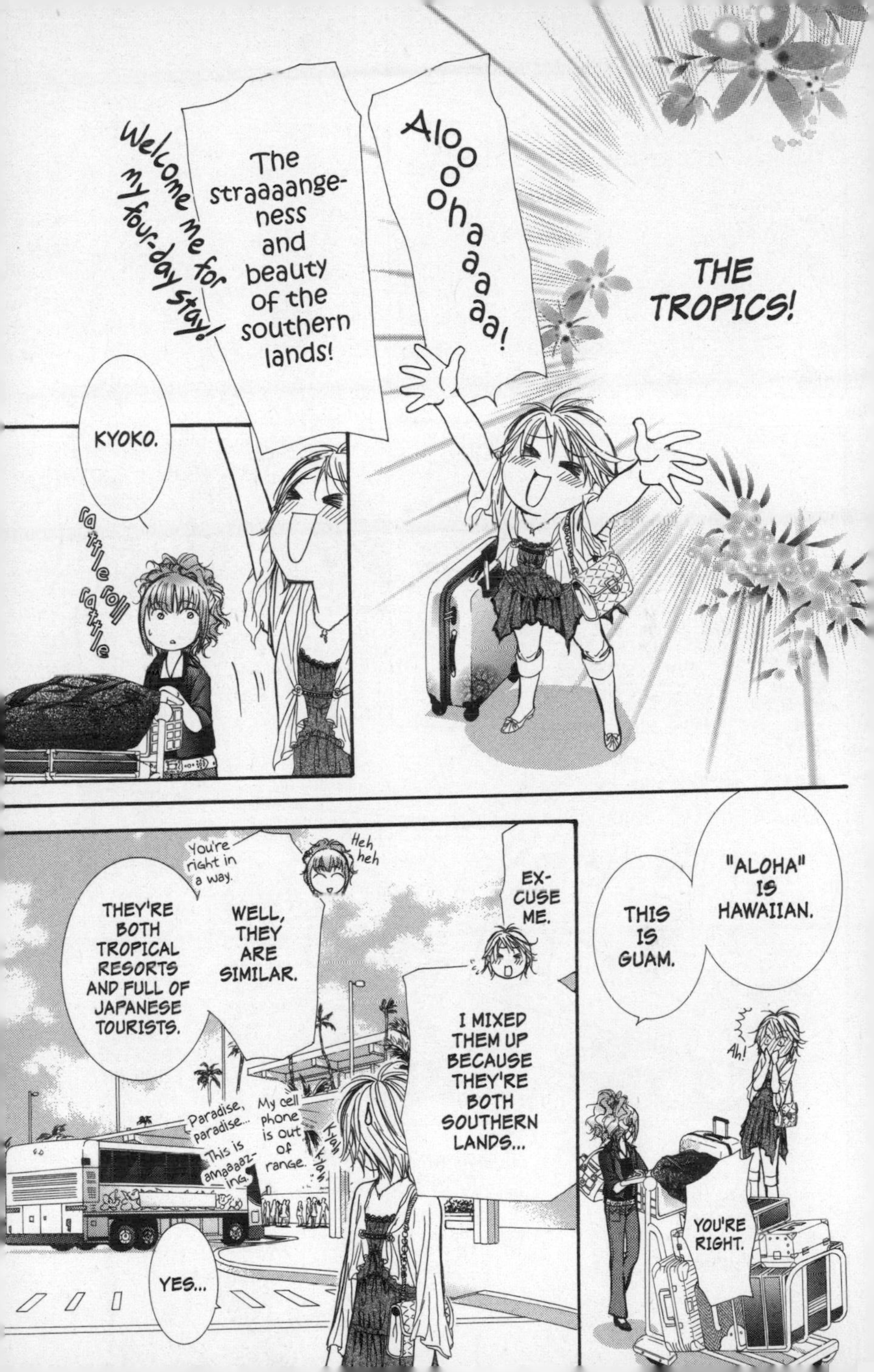
THE TROPICS!
Aloooohaaaaaa!
The straaaange-ness and beauty of the southern lands!
Welcome me for my four-day stay!
KYOKO.
rattle roll rattle
"ALOHA" IS HAWAIIAN.
THIS IS GUAM.
Ah!
YOU'RE RIGHT.
EX-CUSE ME.
I MIXED THEM UP BECAUSE THEY'RE BOTH SOUTHERN LANDS...
Heh heh
You're right in a way.
WELL, THEY ARE SIMILAR.
THEY'RE BOTH TROPICAL RESORTS AND FULL OF JAPANESE TOURISTS.
My cell phone is out of range.
Klah klah
Paradise, paradise...
This is amaaaaz-ing.
YES...

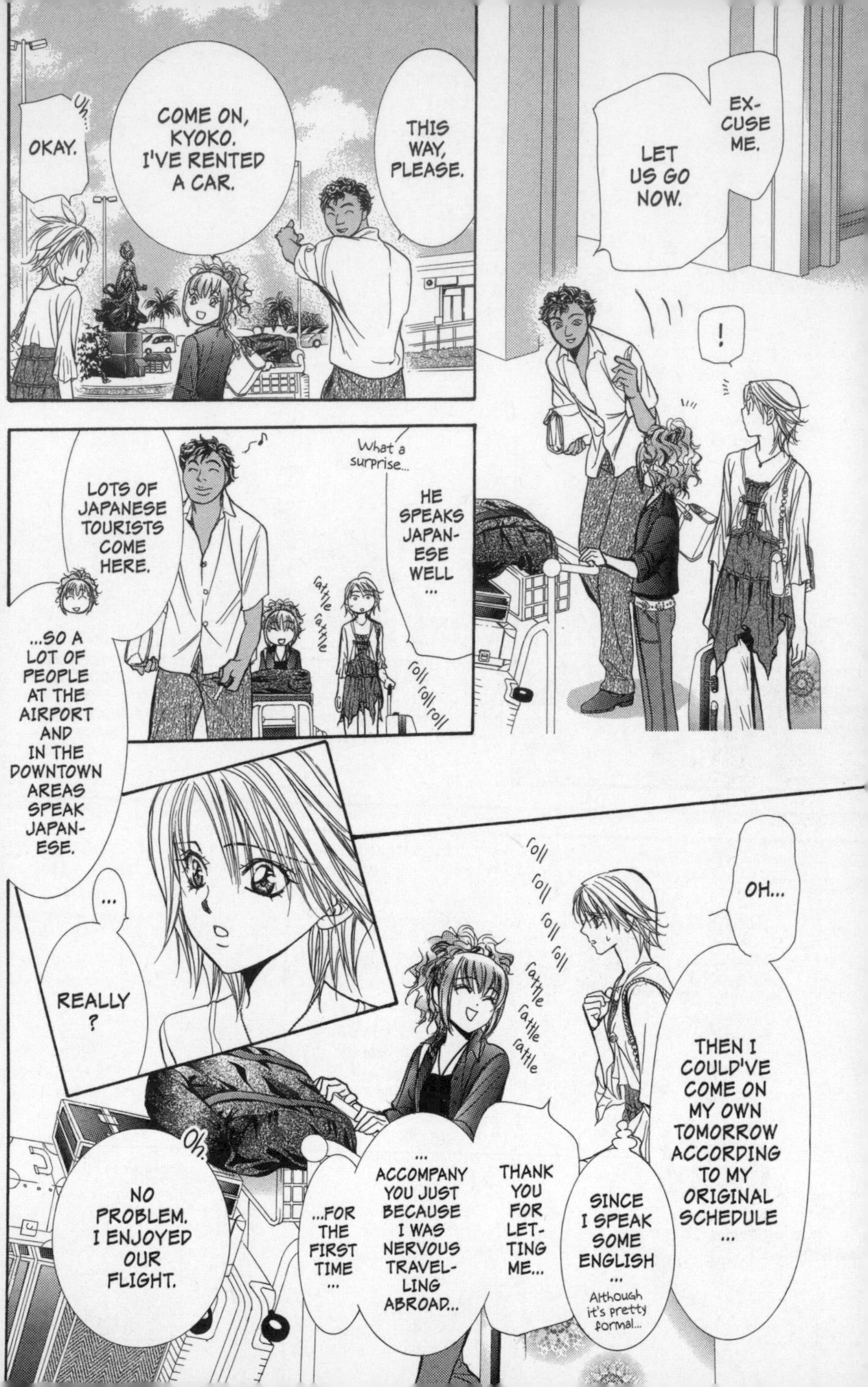

EX-CUSE ME.
LET US GO NOW.
!
THIS WAY, PLEASE.
COME ON, KYOKO. I'VE RENTED A CAR.
Uh...
OKAY.
What a surprise...
HE SPEAKS JAPAN-ESE WELL ...
LOTS OF JAPANESE TOURISTS COME HERE.
...SO A LOT OF PEOPLE AT THE AIRPORT AND IN THE DOWNTOWN AREAS SPEAK JAPAN-ESE.
roll roll roll
rattle rattle
...
REALLY ?
OH...
roll roll roll roll
rattle rattle rattle
THEN I COULD'VE COME ON MY OWN TOMORROW ACCORDING TO MY ORIGINAL SCHEDULE ...
SINCE I SPEAK SOME ENGLISH ...
Although it's pretty formal...
THANK YOU FOR LET-TING ME...
... ACCOMPANY YOU JUST BECAUSE I WAS NERVOUS TRAVEL-LING ABROAD...
...FOR THE FIRST TIME ...
Oh.
NO PROBLEM. I ENJOYED OUR FLIGHT.

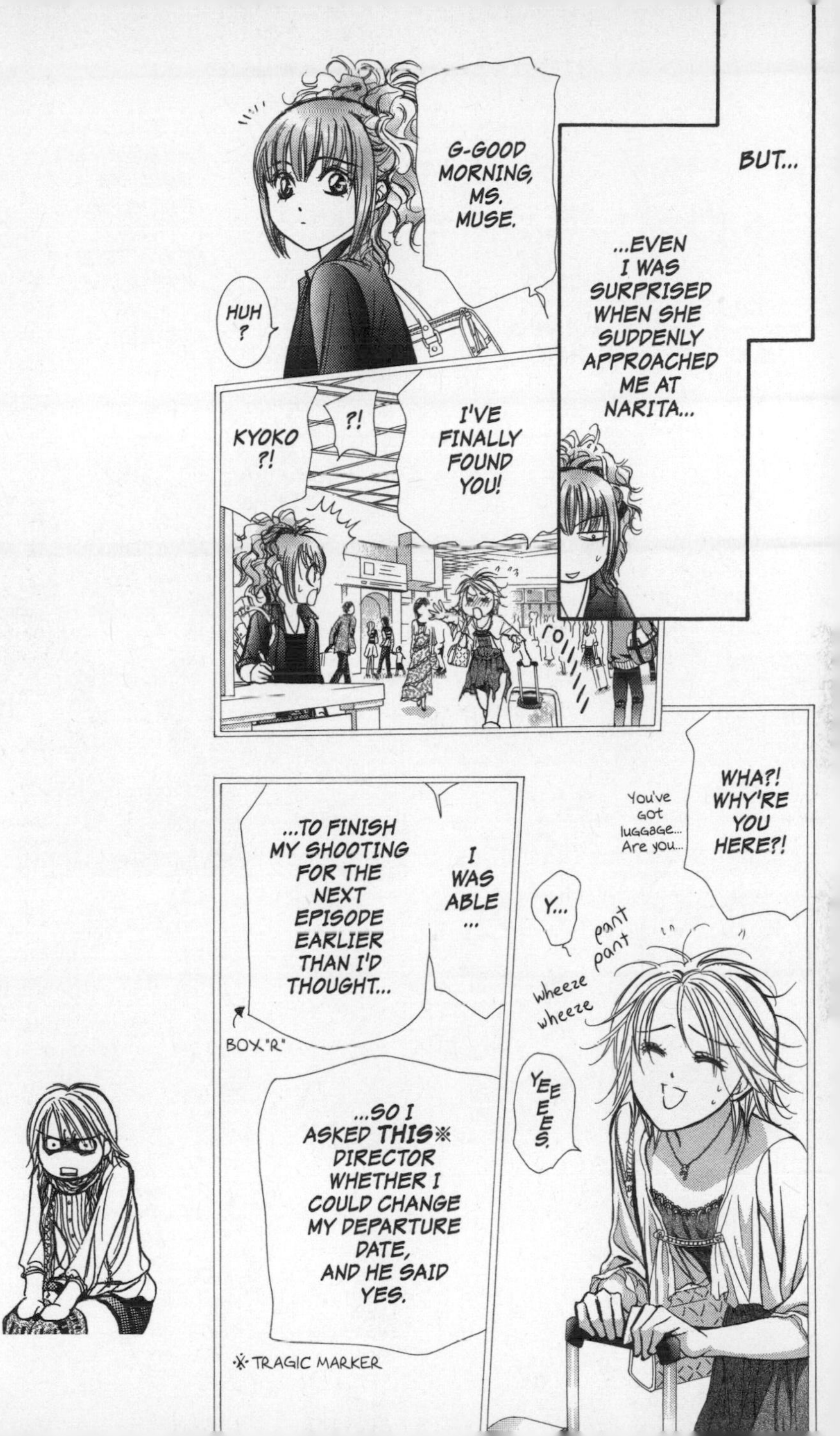
BUT...
...EVEN I WAS SURPRISED WHEN SHE SUDDENLY APPROACHED ME AT NARITA...
G-GOOD MORNING, MS. MUSE.
HUH?
I'VE FINALLY FOUND YOU!
?!
KYOKO?!
roll
WHA?! WHY'RE YOU HERE?!
You've got luggage... Are you...
Y...
pant pant
wheeze wheeze
YEEEES.
I WAS ABLE...
...TO FINISH MY SHOOTING FOR THE NEXT EPISODE EARLIER THAN I'D THOUGHT...
BOX"R"
...SO I ASKED THIS※ DIRECTOR WHETHER I COULD CHANGE MY DEPARTURE DATE, AND HE SAID YES.
※TRAGIC MARKER

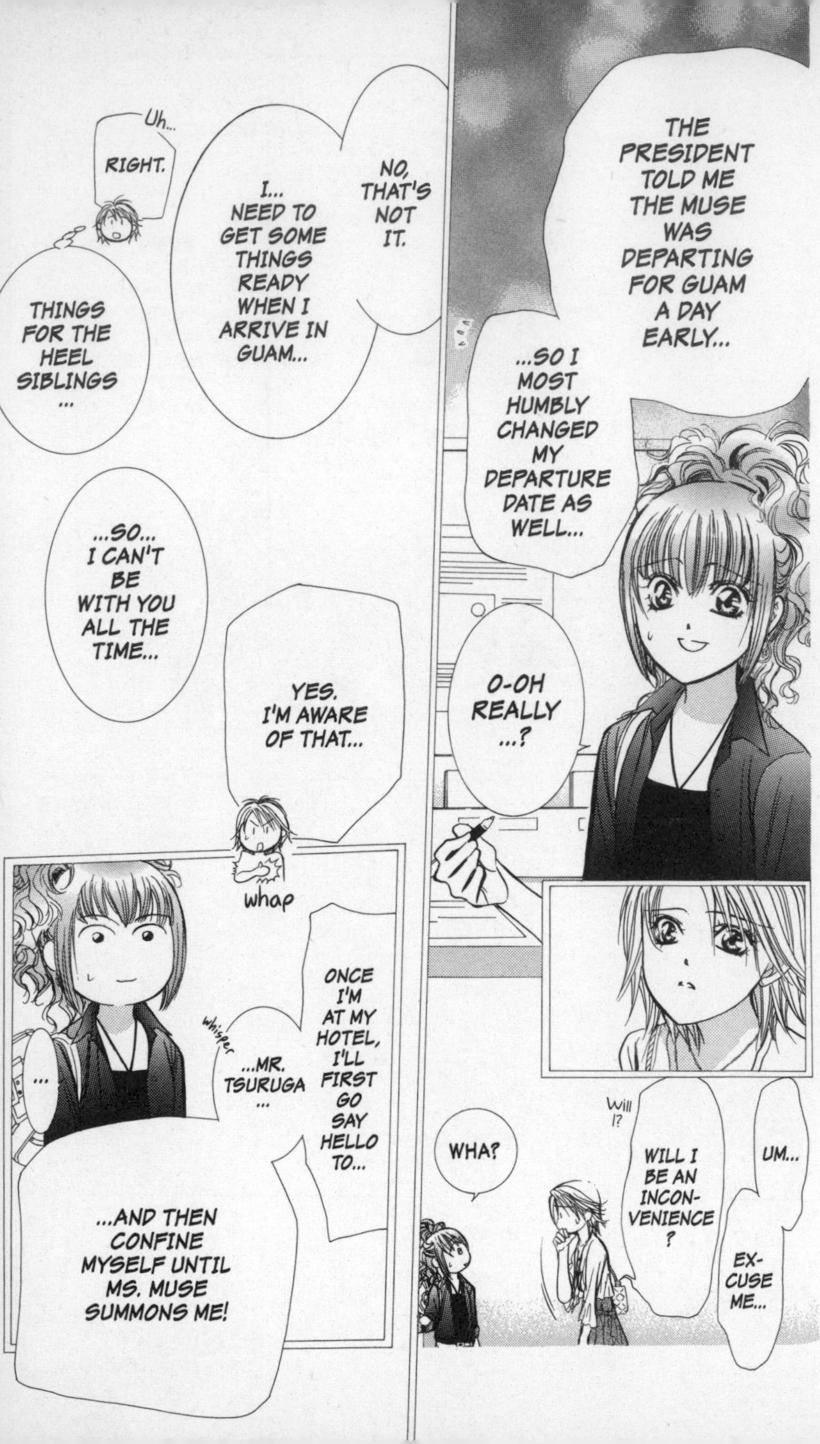
THE PRESIDENT TOLD ME THE MUSE WAS DEPARTING FOR GUAM A DAY EARLY...
...SO I MOST HUMBLY CHANGED MY DEPARTURE DATE AS WELL...
O-OH REALLY ...?
UM...
EXCUSE ME...
Will I?
WILL I BE AN INCON-VENIENCE ?
WHA?
NO, THAT'S NOT IT.
I... NEED TO GET SOME THINGS READY WHEN I ARRIVE IN GUAM...
Uh...
RIGHT.
THINGS FOR THE HEEL SIBLINGS ...
...SO... I CAN'T BE WITH YOU ALL THE TIME...
YES. I'M AWARE OF THAT...
whap
ONCE I'M AT MY HOTEL, I'LL FIRST GO SAY HELLO TO...
whisper
...MR. TSURUGA ...
...
...AND THEN CONFINE MYSELF UNTIL MS. MUSE SUMMONS ME!

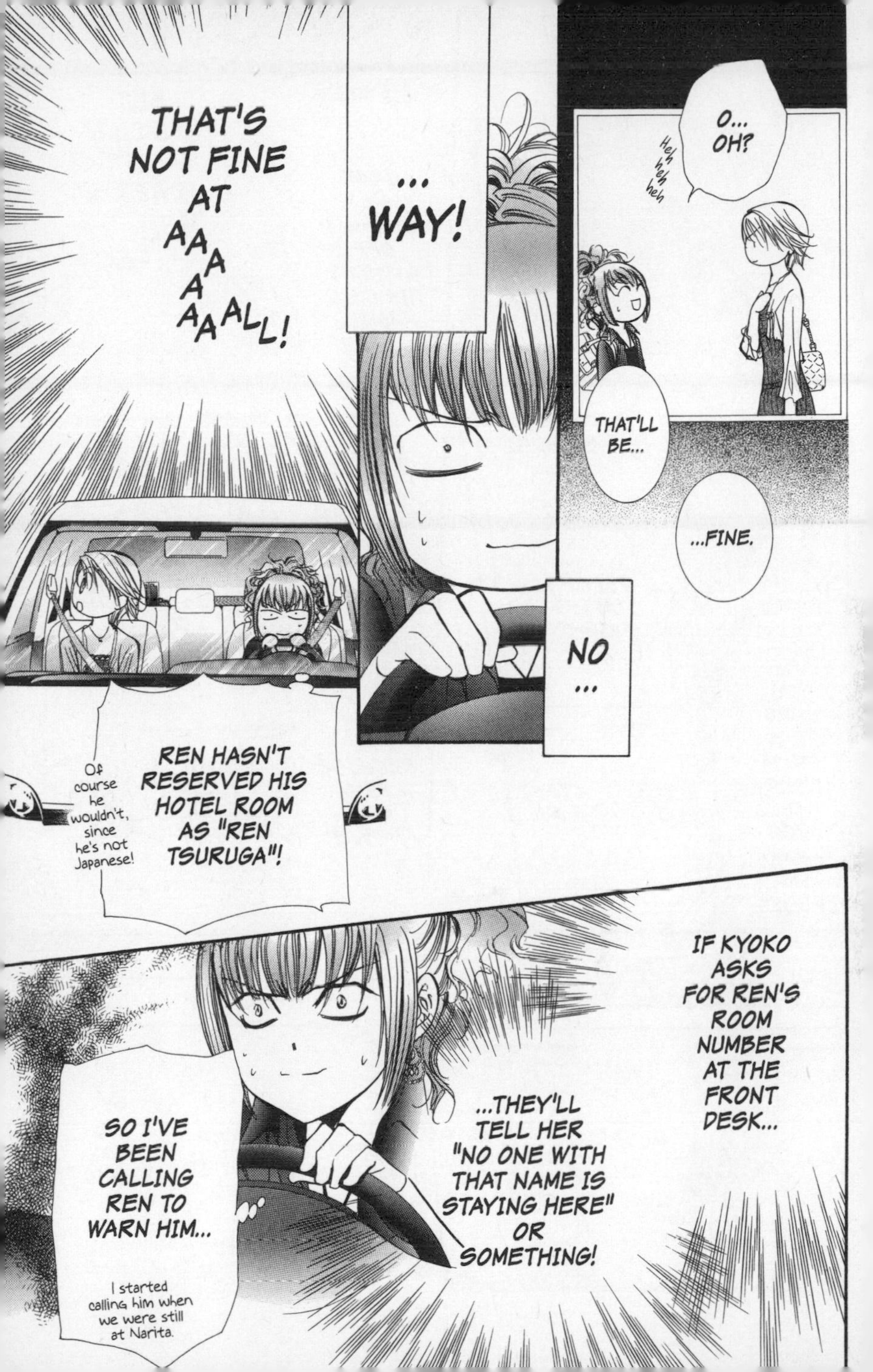

O... OH?
Heh heh heh
THAT'LL BE...
...FINE.
NO...
...WAY!
THAT'S NOT FINE AT AAAAAALL!
REN HASN'T RESERVED HIS HOTEL ROOM AS "REN TSURUGA"!
Of course he wouldn't, since he's not Japanese!
IF KYOKO ASKS FOR REN'S ROOM NUMBER AT THE FRONT DESK...
...THEY'LL TELL HER "NO ONE WITH THAT NAME IS STAYING HERE" OR SOMETHING!
SO I'VE BEEN CALLING REN TO WARN HIM...
I started calling him when we were still at Narita.

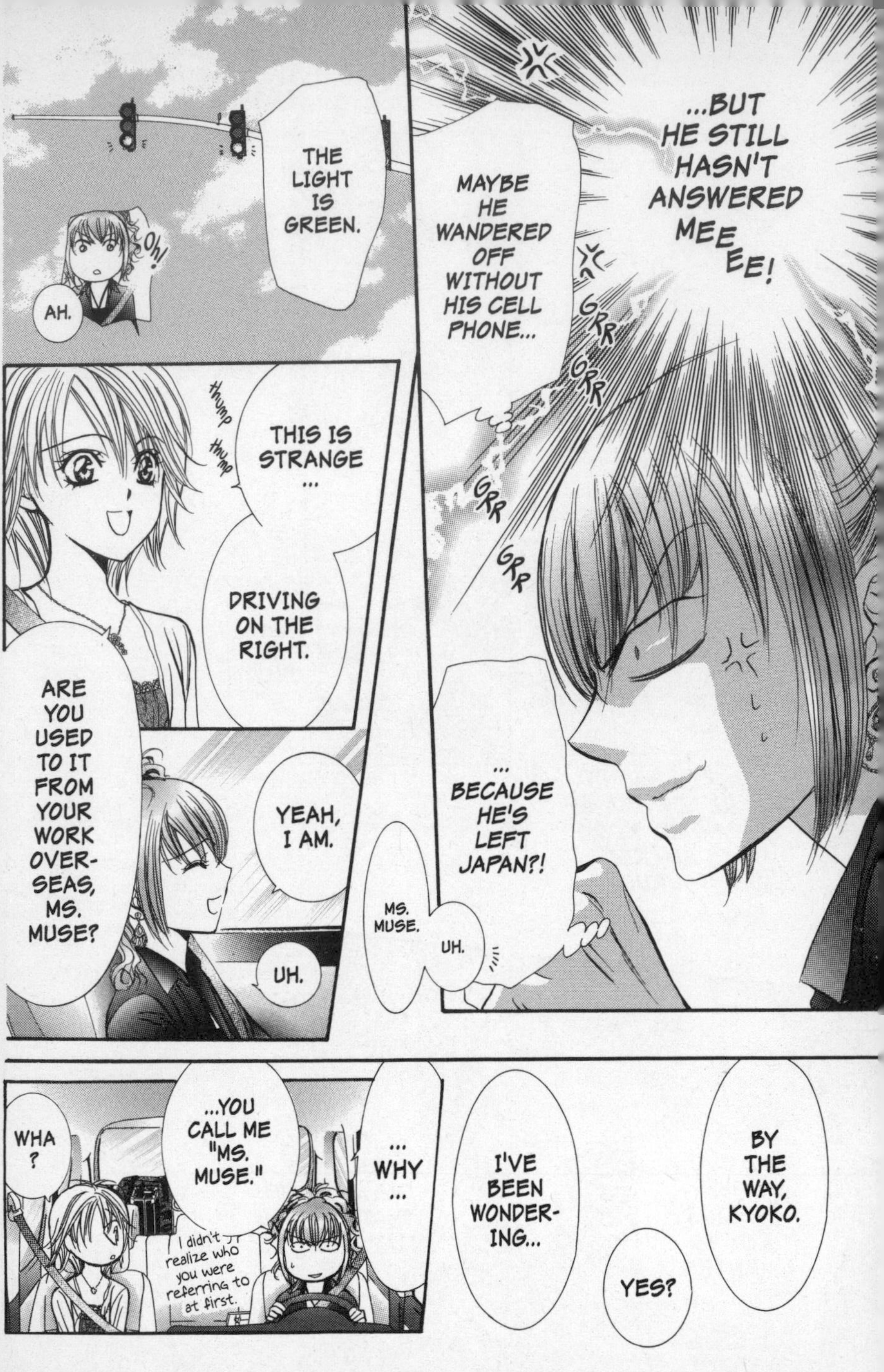
...BUT HE STILL HASN'T ANSWERED MEEEEE!
MAYBE HE WANDERED OFF WITHOUT HIS CELL PHONE...
GRR
GRR
GRR
GRR
... BECAUSE HE'S LEFT JAPAN?!
MS. MUSE.
UH.
THE LIGHT IS GREEN.
Oh!
AH.
THIS IS STRANGE ...
thump thump
DRIVING ON THE RIGHT.
ARE YOU USED TO IT FROM YOUR WORK OVER-SEAS, MS. MUSE?
YEAH, I AM.
UH.
BY THE WAY, KYOKO.
YES?
I'VE BEEN WONDER-ING...
... WHY ...
...YOU CALL ME "MS. MUSE."
WHA?
I didn't realize who you were referring to at first.

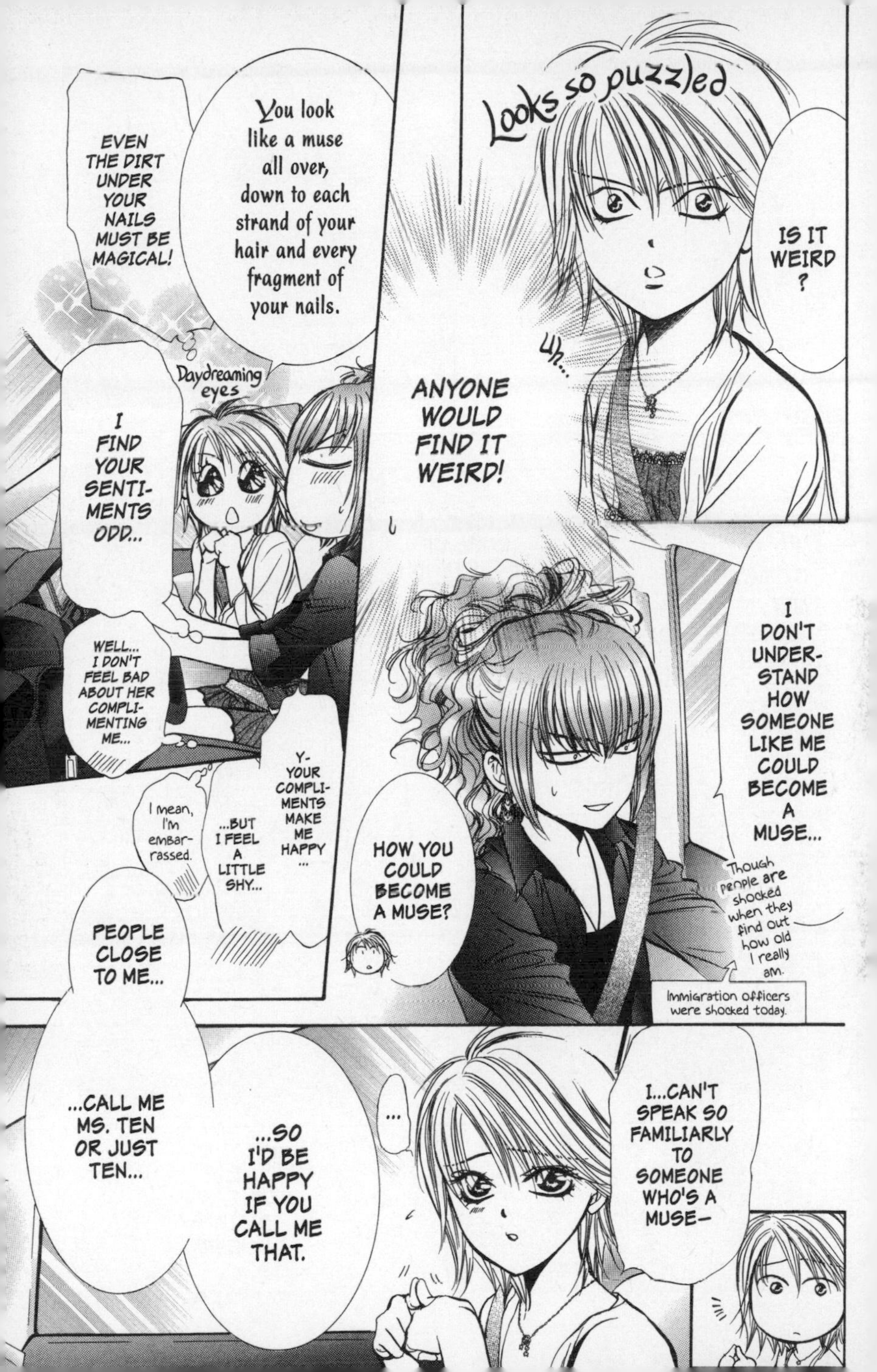
Looks so puzzled
IS IT WEIRD?
Uh...
ANYONE WOULD FIND IT WEIRD!
I DON'T UNDERSTAND HOW SOMEONE LIKE ME COULD BECOME A MUSE...
Though people are shocked when they find out how old I really am.
Immigration officers were shocked today.
HOW YOU COULD BECOME A MUSE?
You look like a muse all over, down to each strand of your hair and every fragment of your nails.
EVEN THE DIRT UNDER YOUR NAILS MUST BE MAGICAL!
Daydreaming eyes
I FIND YOUR SENTIMENTS ODD...
WELL... I DON'T FEEL BAD ABOUT HER COMPLIMENTING ME...
Y-YOUR COMPLIMENTS MAKE ME HAPPY...
...BUT I FEEL A LITTLE SHY...
I mean, I'm embarrassed.
I...CAN'T SPEAK SO FAMILIARLY TO SOMEONE WHO'S A MUSE—
...
PEOPLE CLOSE TO ME...
...CALL ME MS. TEN OR JUST TEN...
...SO I'D BE HAPPY IF YOU CALL ME THAT.

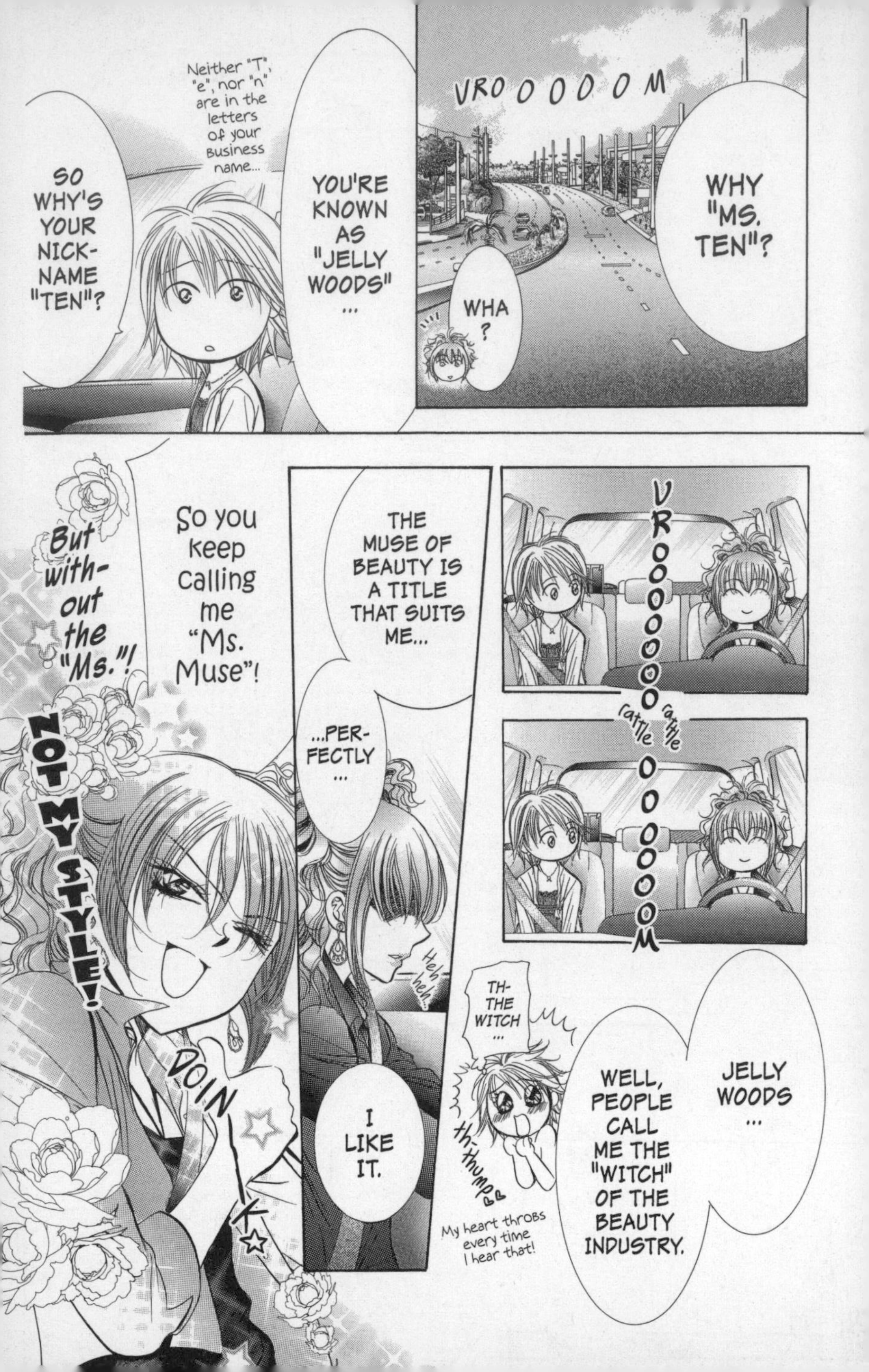
VROOOOOOM
WHY "MS. TEN"?
WHA?
YOU'RE KNOWN AS "JELLY WOODS"...
Neither "T", "e", nor "n" are in the letters of your business name...
SO WHY'S YOUR NICK-NAME "TEN"?
VROOOOOOOOO
rattle rattle
OOOOOOOM
JELLY WOODS...
WELL, PEOPLE CALL ME THE "WITCH" OF THE BEAUTY INDUSTRY.
TH-THE WITCH...
th-thump
My heart throbs every time I hear that!
THE MUSE OF BEAUTY IS A TITLE THAT SUITS ME...
...PER-FECTLY...
Heh heh...
I LIKE IT.
So you keep calling me "Ms. Muse"!
But with-out the "Ms."!
NOT MY STYLE!
DOINK

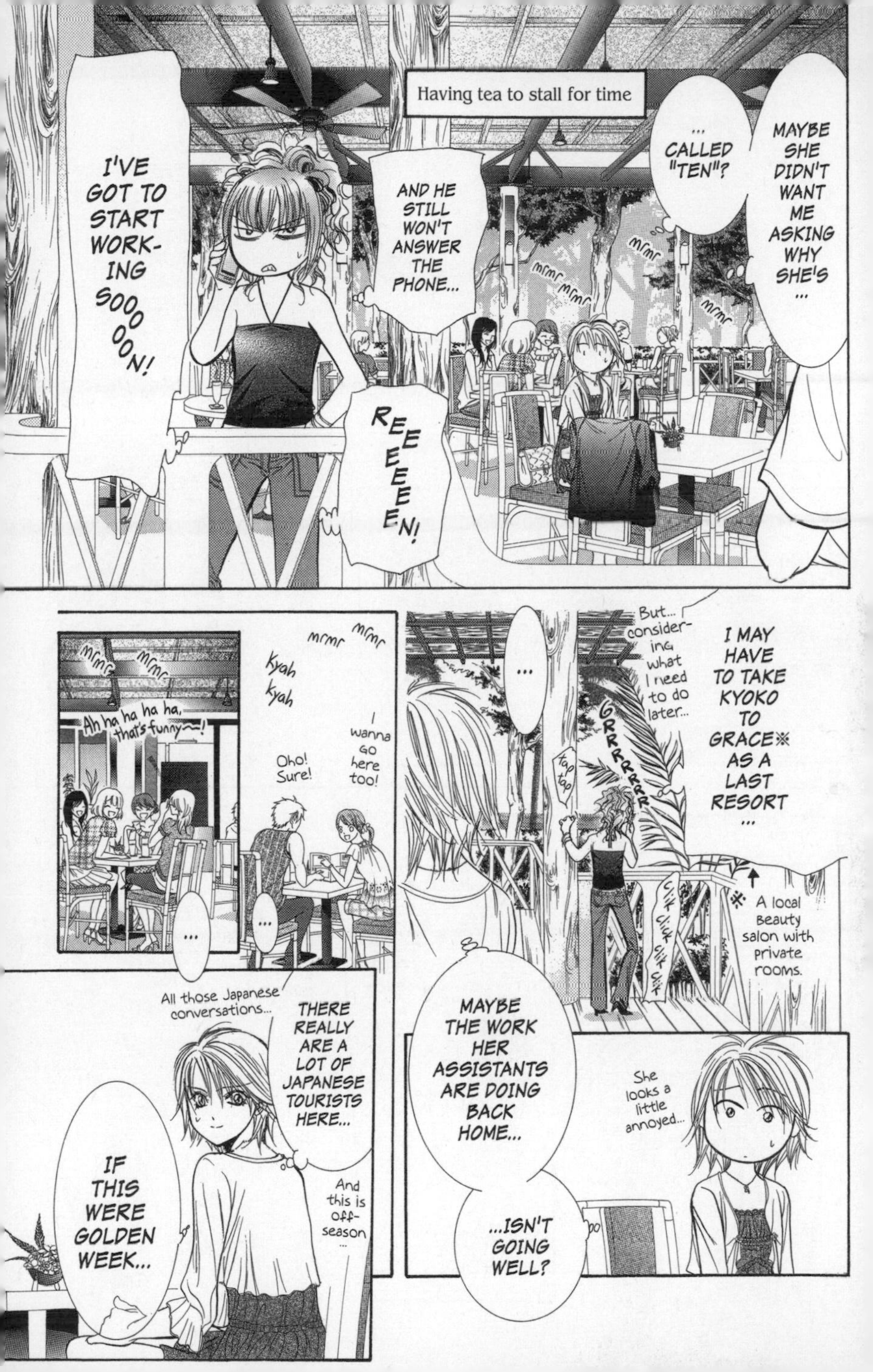
Having tea to stall for time
MAYBE SHE DIDN'T WANT ME ASKING WHY SHE'S ...
... CALLED "TEN"?
mrmr mrmr mrmr mrmr
AND HE STILL WON'T ANSWER THE PHONE...
I'VE GOT TO START WORK-ING SOOOOOON!
REEEEEEN!
I MAY HAVE TO TAKE KYOKO TO GRACE※ AS A LAST RESORT ...
But... consider-ing what I need to do later...
...
GRRRRRRR
tap tap
Click click click click
※ A local Beauty salon with private rooms.
mrmr mrmr mrmr mrmr
Kyah kyah
I wanna go here too!
Oho! Sure!
Ah ha ha ha ha, that's funny~~!
...
...
She looks a little annoyed...
MAYBE THE WORK HER ASSISTANTS ARE DOING BACK HOME...
...ISN'T GOING WELL?
THERE REALLY ARE A LOT OF JAPANESE TOURISTS HERE...
All those Japanese conversations...
And this is off-season ...
IF THIS WERE GOLDEN WEEK...

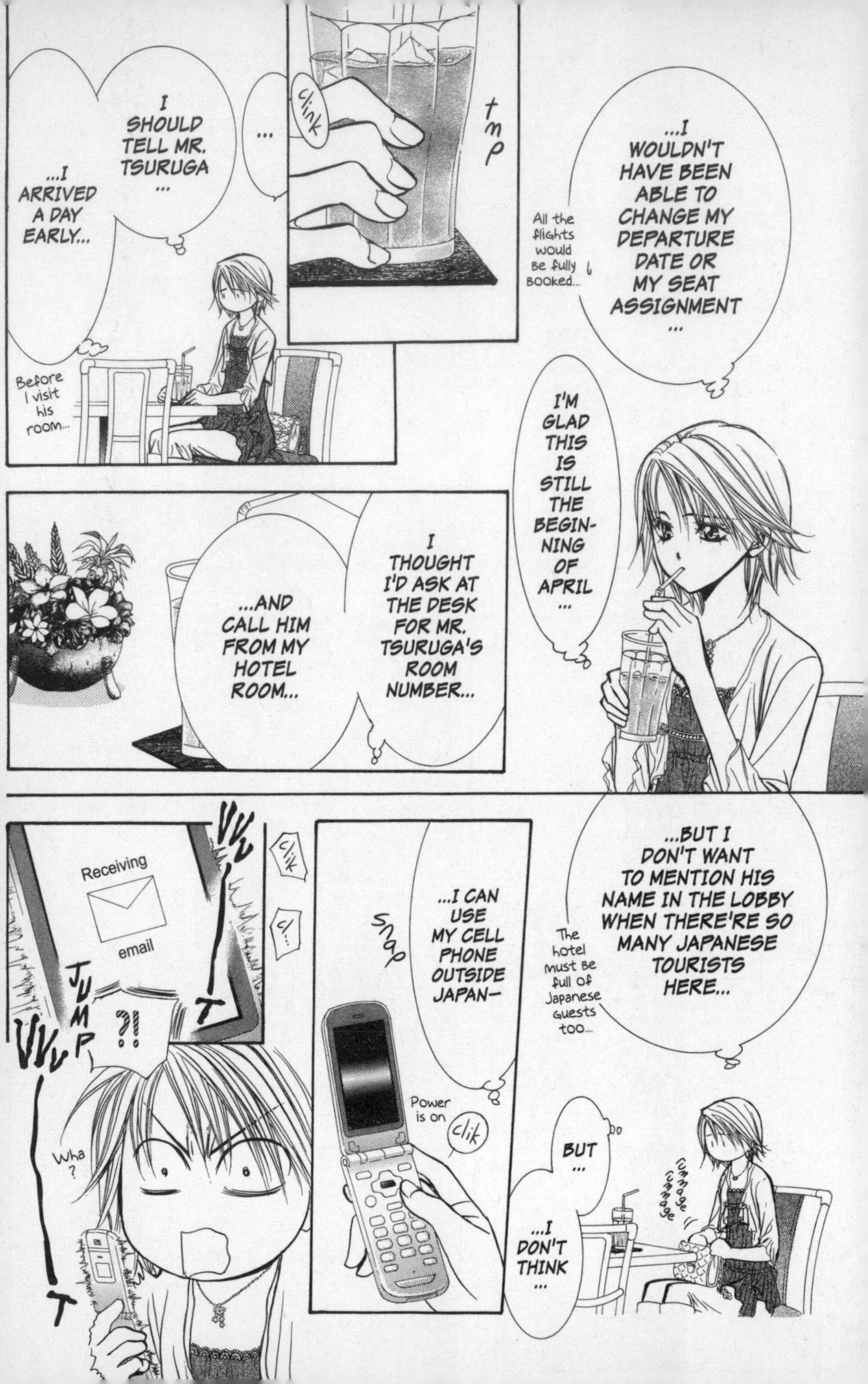
...I WOULDN'T HAVE BEEN ABLE TO CHANGE MY DEPARTURE DATE OR MY SEAT ASSIGNMENT...
All the flights would be fully booked...
tmp
clink
...
I SHOULD TELL MR. TSURUGA...
...I ARRIVED A DAY EARLY...
Before I visit his room...
I'M GLAD THIS IS STILL THE BEGINNING OF APRIL...
I THOUGHT I'D ASK AT THE DESK FOR MR. TSURUGA'S ROOM NUMBER...
...AND CALL HIM FROM MY HOTEL ROOM...
...BUT I DON'T WANT TO MENTION HIS NAME IN THE LOBBY WHEN THERE'RE SO MANY JAPANESE TOURISTS HERE...
The hotel must be full of Japanese guests too...
BUT...
...I DON'T THINK...
rummage rummage
...I CAN USE MY CELL PHONE OUTSIDE JAPAN—
snap
Power is on
clik
VVV
clik
cl...
Receiving email
JUMP
?!
Wha?
VVV

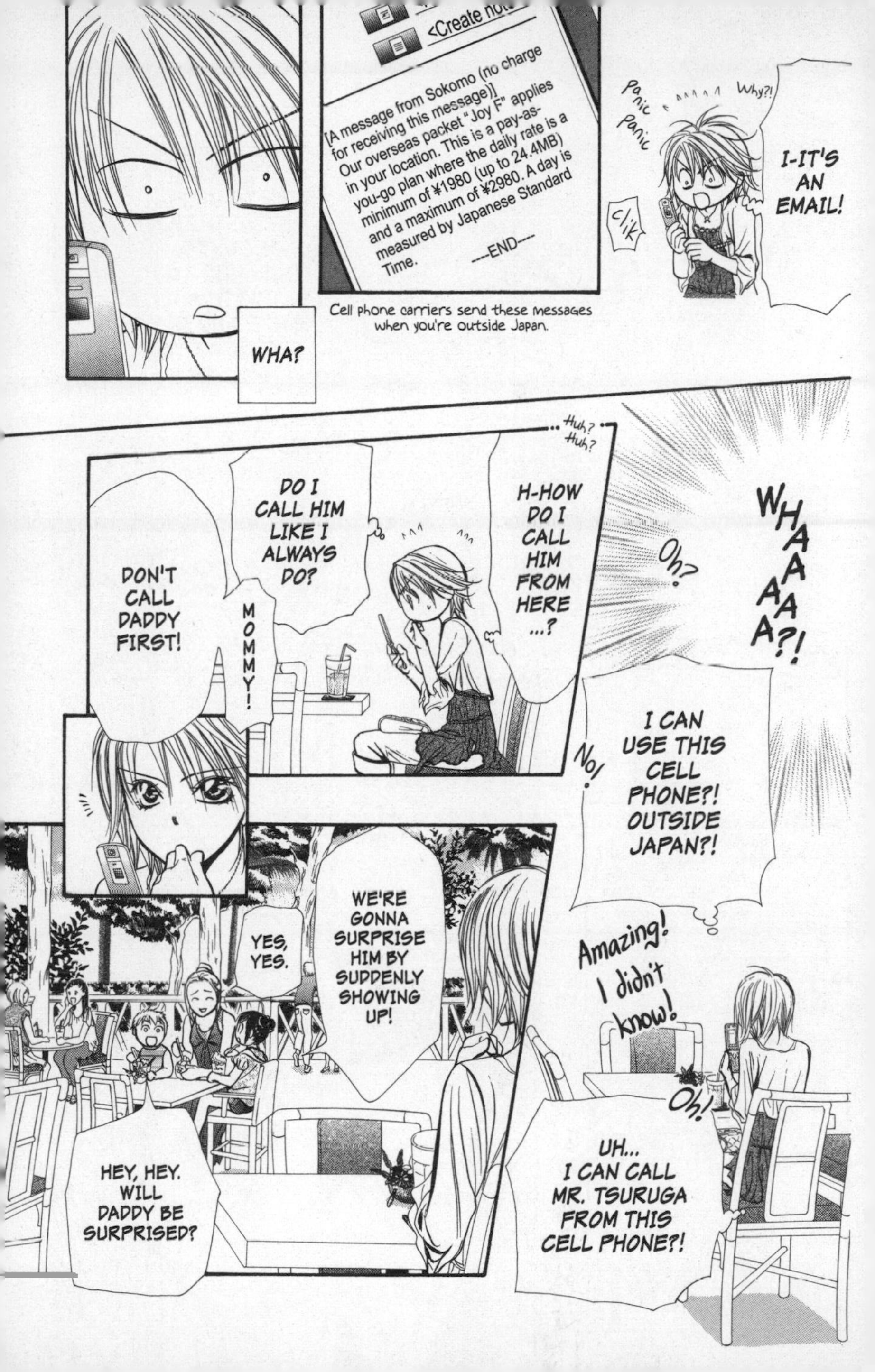
Panic Panic
Why?!
I-IT'S AN EMAIL!
clik
<Create note
[A message from Sokomo (no charge for receiving this message)] Our overseas packet "Joy F" applies in your location. This is a pay-as-you-go plan where the daily rate is a minimum of ¥1980 (up to 24.4MB) and a maximum of ¥2980. A day is measured by Japanese Standard Time. ---END---
Cell phone carriers send these messages when you're outside Japan.
WHA?
WHAAAAA?!
Oh?
No!
I CAN USE THIS CELL PHONE?! OUTSIDE JAPAN?!
Huh? Huh?
H-HOW DO I CALL HIM FROM HERE ...?
DO I CALL HIM LIKE I ALWAYS DO?
MOMMY!
DON'T CALL DADDY FIRST!
Amazing! I didn't know!
Oh!
UH... I CAN CALL MR. TSURUGA FROM THIS CELL PHONE?!
WE'RE GONNA SURPRISE HIM BY SUDDENLY SHOWING UP!
YES, YES.
HEY, HEY. WILL DADDY BE SURPRISED?

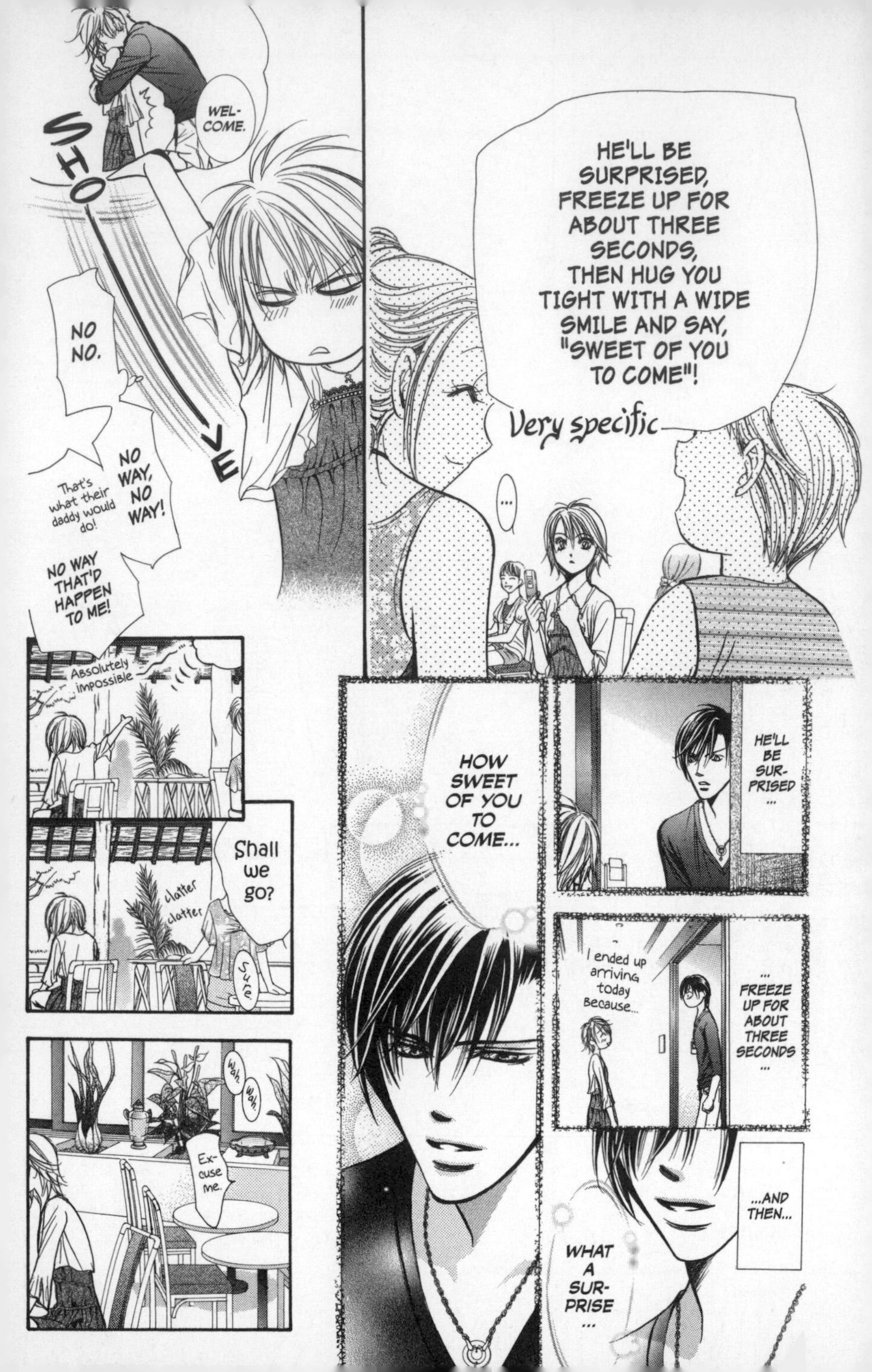
HE'LL BE SURPRISED, FREEZE UP FOR ABOUT THREE SECONDS, THEN HUG YOU TIGHT WITH A WIDE SMILE AND SAY, "SWEET OF YOU TO COME"!
Very specific
...
WEL-COME.
SHOVE
NO NO.
NO WAY, NO WAY!
That's what their daddy would do!
NO WAY THAT'D HAPPEN TO ME!
HE'LL BE SUR-PRISED...
I ended up arriving today because...
...FREEZE UP FOR ABOUT THREE SECONDS...
...AND THEN...
WHAT A SUR-PRISE...
HOW SWEET OF YOU TO COME...
Absolutely impossible
Shall we go?
clatter clatter
Sure.
Wah wah
Ex-cuse me.

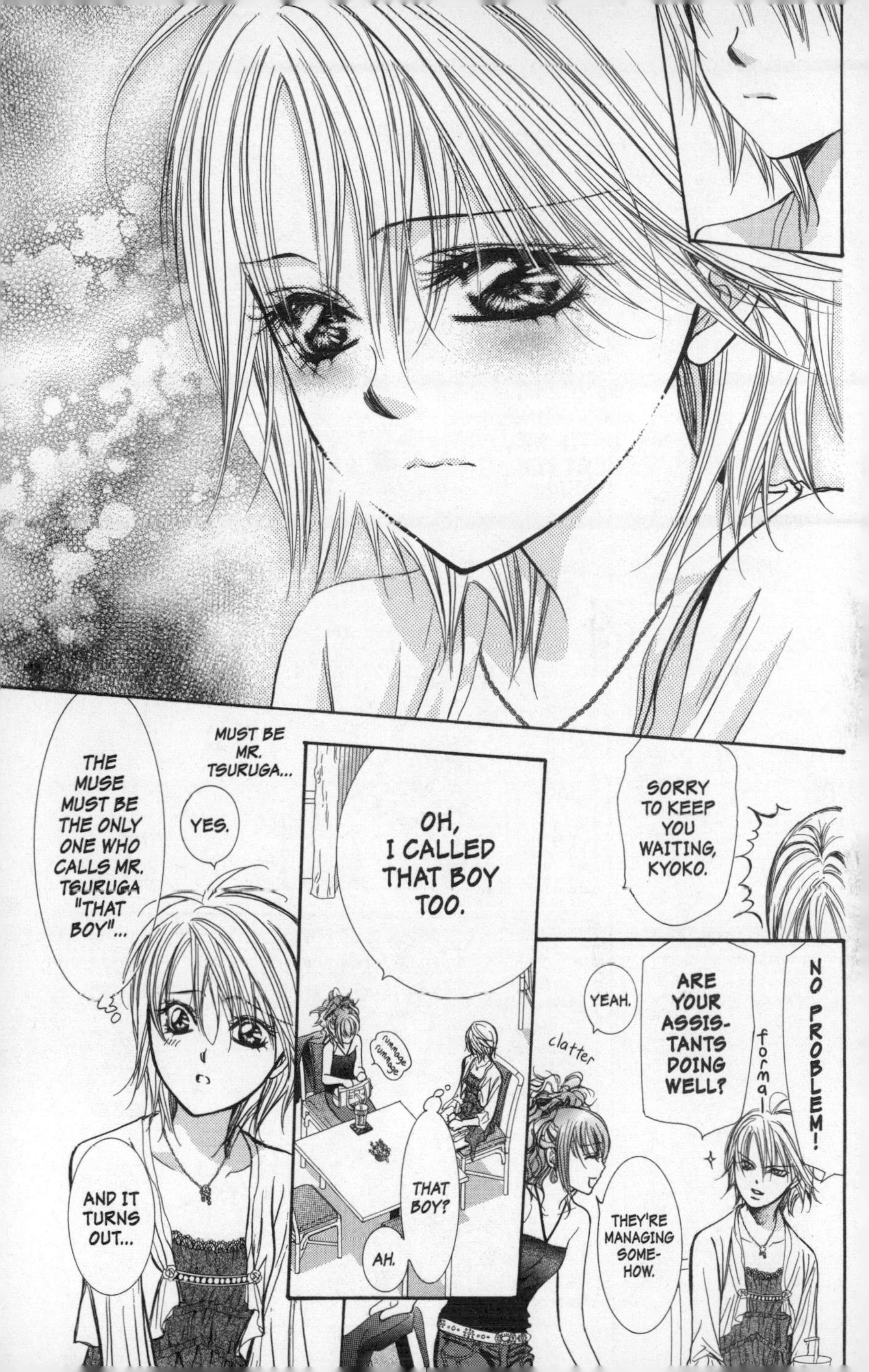
SORRY TO KEEP YOU WAITING, KYOKO.
NO PROBLEM!
formal
ARE YOUR ASSIS-TANTS DOING WELL?
YEAH.
clatter
THEY'RE MANAGING SOME-HOW.
OH, I CALLED THAT BOY TOO.
rummage rummage
THAT BOY?
AH.
MUST BE MR. TSURUGA...
YES.
THE MUSE MUST BE THE ONLY ONE WHO CALLS MR. TSURUGA "THAT BOY"...
AND IT TURNS OUT...

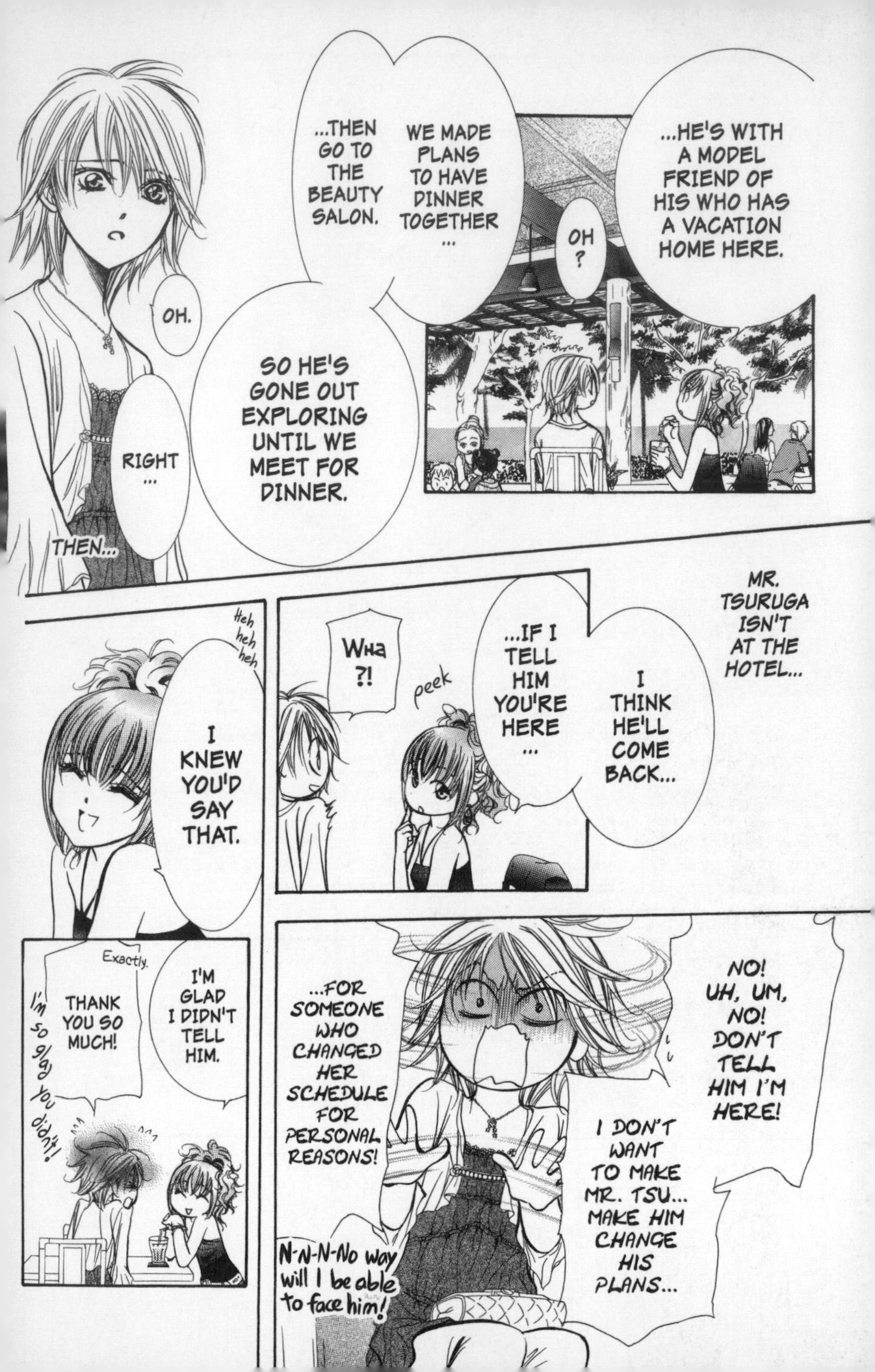
...HE'S WITH A MODEL FRIEND OF HIS WHO HAS A VACATION HOME HERE.
OH?
WE MADE PLANS TO HAVE DINNER TOGETHER...
...THEN GO TO THE BEAUTY SALON.
SO HE'S GONE OUT EXPLORING UNTIL WE MEET FOR DINNER.
OH.
RIGHT...
THEN...
MR. TSURUGA ISN'T AT THE HOTEL...
I THINK HE'LL COME BACK...
...IF I TELL HIM YOU'RE HERE...
peek
Wha?!
Heh heh heh
I KNEW YOU'D SAY THAT.
NO! UH, UM, NO! DON'T TELL HIM I'M HERE!
I DON'T WANT TO MAKE MR. TSU... MAKE HIM CHANGE HIS PLANS...
...FOR SOMEONE WHO CHANGED HER SCHEDULE FOR PERSONAL REASONS!
N-N-N-No way will I be able to face him!
I'M GLAD I DIDN'T TELL HIM.
Exactly.
THANK YOU SO MUCH!
I'm so glad you didn't!

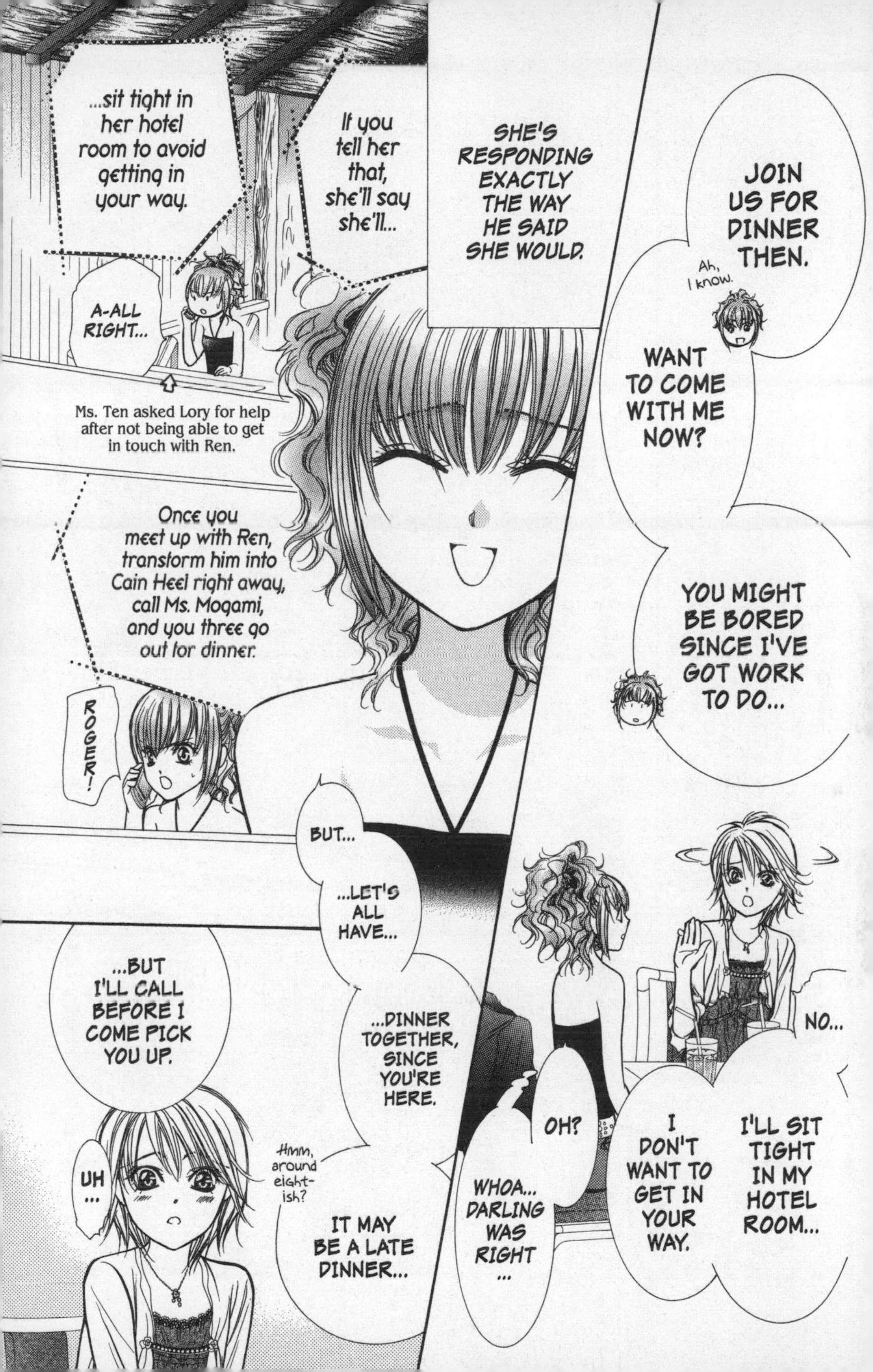
JOIN US FOR DINNER THEN.
Ah, I know.
WANT TO COME WITH ME NOW?
YOU MIGHT BE BORED SINCE I'VE GOT WORK TO DO...
NO...
I'LL SIT TIGHT IN MY HOTEL ROOM...
I DON'T WANT TO GET IN YOUR WAY.
OH?
WHOA... DARLING WAS RIGHT...
If you tell her that, she'll say she'll...
...sit tight in her hotel room to avoid getting in your way.
A-ALL RIGHT...
Ms. Ten asked Lory for help after not being able to get in touch with Ren.
Once you meet up with Ren, transform him into Cain Heel right away, call Ms. Mogami, and you three go out for dinner.
ROGER!
SHE'S RESPONDING EXACTLY THE WAY HE SAID SHE WOULD.
BUT...
...LET'S ALL HAVE...
...DINNER TOGETHER, SINCE YOU'RE HERE.
Hmm, around eight-ish?
IT MAY BE A LATE DINNER...
...BUT I'LL CALL BEFORE I COME PICK YOU UP.
UH...

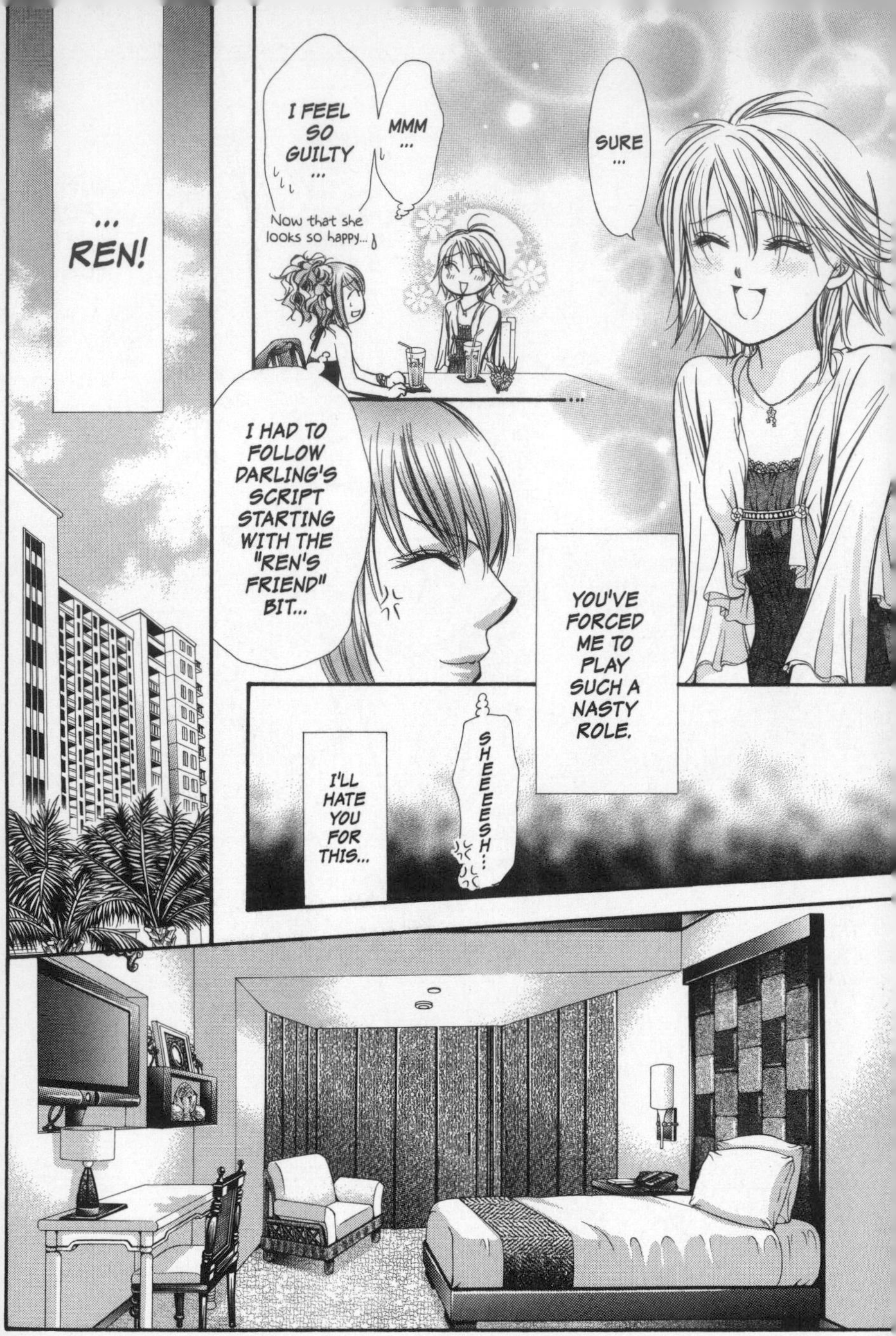
SURE ...
I FEEL SO GUILTY ...
MMM ...
Now that she looks so happy...
I HAD TO FOLLOW DARLING'S SCRIPT STARTING WITH THE "REN'S FRIEND" BIT...
YOU'VE FORCED ME TO PLAY SUCH A NASTY ROLE.
SHEEEESH...
I'LL HATE YOU FOR THIS...
... REN!

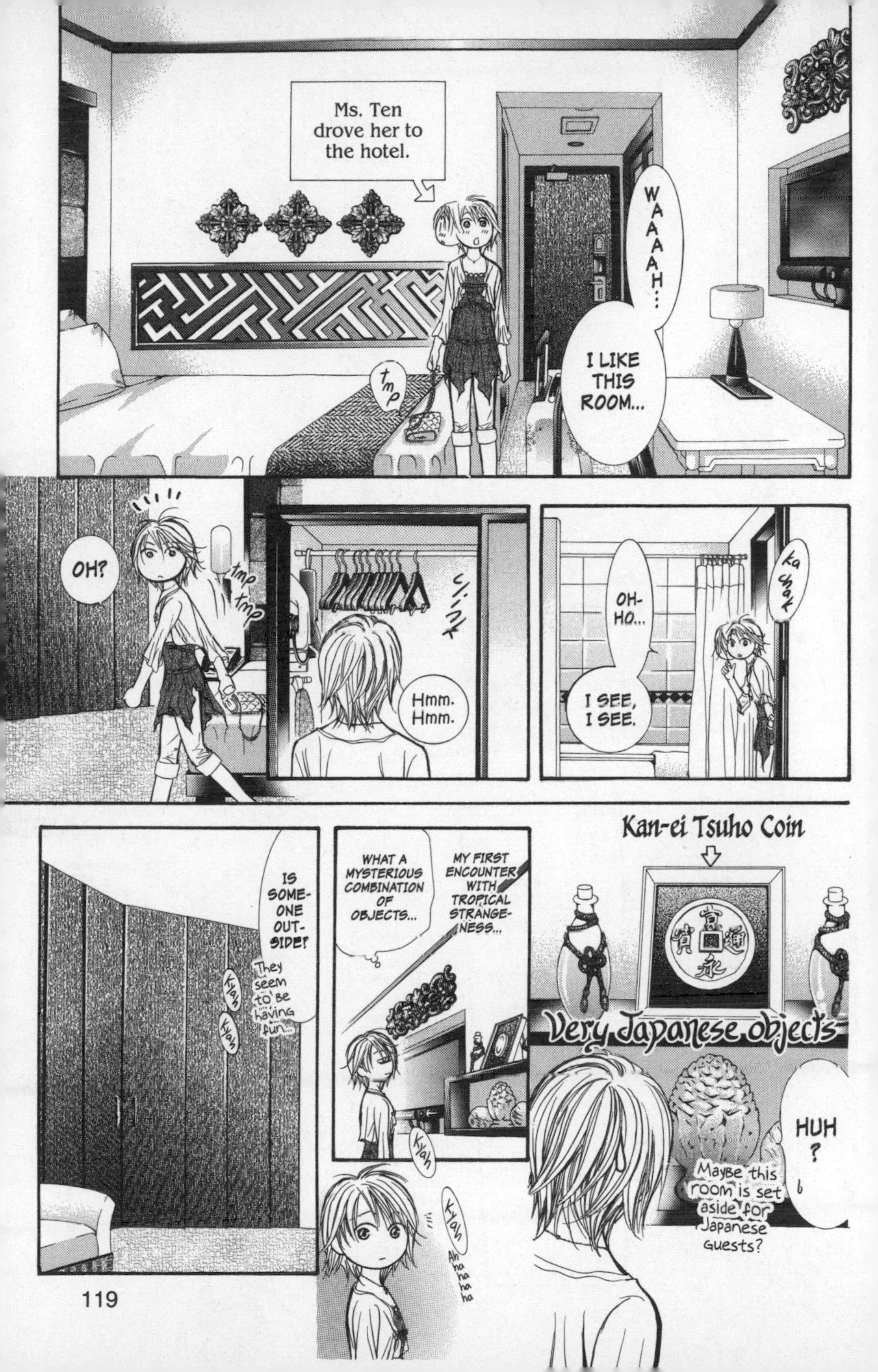
Ms. Ten drove her to the hotel.
WAAAAH...
I LIKE THIS ROOM...
tmp
ka chak
OH-HO...
I SEE, I SEE.
Hmm. Hmm.
OH?
tmp tmp
Kan-ei Tsuho Coin
Very Japanese objects
HUH?
Maybe this room is set aside for Japanese guests?
WHAT A MYSTERIOUS COMBINATION OF OBJECTS...
MY FIRST ENCOUNTER WITH TROPICAL STRANGE-NESS...
Kyah
Kyah
Ah ha ha ha ha
IS SOME-ONE OUT-SIDE!?
They seem to be having fun...
Kyah
Kyah

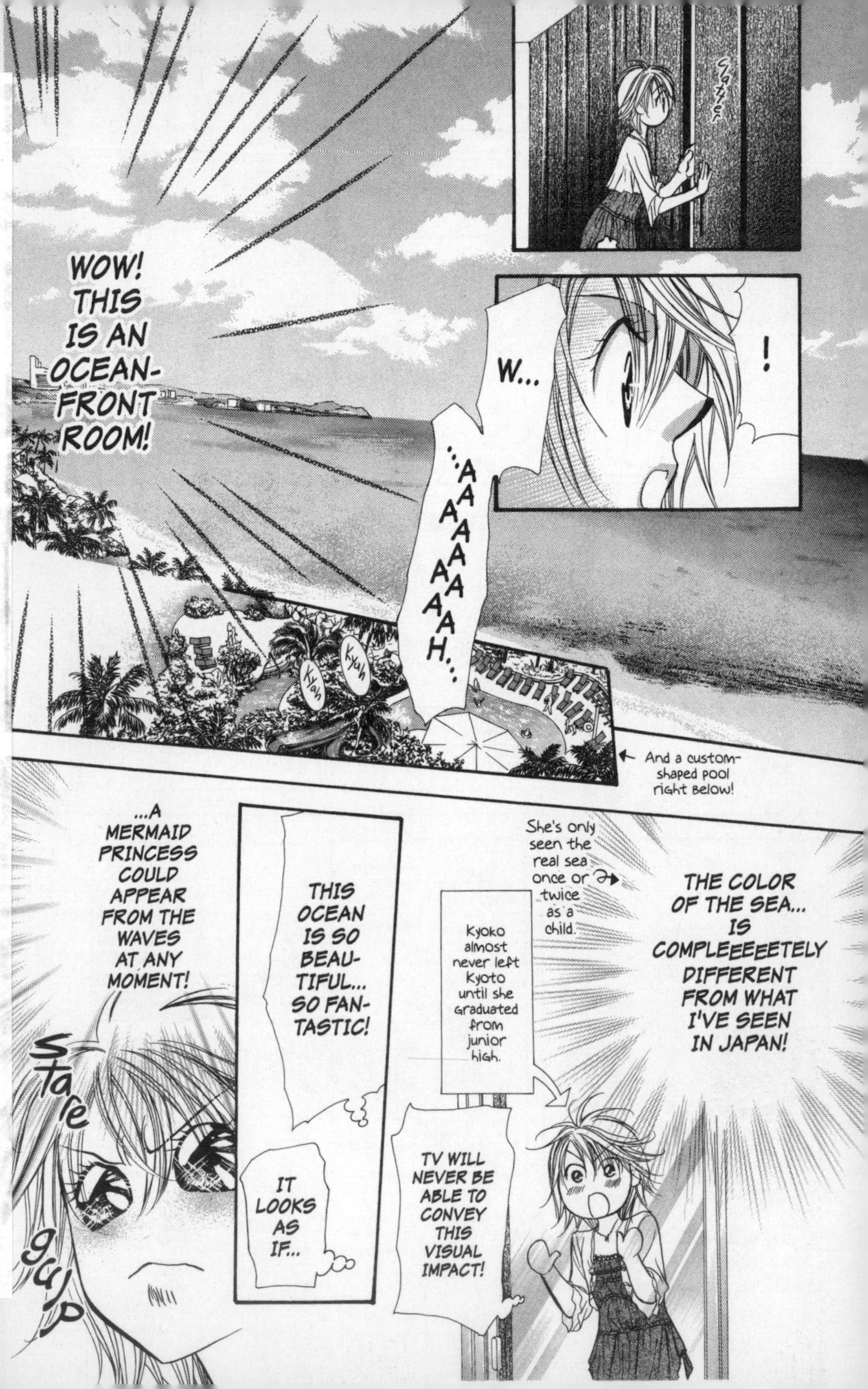
Clatter
!
W...
...AAAAAAAAAH...
WOW! THIS IS AN OCEAN-FRONT ROOM!
Kyah
Kyah
And a custom-shaped pool right below!
THE COLOR OF THE SEA... IS COMPLEEEEETELY DIFFERENT FROM WHAT I'VE SEEN IN JAPAN!
She's only seen the real sea once or twice as a child.
Kyoko almost never left Kyoto until she graduated from junior high.
TV WILL NEVER BE ABLE TO CONVEY THIS VISUAL IMPACT!
THIS OCEAN IS SO BEAUTIFUL... SO FANTASTIC!
IT LOOKS AS IF...
...A MERMAID PRINCESS COULD APPEAR FROM THE WAVES AT ANY MOMENT!
Stare
gulp

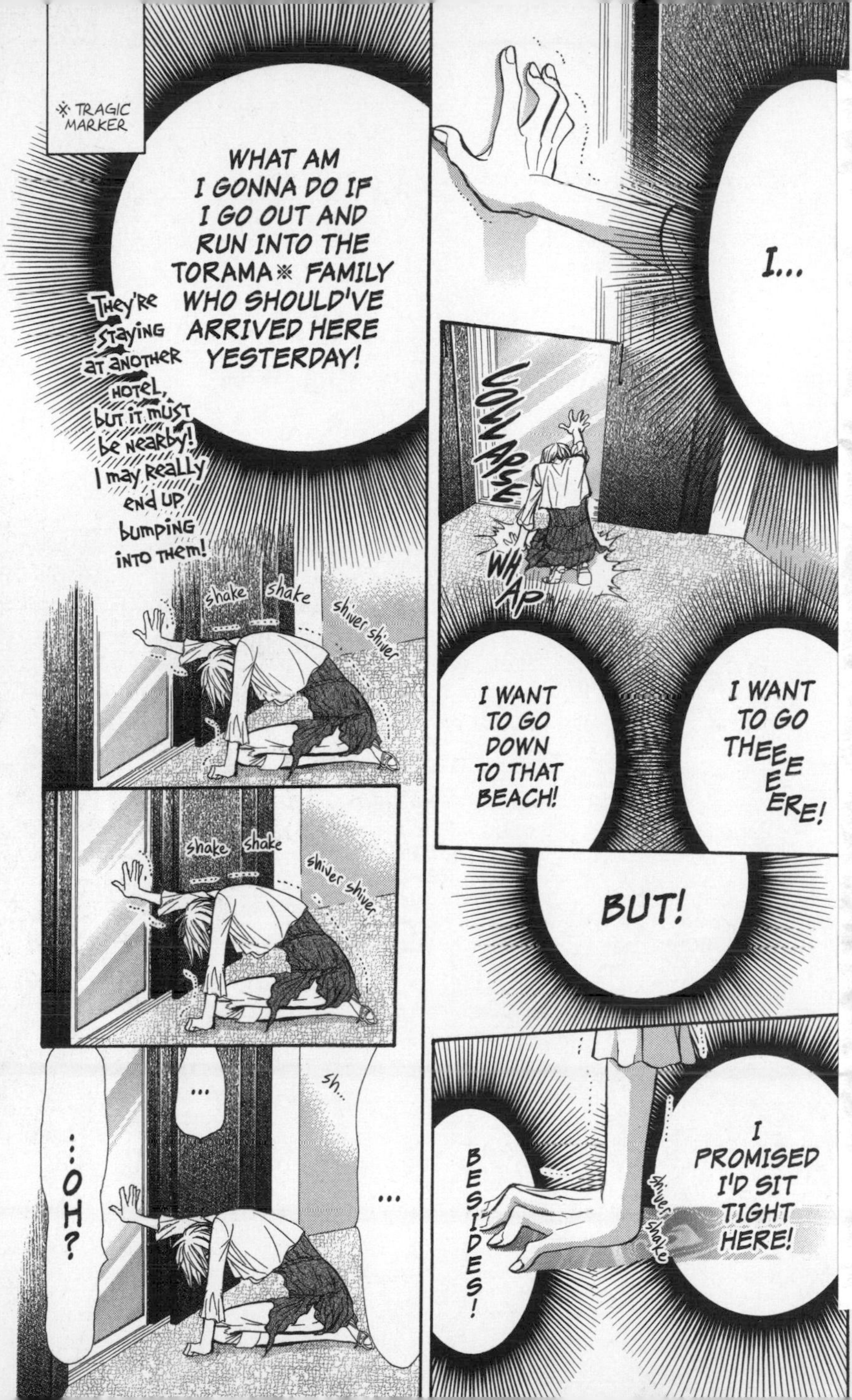
I...
COLLAPSE
WHAP
I WANT TO GO THEEEEERE!
I WANT TO GO DOWN TO THAT BEACH!
BUT!
I PROMISED I'D SIT TIGHT HERE!
shiver shake
BESIDES!
※ TRAGIC MARKER
WHAT AM I GONNA DO IF I GO OUT AND RUN INTO THE TORAMA※ FAMILY WHO SHOULD'VE ARRIVED HERE YESTERDAY!
They're staying at another hotel, but it must be nearby! I may really end up bumping into them!
shake shake
shiver shiver
shake shake
shiver shiver
sh...
...
...
...OH?

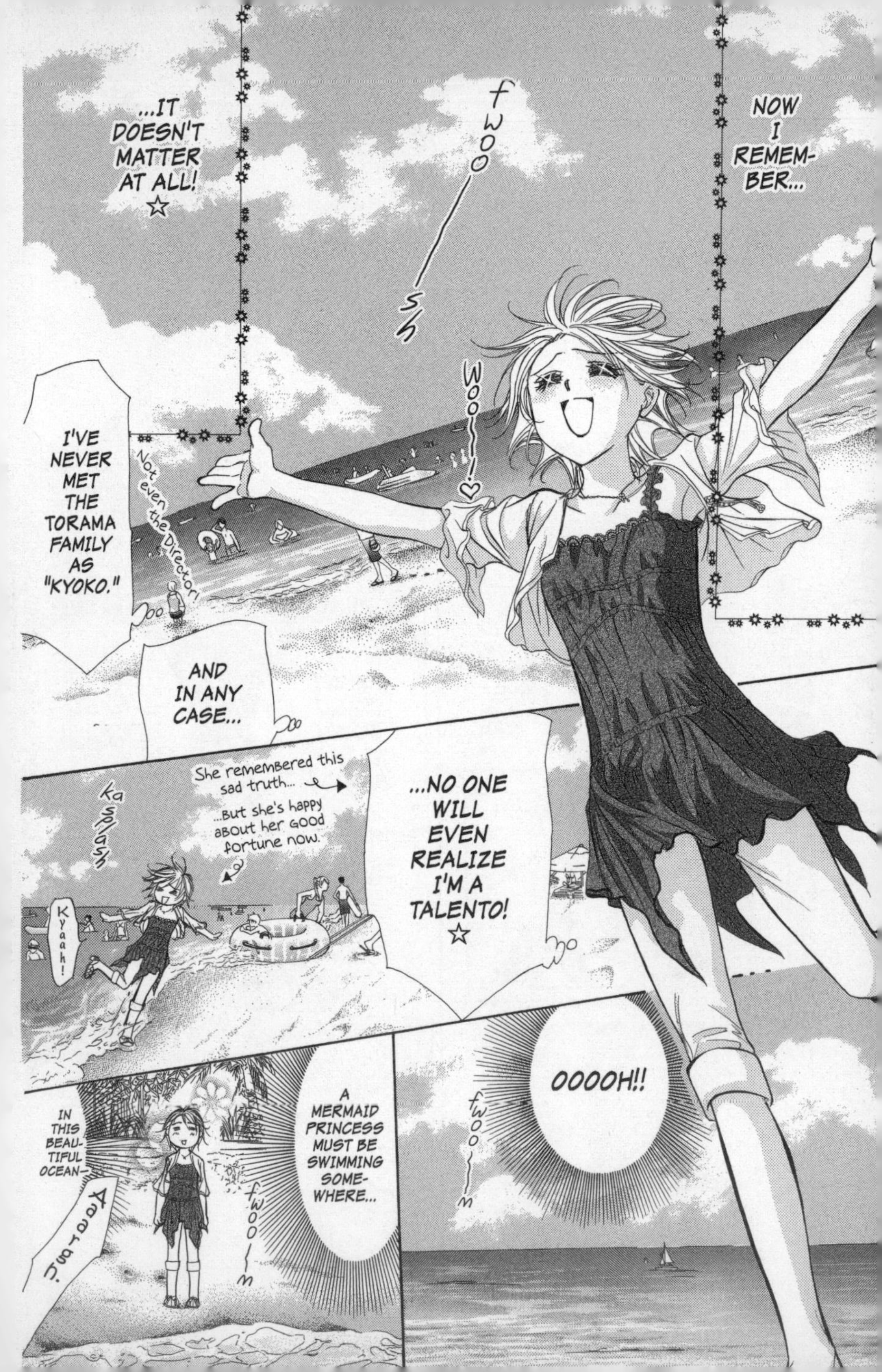
NOW I REMEMBER...
fwoo—sh
Woo—!♡
...IT DOESN'T MATTER AT ALL! ☆
I'VE NEVER MET THE TORAMA FAMILY AS "KYOKO."
Not even the Director!
AND IN ANY CASE...
...NO ONE WILL EVEN REALIZE I'M A TALENTO! ☆
She remembered this sad truth...
...But she's happy about her good fortune now.
kasplash
Kyaah!
OOOOH!!
fwoo—m
A MERMAID PRINCESS MUST BE SWIMMING SOME-WHERE...
fwoo—m
IN THIS BEAU-TIFUL OCEAN—

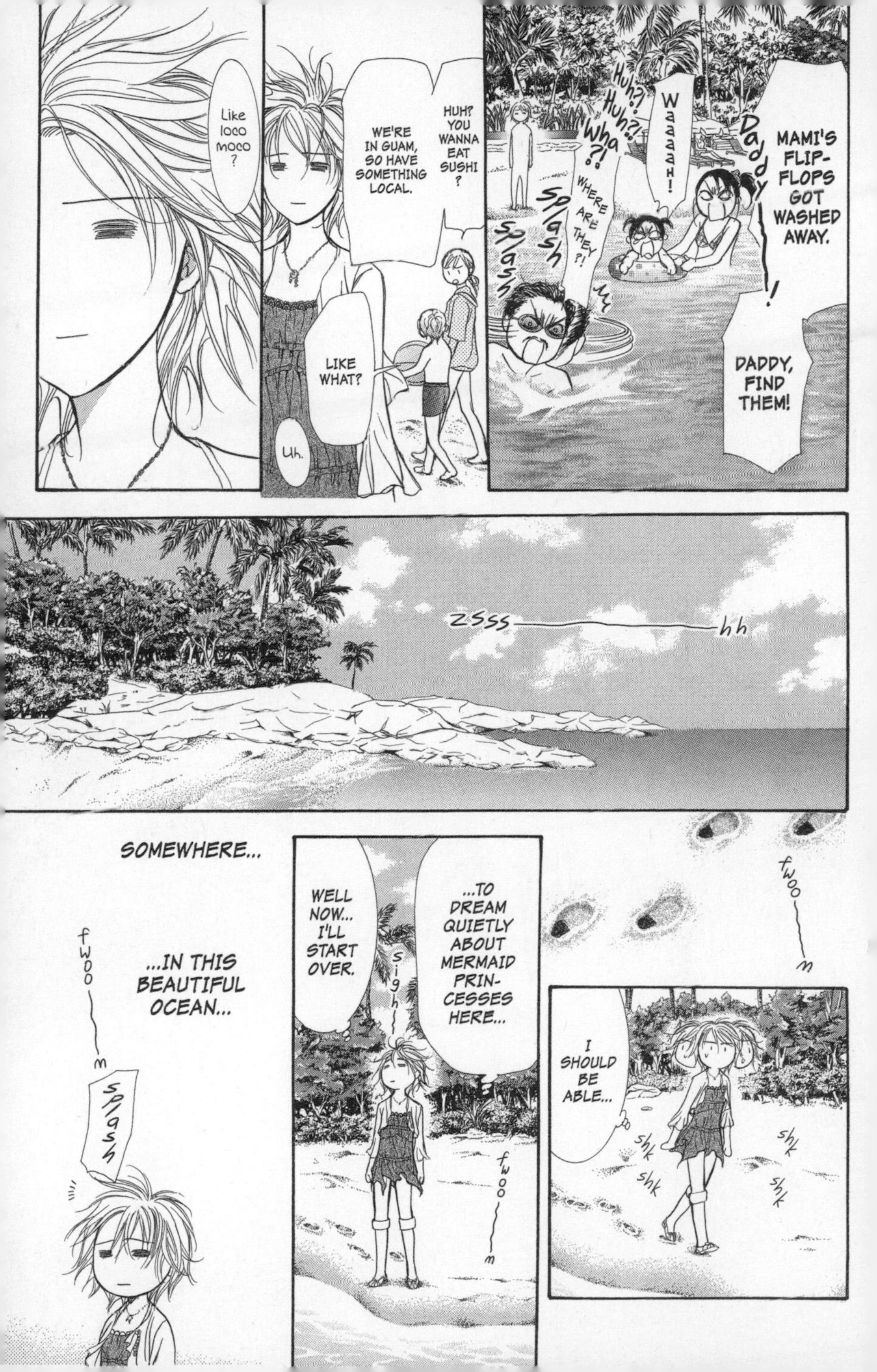
MAMI'S FLIP-FLOPS GOT WASHED AWAY.
Daddy—!
DADDY, FIND THEM!
Waaaaah!
Huh?! Huh?! Wha?!
WHERE ARE THEY?!
Splash
Splash
HUH? YOU WANNA EAT SUSHI?
WE'RE IN GUAM, SO HAVE SOMETHING LOCAL.
LIKE WHAT?
Uh.
Like loco moco?
ZSSS———hh
fwoo——m
I SHOULD BE ABLE...
shk
shk
shk
shk
...TO DREAM QUIETLY ABOUT MERMAID PRINCESSES HERE...
WELL NOW... I'LL START OVER.
sigh
fwoo——m
SOMEWHERE...
...IN THIS BEAUTIFUL OCEAN...
fwoo——m
splash

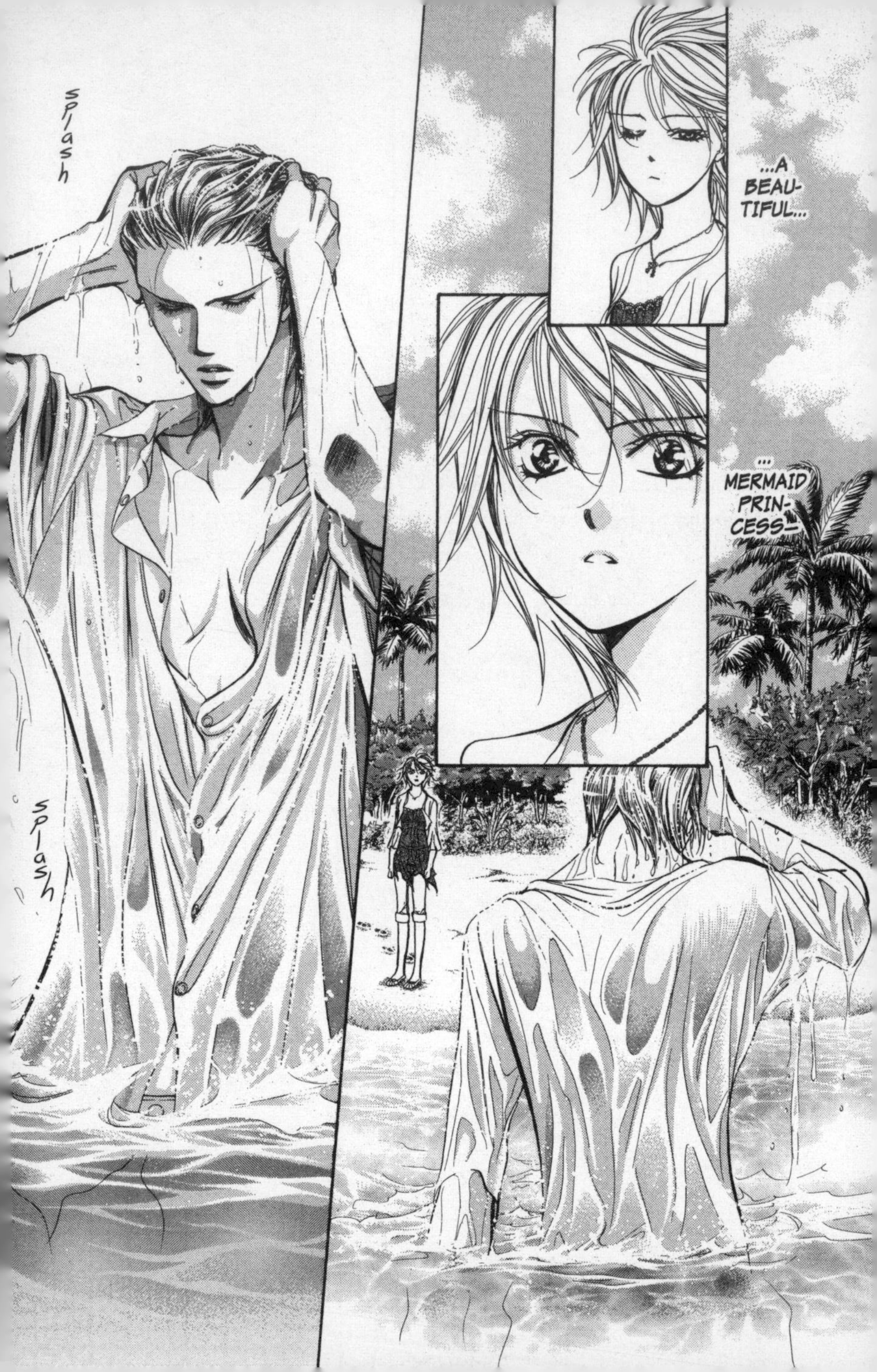
...A BEAU-TIFUL...
...MERMAID PRIN-CESS—
splash
splash

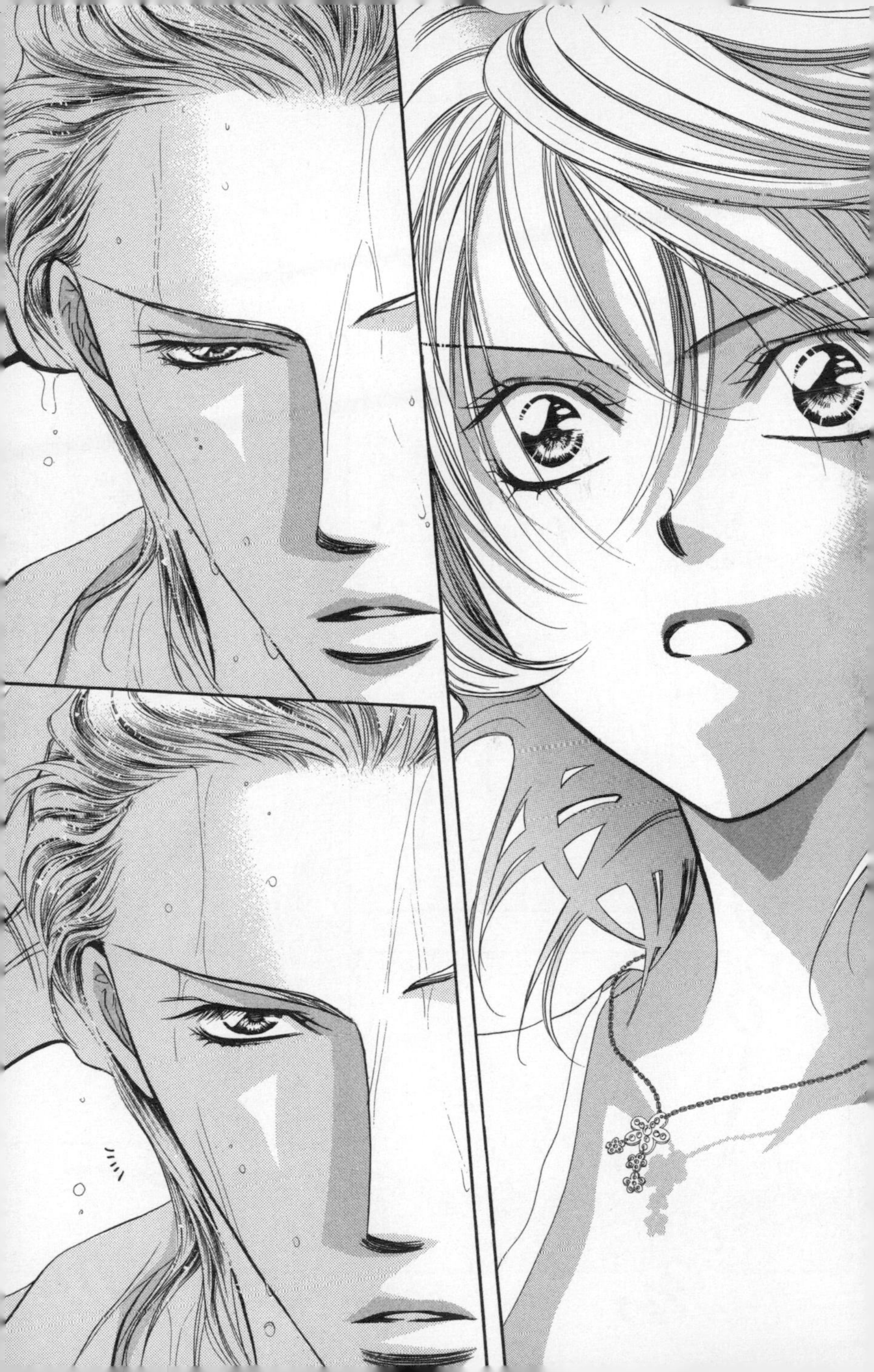

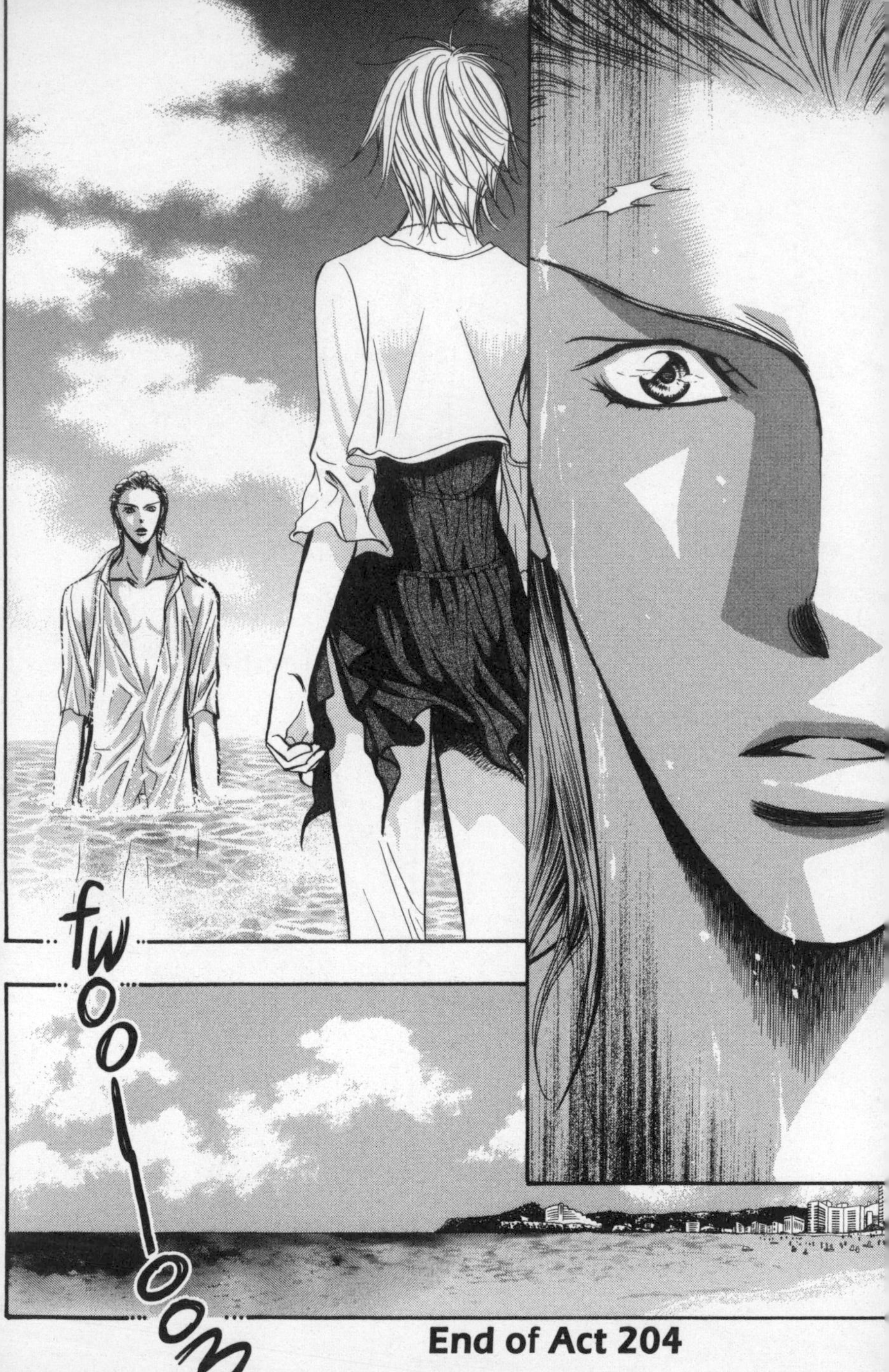
fwoo—ooom

End of Act 204

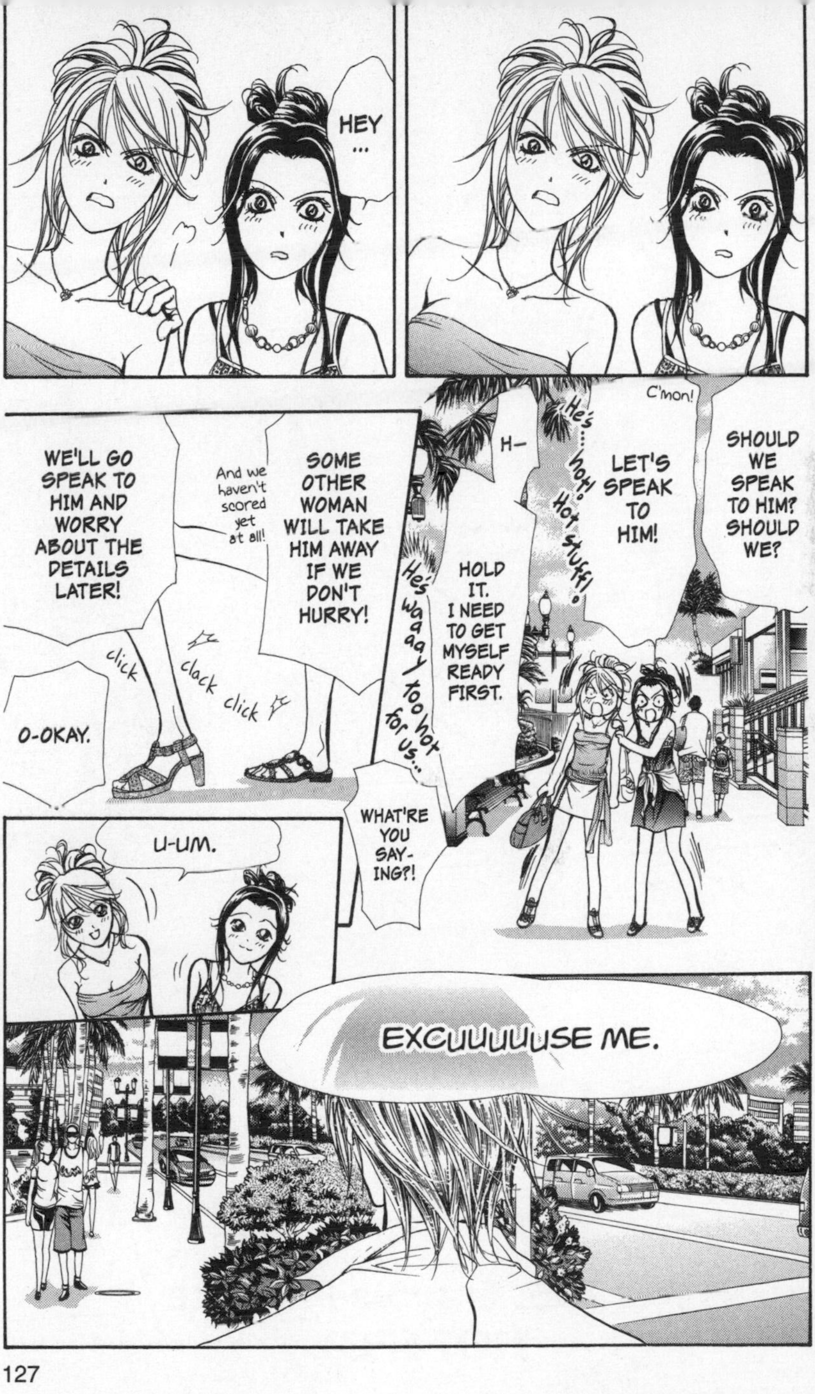
HEY ...
C'mon!
SHOULD WE SPEAK TO HIM? SHOULD WE?
He's... hot! Hot stuff!
LET'S SPEAK TO HIM!
H—
HOLD IT. I NEED TO GET MYSELF READY FIRST.
He's waaay too hot for us...
WHAT'RE YOU SAYING?!
SOME OTHER WOMAN WILL TAKE HIM AWAY IF WE DON'T HURRY!
And we haven't scored yet at all!
WE'LL GO SPEAK TO HIM AND WORRY ABOUT THE DETAILS LATER!
click
clack
click
O-OKAY.
U-UM.
EXCUUUUUUSE ME.

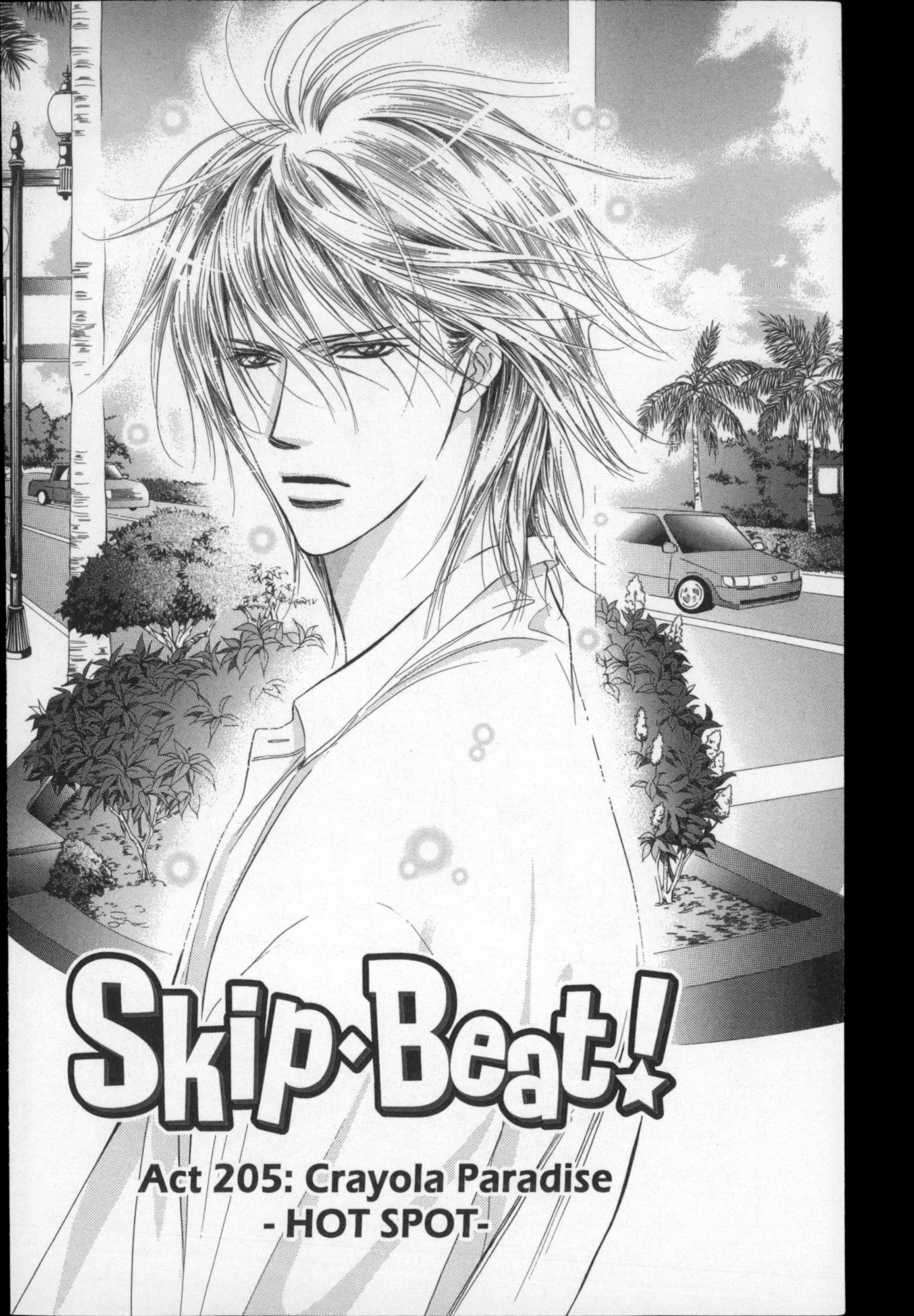
Skip·Beat!
Act 205: Crayola Paradise
- HOT SPOT-

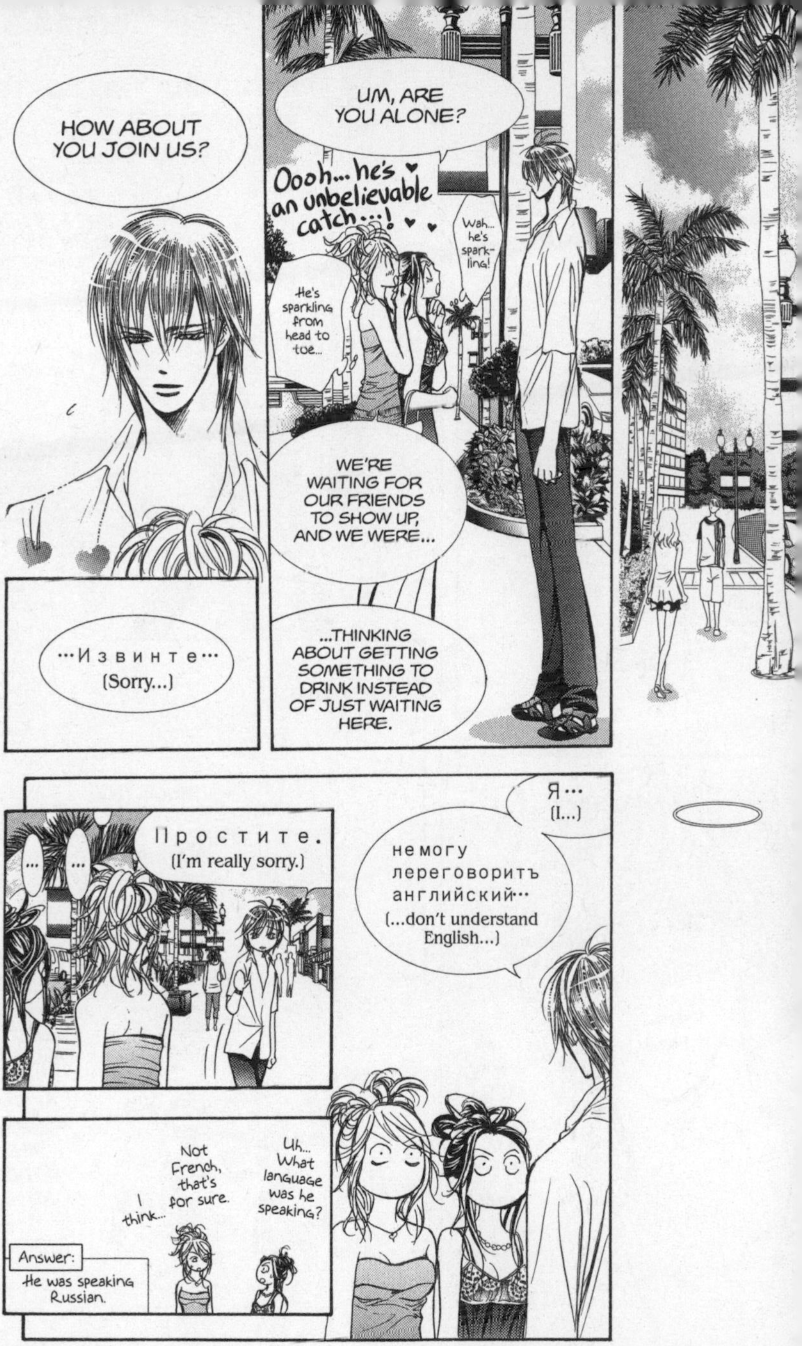
UM, ARE YOU ALONE?
Oooh... he's an unbelievable catch...!
Wah... he's sparkling!
He's sparkling from head to toe...
WE'RE WAITING FOR OUR FRIENDS TO SHOW UP, AND WE WERE...
...THINKING ABOUT GETTING SOMETHING TO DRINK INSTEAD OF JUST WAITING HERE.
HOW ABOUT YOU JOIN US?
...Извините...
(Sorry...)
Я...
(I...)
не могу лереговоритъ английский...
(...don't understand English...)
Простите.
(I'm really sorry.)
...
...
Uh... What language was he speaking?
Not French, that's for sure.
I think...
Answer:
He was speaking Russian.

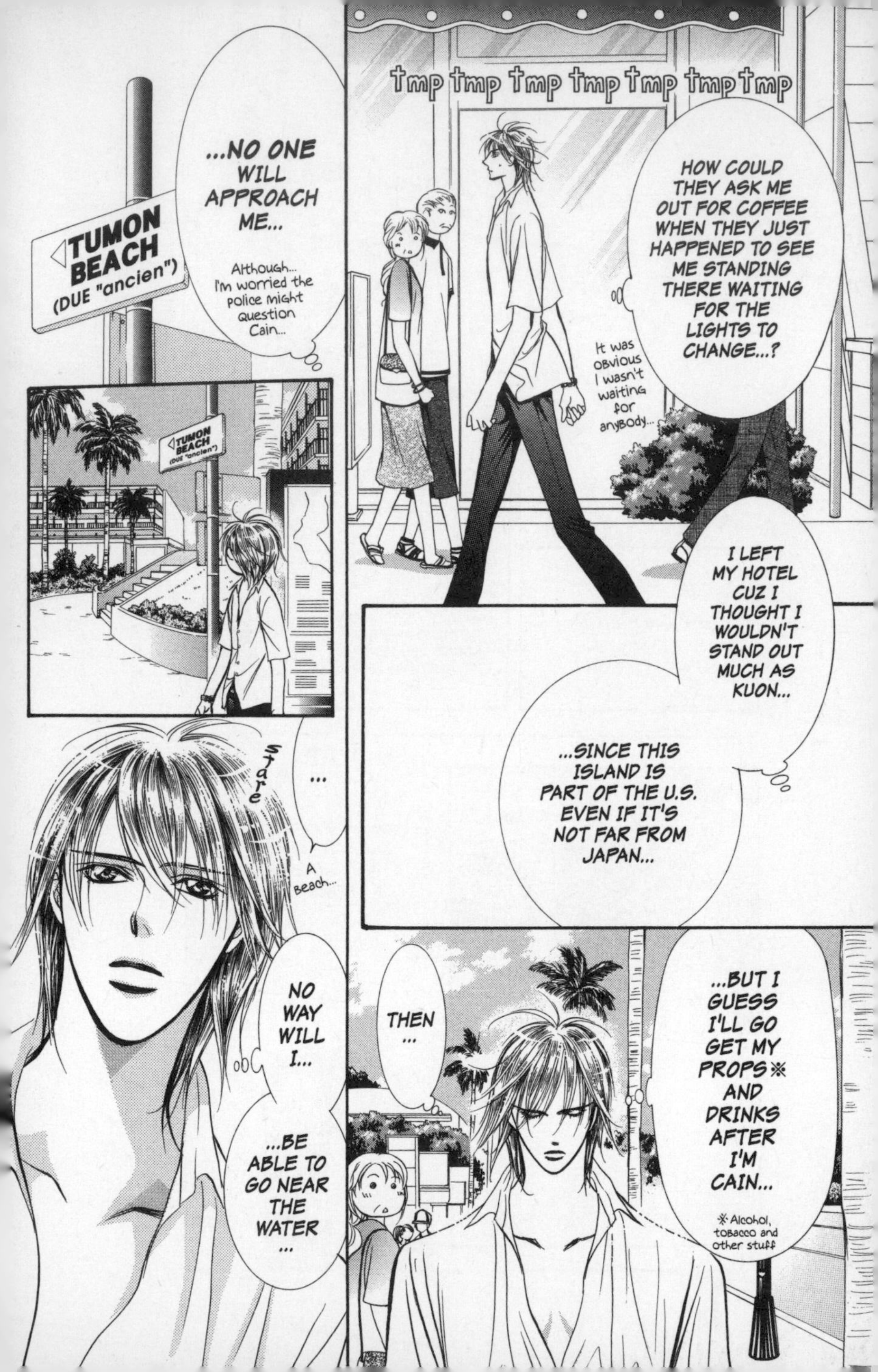
tmp tmp tmp tmp tmp tmp tmp
HOW COULD THEY ASK ME OUT FOR COFFEE WHEN THEY JUST HAPPENED TO SEE ME STANDING THERE WAITING FOR THE LIGHTS TO CHANGE...?
It was obvious I wasn't waiting for anybody...
I LEFT MY HOTEL CUZ I THOUGHT I WOULDN'T STAND OUT MUCH AS KUON...
...SINCE THIS ISLAND IS PART OF THE U.S. EVEN IF IT'S NOT FAR FROM JAPAN...
...BUT I GUESS I'LL GO GET MY PROPS※ AND DRINKS AFTER I'M CAIN...
※Alcohol, tobacco and other stuff
THEN...
...NO ONE WILL APPROACH ME...
Although... I'm worried the police might question Cain...
TUMON BEACH (DUE "ancien")
TUMON BEACH (DUE "ancien")
Stare
...
A Beach...
NO WAY WILL I...
...BE ABLE TO GO NEAR THE WATER...

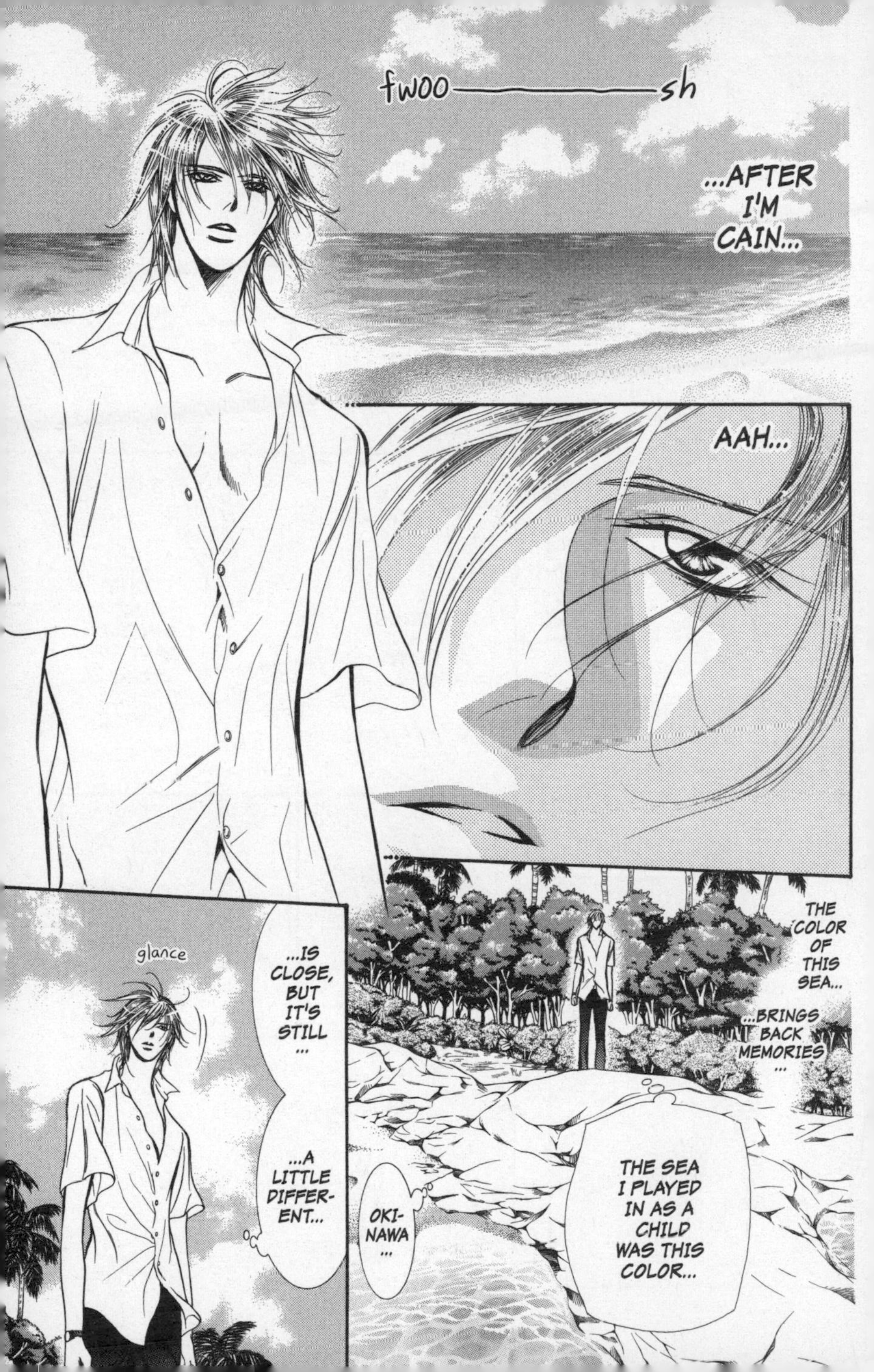
fwoo————sh
...AFTER I'M CAIN...
AAH...
THE COLOR OF THIS SEA...
...BRINGS BACK MEMORIES...
THE SEA I PLAYED IN AS A CHILD WAS THIS COLOR...
OKI-NAWA...
glance
...IS CLOSE, BUT IT'S STILL...
...A LITTLE DIFFER-ENT...

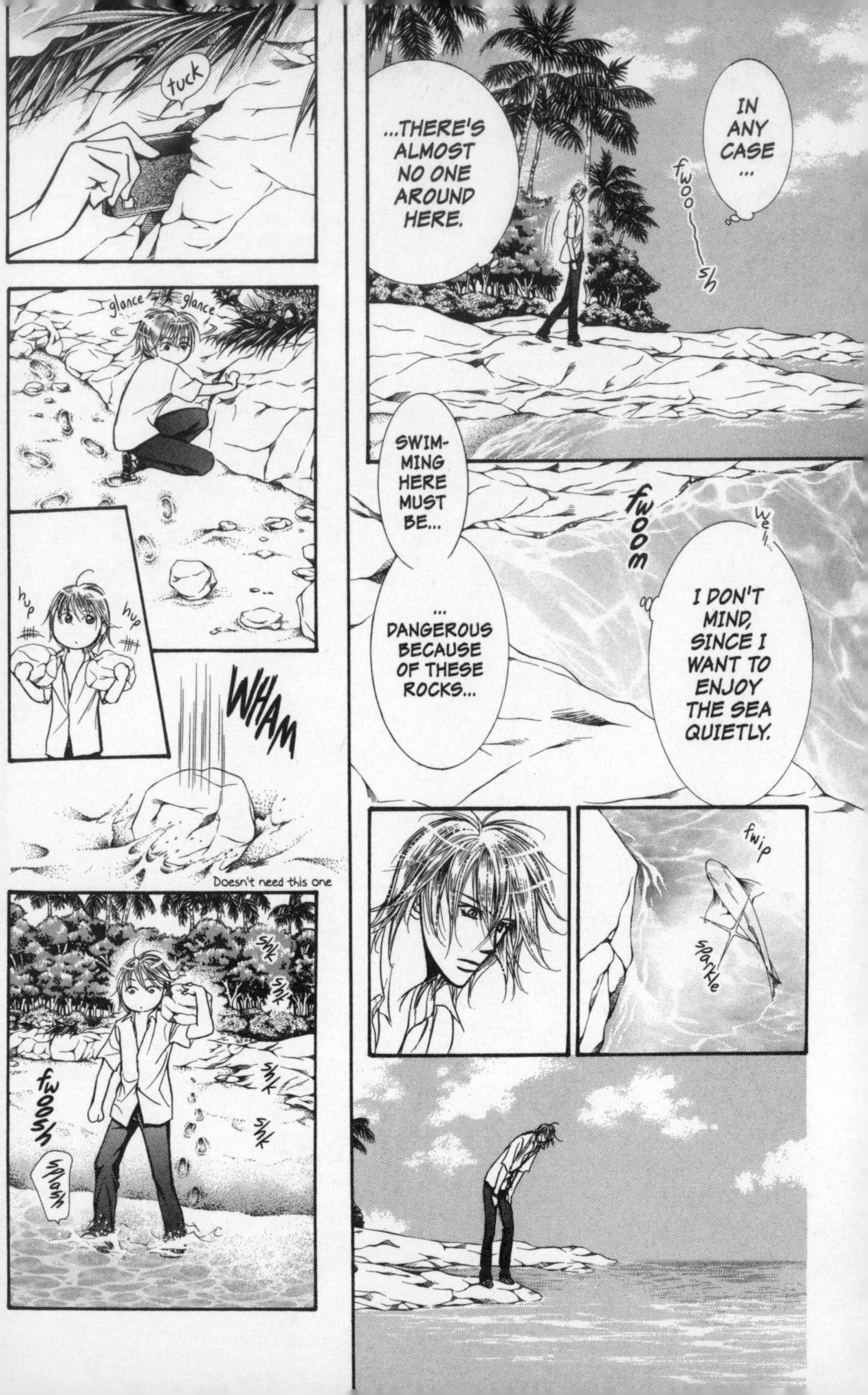
IN ANY CASE ...
fwoo—sh
...THERE'S ALMOST NO ONE AROUND HERE.
SWIMMING HERE MUST BE...
... DANGEROUS BECAUSE OF THESE ROCKS...
fwoom
well...
I DON'T MIND, SINCE I WANT TO ENJOY THE SEA QUIETLY.
fwip
sparkle
tuck
glance glance
hup hup
WHAM
Doesn't need this one
shk
shk
shk
shk
fwoosh
splash

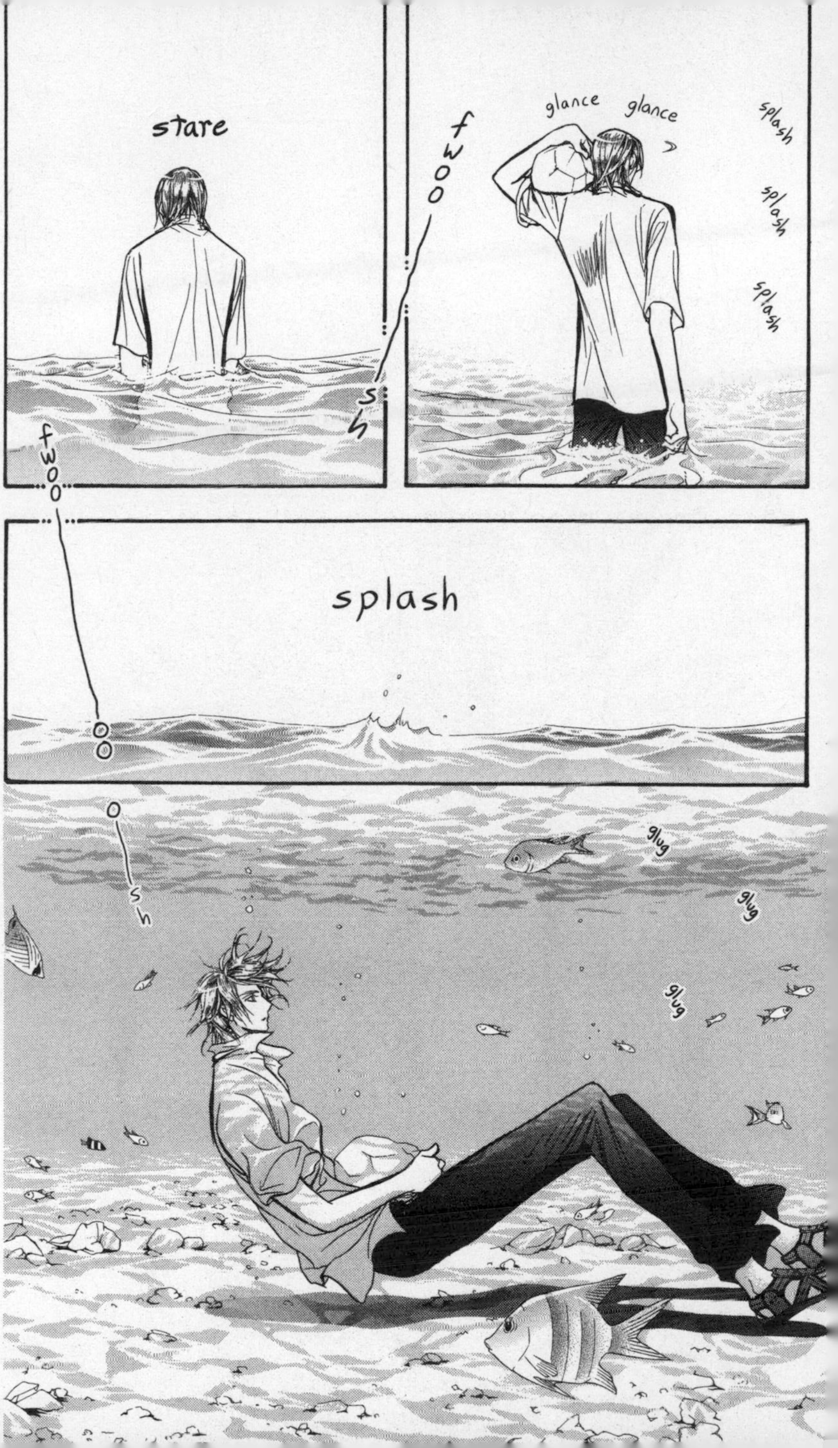
glance
glance
splash
splash
splash
fwoosh
stare
fwoo
splash
oosh
glug
glug
glug

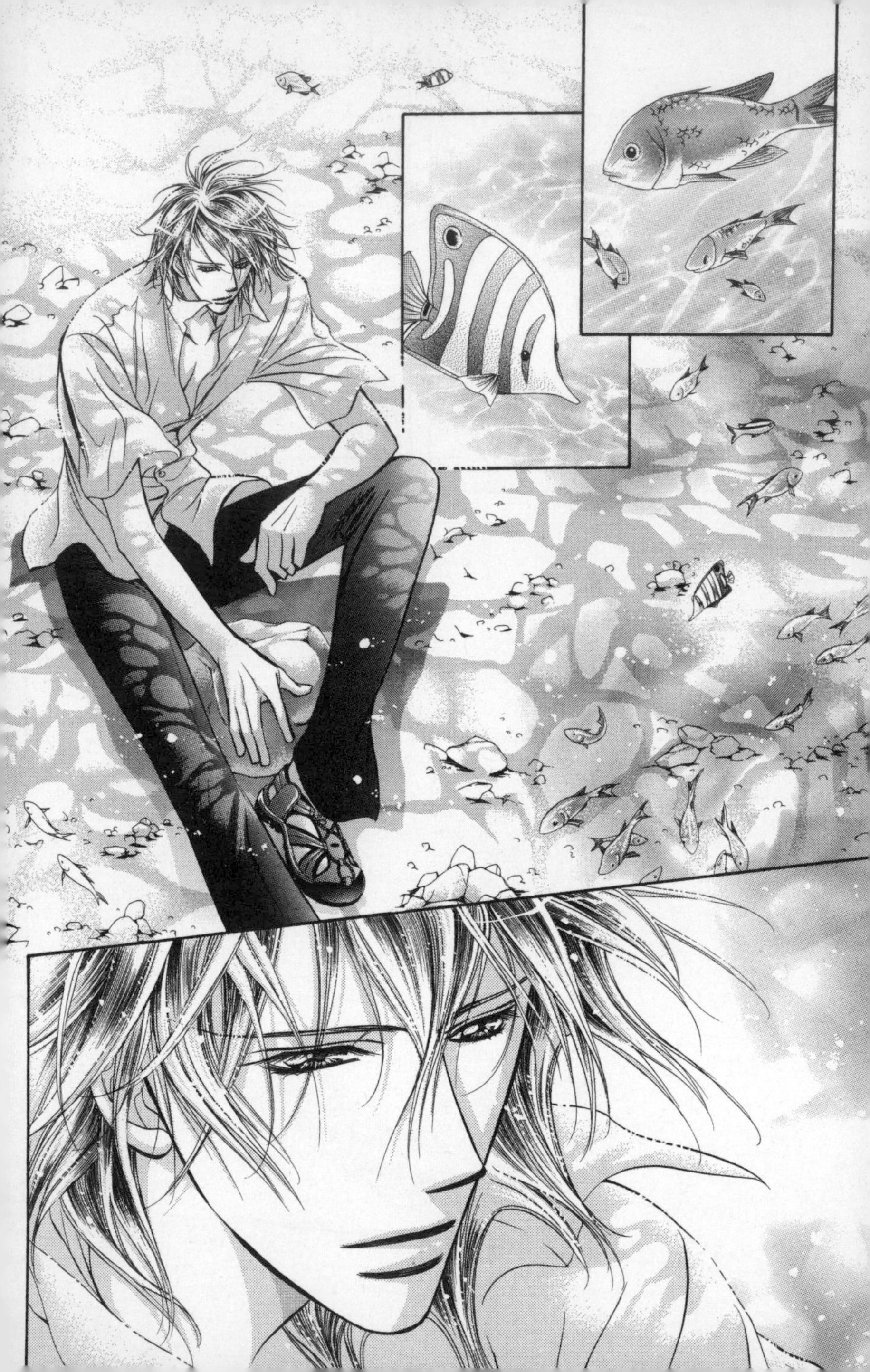

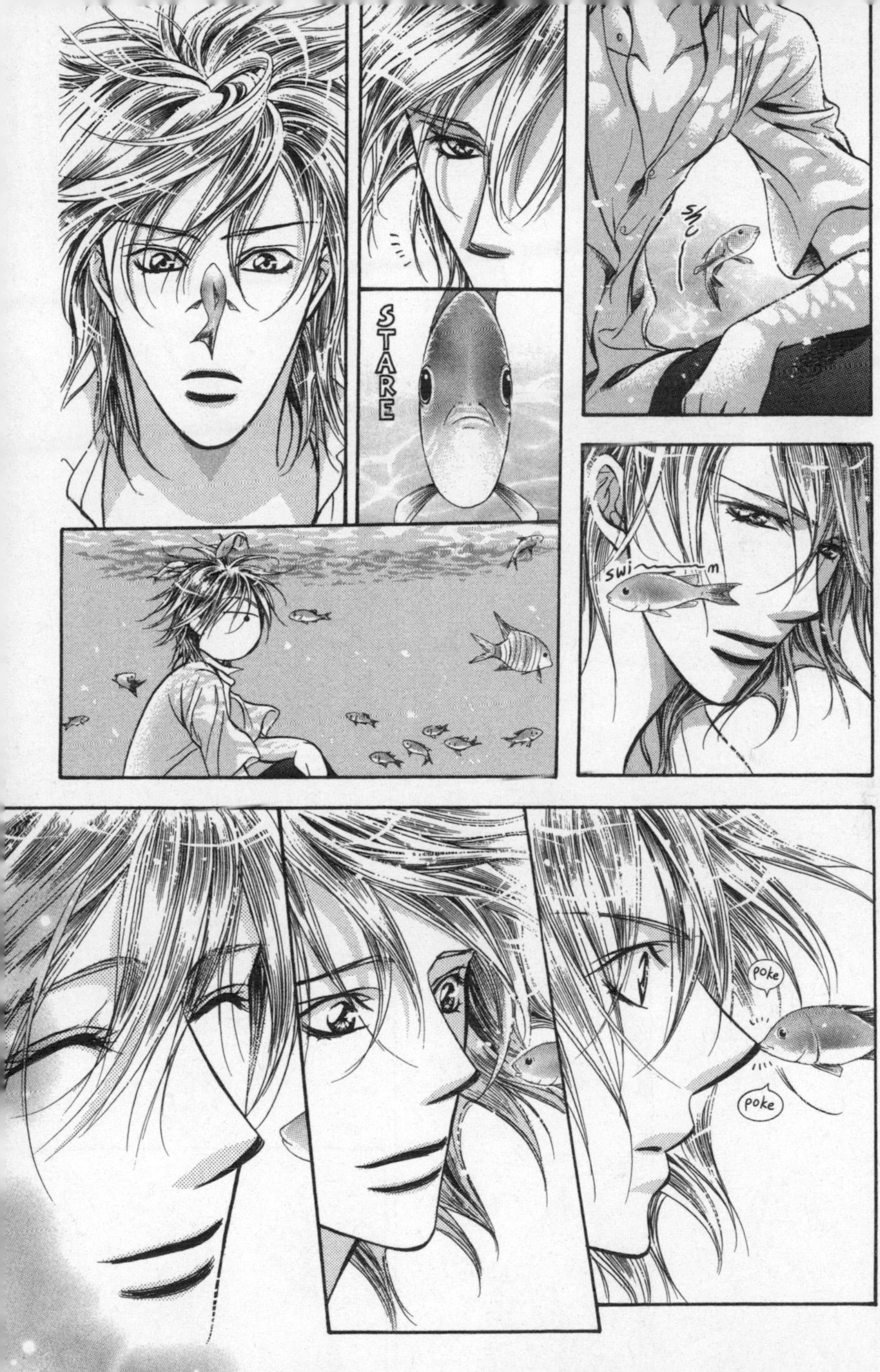
shu
STARE
swi~m
poke
poke

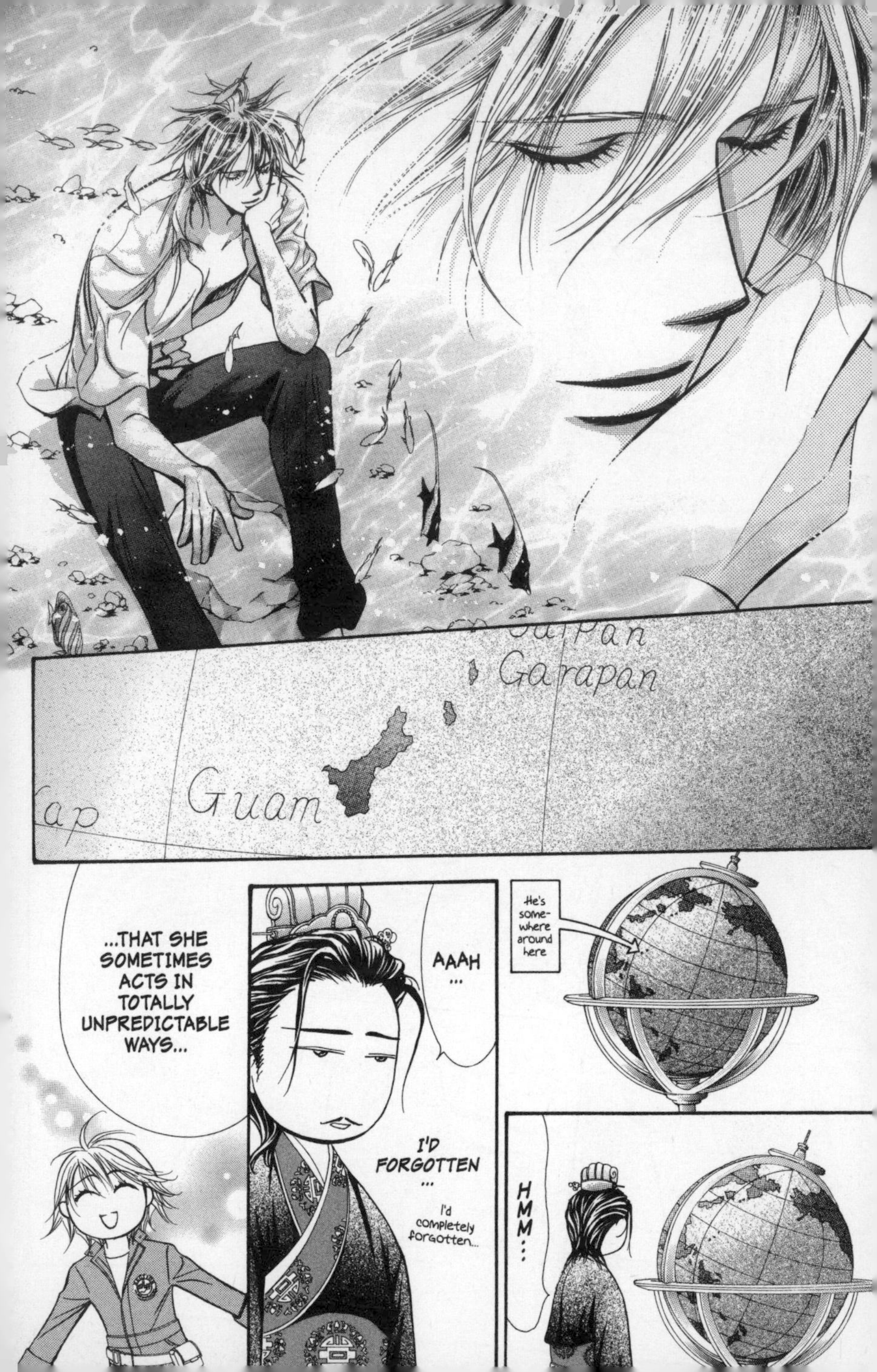
Garapan
Guam
He's some-where around here
HMM...
AAAH ...
I'D FORGOTTEN ...
I'd completely forgotten...
...THAT SHE SOMETIMES ACTS IN TOTALLY UNPREDICTABLE WAYS...

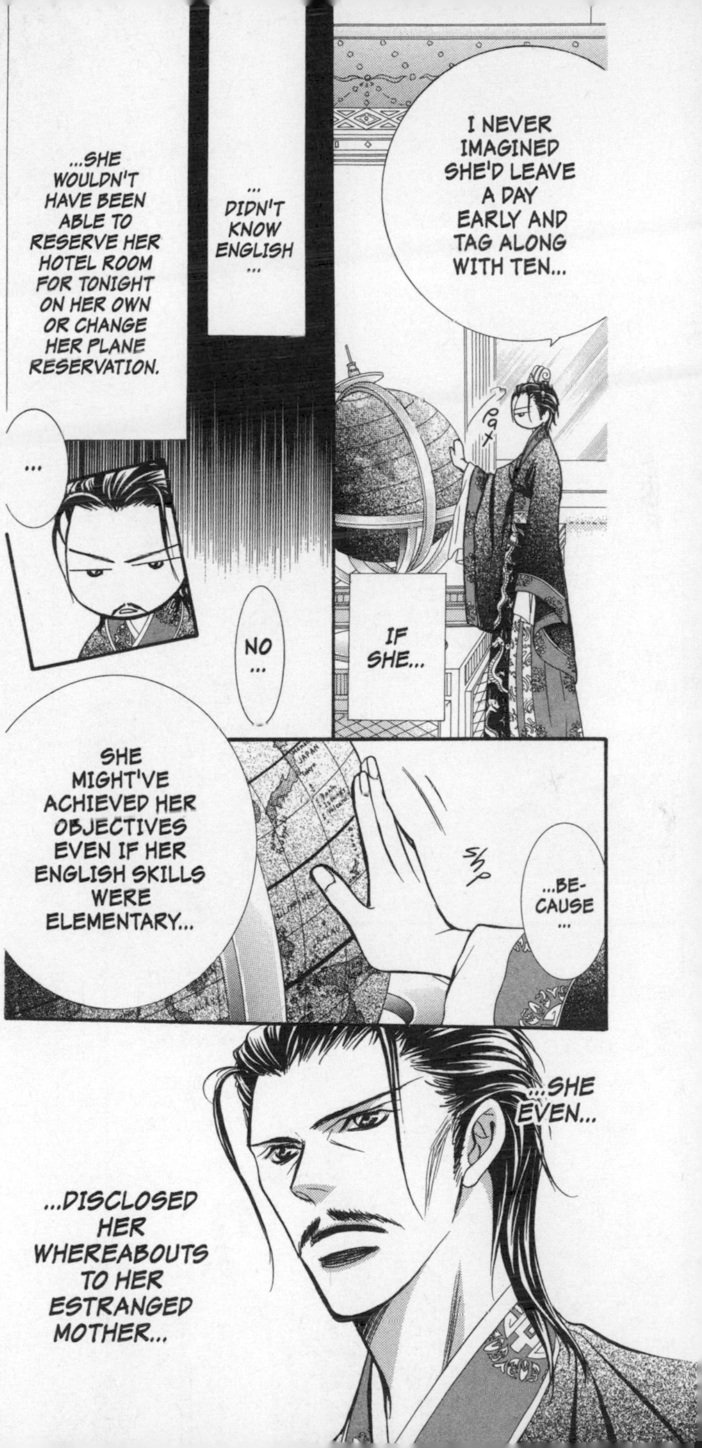
I NEVER IMAGINED SHE'D LEAVE A DAY EARLY AND TAG ALONG WITH TEN...
Pat
IF SHE...
...DIDN'T KNOW ENGLISH...
...SHE WOULDN'T HAVE BEEN ABLE TO RESERVE HER HOTEL ROOM FOR TONIGHT ON HER OWN OR CHANGE HER PLANE RESERVATION.
...
NO...
...BE-CAUSE...
SHE MIGHT'VE ACHIEVED HER OBJECTIVES EVEN IF HER ENGLISH SKILLS WERE ELEMENTARY...
...SHE EVEN...
...DISCLOSED HER WHEREABOUTS TO HER ESTRANGED MOTHER...

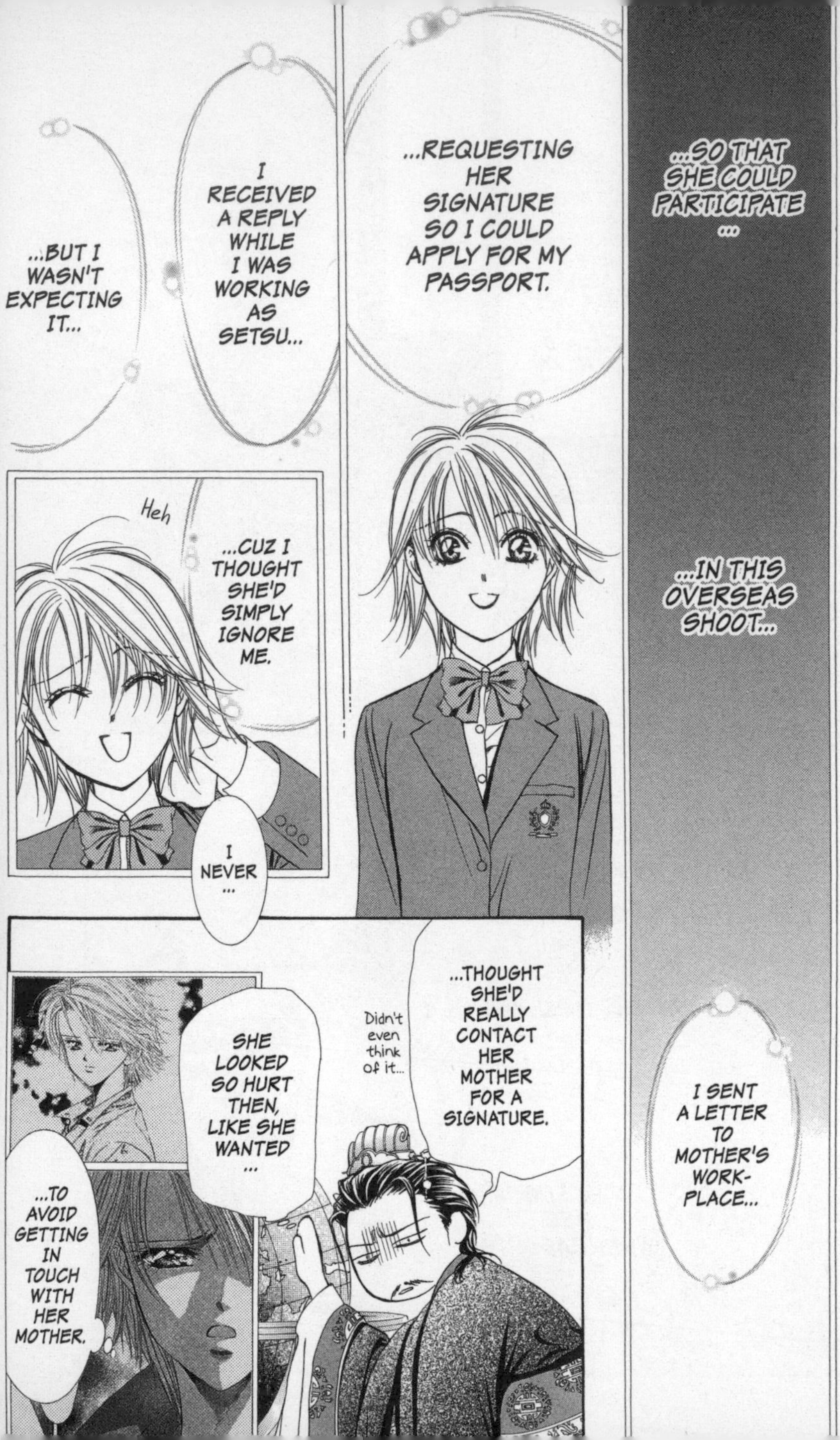
...SO THAT SHE COULD PARTICIPATE ...
...IN THIS OVERSEAS SHOOT...
I SENT A LETTER TO MOTHER'S WORKPLACE...
...REQUESTING HER SIGNATURE SO I COULD APPLY FOR MY PASSPORT.
I RECEIVED A REPLY WHILE I WAS WORKING AS SETSU...
...BUT I WASN'T EXPECTING IT...
Heh
...CUZ I THOUGHT SHE'D SIMPLY IGNORE ME.
I NEVER ...
...THOUGHT SHE'D REALLY CONTACT HER MOTHER FOR A SIGNATURE.
Didn't even think of it...
SHE LOOKED SO HURT THEN, LIKE SHE WANTED ...
...TO AVOID GETTING IN TOUCH WITH HER MOTHER.

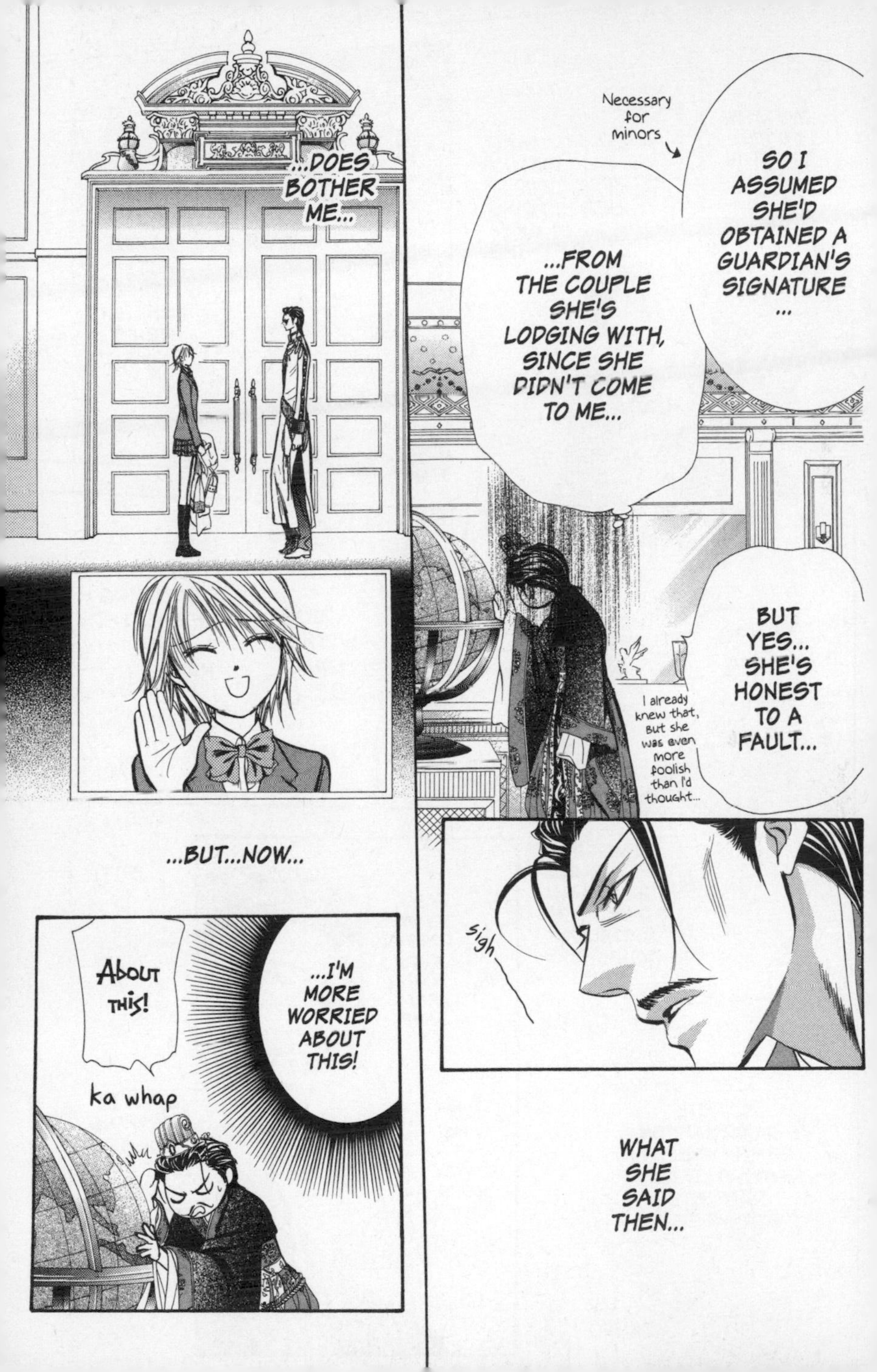
Necessary for minors
SO I ASSUMED SHE'D OBTAINED A GUARDIAN'S SIGNATURE ...
...FROM THE COUPLE SHE'S LODGING WITH, SINCE SHE DIDN'T COME TO ME...
BUT YES... SHE'S HONEST TO A FAULT...
I already knew that, but she was even more foolish than I'd thought...
sigh
WHAT SHE SAID THEN...
...DOES BOTHER ME...
...BUT...NOW...
...I'M MORE WORRIED ABOUT THIS!
About this!
ka whap

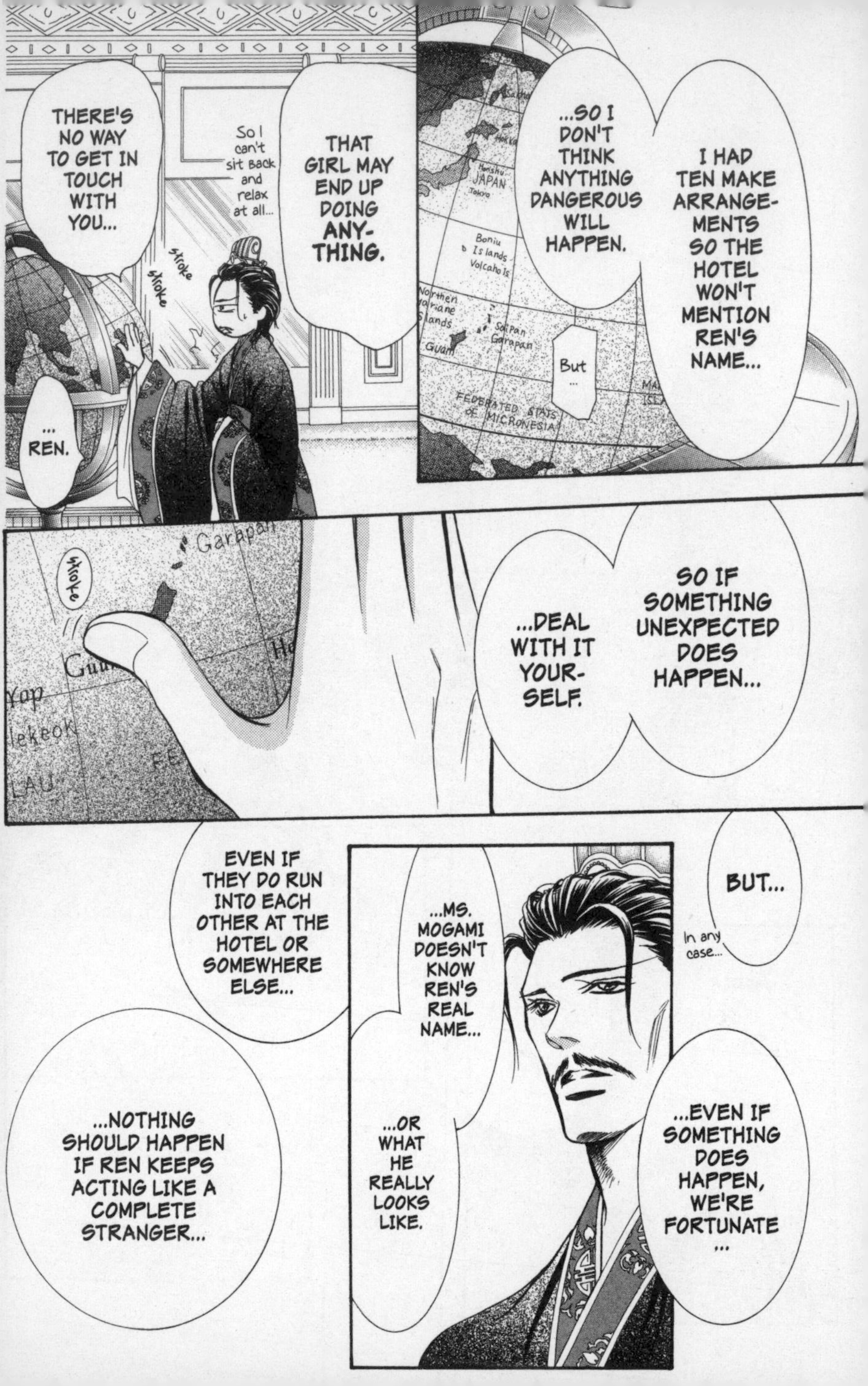
I HAD TEN MAKE ARRANGE-MENTS SO THE HOTEL WON'T MENTION REN'S NAME...
...SO I DON'T THINK ANYTHING DANGEROUS WILL HAPPEN.
But...
JAPAN
Honshu
Tokyo
Boniu Islands
Volcano Is
Northern Mariane Islands
Saipan
Garapan
Guam
FEDERATED STATS OF MICRONESIA
THAT GIRL MAY END UP DOING ANY-THING.
So I can't sit back and relax at all...
THERE'S NO WAY TO GET IN TOUCH WITH YOU...
stroke
stroke
... REN.
SO IF SOMETHING UNEXPECTED DOES HAPPEN...
...DEAL WITH IT YOUR-SELF.
Garapan
stroke
Guam
Yap
BUT...
In any case...
...MS. MOGAMI DOESN'T KNOW REN'S REAL NAME...
...OR WHAT HE REALLY LOOKS LIKE.
...EVEN IF SOMETHING DOES HAPPEN, WE'RE FORTUNATE...
EVEN IF THEY DO RUN INTO EACH OTHER AT THE HOTEL OR SOMEWHERE ELSE...
...NOTHING SHOULD HAPPEN IF REN KEEPS ACTING LIKE A COMPLETE STRANGER...

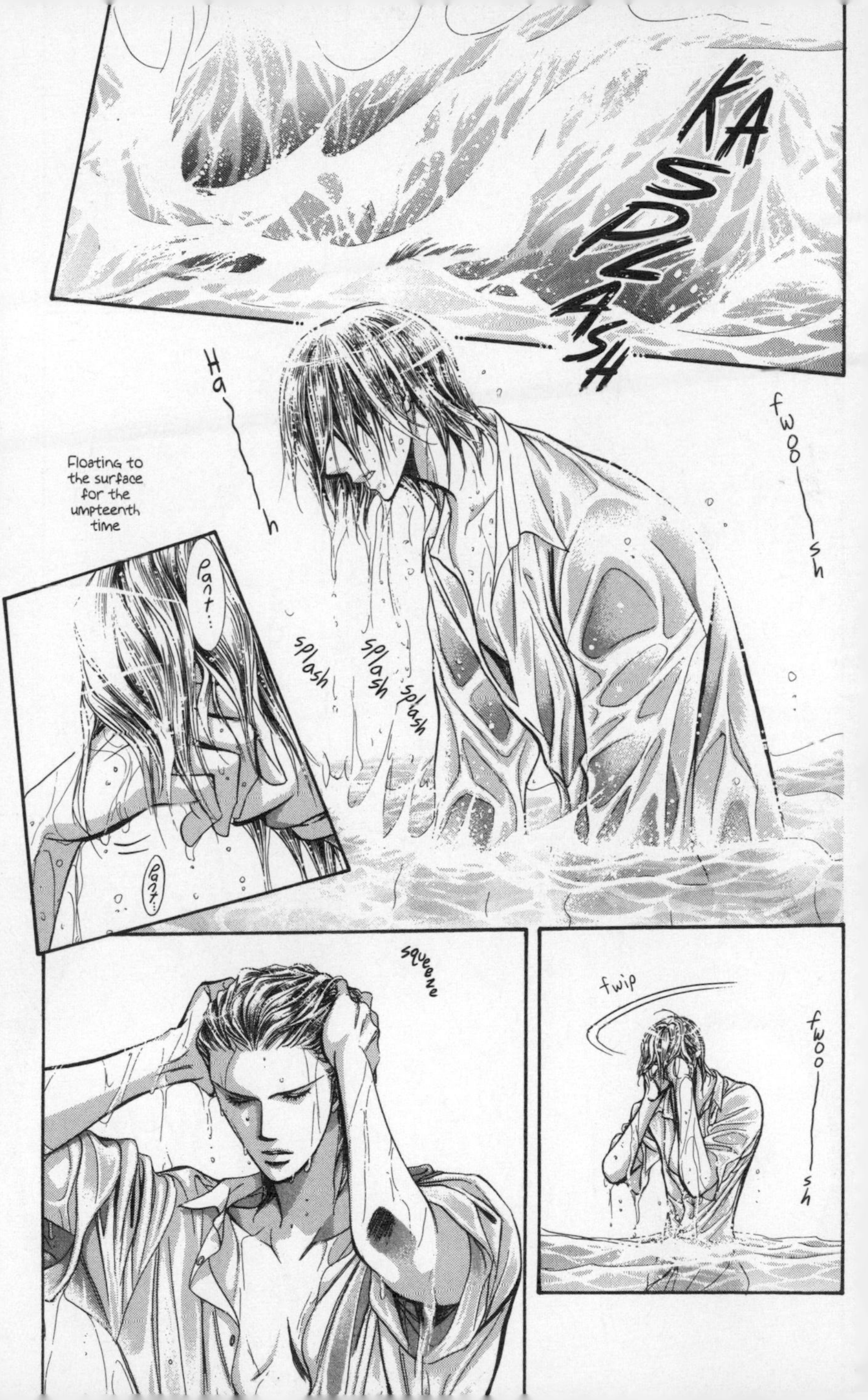
KASPLASH
fwoo——sh
Ha——h
Floating to the surface for the umpteenth time
splash
splash
splash
Pant...
Pant...
fwoo——sh
fwip
squeeze

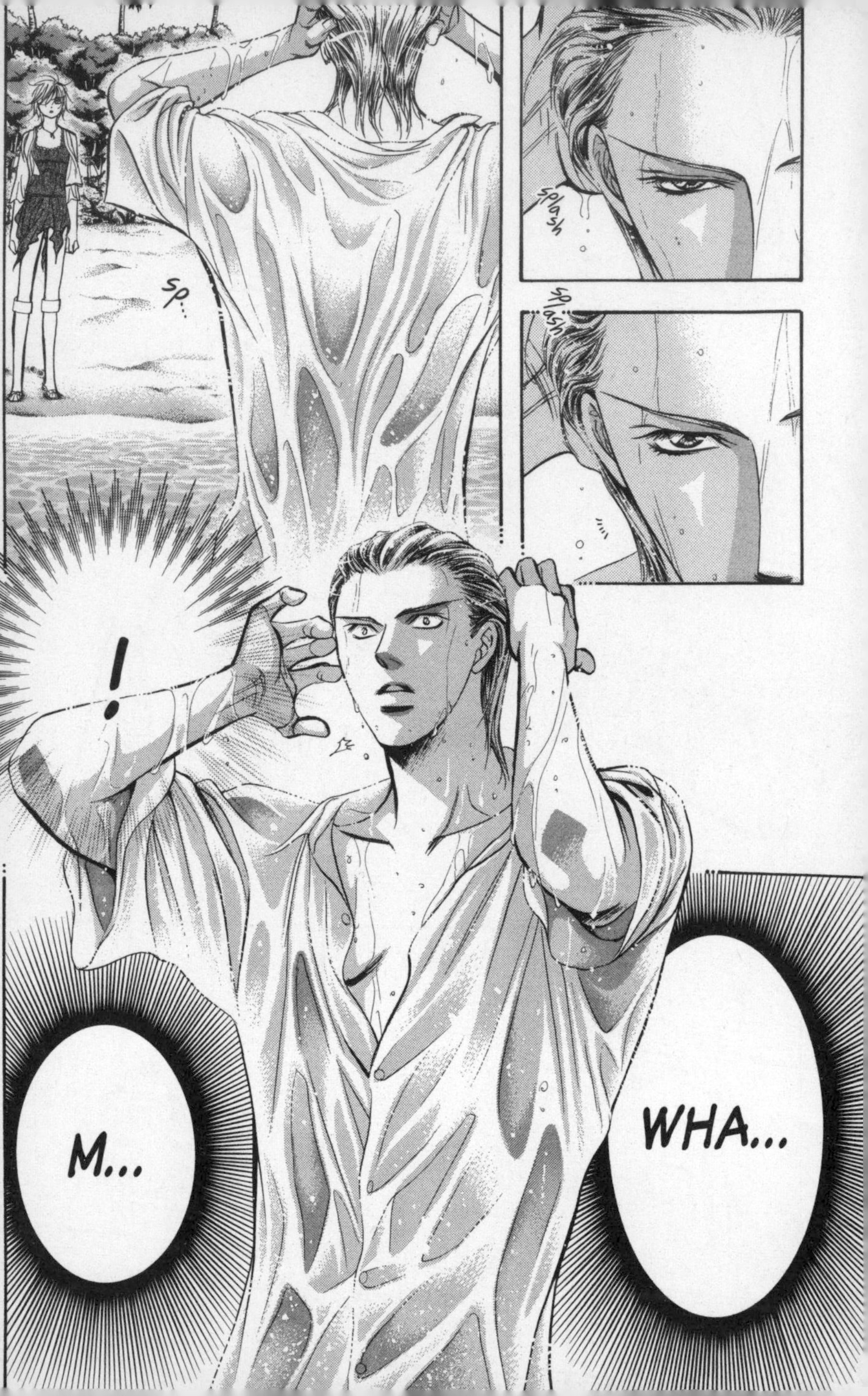
splash
splash
sp...
!
WHA...
M...

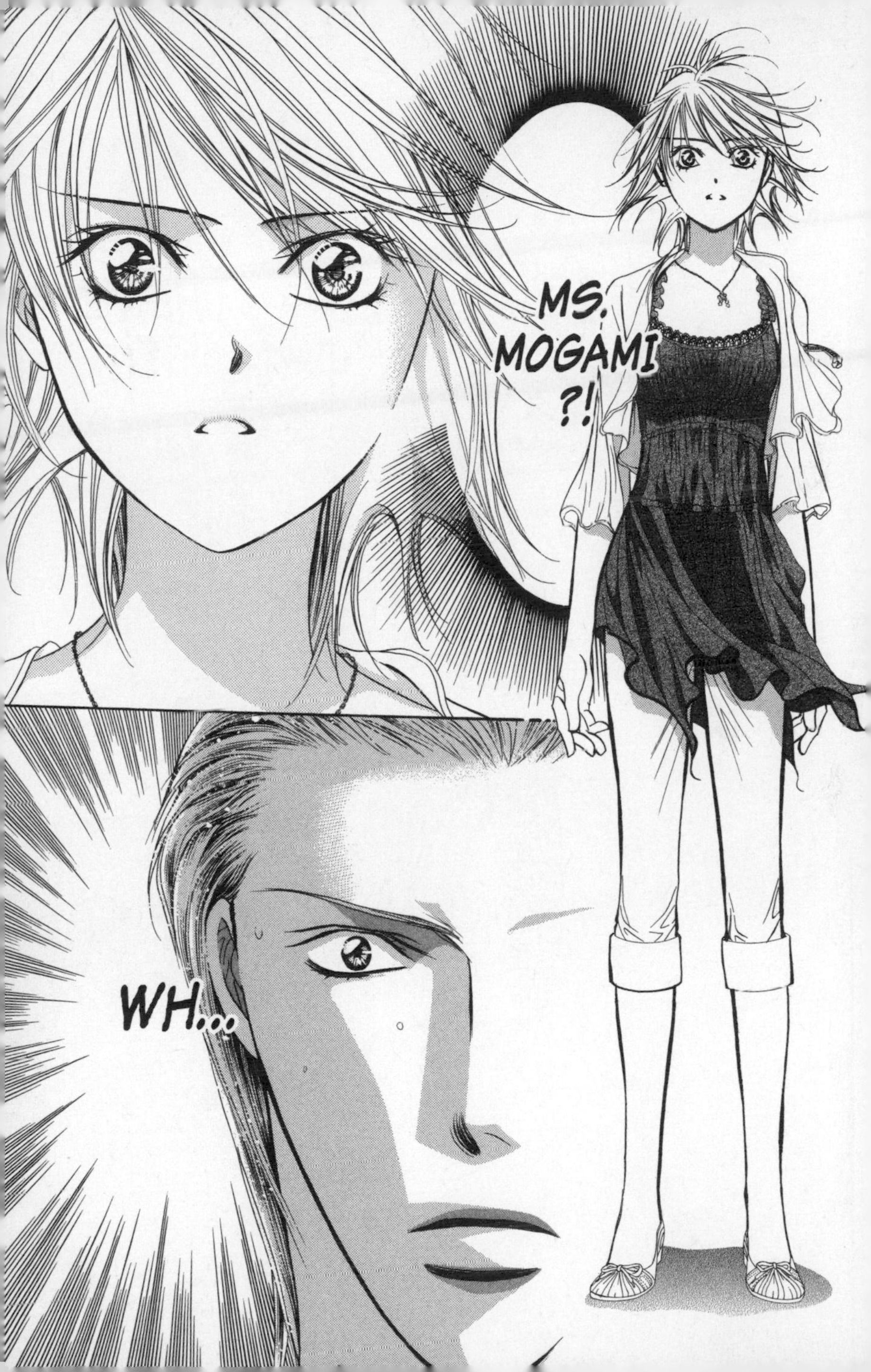
MS. MOGAMI ?!
WH...

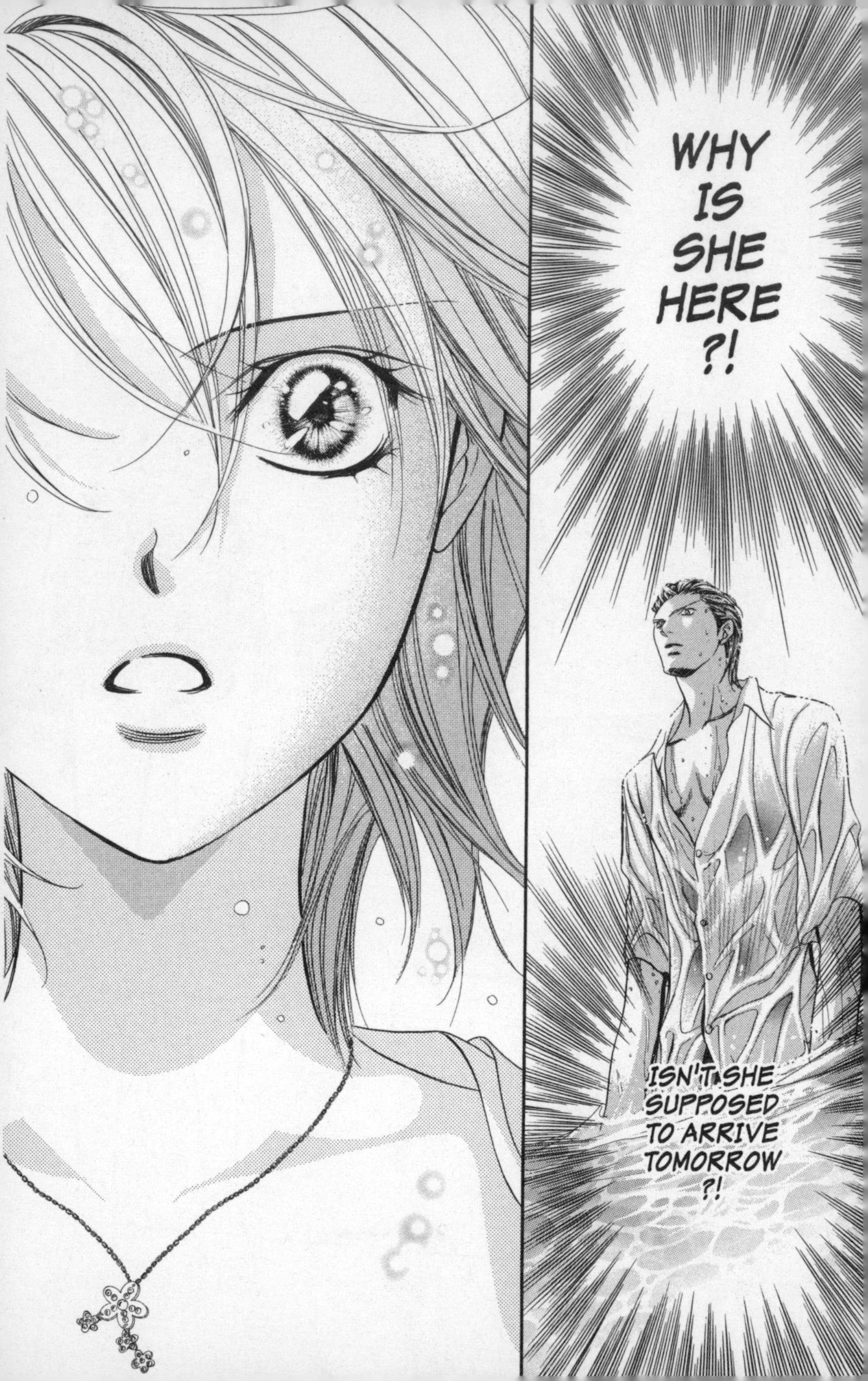
WHY IS SHE HERE ?!
ISN'T SHE SUPPOSED TO ARRIVE TOMORROW ?!

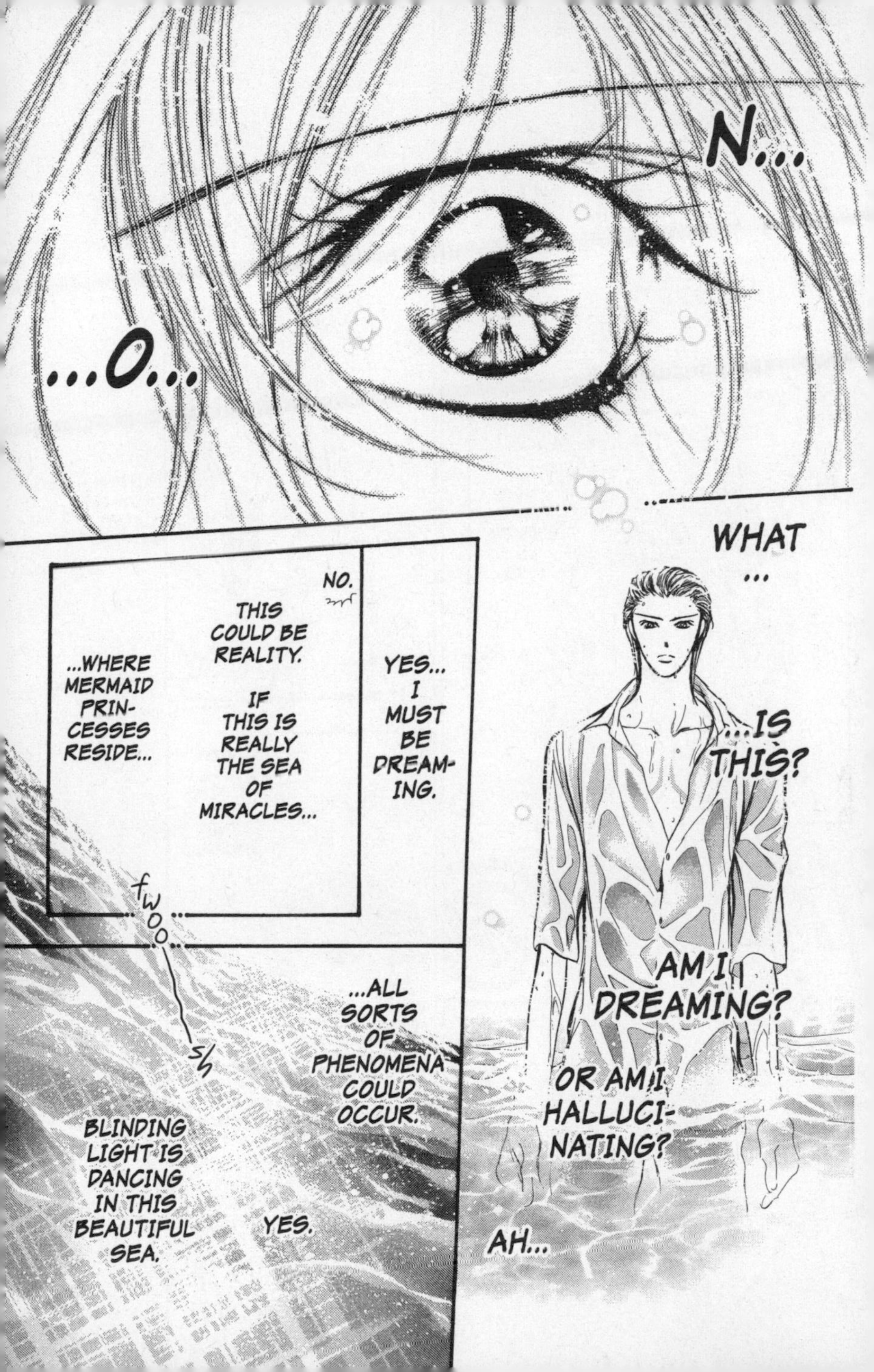
N...
...O...
WHAT ...
...IS THIS?
AM I DREAMING?
OR AM I HALLUCI-NATING?
AH...
YES... I MUST BE DREAM-ING.
NO.
THIS COULD BE REALITY.
IF THIS IS REALLY THE SEA OF MIRACLES...
...WHERE MERMAID PRIN-CESSES RESIDE...
FWOOO—SH
...ALL SORTS OF PHENOMENA COULD OCCUR.
YES.
BLINDING LIGHT IS DANCING IN THIS BEAUTIFUL SEA.

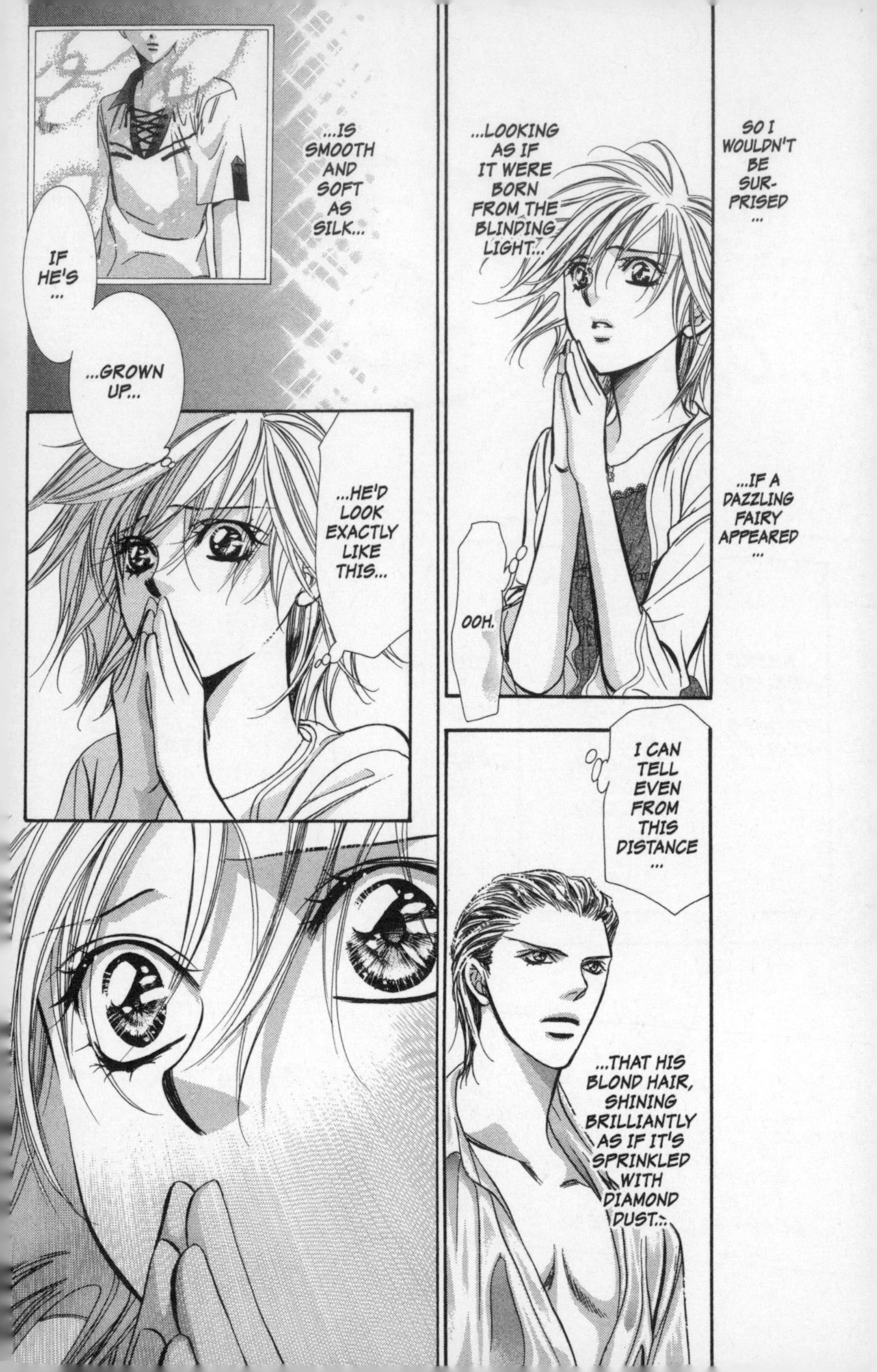
SO I WOULDN'T BE SUR-PRISED...
...IF A DAZZLING FAIRY APPEARED...
...LOOKING AS IF IT WERE BORN FROM THE BLINDING LIGHT...
OOH.
I CAN TELL EVEN FROM THIS DISTANCE...
...THAT HIS BLOND HAIR, SHINING BRILLIANTLY AS IF IT'S SPRINKLED WITH DIAMOND DUST...
...IS SMOOTH AND SOFT AS SILK...
IF HE'S...
...GROWN UP...
...HE'D LOOK EXACTLY LIKE THIS...

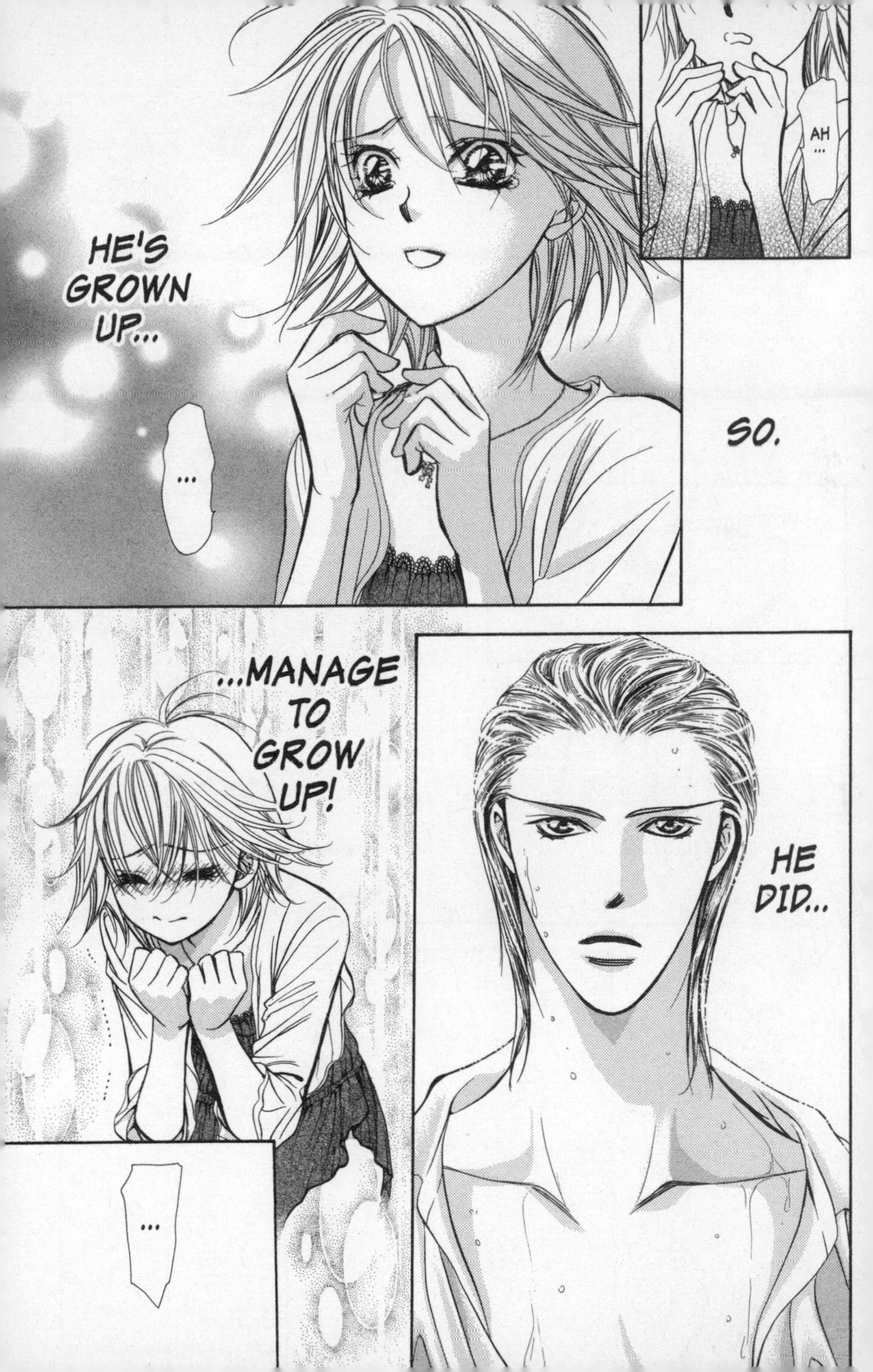
AH ...
HE'S GROWN UP...
...
SO.
HE DID...
...MANAGE TO GROW UP!
...

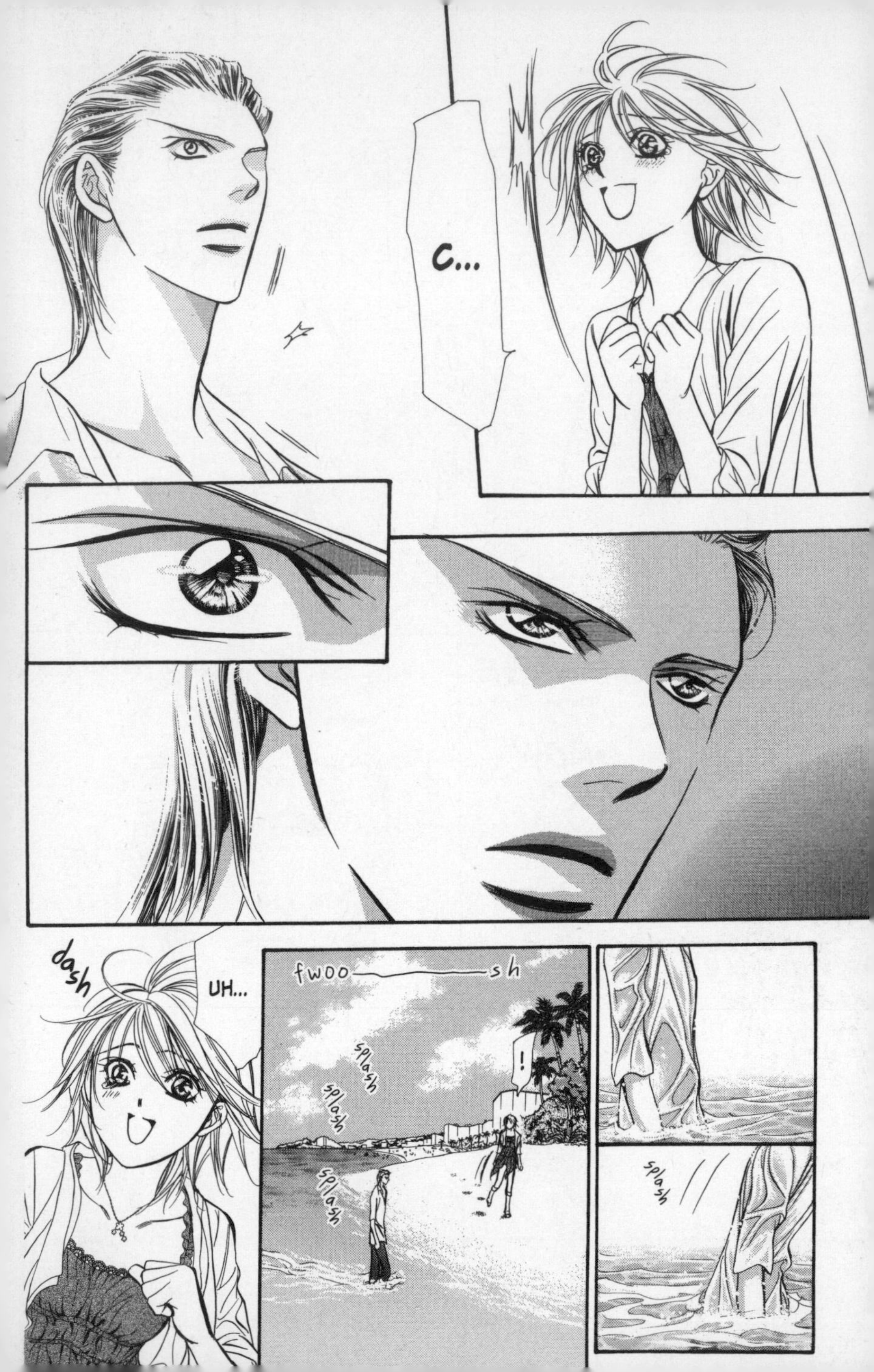
C...
UH...
dash
fwoo———————sh
!
splash
splash
splash
splash

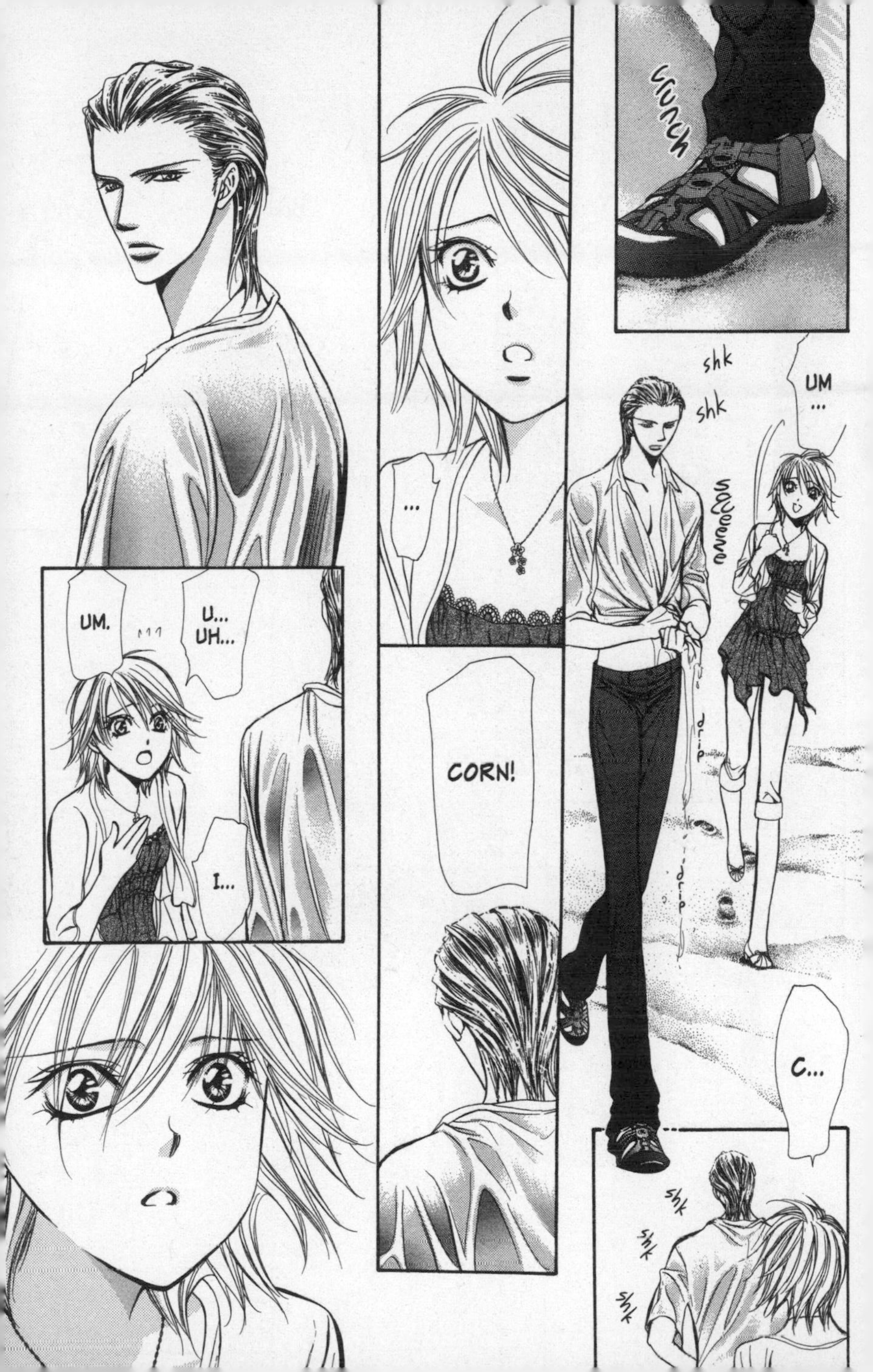
crunch
shk
shk
UM ...
squeeze
drip
drip
C...
shk
shk
shk
...
CORN!
UM.
U... UH...
I...

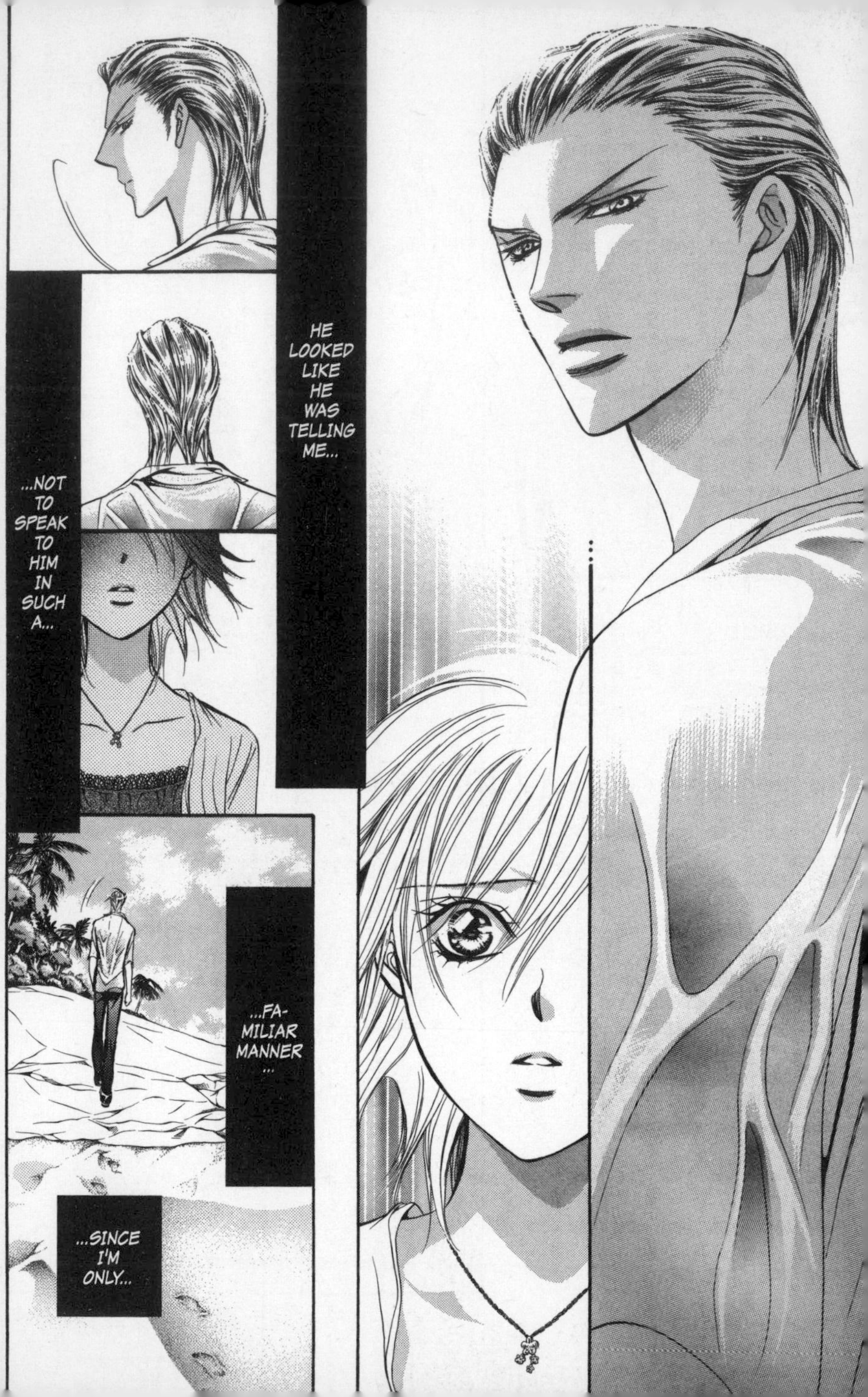
HE LOOKED LIKE HE WAS TELLING ME...
...NOT TO SPEAK TO HIM IN SUCH A...
...FA-MILIAR MANNER ...
...SINCE I'M ONLY...

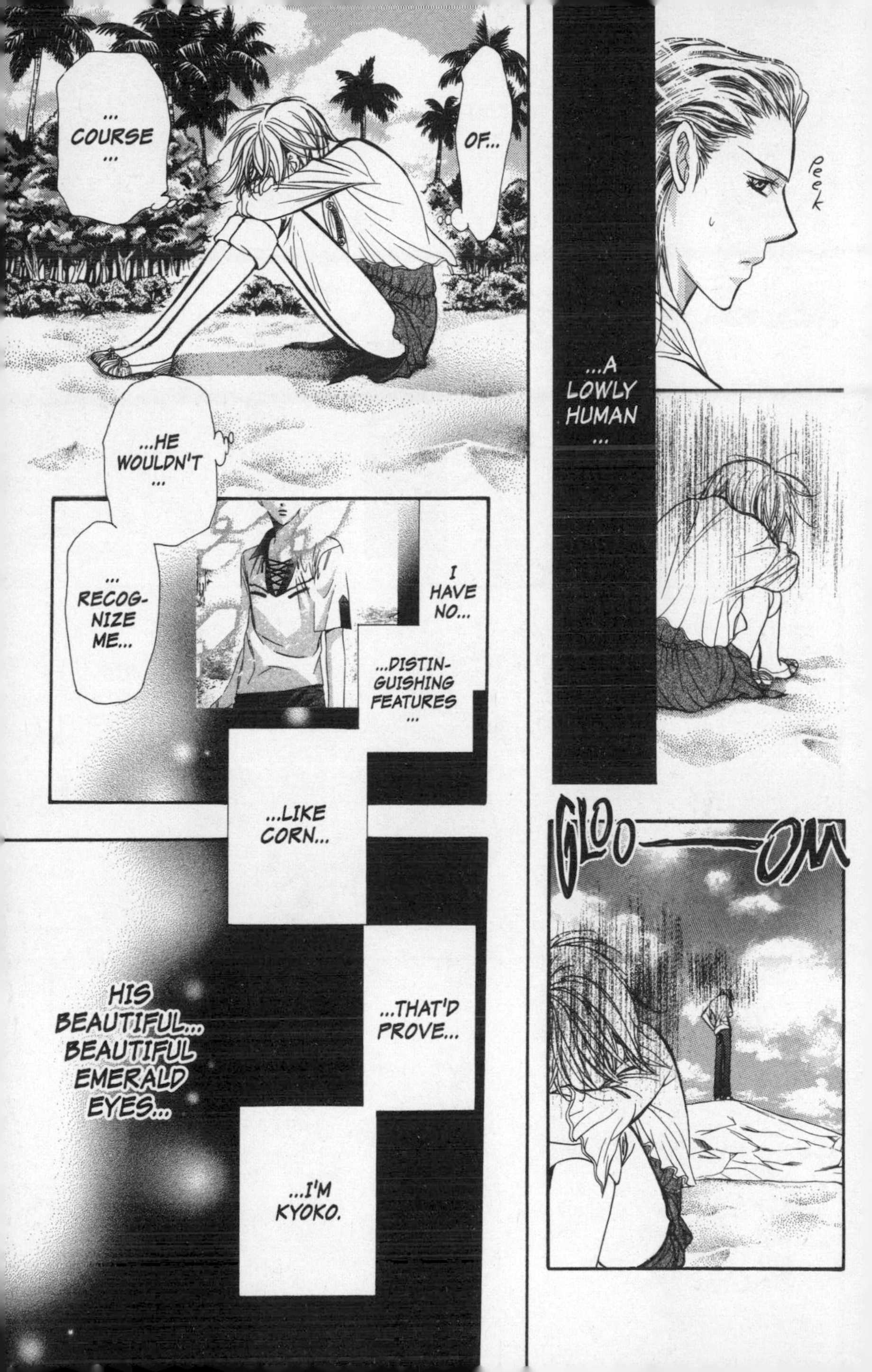
Peek
...A LOWLY HUMAN...
GLOO——OM
OF...
...COURSE...
...HE WOULDN'T...
...RECOG-NIZE ME...
I HAVE NO...
...DISTIN-GUISHING FEATURES...
...LIKE CORN...
...THAT'D PROVE...
...I'M KYOKO.
HIS BEAUTIFUL... BEAUTIFUL EMERALD EYES...

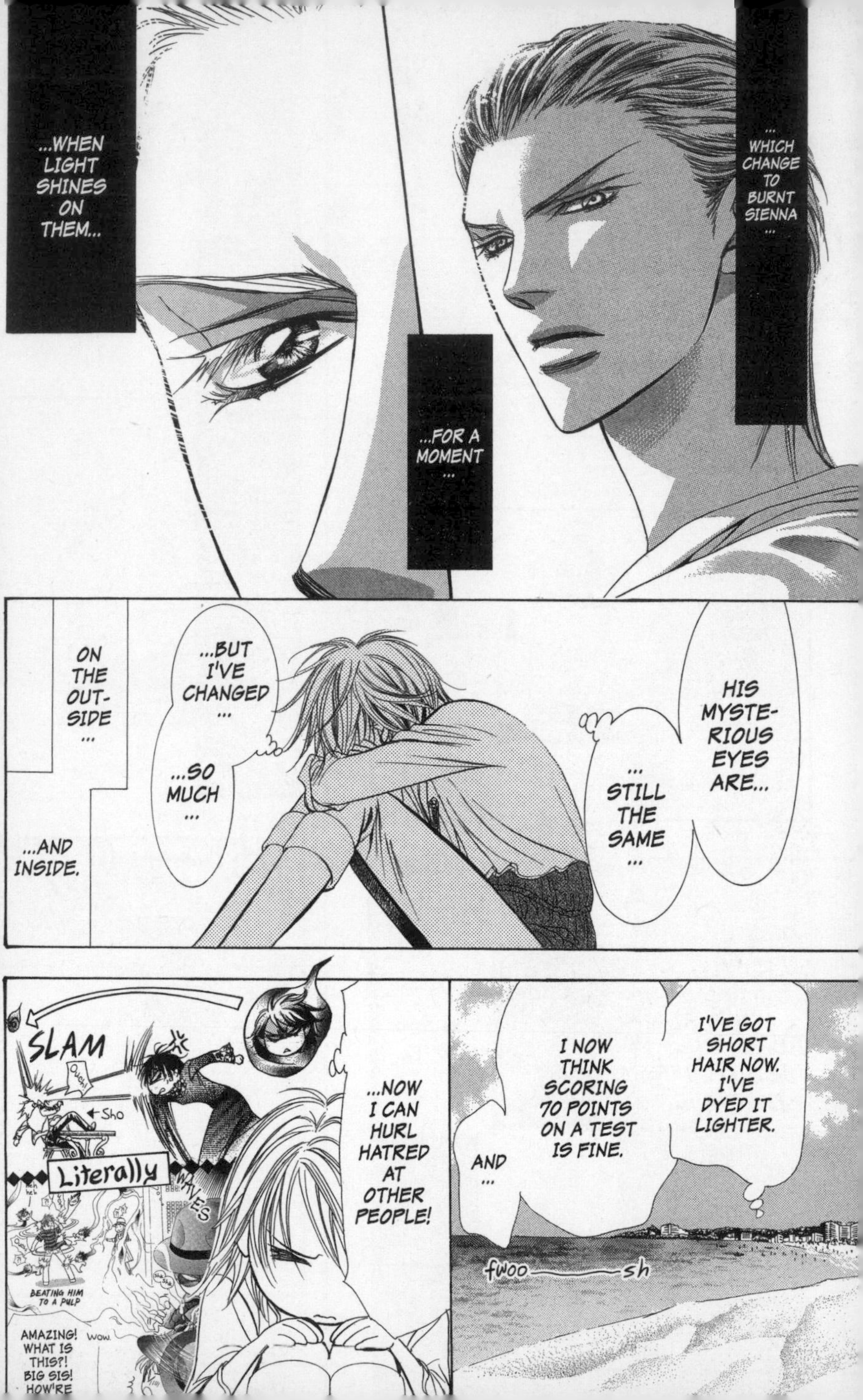
...WHICH CHANGE TO BURNT SIENNA...
...FOR A MOMENT...
...WHEN LIGHT SHINES ON THEM...
HIS MYSTERIOUS EYES ARE...
...STILL THE SAME...
...BUT I'VE CHANGED...
...SO MUCH...
ON THE OUTSIDE...
...AND INSIDE.
I'VE GOT SHORT HAIR NOW. I'VE DYED IT LIGHTER.
I NOW THINK SCORING 70 POINTS ON A TEST IS FINE.
AND...
fwoo——sh
...NOW I CAN HURL HATRED AT OTHER PEOPLE!
SLAM
Ouch!
Sho
Literally
WAVES
BEATING HIM TO A PULP
AMAZING! WHAT IS THIS?! BIG SIS! HOW'RE
Wow.

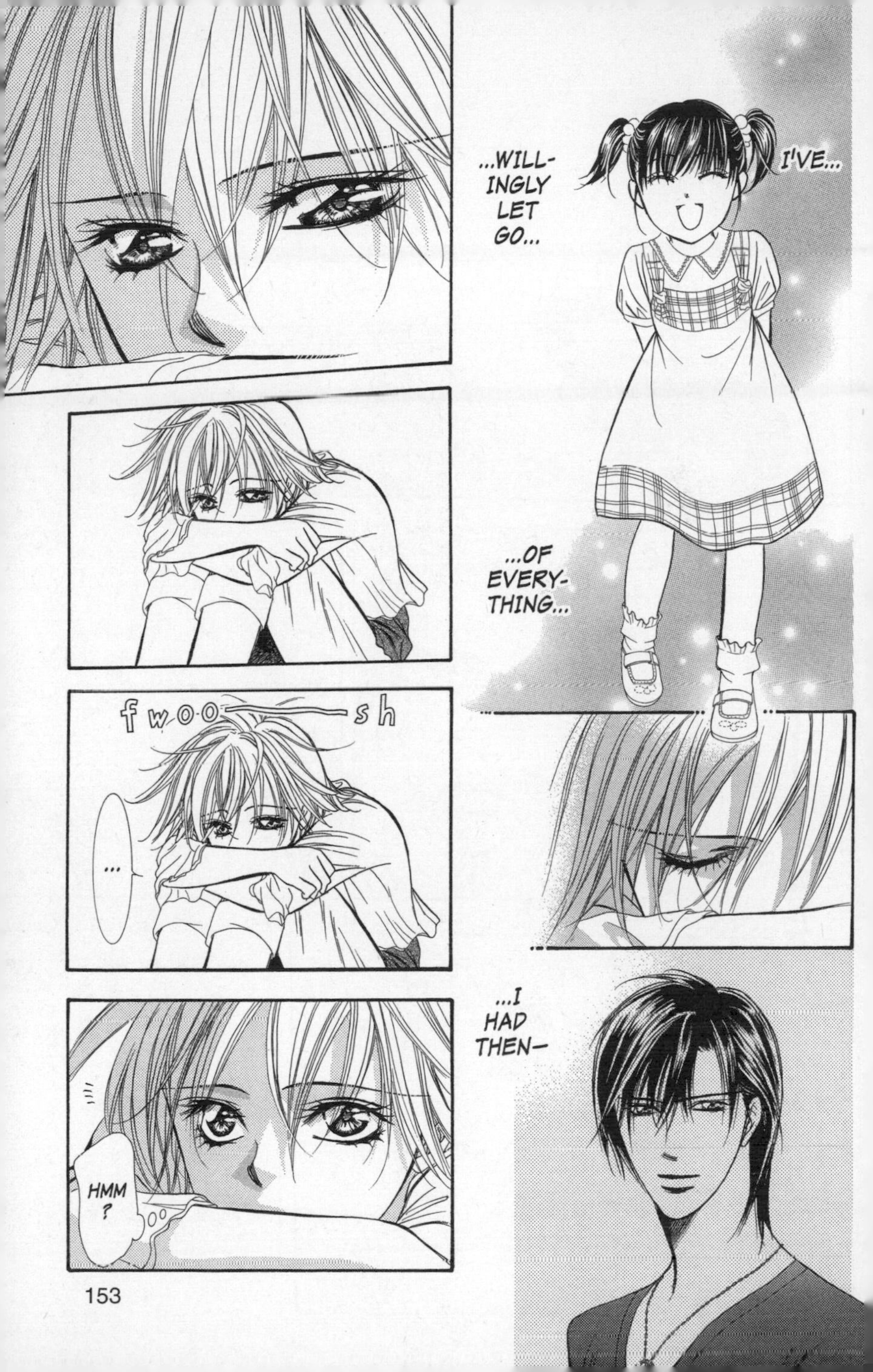
I'VE...
...WILLINGLY LET GO...
...OF EVERYTHING...
...I HAD THEN—
fwoo—sh
...
HMM?

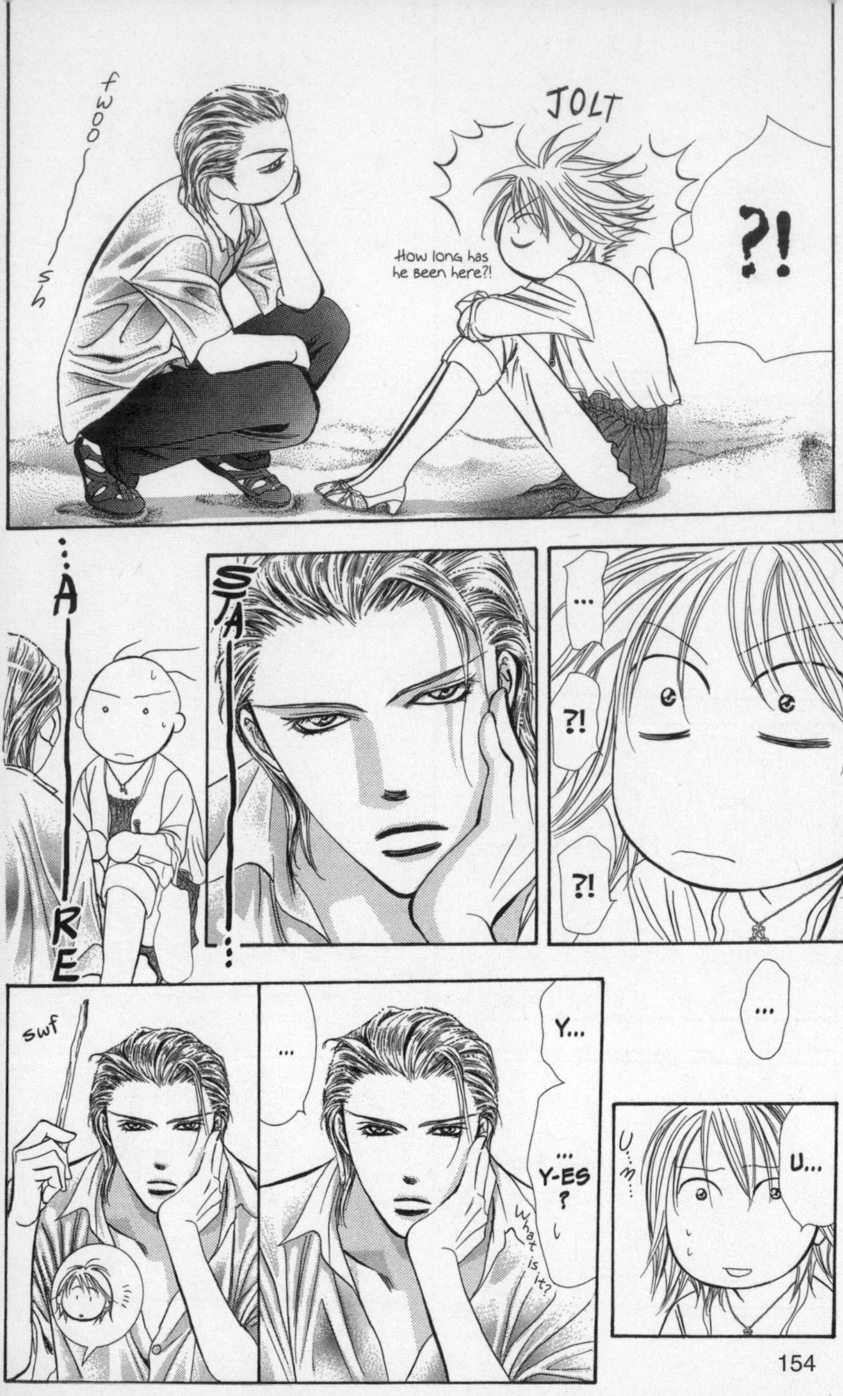
?!
JOLT
How long has he been here?!
fwoo—sh
...
?!
?!
STA—...
...A—RE
...
U...
U...m...
Y...
...Y-ES?
What is it?
...
swf

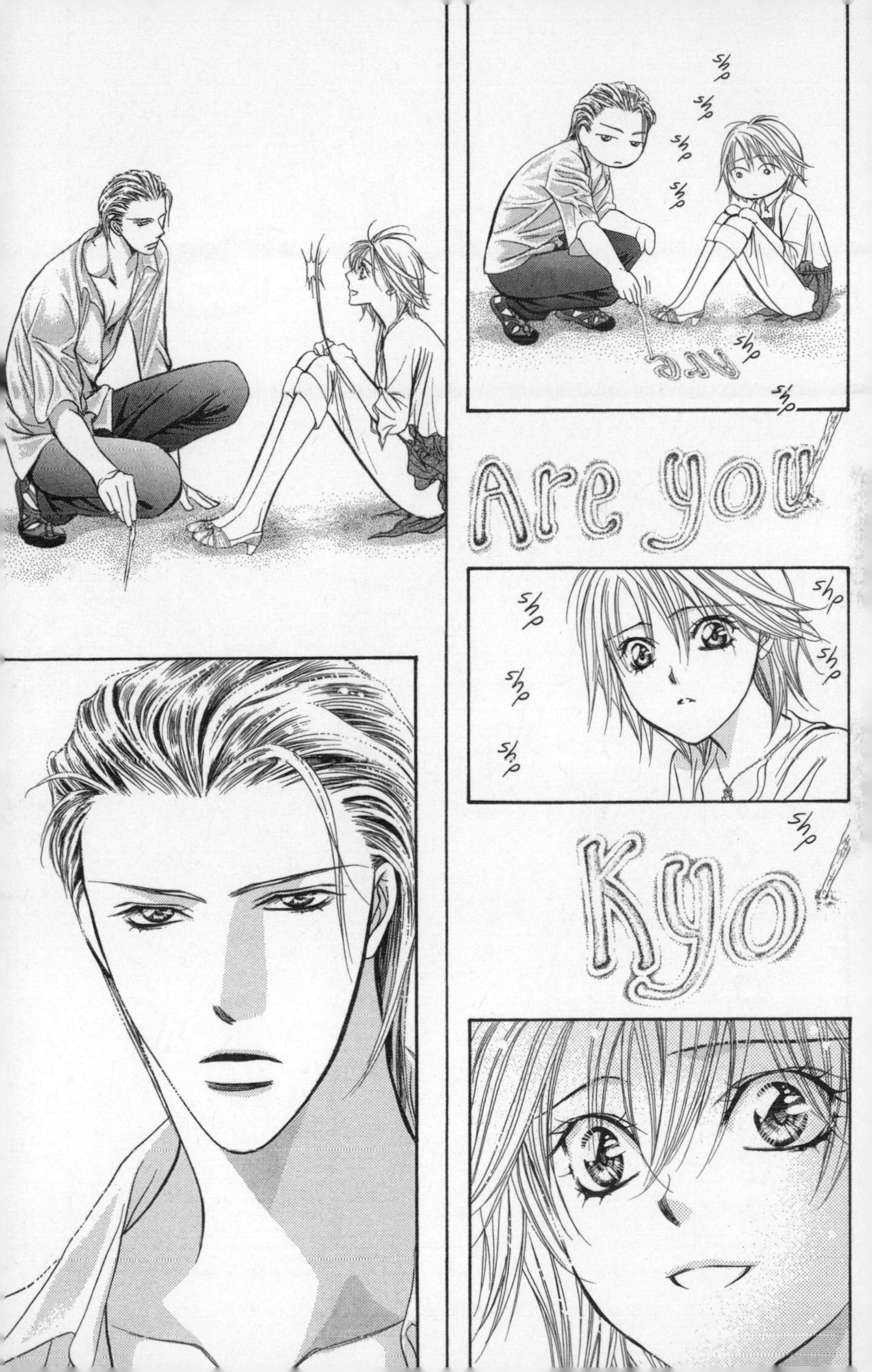
shp
shp
shp
shp
are
shp
shp
Are you
shp
shp
shp
shp
shp
shp
Kyo

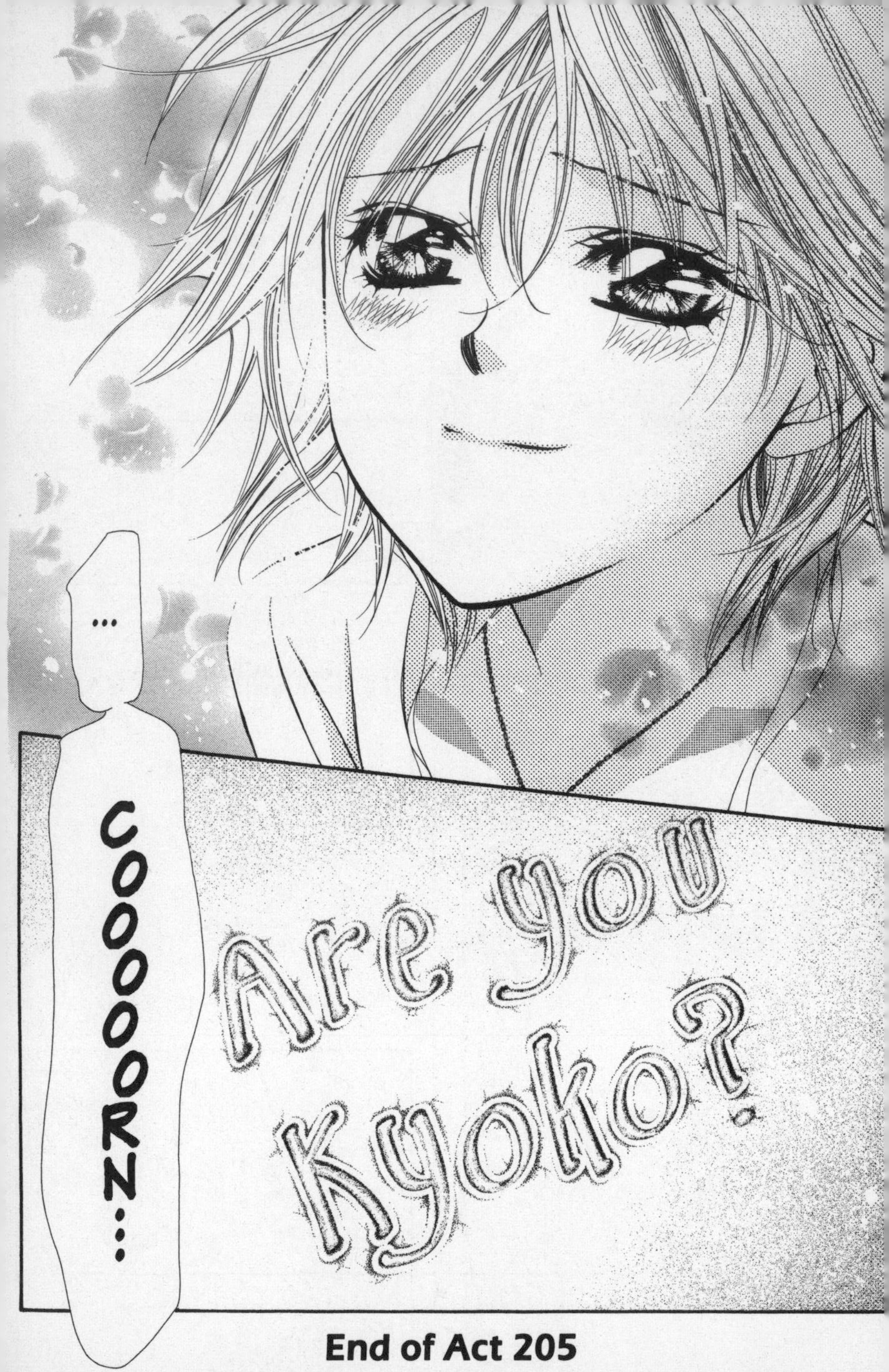
... COOOOOORN...
Are you Kyoko?
End of Act 205

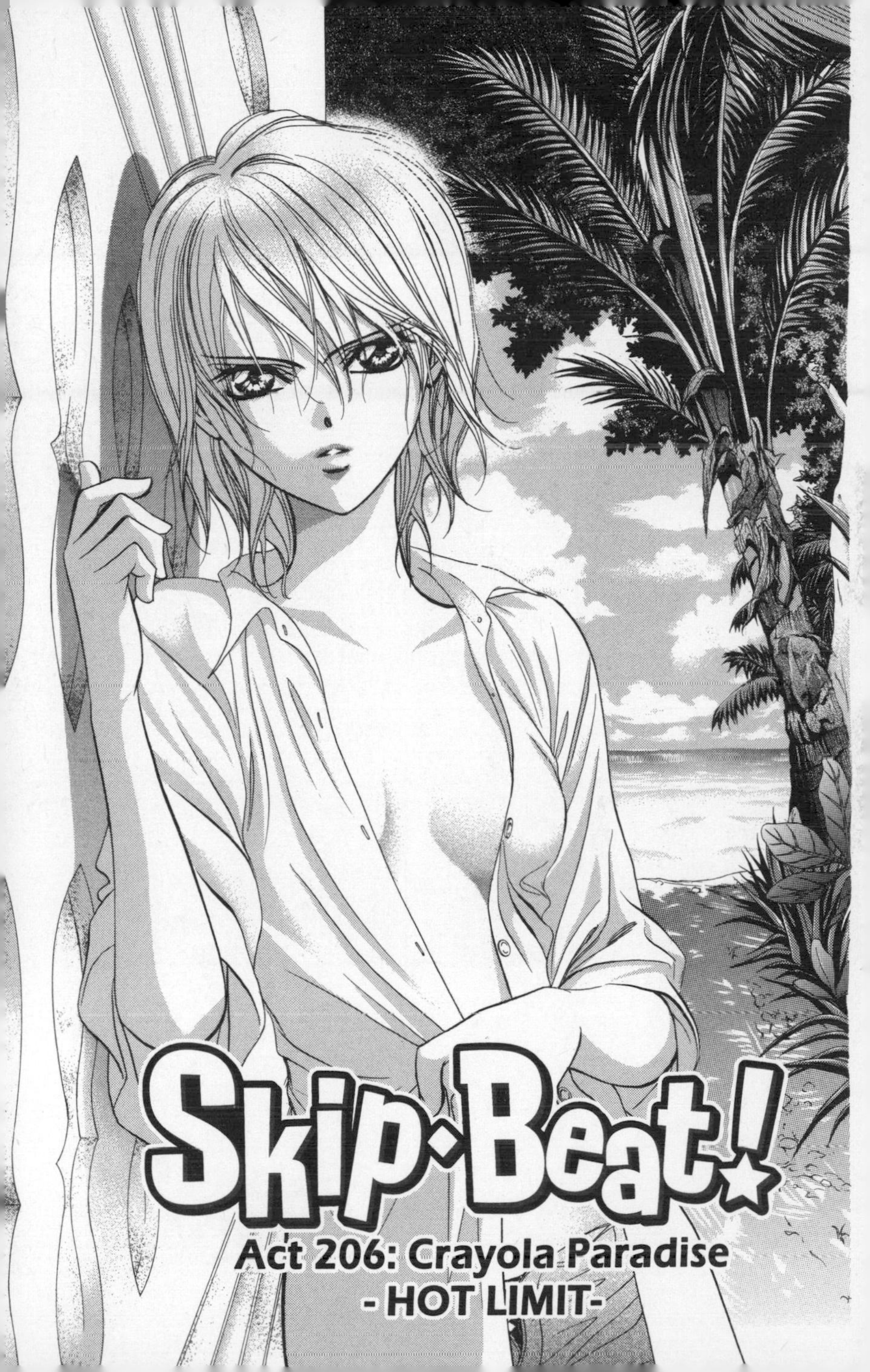
Skip·Beat!
Act 206: Crayola Paradise
- HOT LIMIT -

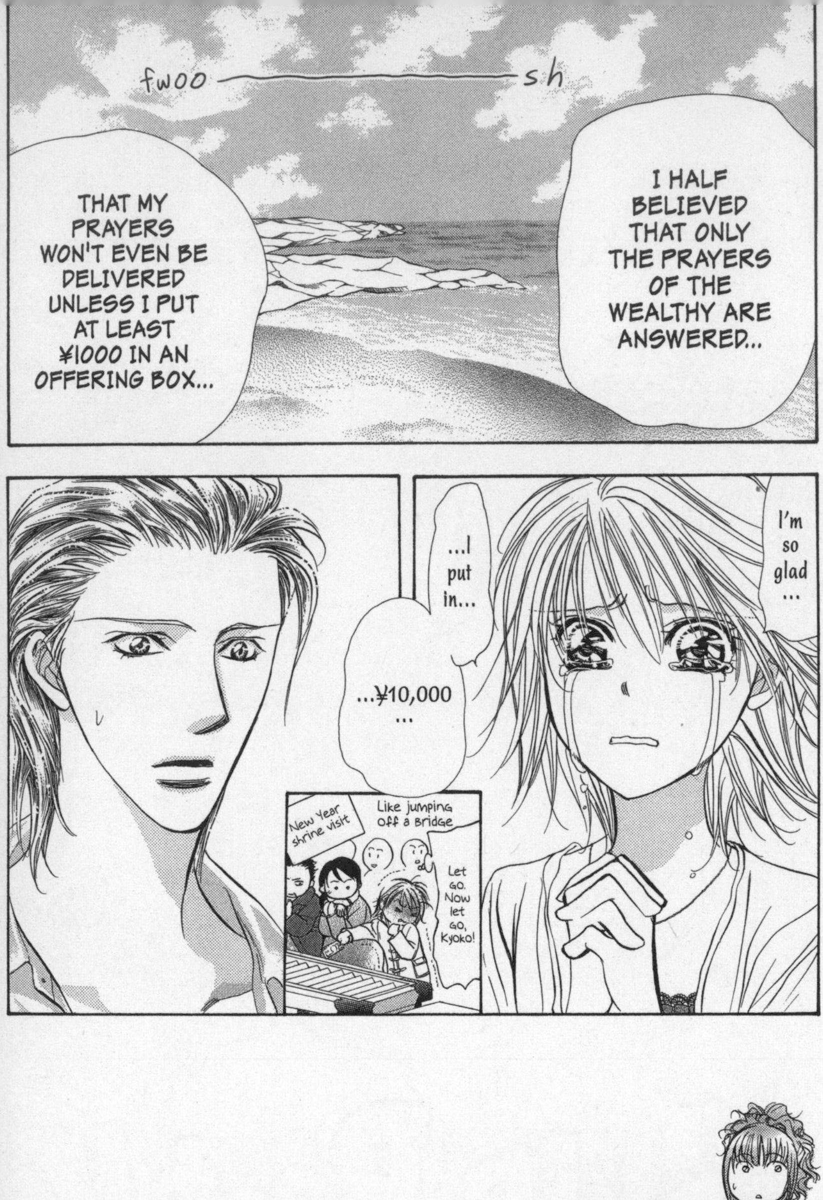
fwoo——sh
I HALF BELIEVED THAT ONLY THE PRAYERS OF THE WEALTHY ARE ANSWERED...
THAT MY PRAYERS WON'T EVEN BE DELIVERED UNLESS I PUT AT LEAST ¥1000 IN AN OFFERING BOX...
I'm so glad...
...I put in...
...¥10,000...
New Year shrine visit
Like jumping off a Bridge
Let GO. Now let GO, Kyoko!

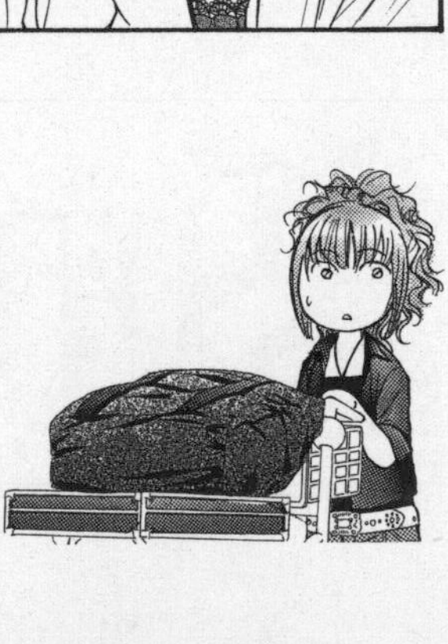

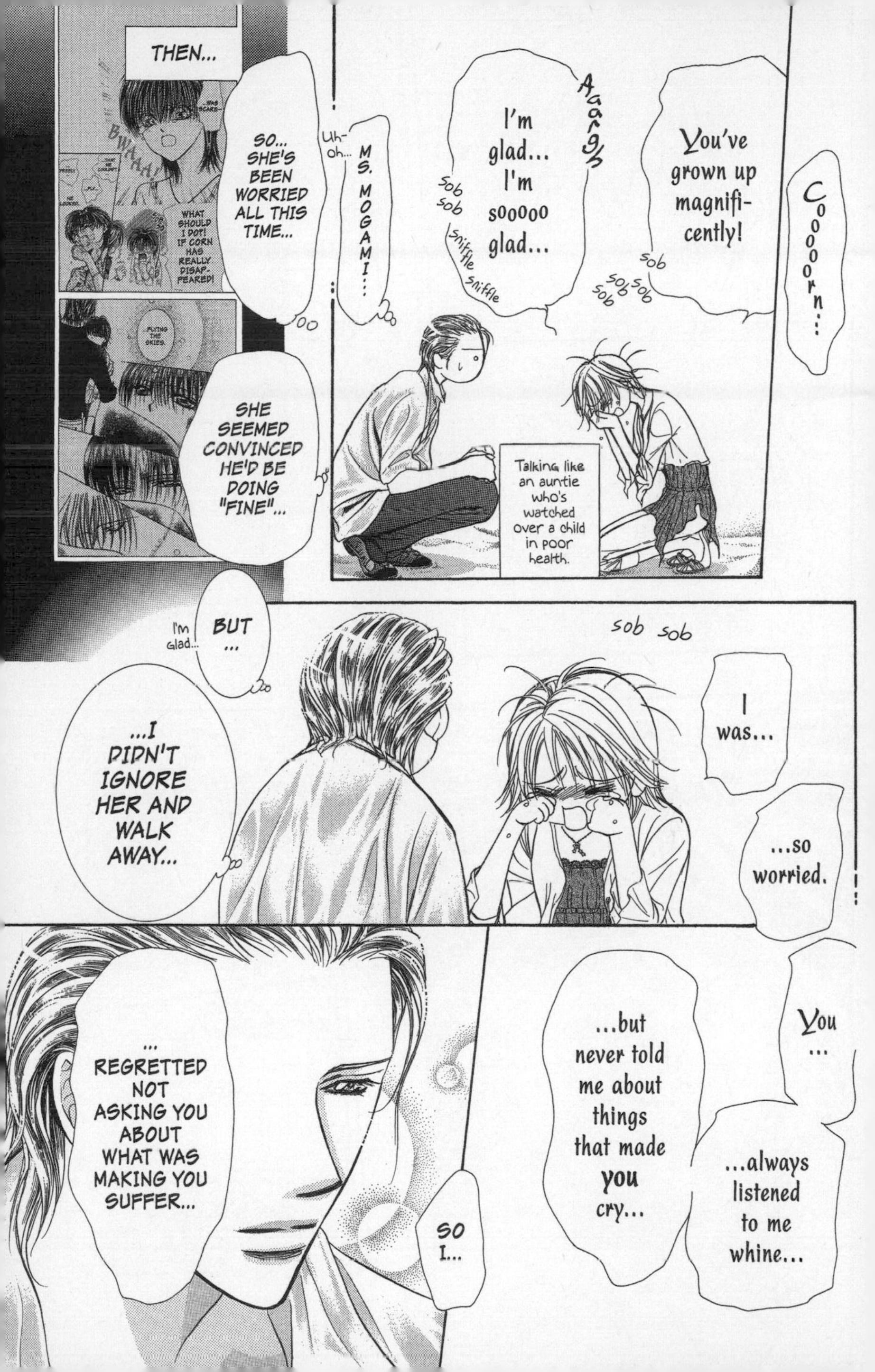
Cooooorn...
You've grown up magnificently!
sob sob sob sob
I'm glad... I'm sooooo glad...
Aaargh
sniffle sniffle
sob sob
Uh-oh...
MS. MOGAMI...
Talking like an auntie who's watched over a child in poor health.
THEN...
...WAS SCARE-
BWAAA!
WHAT SHOULD I DO? IF CORN HAS REALLY DISAPPEARED!
SO... SHE'S BEEN WORRIED ALL THIS TIME...
...FLYING THE SKIES.
SHE SEEMED CONVINCED HE'D BE DOING "FINE"...
sob sob
I was...
...so worried.
BUT...
I'm Glad...
...I DIDN'T IGNORE HER AND WALK AWAY...
You...
...always listened to me whine...
...but never told me about things that made you cry...
SO I...
...REGRETTED NOT ASKING YOU ABOUT WHAT WAS MAKING YOU SUFFER...

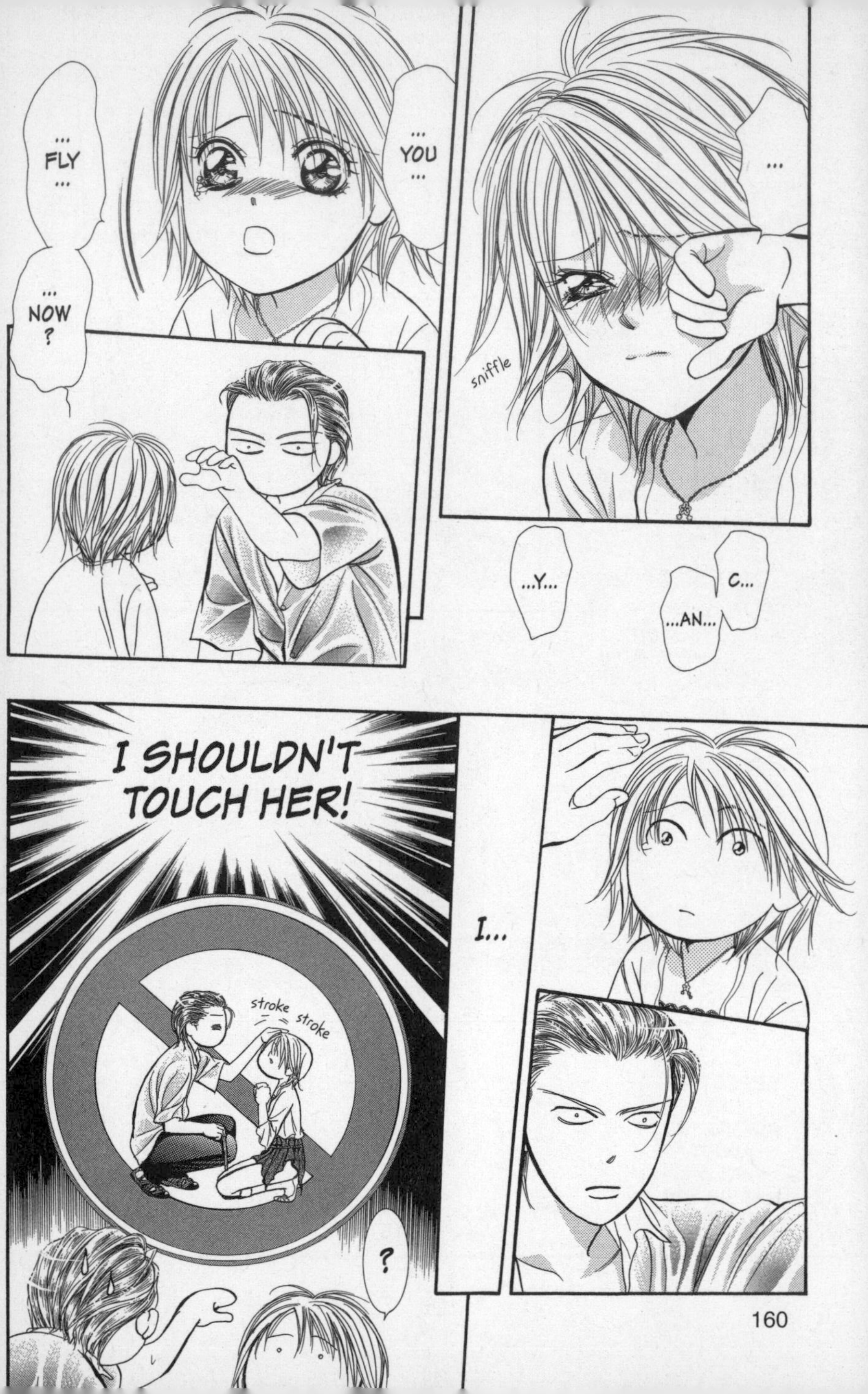
...
sniffle
C...
...AN...
...Y...
... YOU ...
... FLY ...
... NOW ?
I...
I SHOULDN'T TOUCH HER!
stroke stroke
?

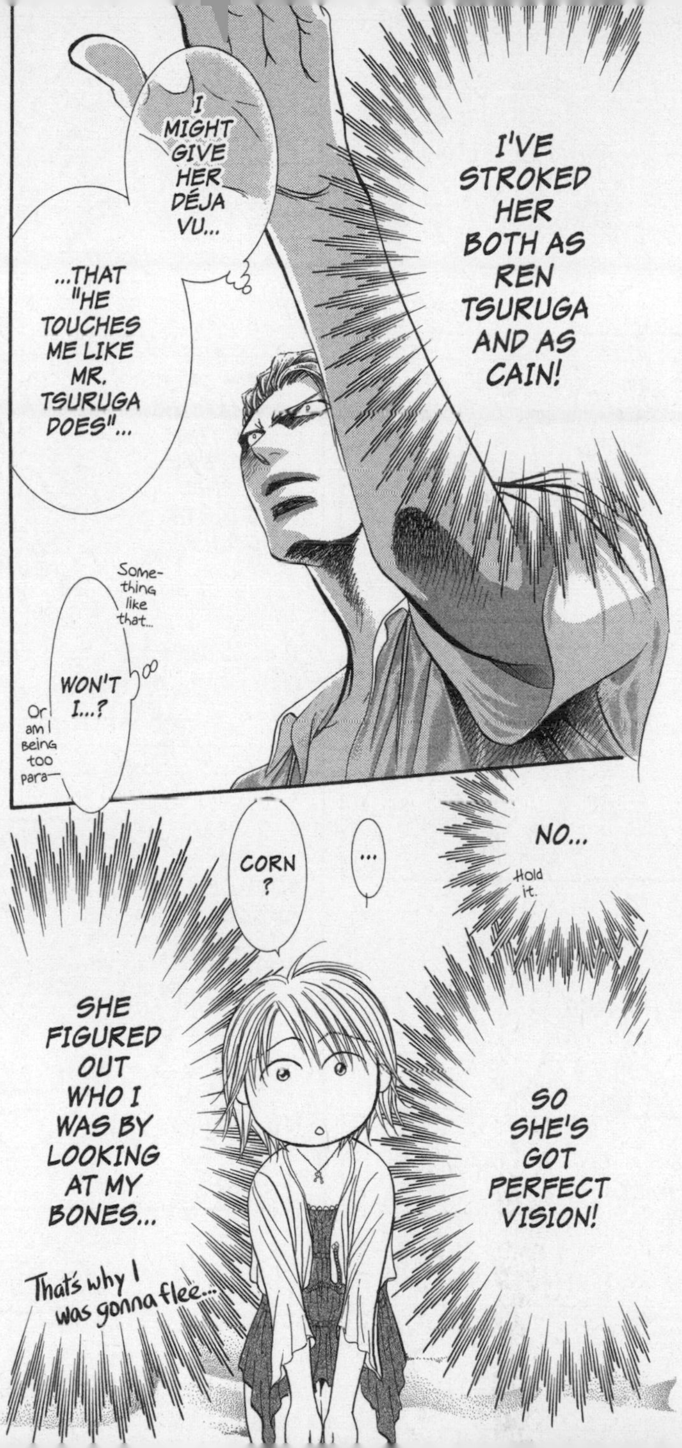
I'VE STROKED HER BOTH AS REN TSURUGA AND AS CAIN!
I MIGHT GIVE HER DÉJA VU...
...THAT "HE TOUCHES ME LIKE MR. TSURUGA DOES"...
Something like that...
WON'T I...?
Or am I being too para—
NO...
Hold it.
...
CORN?
SO SHE'S GOT PERFECT VISION!
SHE FIGURED OUT WHO I WAS BY LOOKING AT MY BONES...
That's why I was gonna flee...

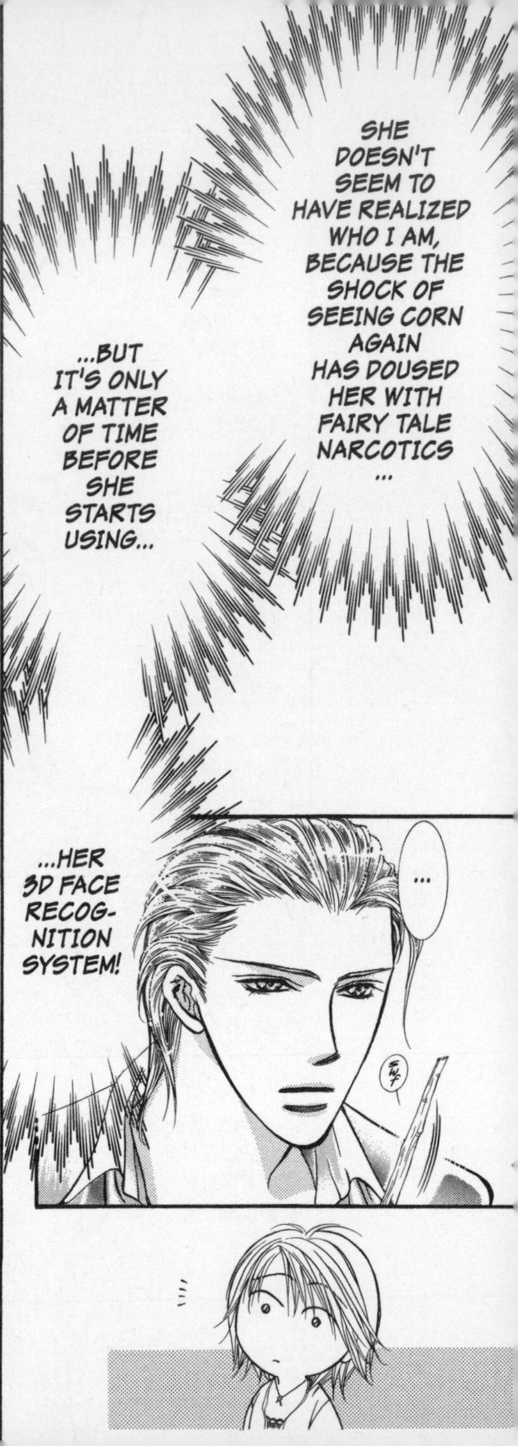
SHE DOESN'T SEEM TO HAVE REALIZED WHO I AM, BECAUSE THE SHOCK OF SEEING CORN AGAIN HAS DOUSED HER WITH FAIRY TALE NARCOTICS...
...BUT IT'S ONLY A MATTER OF TIME BEFORE SHE STARTS USING...
...
...HER 3D FACE RECOG-NITION SYSTEM!
SWF
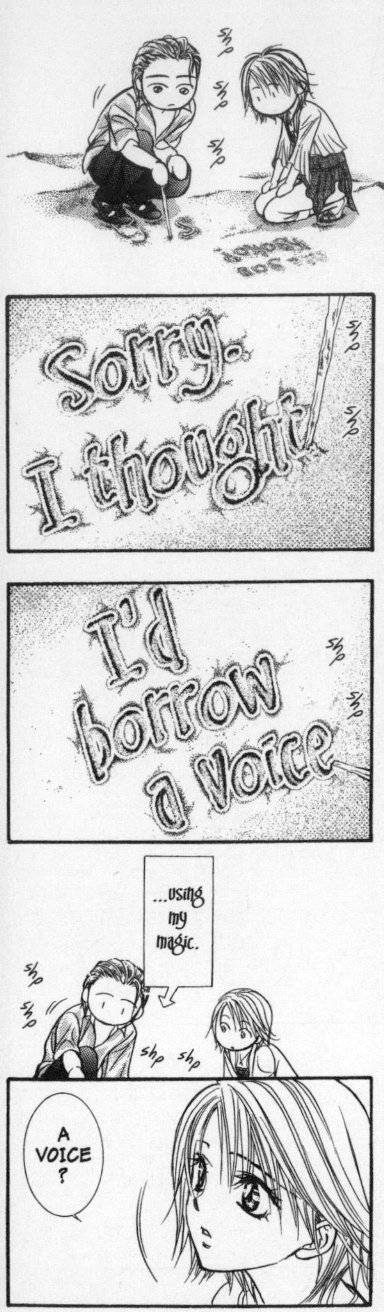
shp
shp
shp
Sorry. I thought
shp
shp
I'd borrow a voice
shp
shp
...using my magic.
shp
shp
shp
shp
A VOICE?

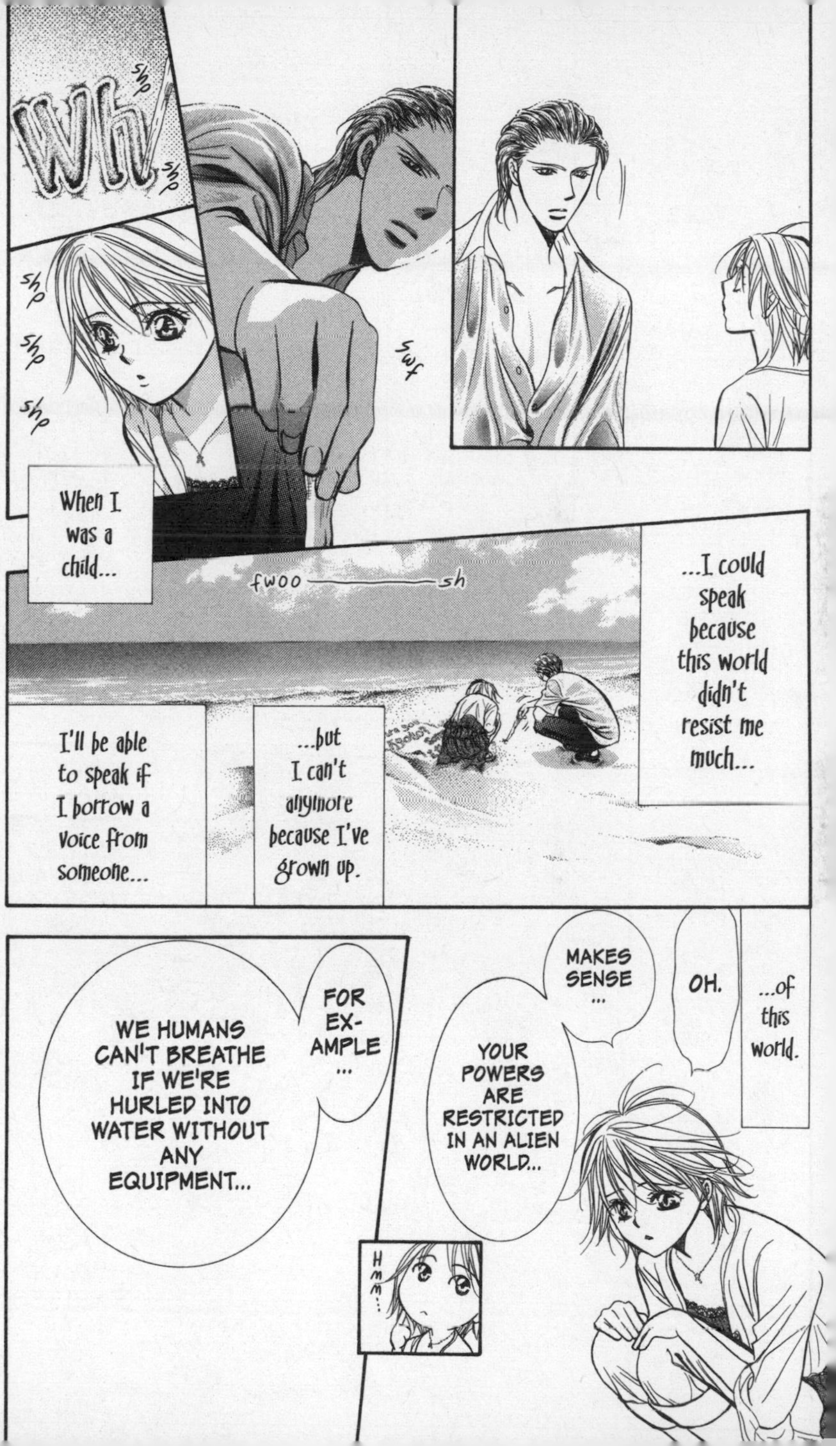
Wh
shp shp
shp shp shp
swf
When I was a child...
fwoo——sh
...I could speak because this world didn't resist me much...
...but I can't anymore because I've grown up.
I'll be able to speak if I borrow a voice from someone...
...of this world.
OH.
MAKES SENSE...
YOUR POWERS ARE RESTRICTED IN AN ALIEN WORLD...
Hmm...
FOR EX-AMPLE...
WE HUMANS CAN'T BREATHE IF WE'RE HURLED INTO WATER WITHOUT ANY EQUIPMENT...

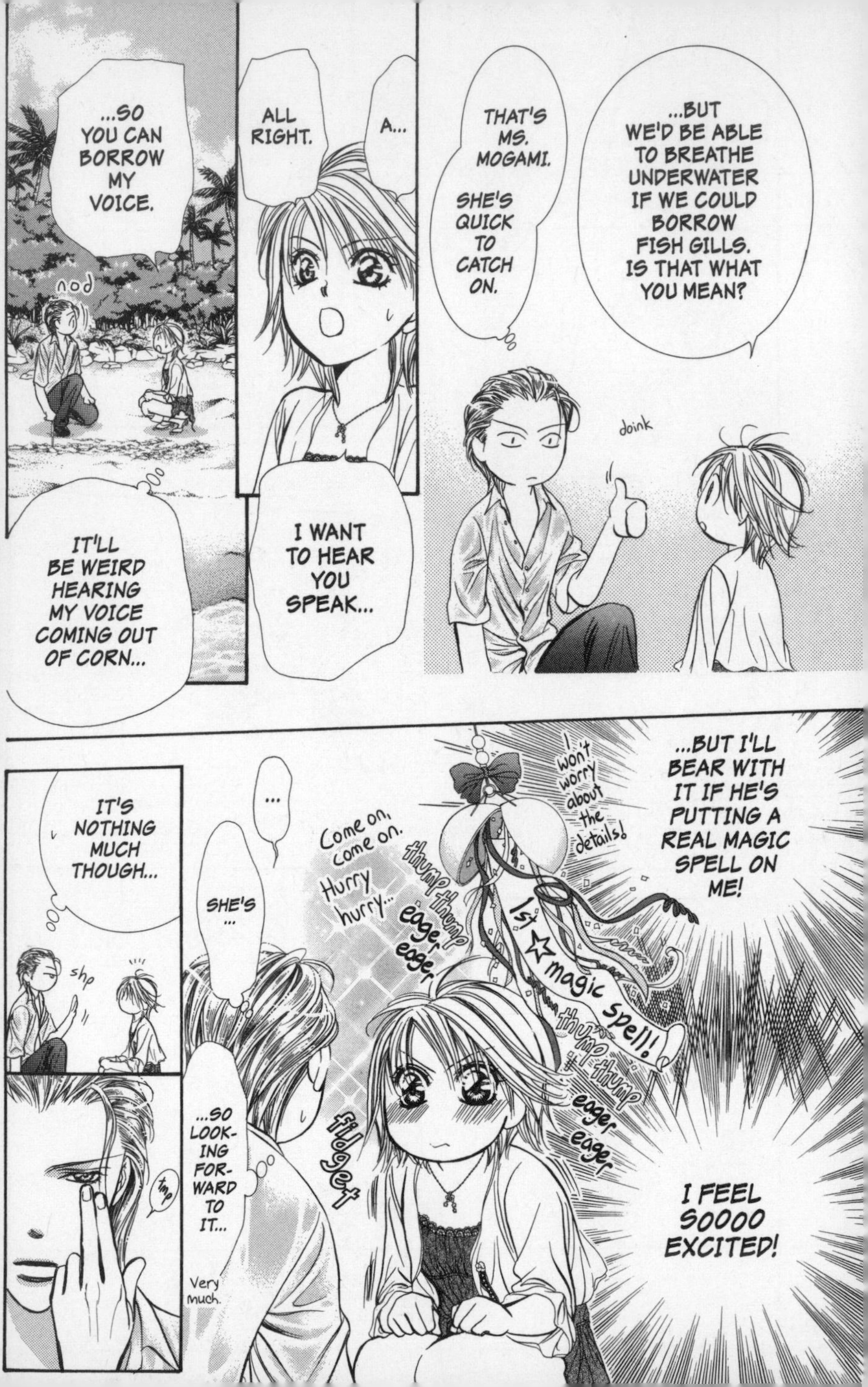
...BUT WE'D BE ABLE TO BREATHE UNDERWATER IF WE COULD BORROW FISH GILLS. IS THAT WHAT YOU MEAN?
THAT'S MS. MOGAMI.
SHE'S QUICK TO CATCH ON.
doink
A...
ALL RIGHT.
I WANT TO HEAR YOU SPEAK...
...SO YOU CAN BORROW MY VOICE.
nod
IT'LL BE WEIRD HEARING MY VOICE COMING OUT OF CORN...
...BUT I'LL BEAR WITH IT IF HE'S PUTTING A REAL MAGIC SPELL ON ME!
I won't worry about the details!
Come on, come on. Hurry hurry...
thump thump
eager eager
1st ☆ magic spell!
thump thump
eager eager
fidget
I FEEL SOOOO EXCITED!
...
SHE'S ...
...SO LOOKING FORWARD TO IT...
Very much.
IT'S NOTHING MUCH THOUGH...
shp
tmp

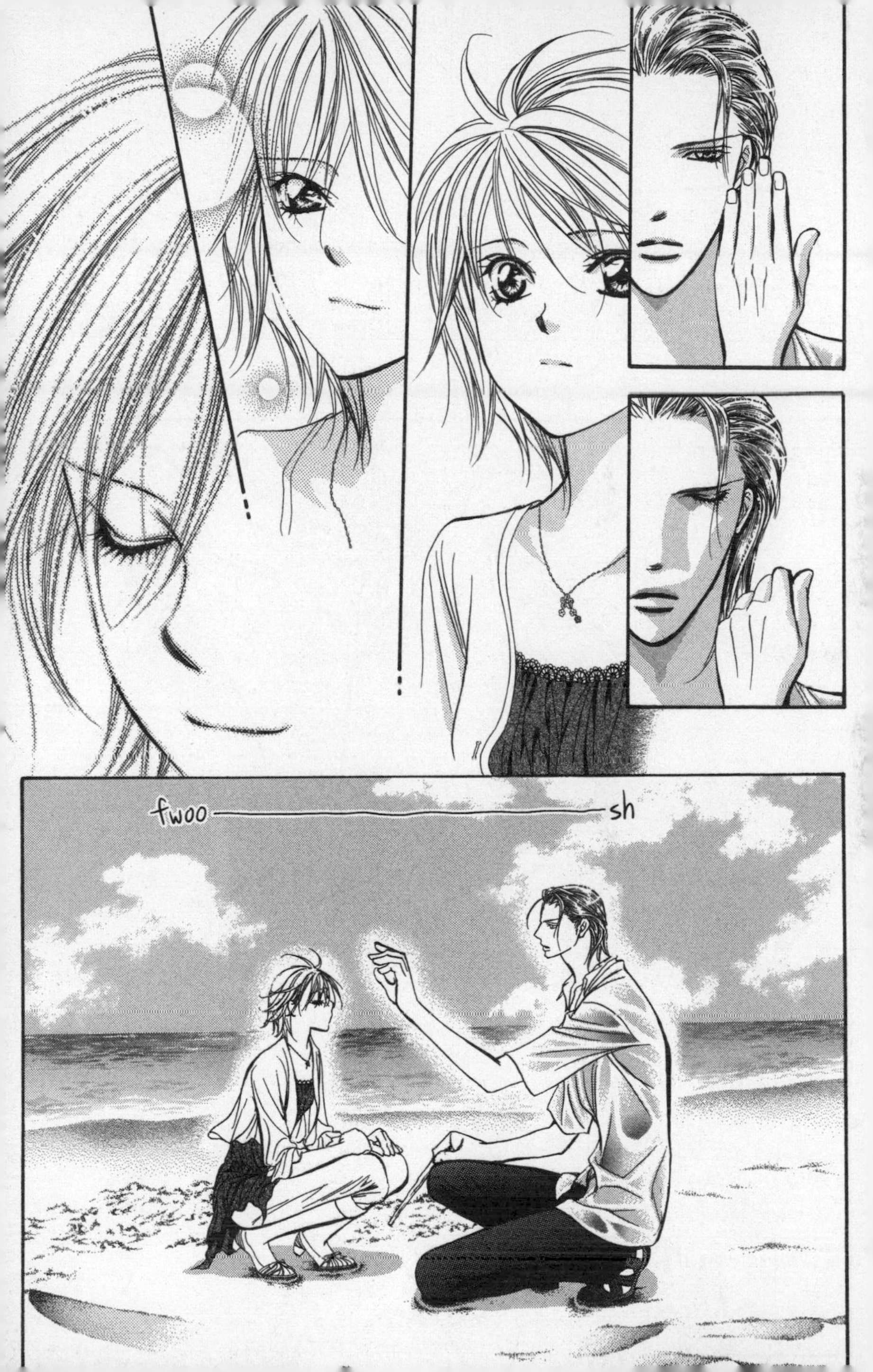
fwoo———sh

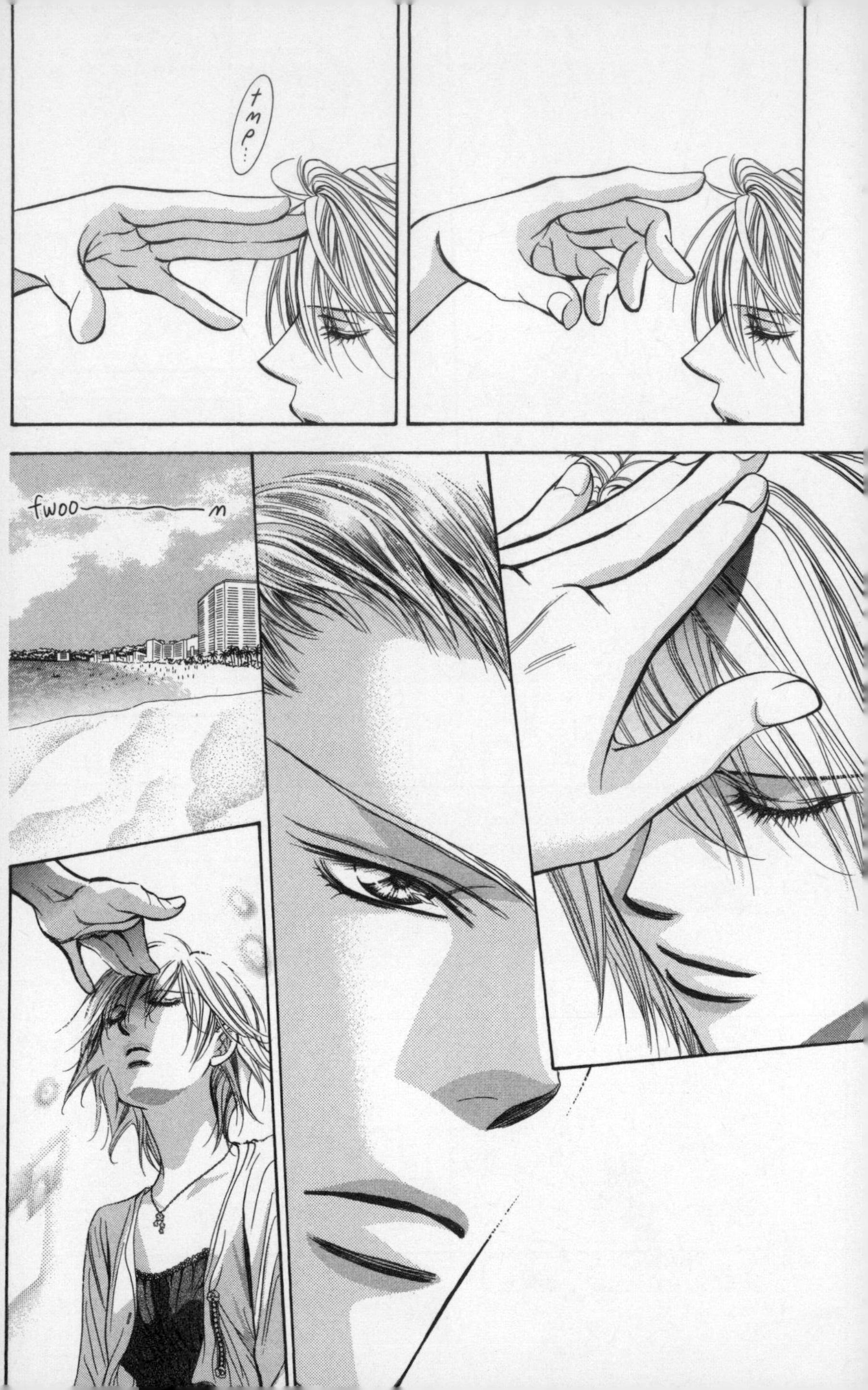
tmp...
fwoo——n

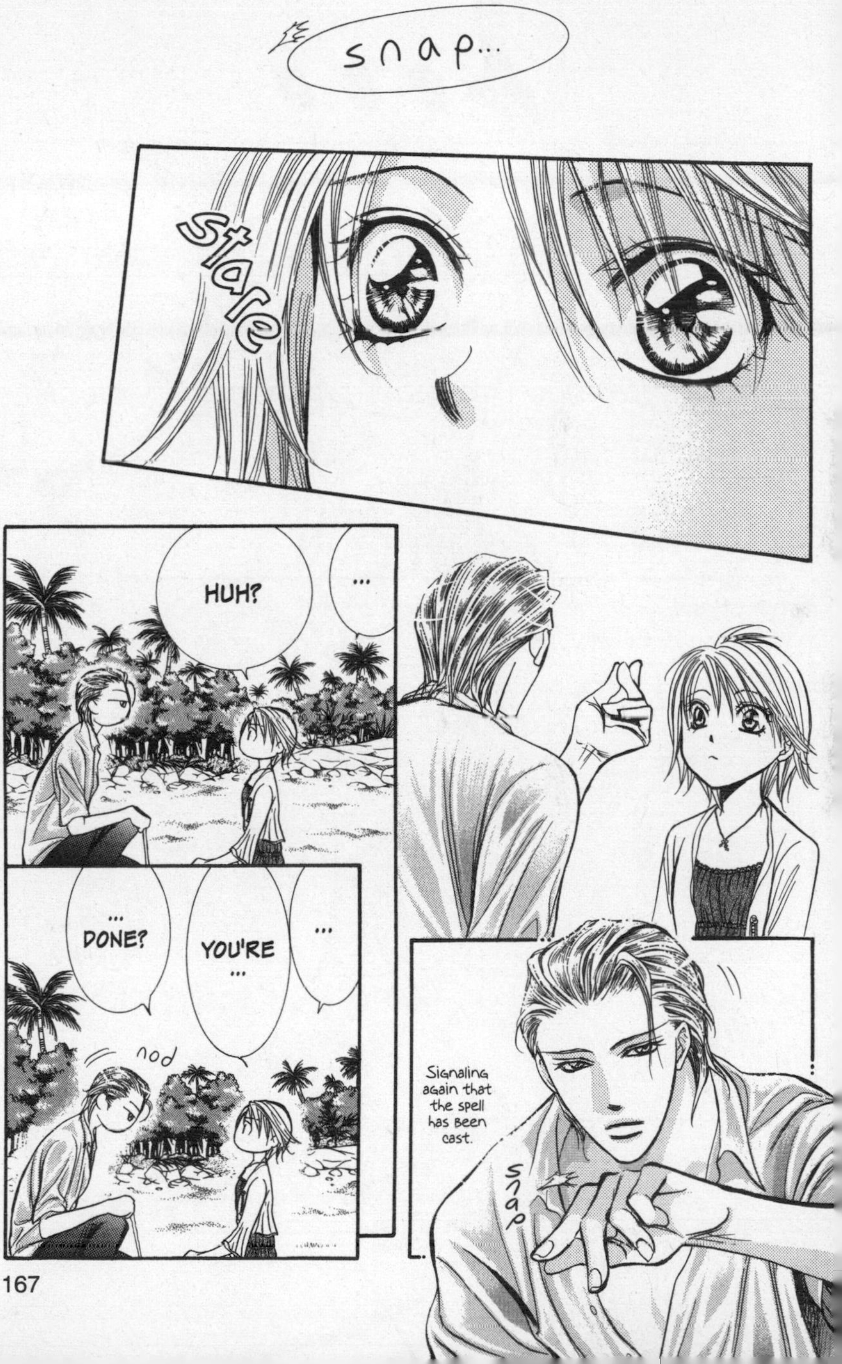
snap...
stare
...
HUH?
...
YOU'RE ...
... DONE?
nod
Signaling again that the spell has been cast.
snap

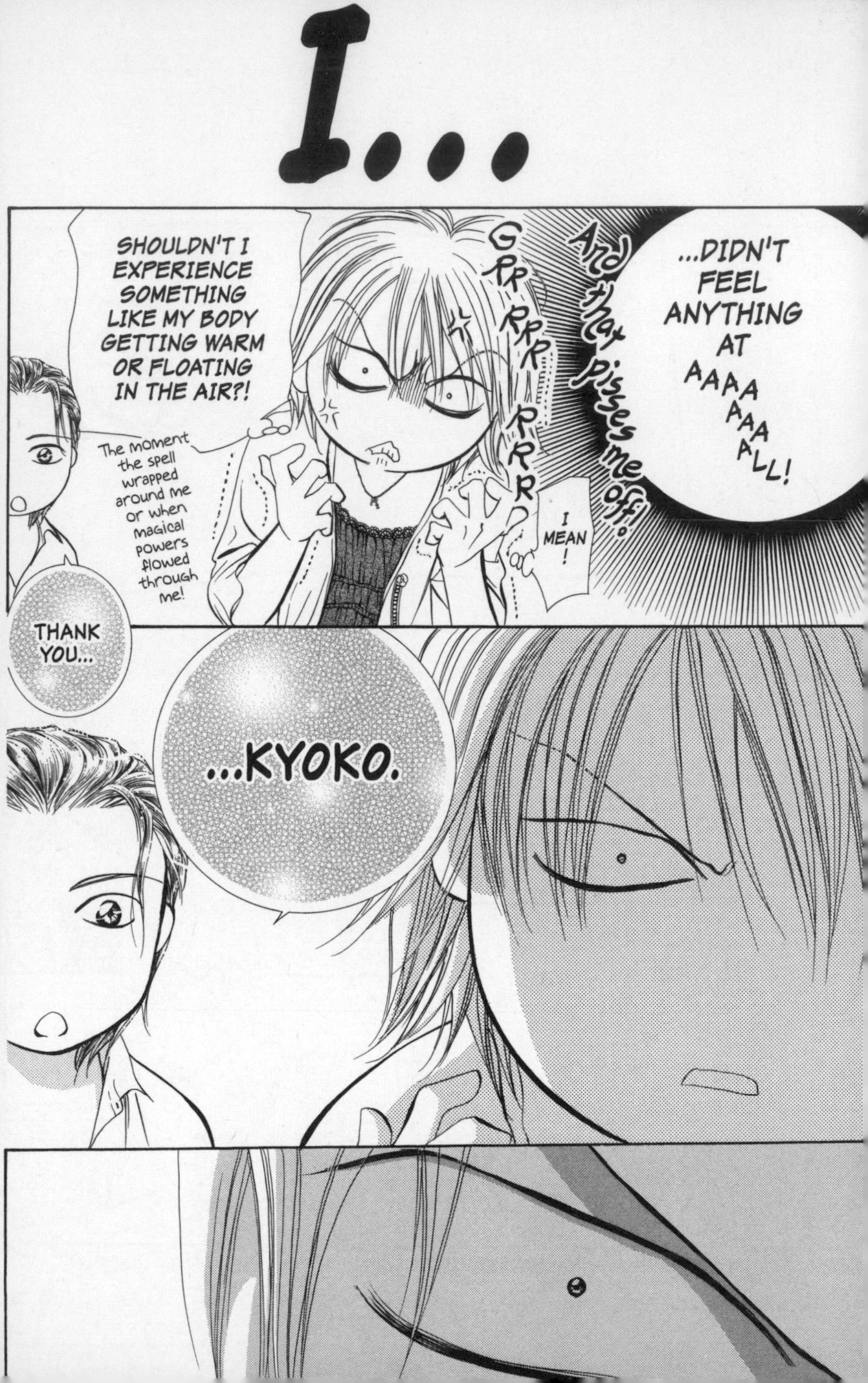
I...
...DIDN'T FEEL ANYTHING AT AAAAAAAALL!
And that pisses me off!
GRRRRRRRR
I MEAN!
SHOULDN'T I EXPERIENCE SOMETHING LIKE MY BODY GETTING WARM OR FLOATING IN THE AIR?!
The moment the spell wrapped around me or when magical powers flowed through me!
THANK YOU...
...KYOKO.

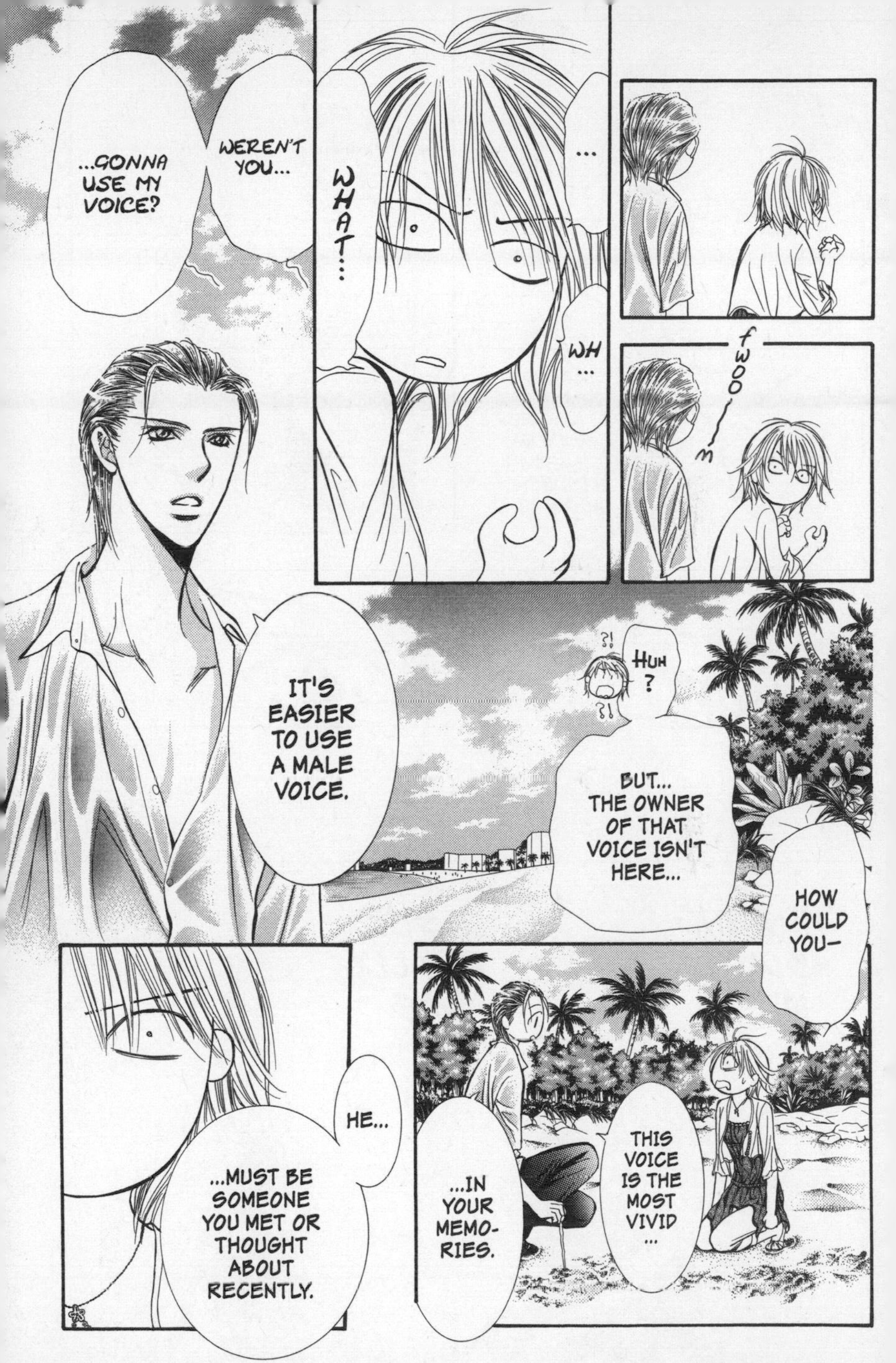
FWOO—M
...
WH ...
WHAT...
WEREN'T YOU...
...GONNA USE MY VOICE?
IT'S EASIER TO USE A MALE VOICE.
?! ?!
HUH?
BUT... THE OWNER OF THAT VOICE ISN'T HERE...
HOW COULD YOU—
THIS VOICE IS THE MOST VIVID ...
...IN YOUR MEMORIES.
HE...
...MUST BE SOMEONE YOU MET OR THOUGHT ABOUT RECENTLY.

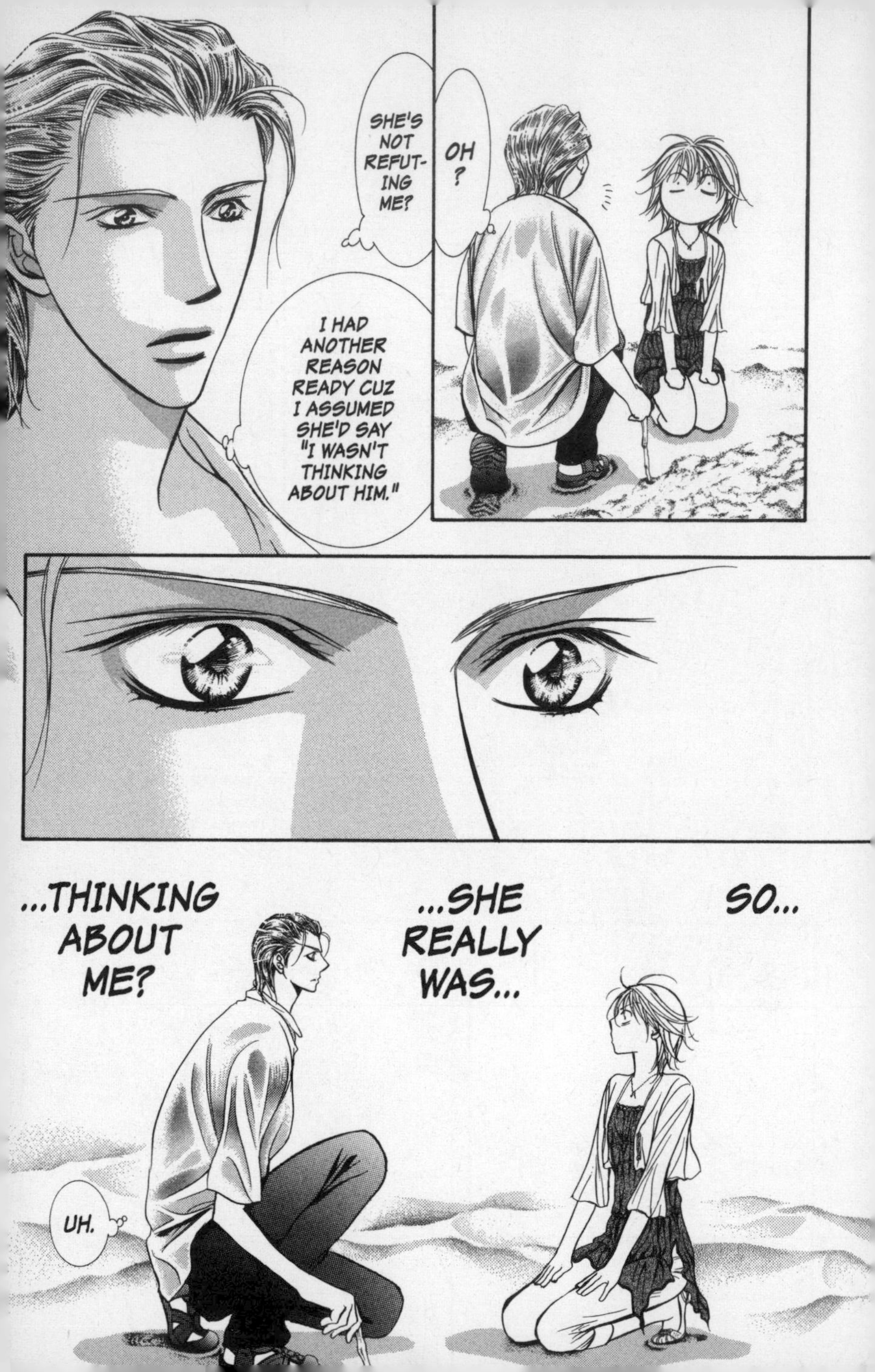
OH ?
SHE'S NOT REFUTING ME?
I HAD ANOTHER REASON READY CUZ I ASSUMED SHE'D SAY "I WASN'T THINKING ABOUT HIM."
SO...
...SHE REALLY WAS...
...THINKING ABOUT ME?
UH.

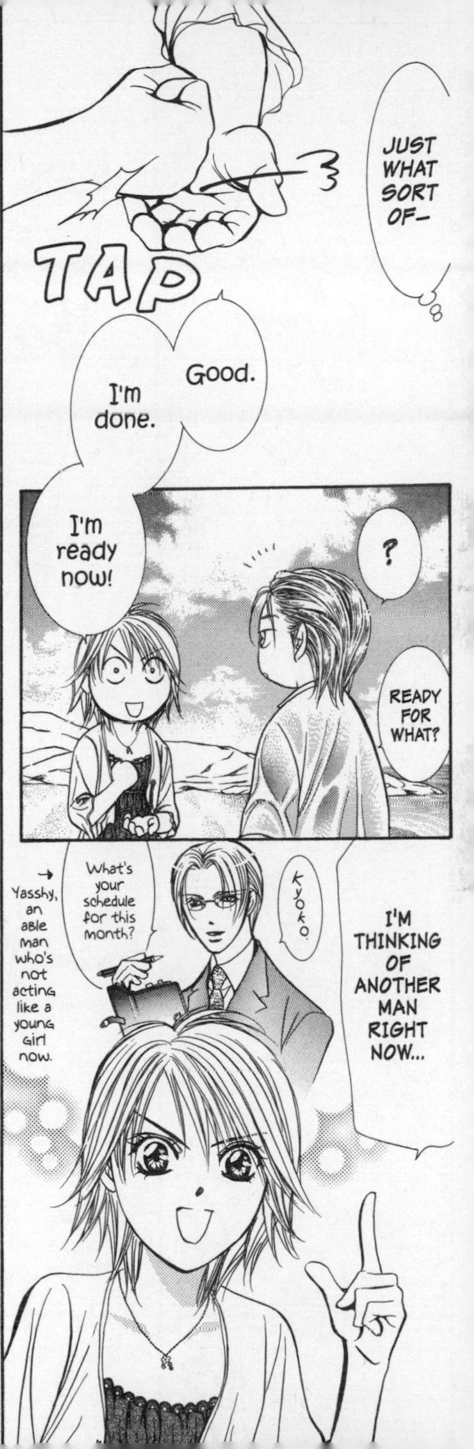
JUST WHAT SORT OF–
TAP
Good.
I'm done.
I'm ready now!
?
READY FOR WHAT?
I'M THINKING OF ANOTHER MAN RIGHT NOW...
Kyoko.
What's your schedule for this month?
Yasshy, an able man who's not acting like a young girl now.
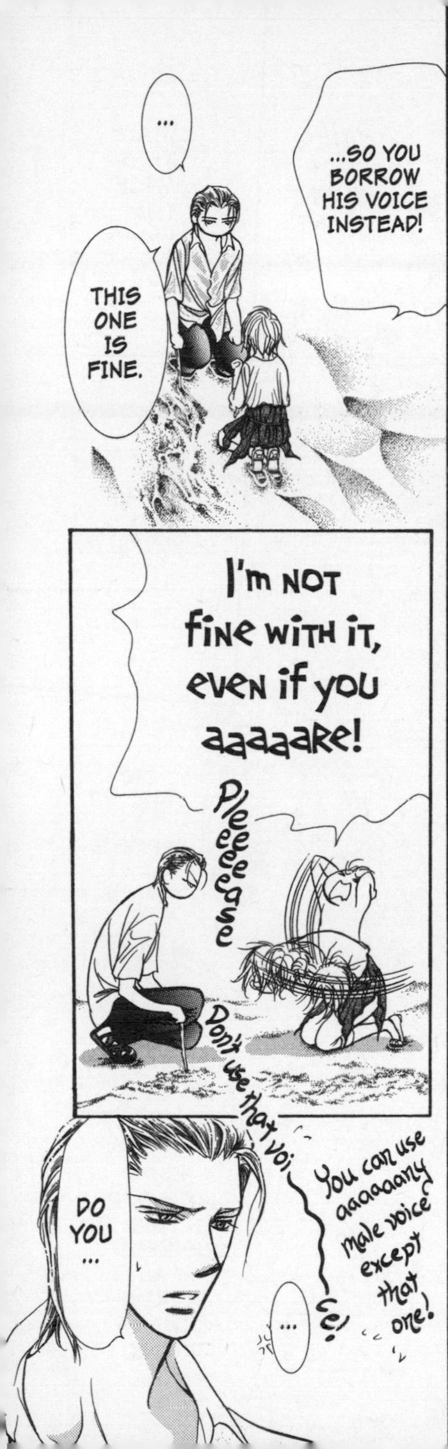
...SO YOU BORROW HIS VOICE INSTEAD!
...
THIS ONE IS FINE.
I'm NOT fine with it, even if you aaaaare!
Pleeeeeease
Don't use that voi–ce!
You can use aaaaaany male voice except that one!
...
DO YOU ...

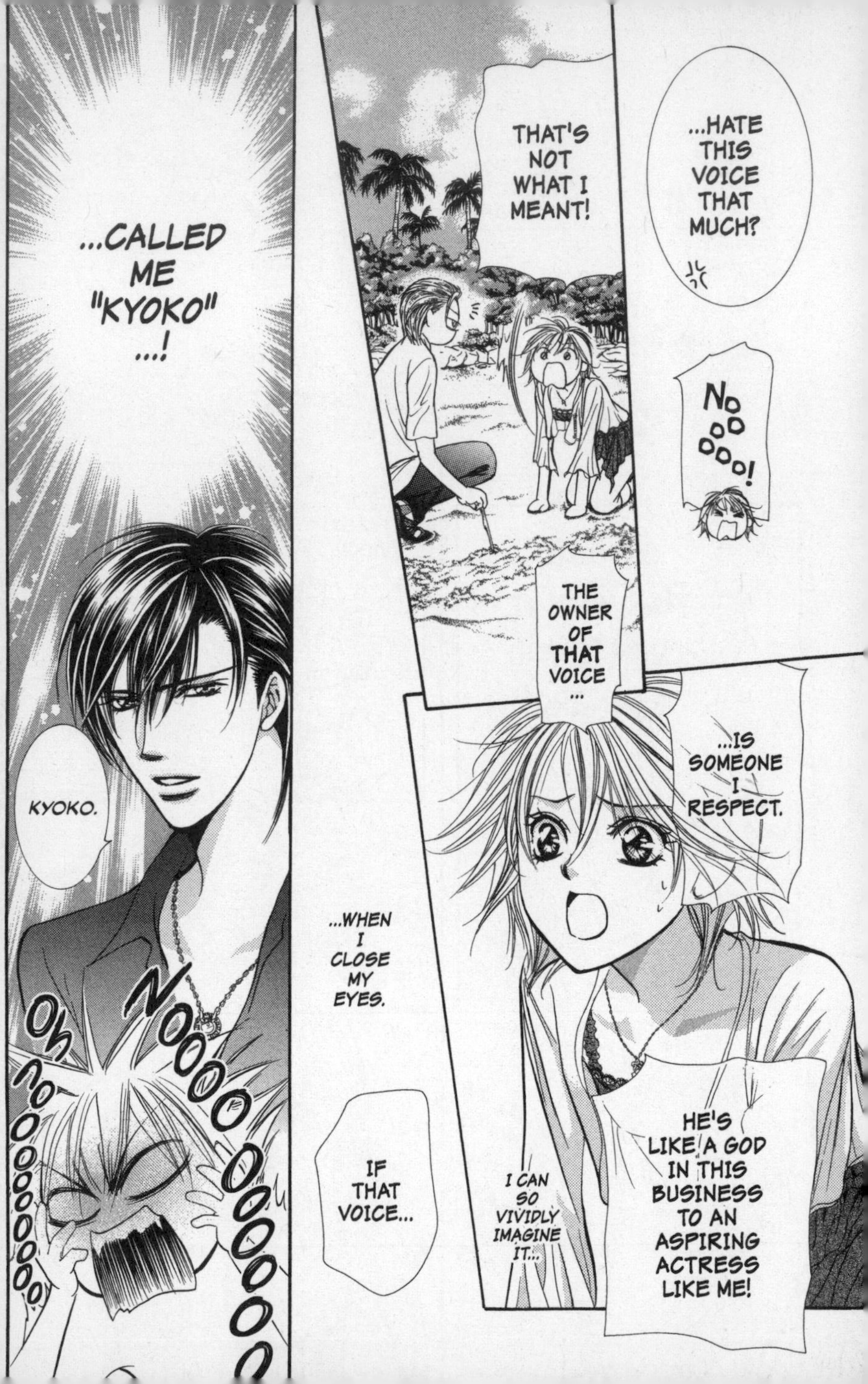
...HATE THIS VOICE THAT MUCH?
THAT'S NOT WHAT I MEANT!
NOOOOOOO!
THE OWNER OF THAT VOICE...
...IS SOMEONE I RESPECT.
HE'S LIKE A GOD IN THIS BUSINESS TO AN ASPIRING ACTRESS LIKE ME!
I CAN SO VIVIDLY IMAGINE IT...
...WHEN I CLOSE MY EYES.
IF THAT VOICE...
...CALLED ME "KYOKO" ...!
KYOKO.
NOOOOOOOOOOOOOO
OH NO NOOOOOOOOOO

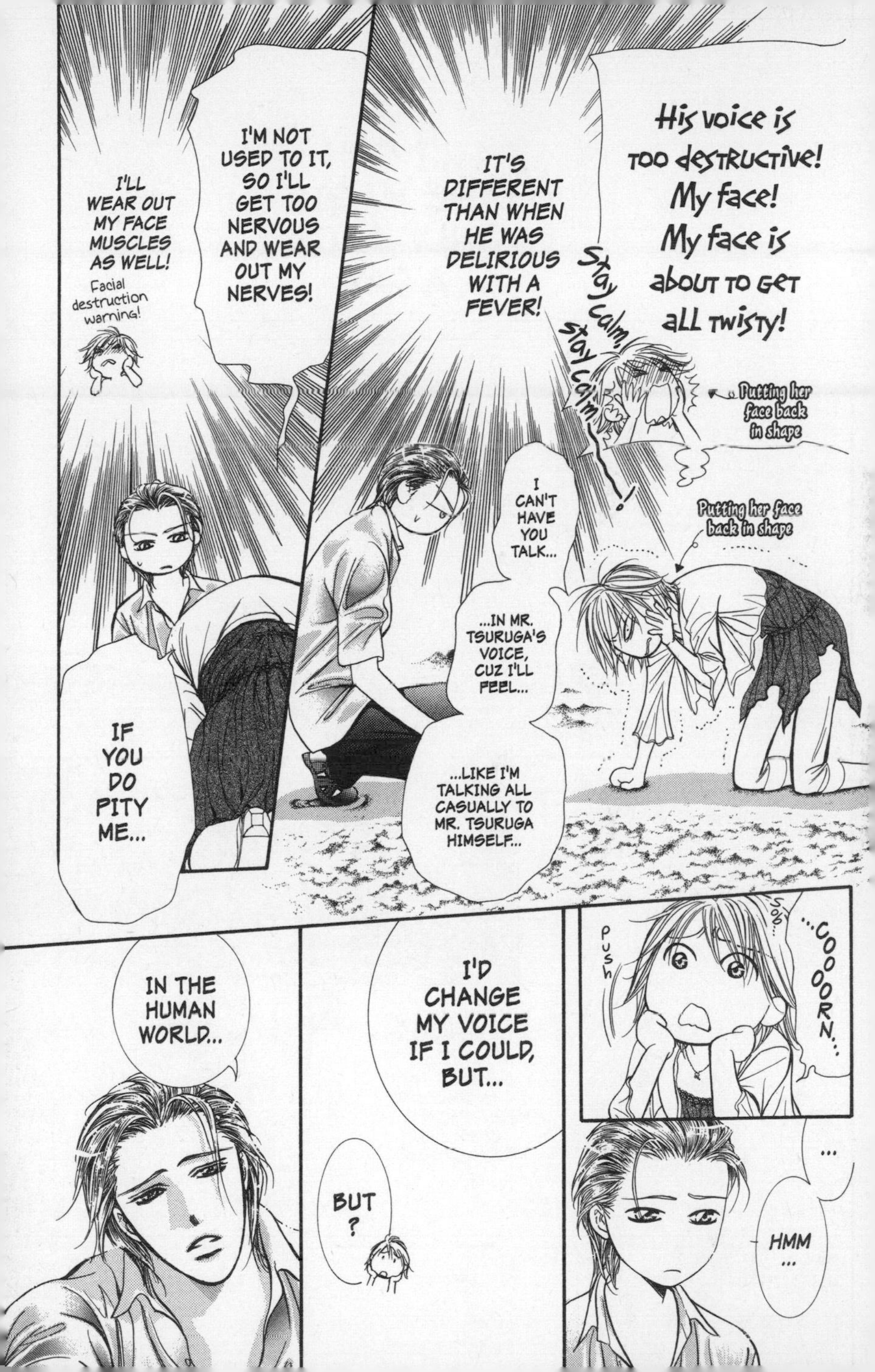
His voice is too destructive! My face! My face is about to get all twisty!
Stay calm, stay calm...!
Putting her face back in shape
Putting her face back in shape
IT'S DIFFERENT THAN WHEN HE WAS DELIRIOUS WITH A FEVER!
I CAN'T HAVE YOU TALK...
...IN MR. TSURUGA'S VOICE, CUZ I'LL FEEL...
...LIKE I'M TALKING ALL CASUALLY TO MR. TSURUGA HIMSELF...
I'M NOT USED TO IT, SO I'LL GET TOO NERVOUS AND WEAR OUT MY NERVES!
I'LL WEAR OUT MY FACE MUSCLES AS WELL!
Facial destruction warning!
IF YOU DO PITY ME...
Push
...COOOOORN...
...
HMM...
I'D CHANGE MY VOICE IF I COULD, BUT...
BUT?
IN THE HUMAN WORLD...

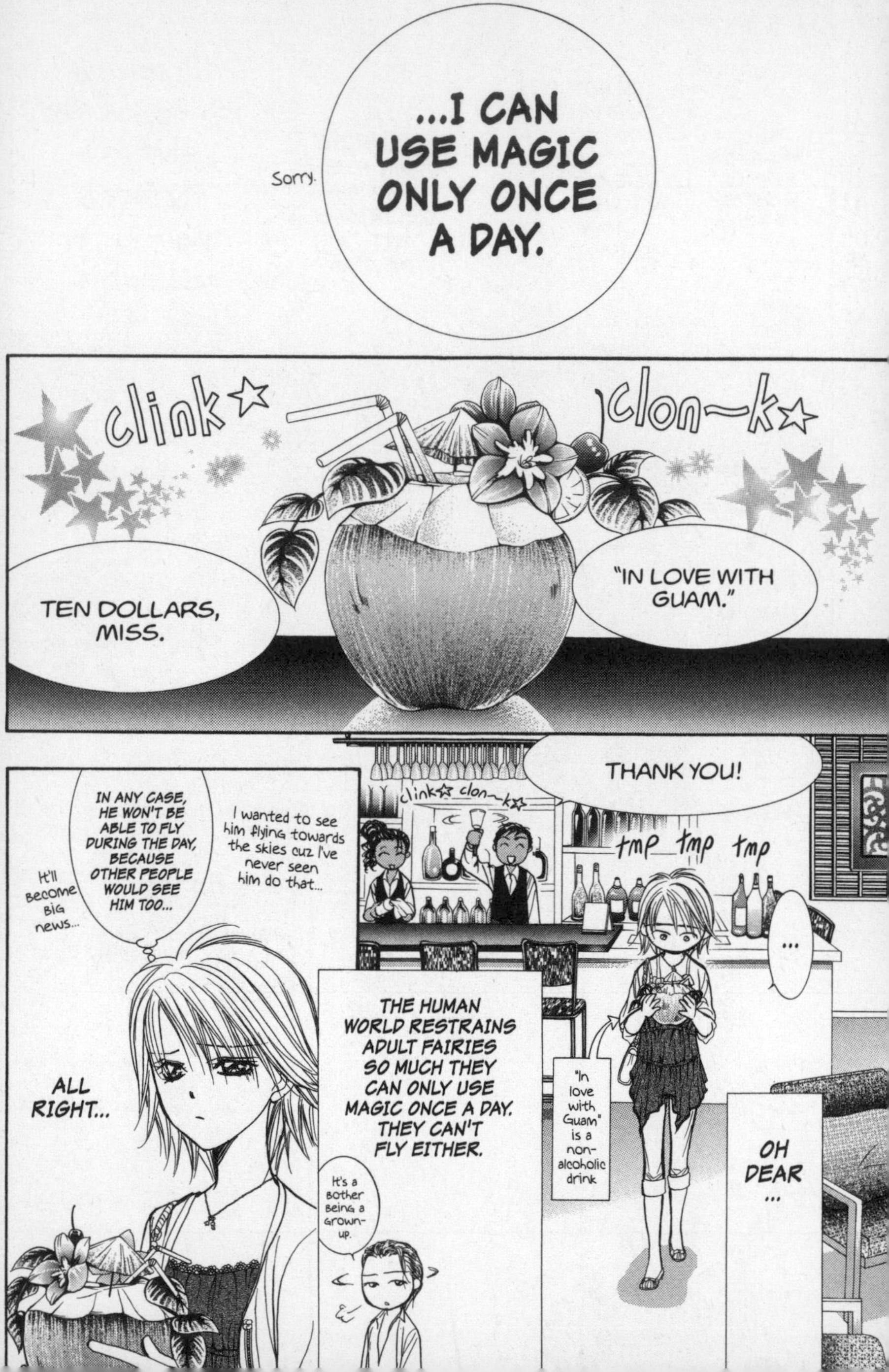
...I CAN USE MAGIC ONLY ONCE A DAY.
Sorry.
clon~k☆
"IN LOVE WITH GUAM."
clink☆
TEN DOLLARS, MISS.
THANK YOU!
clink☆ clon~k☆
tmp tmp tmp
...
"In love with Guam" is a non-alcoholic drink
OH DEAR ...
THE HUMAN WORLD RESTRAINS ADULT FAIRIES SO MUCH THEY CAN ONLY USE MAGIC ONCE A DAY. THEY CAN'T FLY EITHER.
It's a bother being a grown-up.
IN ANY CASE, HE WON'T BE ABLE TO FLY DURING THE DAY, BECAUSE OTHER PEOPLE WOULD SEE HIM TOO...
I wanted to see him flying towards the skies cuz I've never seen him do that...
It'll become big news...
ALL RIGHT...

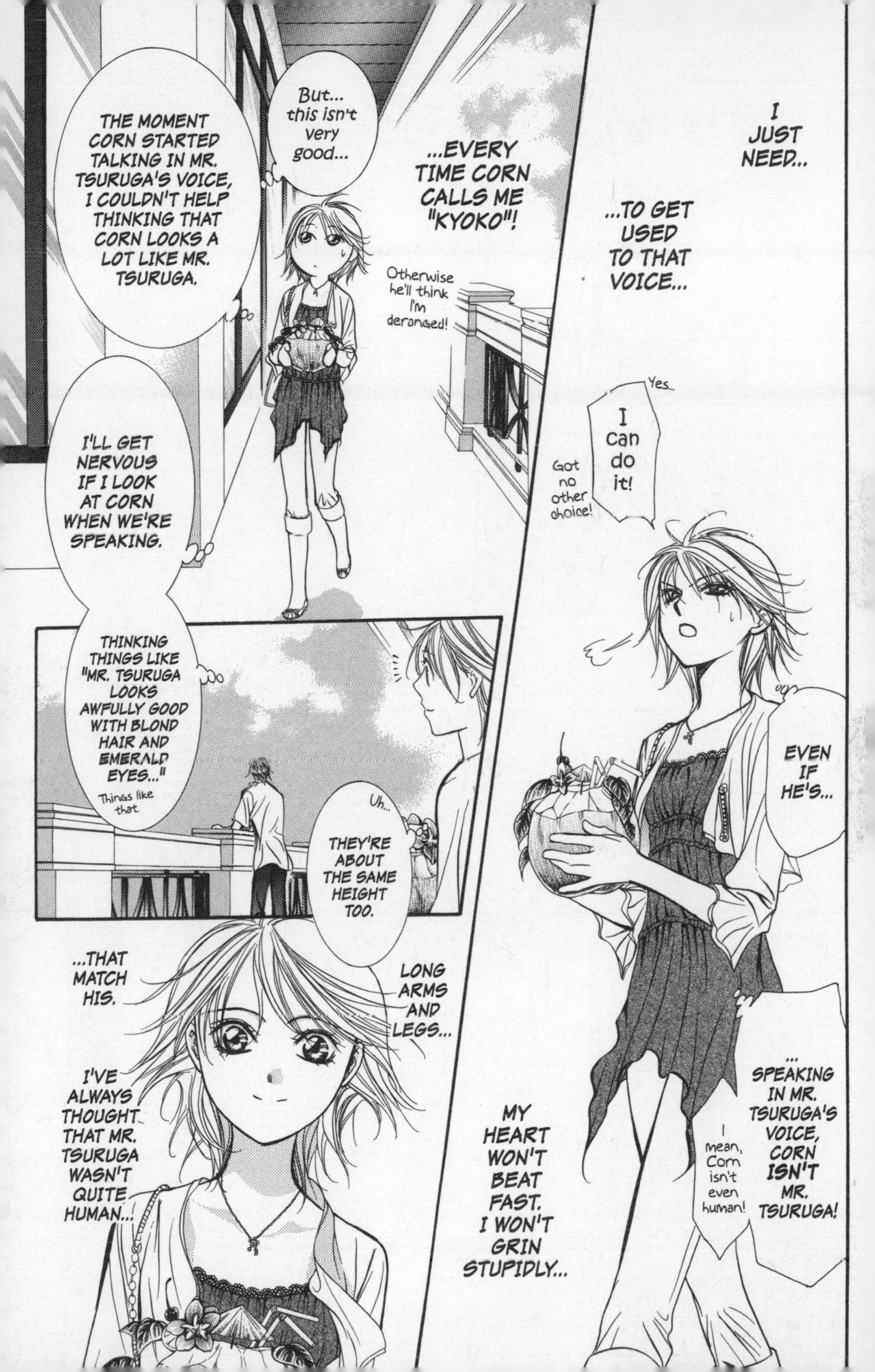

I JUST NEED...
...TO GET USED TO THAT VOICE...
...EVERY TIME CORN CALLS ME "KYOKO"!
Otherwise he'll think I'm deranged!
Yes...
I can do it!
Got no other choice!
EVEN IF HE'S...
...SPEAKING IN MR. TSURUGA'S VOICE, CORN ISN'T MR. TSURUGA!
I mean, Corn isn't even human!
MY HEART WON'T BEAT FAST. I WON'T GRIN STUPIDLY...
But... this isn't very good...
THE MOMENT CORN STARTED TALKING IN MR. TSURUGA'S VOICE, I COULDN'T HELP THINKING THAT CORN LOOKS A LOT LIKE MR. TSURUGA.
I'LL GET NERVOUS IF I LOOK AT CORN WHEN WE'RE SPEAKING.
THINKING THINGS LIKE "MR. TSURUGA LOOKS AWFULLY GOOD WITH BLOND HAIR AND EMERALD EYES..."
Things like that.
Uh...
THEY'RE ABOUT THE SAME HEIGHT TOO.
LONG ARMS AND LEGS...
...THAT MATCH HIS.
I'VE ALWAYS THOUGHT THAT MR. TSURUGA WASN'T QUITE HUMAN...

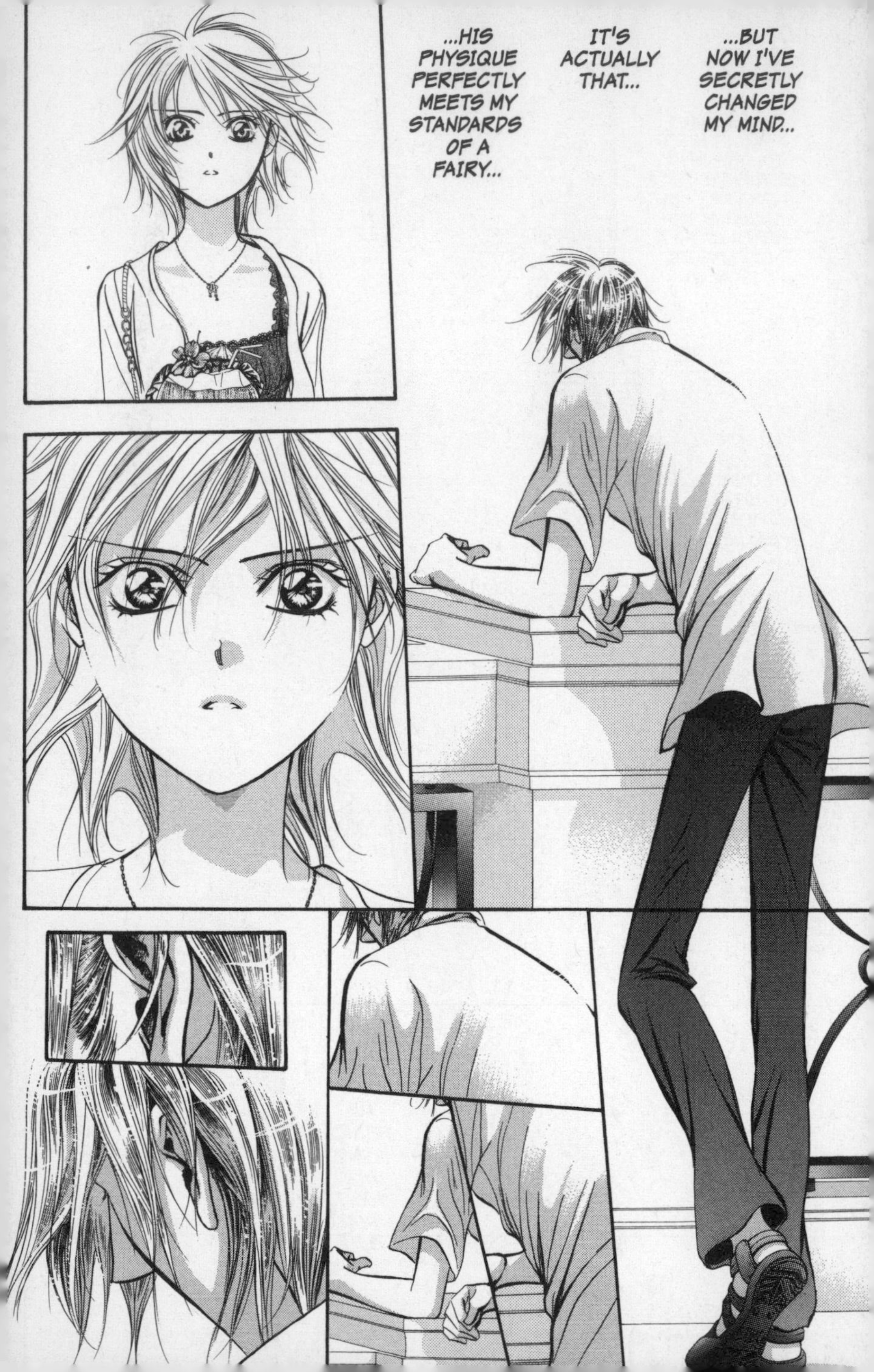
...BUT NOW I'VE SECRETLY CHANGED MY MIND...
IT'S ACTUALLY THAT...
...HIS PHYSIQUE PERFECTLY MEETS MY STANDARDS OF A FAIRY...

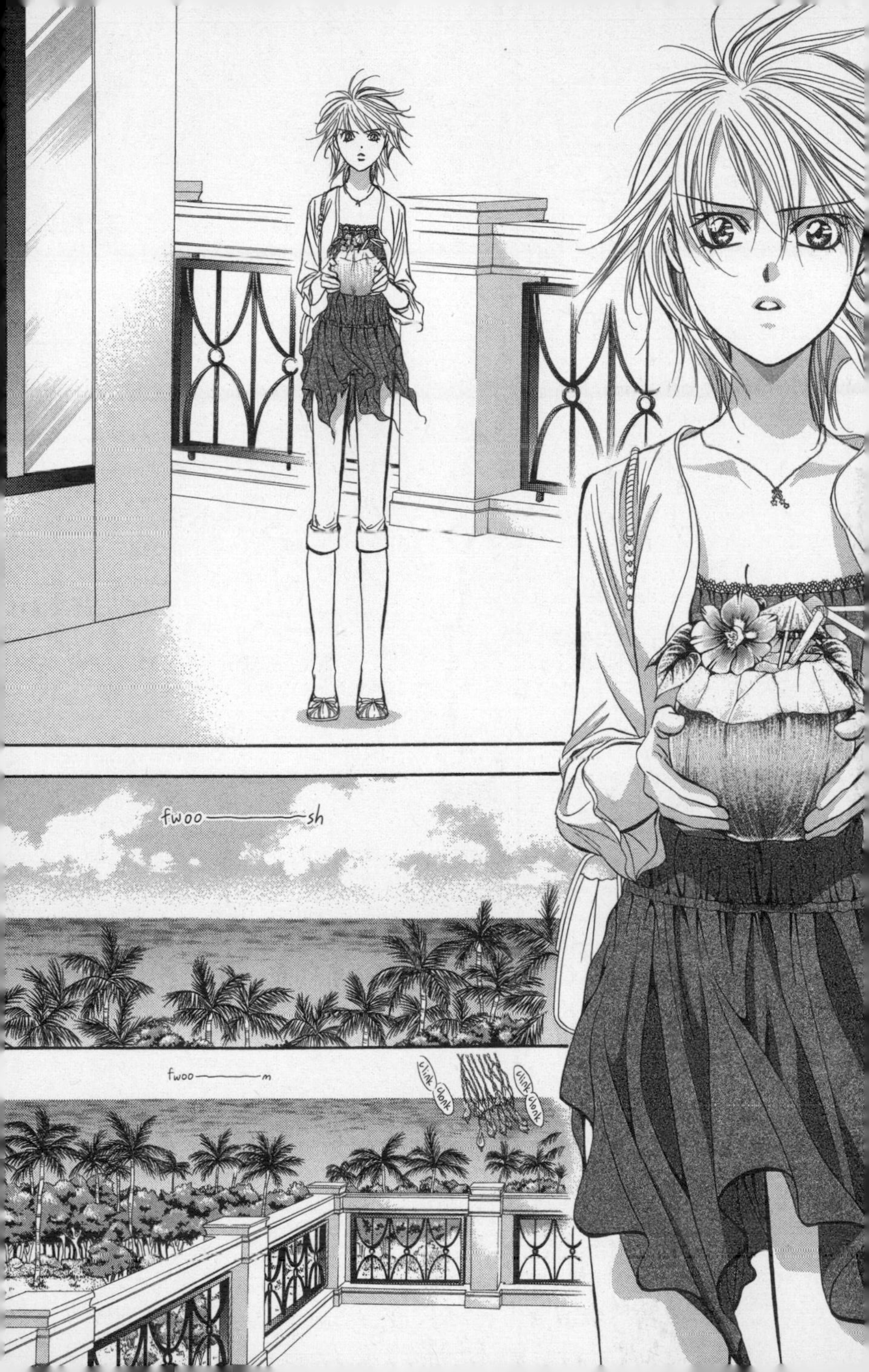
fwoo———sh
clink clonk
clink clonk
fwoo———m

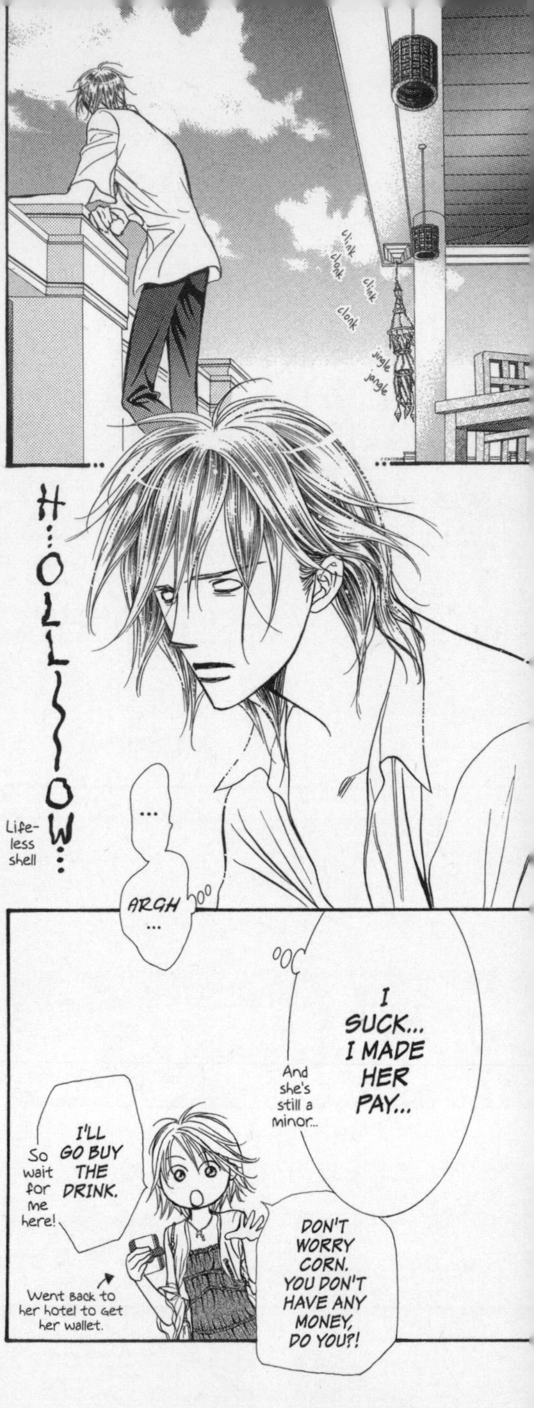
clink
clonk
clink
clonk
jingle
jangle
H...OLLOW...
Life-less shell
...
ARGH ...
I SUCK... I MADE HER PAY...
And she's still a minor...
I'LL GO BUY THE DRINK.
So wait for me here!
DON'T WORRY CORN. YOU DON'T HAVE ANY MONEY, DO YOU?!
Went back to her hotel to get her wallet.

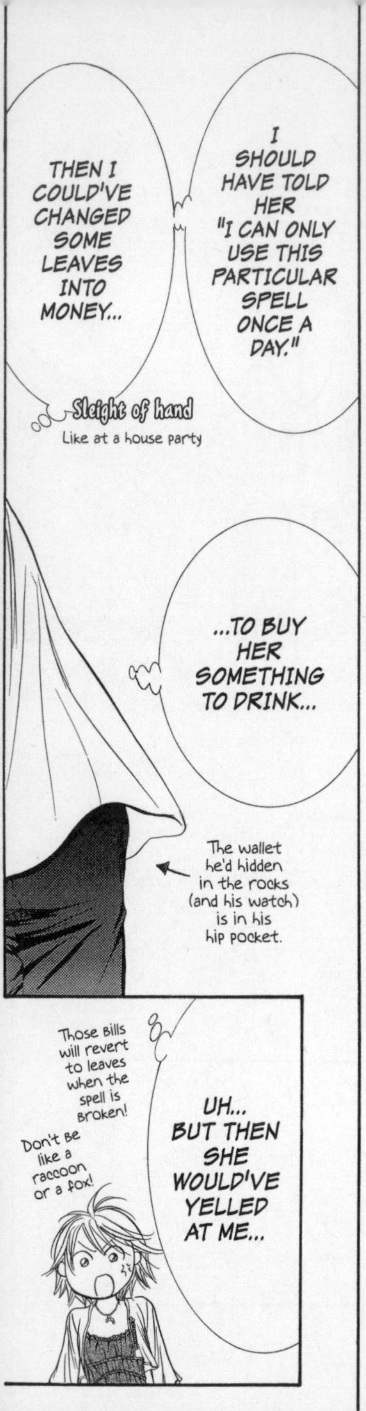
I SHOULD HAVE TOLD HER "I CAN ONLY USE THIS PARTICULAR SPELL ONCE A DAY."
THEN I COULD'VE CHANGED SOME LEAVES INTO MONEY...
Sleight of hand
Like at a house party
...TO BUY HER SOMETHING TO DRINK...
The wallet he'd hidden in the rocks (and his watch) is in his hip pocket.
UH... BUT THEN SHE WOULD'VE YELLED AT ME...
Those bills will revert to leaves when the spell is broken!
Don't be like a raccoon or a fox!

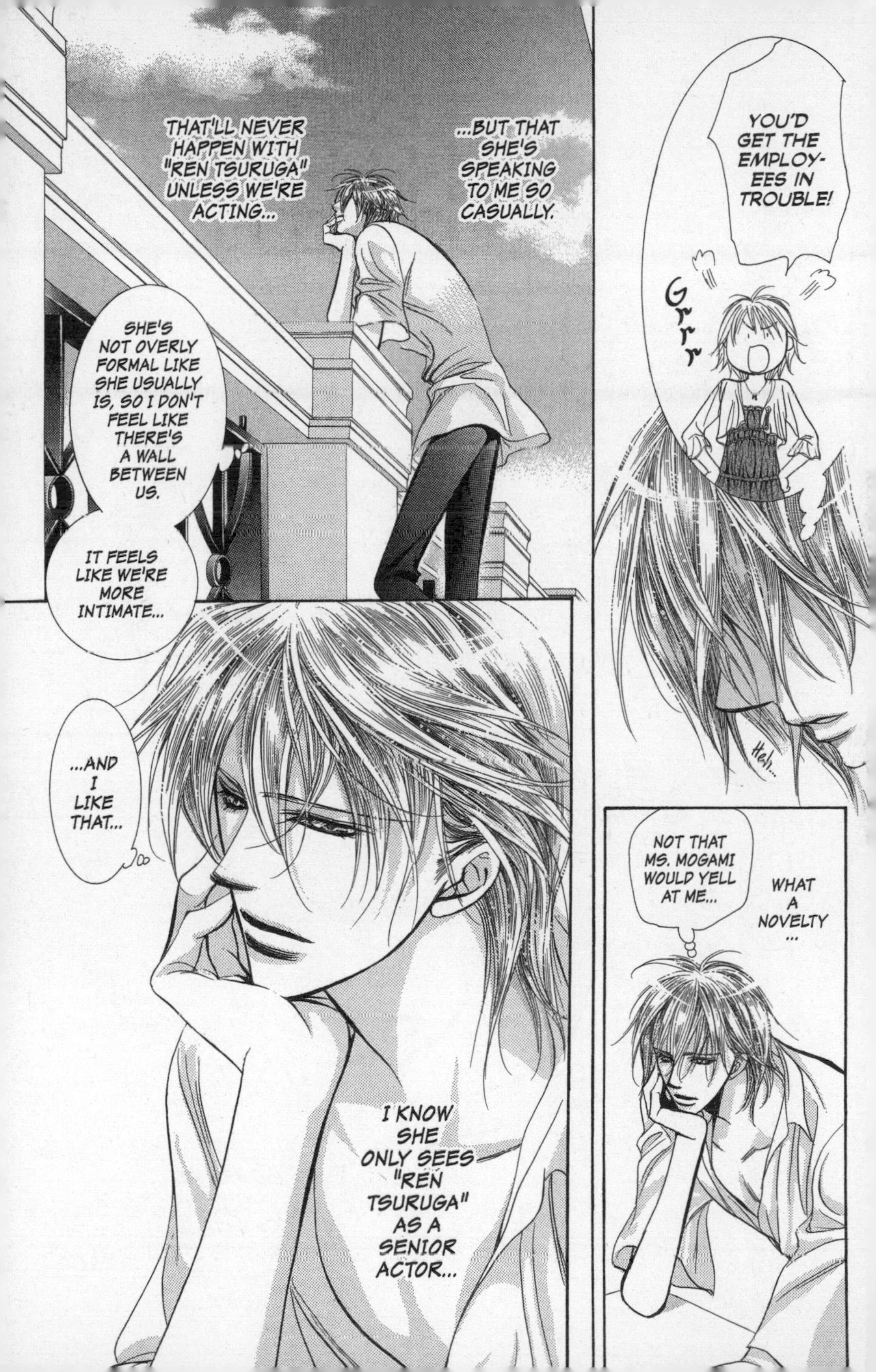
YOU'D GET THE EMPLOY-EES IN TROUBLE!
Grrr
Heh...
NOT THAT MS. MOGAMI WOULD YELL AT ME...
WHAT A NOVELTY...
THAT'LL NEVER HAPPEN WITH "REN TSURUGA" UNLESS WE'RE ACTING...
...BUT THAT SHE'S SPEAKING TO ME SO CASUALLY.
SHE'S NOT OVERLY FORMAL LIKE SHE USUALLY IS, SO I DON'T FEEL LIKE THERE'S A WALL BETWEEN US.
IT FEELS LIKE WE'RE MORE INTIMATE...
...AND I LIKE THAT...
I KNOW SHE ONLY SEES "REN TSURUGA" AS A SENIOR ACTOR...

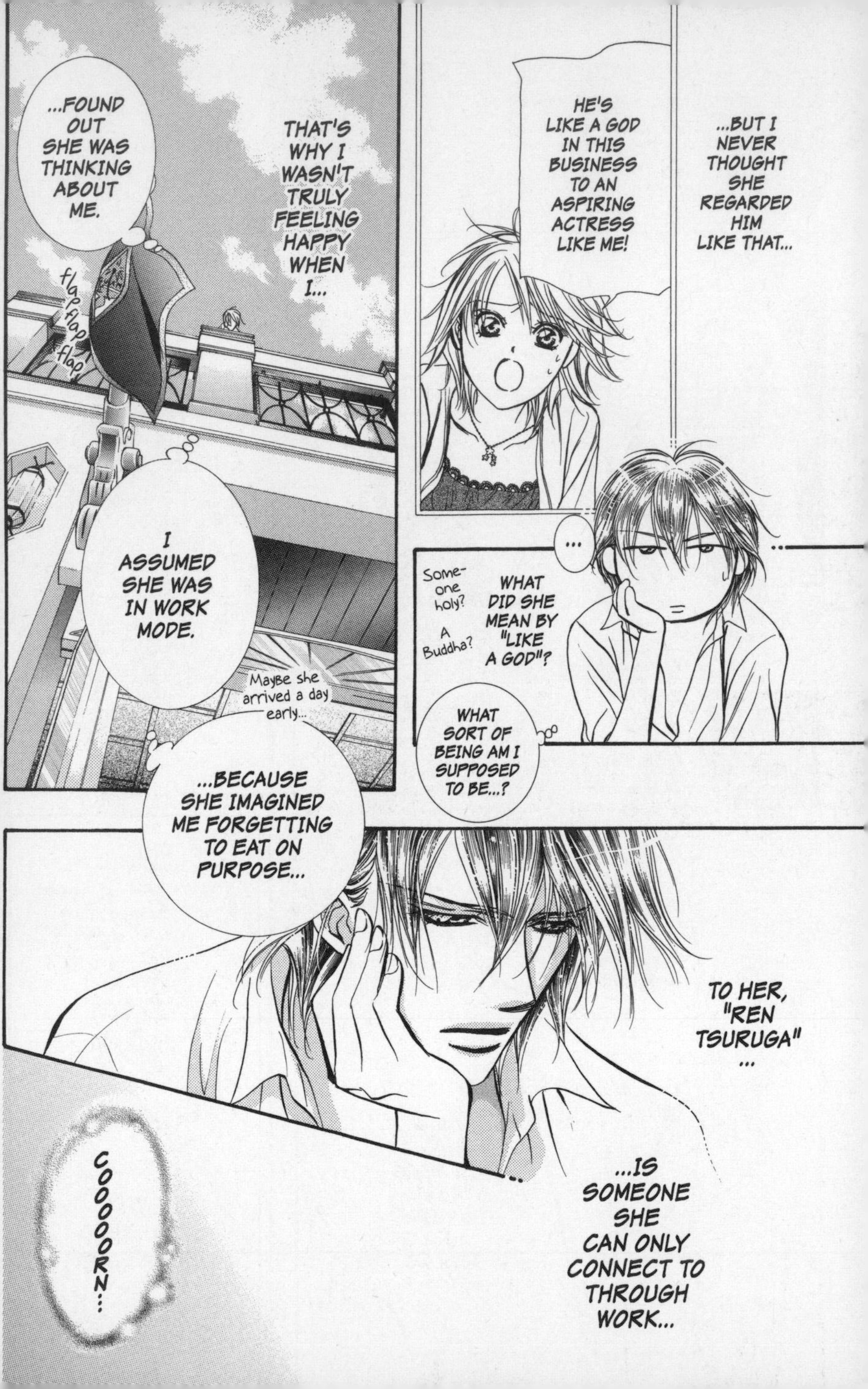
...BUT I NEVER THOUGHT SHE REGARDED HIM LIKE THAT...
HE'S LIKE A GOD IN THIS BUSINESS TO AN ASPIRING ACTRESS LIKE ME!
...
WHAT DID SHE MEAN BY "LIKE A GOD"?
Some-one holy? A Buddha?
WHAT SORT OF BEING AM I SUPPOSED TO BE...?
THAT'S WHY I WASN'T TRULY FEELING HAPPY WHEN I...
...FOUND OUT SHE WAS THINKING ABOUT ME.
flap flap flap
I ASSUMED SHE WAS IN WORK MODE.
Maybe she arrived a day early...
...BECAUSE SHE IMAGINED ME FORGETTING TO EAT ON PURPOSE...
TO HER, "REN TSURUGA" ...
...IS SOMEONE SHE CAN ONLY CONNECT TO THROUGH WORK...
COOOOORN...

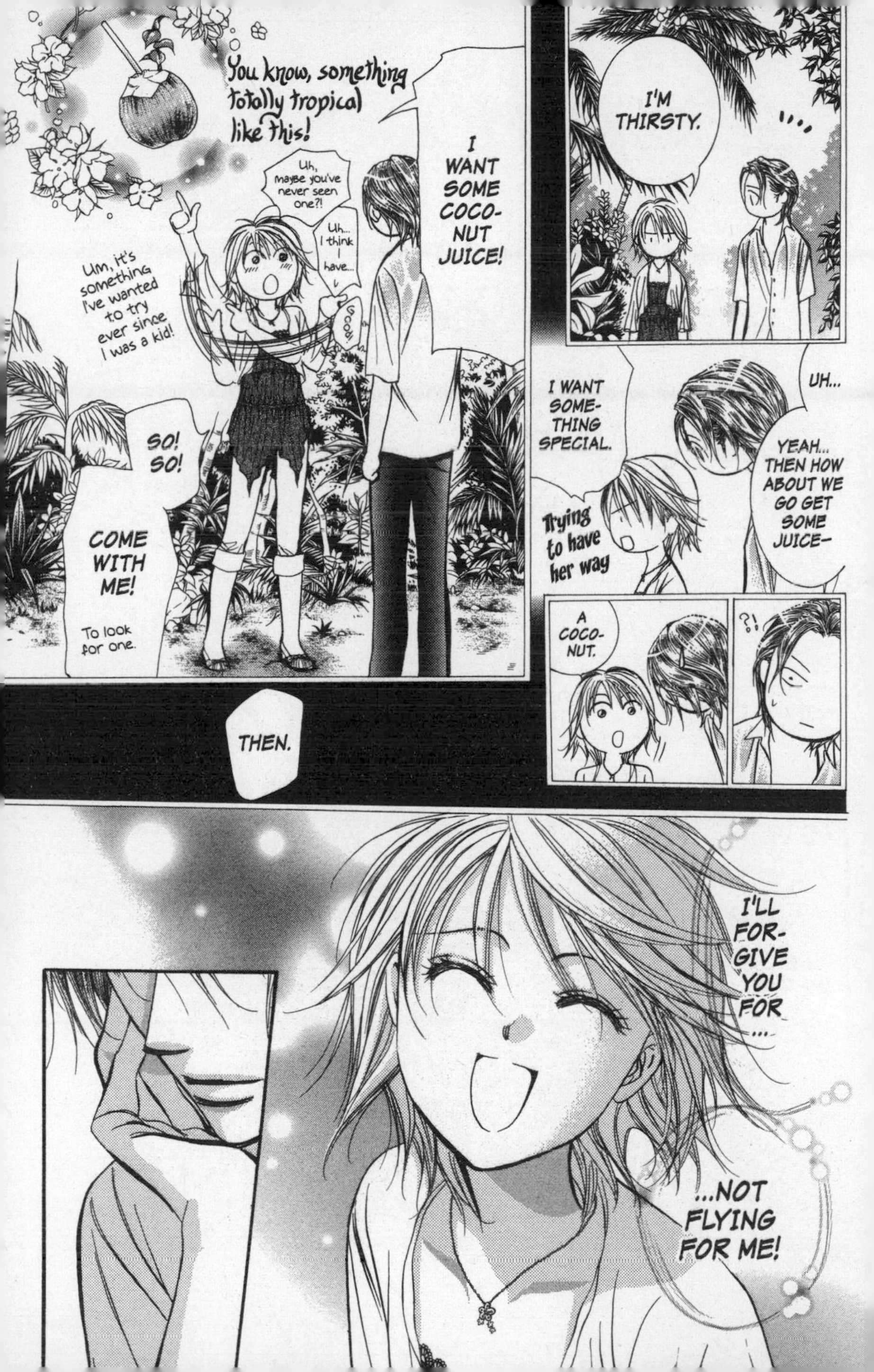
I'M THIRSTY.
...,
UH...
YEAH... THEN HOW ABOUT WE GO GET SOME JUICE-
I WANT SOMETHING SPECIAL.
Trying to have her way
?!
A COCONUT.
I WANT SOME COCONUT JUICE!
You know, something totally tropical like this!
Uh, maybe you've never seen one?!
Uh... I think I have...
Good!
Um, it's something I've wanted to try ever since I was a kid!
SO! SO!
COME WITH ME!
To look for one.
THEN.
I'LL FORGIVE YOU FOR...
...NOT FLYING FOR ME!

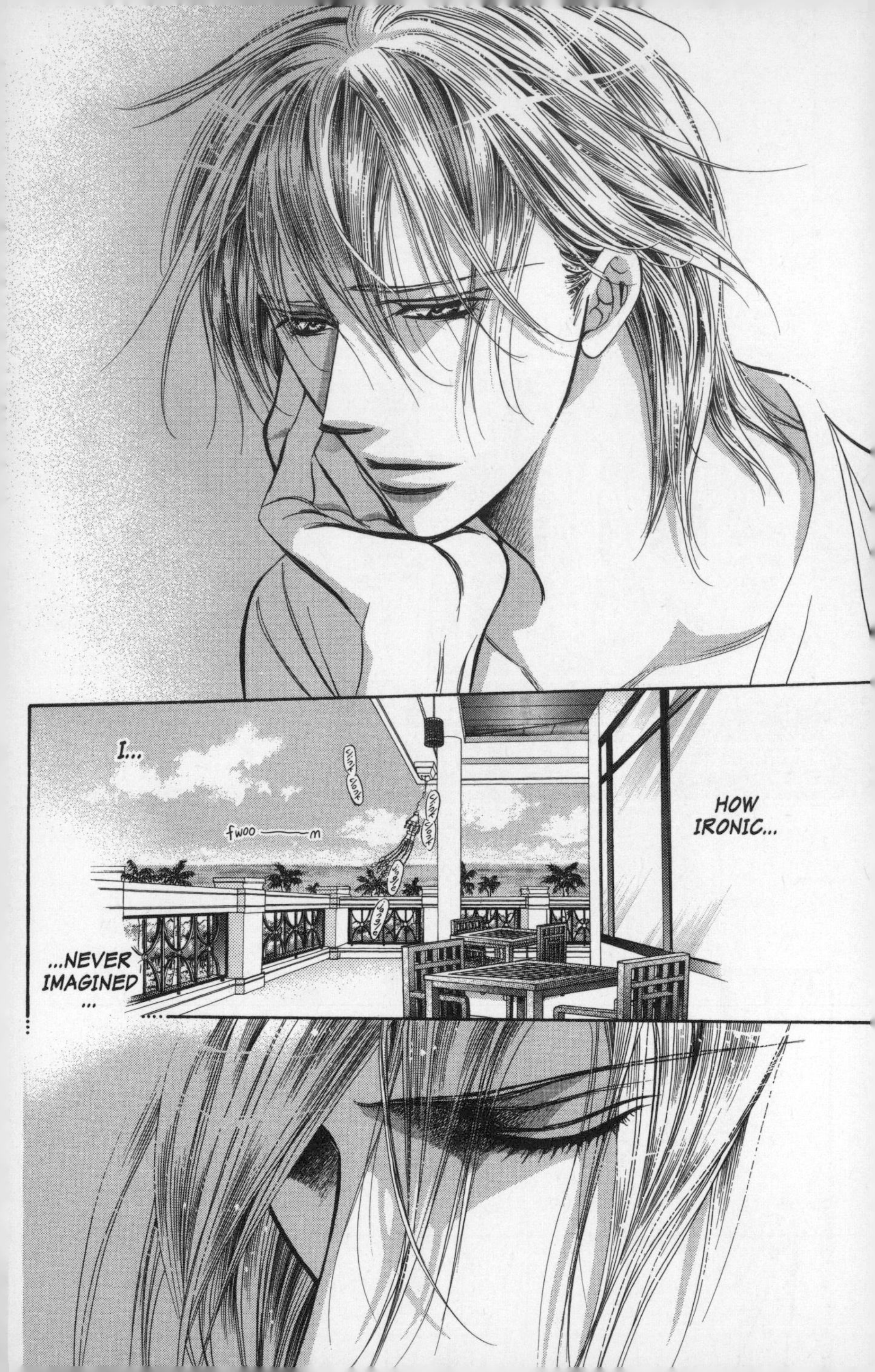
HOW IRONIC...
clink clonk
clink clonk
jingle jangle
I...
fwoo——m
...NEVER IMAGINED
...

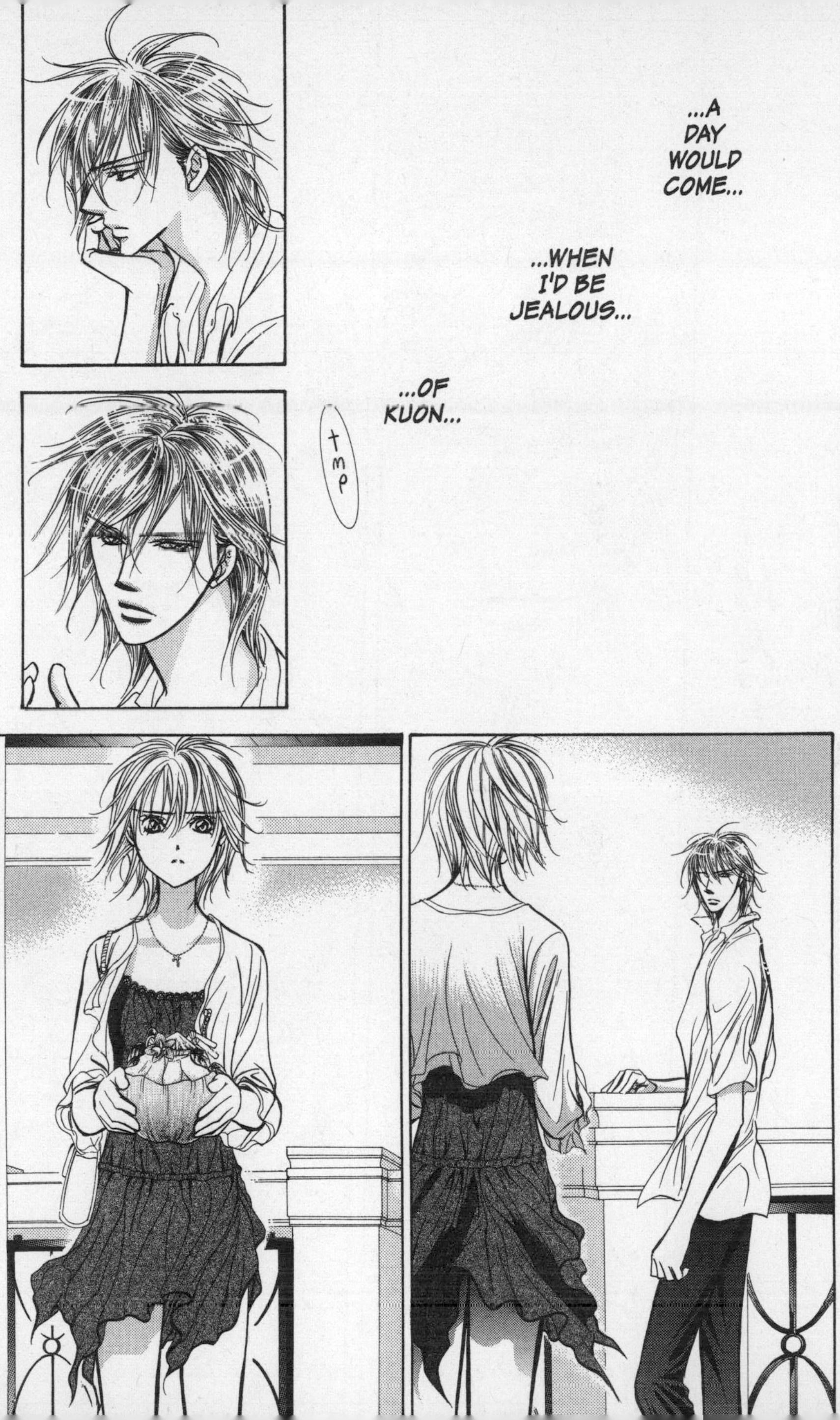
...A DAY WOULD COME...
...WHEN I'D BE JEALOUS...
...OF KUON...
tmp

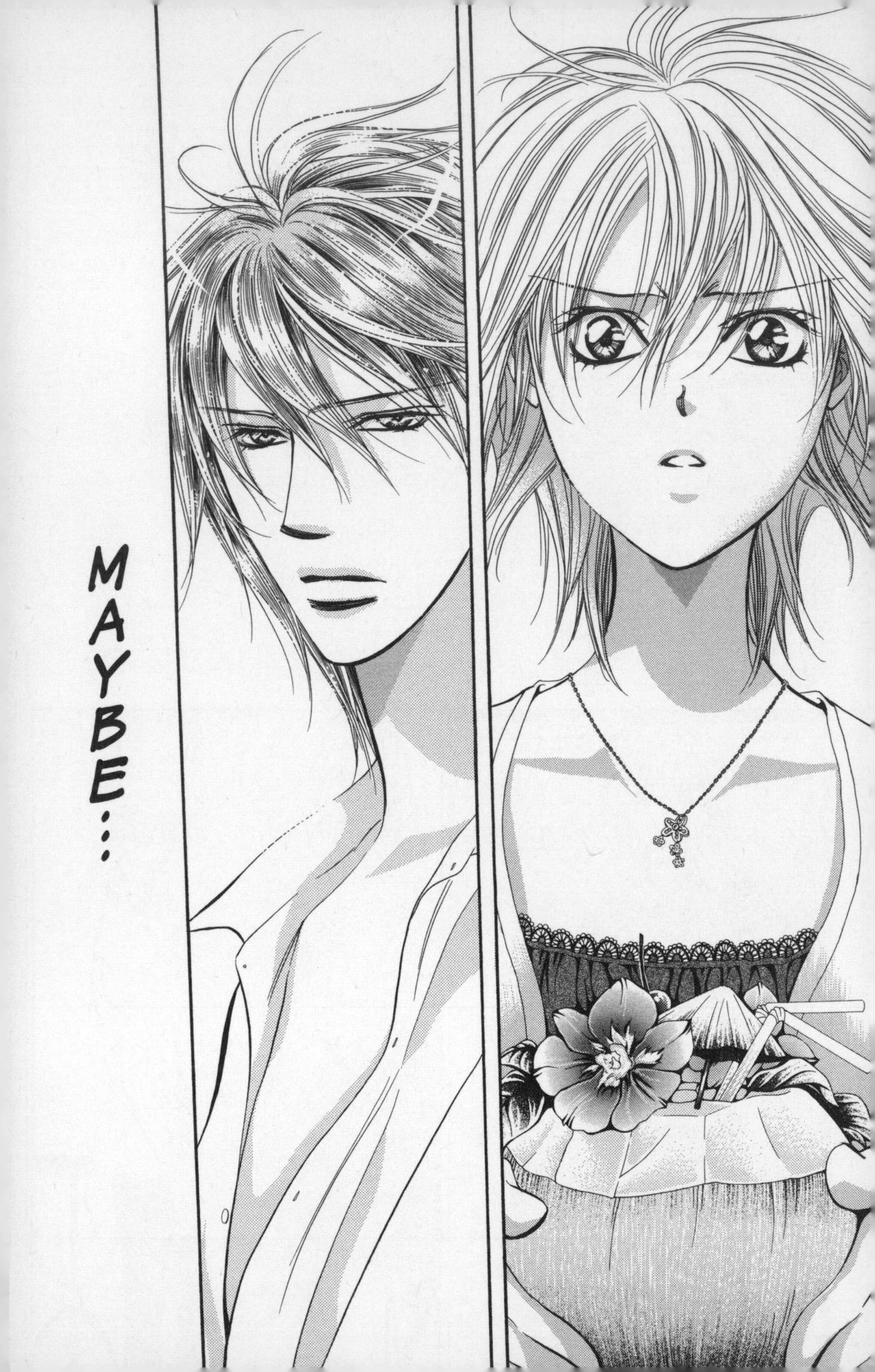
MAYBE...

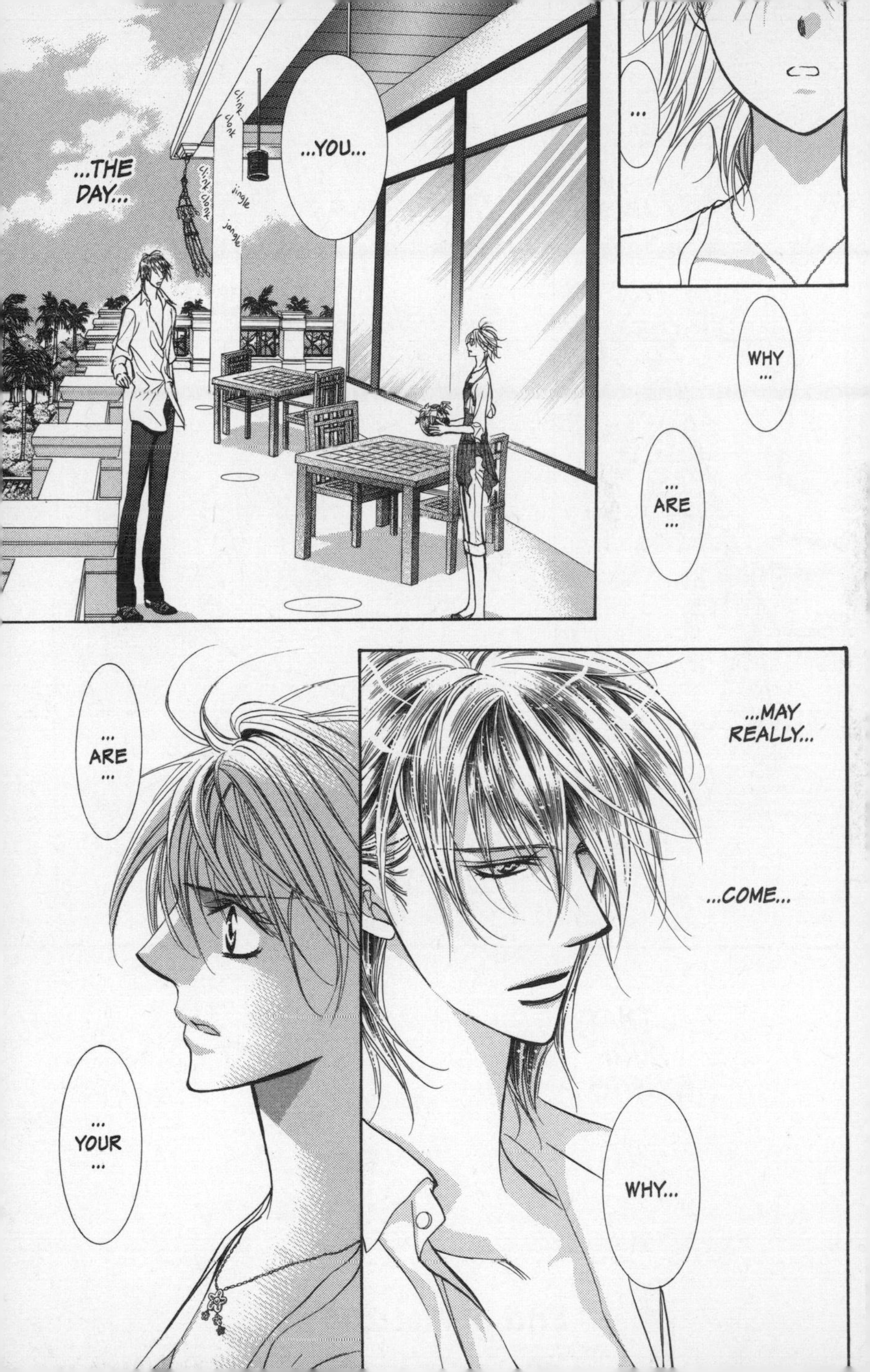
...
WHY...
...ARE...
...YOU...
...THE DAY...
clink clank
clink clank
jingle
jangle
...MAY REALLY...
...COME...
WHY...
...ARE...
...YOUR...

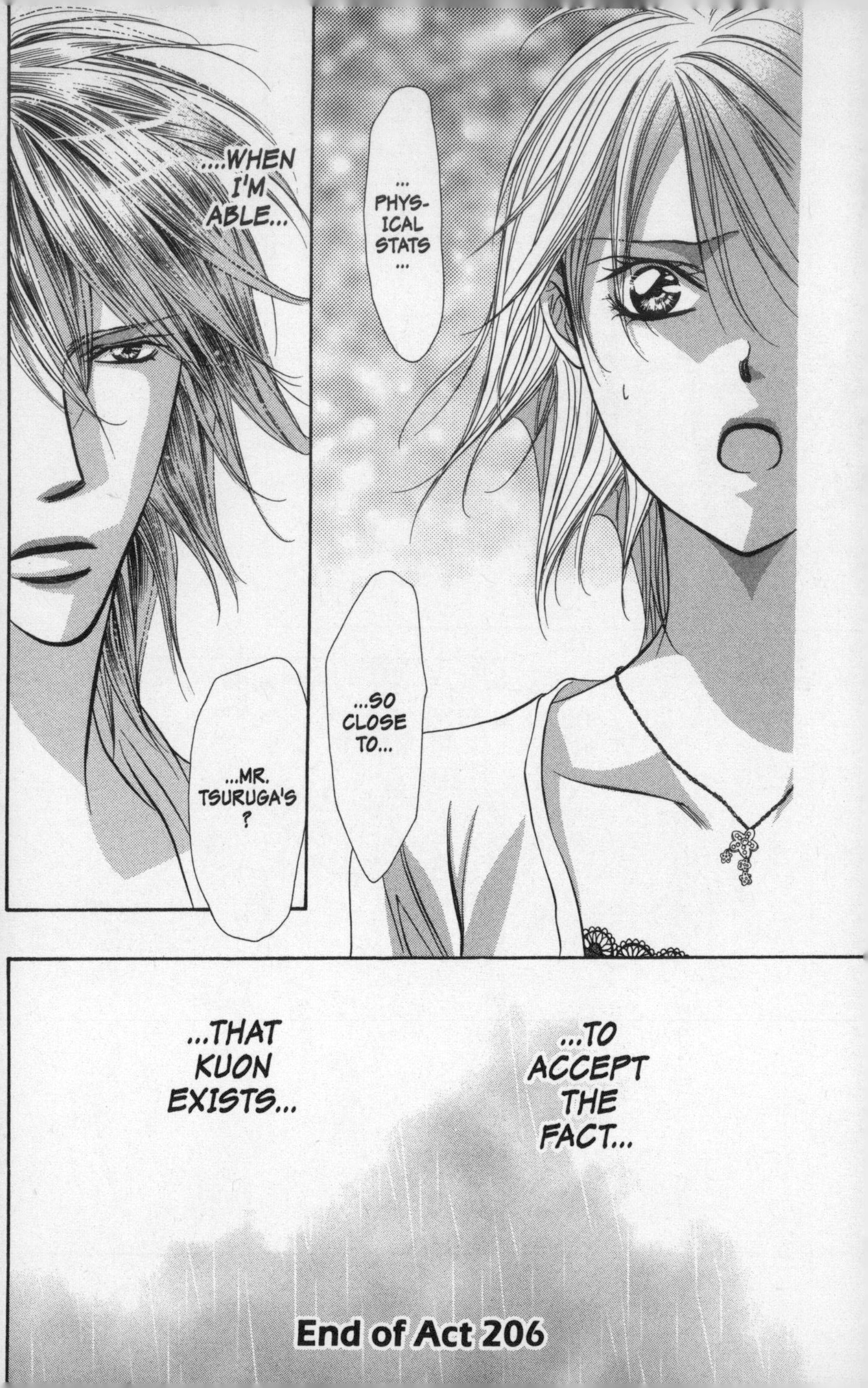

...PHYSICAL STATS...
...SO CLOSE TO...
...MR. TSURUGA'S?
....WHEN I'M ABLE...
...TO ACCEPT THE FACT...
...THAT KUON EXISTS...
End of Act 206

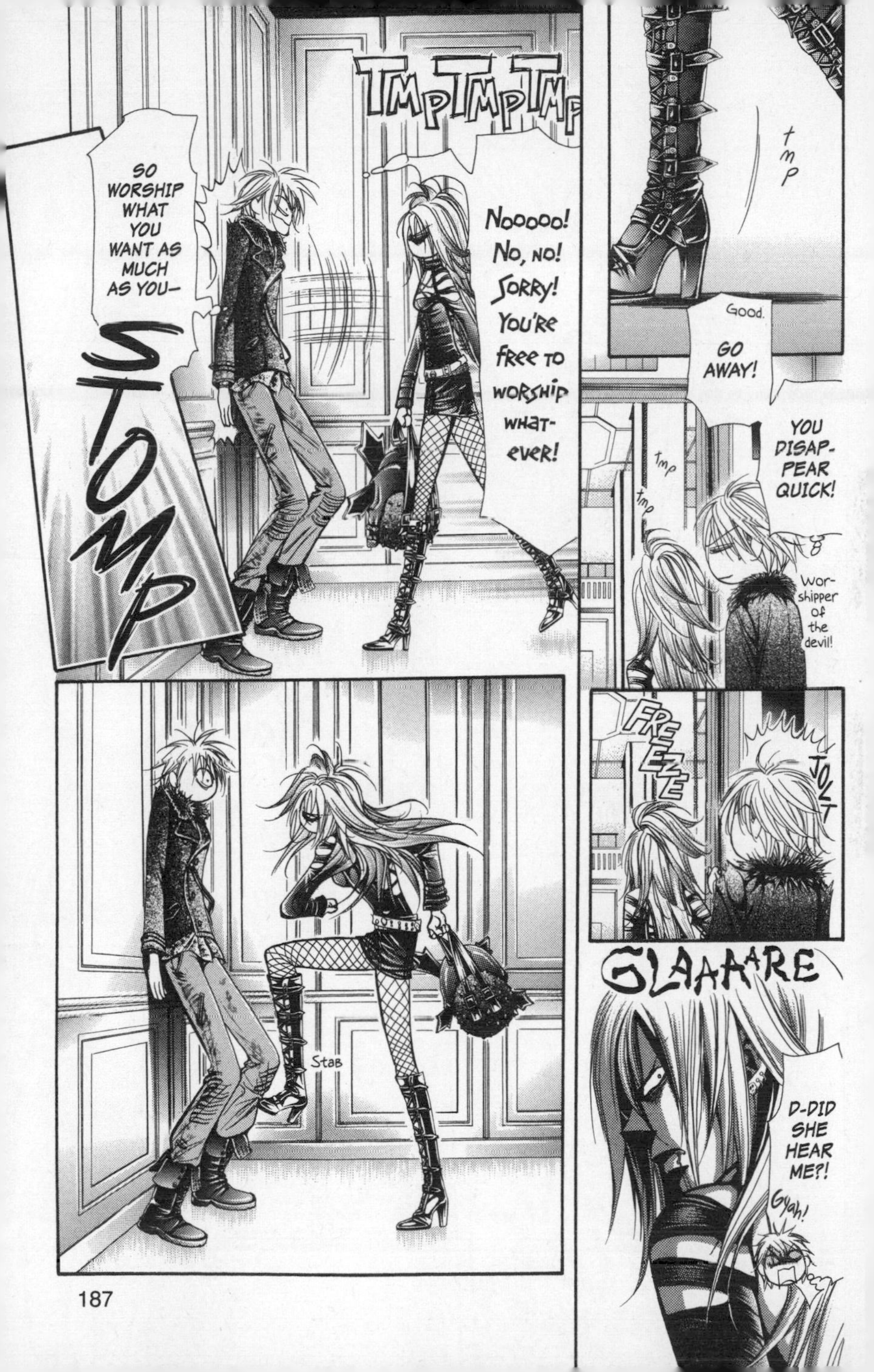
tmp
Good.
GO AWAY!
tmp
tmp
YOU DISAPPEAR QUICK!
Worshipper of the devil!
FREEZE
JOLT
GLAAARE
D-DID SHE HEAR ME?!
Gyah!
TMPTMPTMP
SO WORSHIP WHAT YOU WANT AS MUCH AS YOU—
STOMP
Noooooo! No, no! Sorry! You're free to worship whatever!
Stab

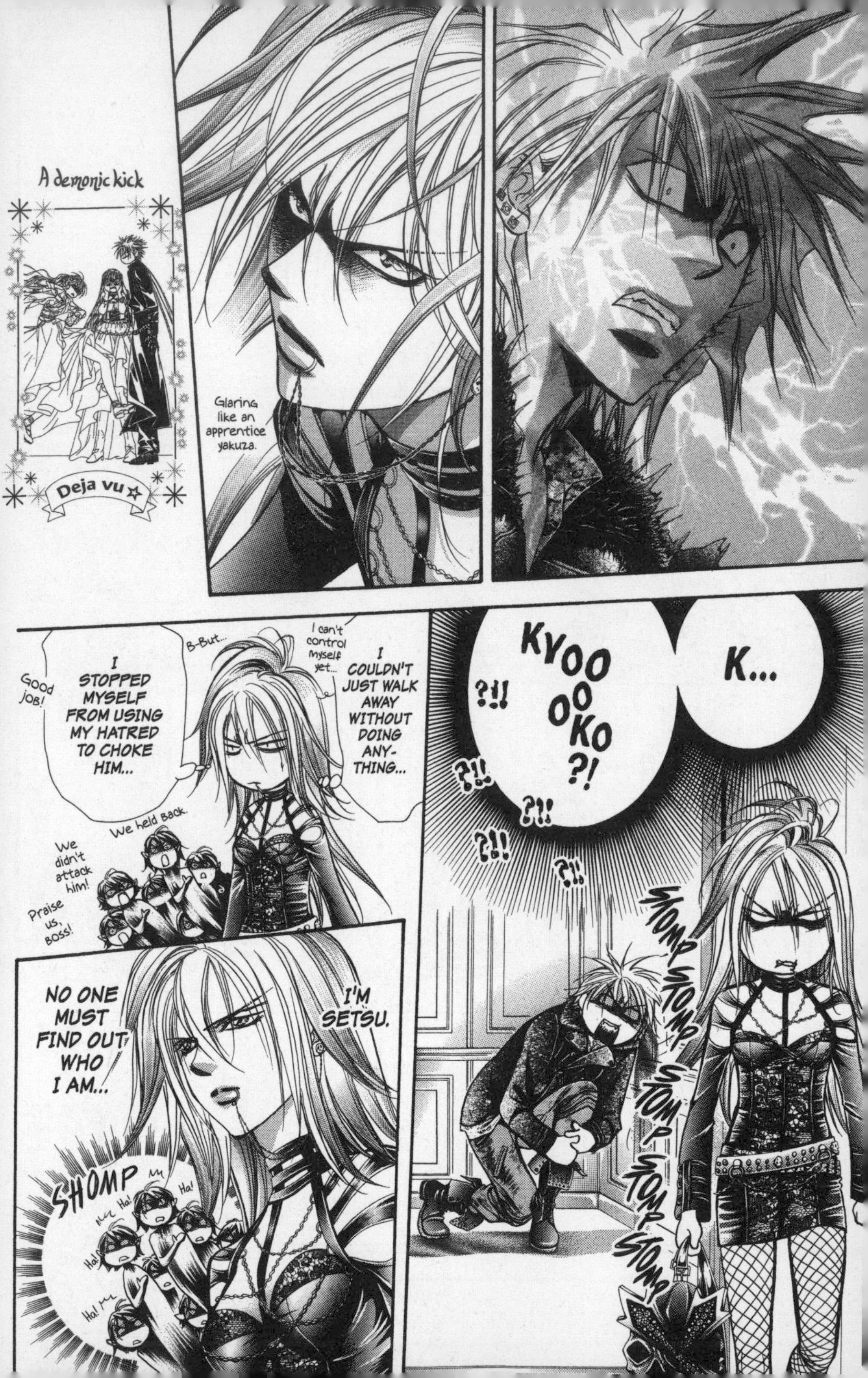
Glaring like an apprentice yakuza.
A demonic kick
Deja vu☆
K...
KYOOOOKO?!
?!!
?!!
?!!
?!!
?!!
STOMP STOMP STOMP STOMP STOMP STOMP
I can't control myself yet...
I COULDN'T JUST WALK AWAY WITHOUT DOING ANYTHING...
B-But...
I STOPPED MYSELF FROM USING MY HATRED TO CHOKE HIM...
Good job!
We held back.
We didn't attack him!
Praise us, BOSS!
I'M SETSU.
NO ONE MUST FIND OUT WHO I AM...
SHOMP
Ha! Ha! Ha! Ha! Ha!

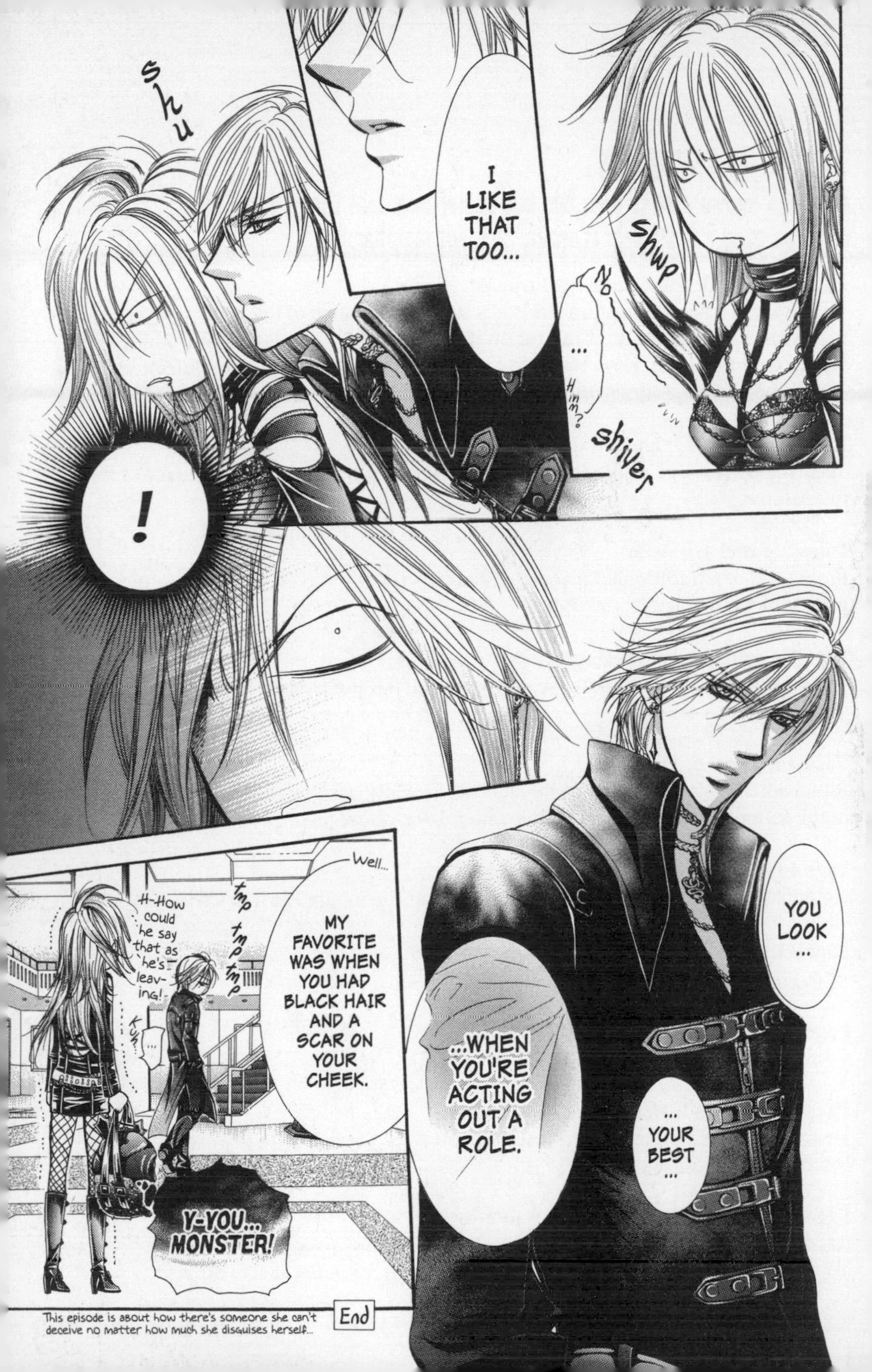
Shwp
No...
... Hmm?
shiver
I LIKE THAT TOO...
shu
!
YOU LOOK ...
... YOUR BEST ...
...WHEN YOU'RE ACTING OUT A ROLE.
Well...
MY FAVORITE WAS WHEN YOU HAD BLACK HAIR AND A SCAR ON YOUR CHEEK.
tmp tmp tmp tmp
H-How could he say that as he's leaving!
Kuh...
...
Y-YOU... MONSTER!
End

This episode is about how there's someone she can't deceive no matter how much she disguises herself...

Skip·Beat! End Notes
Everyone knows how to be a fan, but sometimes cool things from other cultures need a little help crossing the language barrier.

Page 5, panel 3: Mt. Osore. Mt Fuji, Mt. Koya
Mt. Osore is a volcano in Aomori Prefecture where souls of the deceased are believed to go. Mt. Fuji is the highest mountain in Japan and is sacred in both Buddhist and Shinto traditions. Mt. Koya refers to a group of mountains in Nara Prefecture and is one of the sacred grounds of Japanese Buddhism.

Page 6, panel 1: Okamisan
The proprietress of a traditional Japanese restaurant. Okami act as the face of the restaurant.

Page 7, panel 4: Taisho
Proprietor of a traditional Japanese restaurant. Taisho stay in the background to deal with cooking or managerial duties.

Page 34, panel 3: White Day
The day when boys and men give small presents to the women who gave them something on Valentine's.

Page 44, panel 5: Hara-kiri
Ritual suicide by slitting the stomach. Traditionally used by samurai to regain honor in the face of defeat or disgrace. It is also known as *seppuku*.

Page 111, panel 6: Golden Week
Golden Week is a holiday week in Japan that starts in late April or early May.

Page 113, panel 2: 1980 yen, 2980 yen
About $19.40 USD and $29.20 USD.

Page 119, panel 5: Kan-ei Tsuho Coin
Coins used during the Kan-ei era (1624–1643).

Page 158, panel 3: New Year's shrine visit
Japanese people visit local Shinto shrines on New Year's Day to pray for luck and health in the coming year.

Page 178, panel 5: Like a raccoon or a fox
Raccoons and foxes are believed to be able to transform leaves into money. They are also known as tricksters who don't care how false currency affects others.

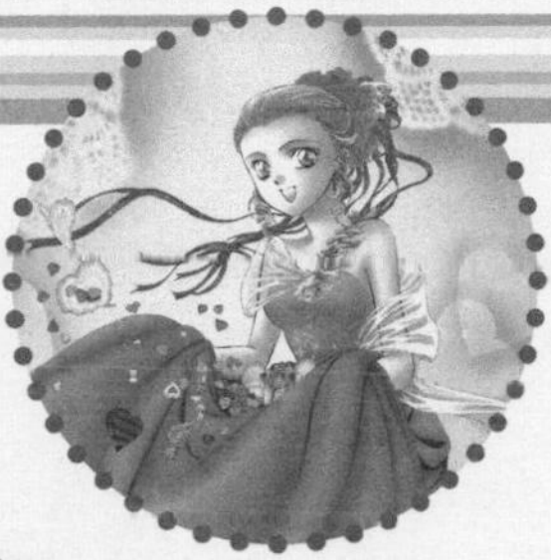

Yoshiki Nakamura is originally from Tokushima Prefecture. She started drawing manga in elementary school, which eventually led to her 1993 debut of *Yume de Au yori Suteki* (Better than Seeing in a Dream) in *Hana to Yume* magazine. Her other works include the basketball series *Saint Love*, *MVP wa Yuzurenai* (Can't Give Up MVP), *Blue Wars* and *Tokyo Crazy Paradise*, a series about a female bodyguard in 2020 Tokyo.

SKIP·BEAT!

Vol. 34

Shojo Beat Edition

STORY AND ART BY YOSHIKI NAKAMURA

English Translation & Adaptation/Tomo Kimura
Touch-up Art & Lettering/Sabrina Heep
Design/Veronica Casson
Editor/Pancha Diaz

Printed in the U.S.A.

Published by VIZ Media, LLC
P.O. Box 77010
San Francisco, CA 94107

www.viz.com

www.shojobeat.com

10 9 8 7 6 5 4 3 2 1
First printing, April 2015

PARENTAL ADVISORY
SKIP·BEAT! is rated T for Teen and is recommended for ages 13 and up. This volume contains a grudge.
ratings.viz.com

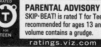